QUALITATIVE RESEARCH
FROM START TO FINISH

Qualitative Research from Start to Finish

◆

ROBERT K. YIN

THE GUILFORD PRESS
New York   London

To Karen and Andrew,

*for many years of love, devotion, and tolerance,
and for being willing to entertain the possibility that
social science can be a lifelong and stimulating endeavor*

© 2011 The Guilford Press
A Division of Guilford Publications, Inc.
72 Spring Street, New York, NY 10012
www.guilford.com

Printed in the United States of America

This book is printed on acid-free paper.

Last digit is print number: 9   8   7   6   5   4   3   2

Library of Congress Cataloging-in-Publication Data is available
from the Publisher.
ISBN 978-1-60623-701-4 (pbk.)
ISBN 978-1-60623-977-3 (hardcover)

Preface

Qualitative research has come of age. Published studies abound. Their findings cover nearly every worldly topic. Of equal importance, compelling methodological works now define the craft, placing it in the mainstream of social science. Your interest in qualitative research may reflect a desire to do it, teach it, or just learn about it. In any of these situations, this book can help you.

THE BOOK

A Practical Approach

As its main theme, the book presents qualitative research from a practical perspective. Such a view reveals insights into how qualitative research is done, at the ground level. The approach should be especially useful if in fact you are actually wanting to conduct a qualitative study—whether it is to be self-standing, part of a larger study, or an academic or training assignment for an undergraduate, graduate, or continuing education course.

An Inductive Approach

Along the way, the book presents numerous examples of successfully completed and published qualitative studies, covering many different academic disciplines and professions such as sociology, anthropology, psychology, education, public health, social work, community development, evaluation, and international affairs. The examples typically take the form of *vignettes* and *quick studies*, strewn throughout the book. Both provide more details about individual studies than the standard citations often found in other texts. Moreover, the studies come from widely available journals and books. Their ready availability enables you to inspect these materials in greater detail, if you wish.

Besides providing a more concrete foundation for understanding how qualitative research has been done by a broad variety of scholars, the numerous examples also convey the breadth of qualitative research. The topics extend over many different types of social settings and everyday lives, while also covering the major variations in qualitative research, including action research, grounded theory, case studies, feminist works, narrative inquiry, and phenomenology. As a most important characteristic, all of the illustrative studies are completed ones. As such, they should boost your confidence in being able to finish (and publish) your own qualitative research.

Similarly, two completed studies, and how they were conducted in relation to the material in Chapters 8, 9, and 12, are presented in depth at the end of those chapters. The studies examine two topics (K–12 in one case and university administration in the other) intended to appeal to all readers because everyone has experienced the two environments.

An Adaptive Approach

The book deliberately presents qualitative research in an adaptive fashion, which actually befits the craft. Rather than conveying it in a dogmatic, much less ideological manner, the book presents critical methodological topics—such as how to design or analyze qualitative research—in the form of optional choices. These choices will enable you to customize your own study.

For instance, you can create your own design, based on the eight choices presented in Chapter 4. The result can be a qualitative study that will range from the old-fashioned way of doing qualitative research to a more pragmatic approach that takes advantage of current techniques and tools. Similarly, you have the choice of starting fieldwork before finalizing your research questions—an option examined in Chapter 3. You also can decide whether or not to code your data, and whether or not to use computer software to assist in analyzing your data, as discussed in Chapters 8 and 9. If you have trouble starting a qualitative study in the first place, the ideas in Chapter 3 about creating a "study bank" offer insightful options.

THE AUTHOR

My own experiences probably account for the book's three preceding features—its practical theme, devotion to understanding how other studies have been done, and need for being adaptive. The practical guidance and inductive orientation come from having done over 30 years of social science research. During this time, I have directly overseen, led, or participated in nearly 200 studies—including those that deliberately mixed qualitative and nonqualitative methods. The adaptive orientation reflects the fact that the studies have covered a wide array of fields, such as primary, secondary, and postsecondary education; health promotion, HIV/AIDS prevention, and substance abuse prevention; neighborhood, community, and urban development; crime prevention; technological innovation and diffusion; communications; and organizational development and program evaluation.

All of the studies came to a formal written conclusion, either as an academic publication or as a final report of some sort. Successfully arriving at such a concluding step means that I have practiced the entire research cycle many times—from start to finish. Each study started with an intensive scan and review of other comparable studies, which exposed me to the ways in which other scholars have designed and conducted their research. Because each of my own studies was done under different circumstances and addressed different research questions, I became exposed to the diverse ways in which studies can be designed, analyzed, and presented.

Only in retrospect have I realized that these career experiences, along with research questions that inevitably address "how and why" questions, have included an extensive amount of work with qualitative methods. Although I have not spent long periods of time doing ethnography in the field, I have directed or conducted numerous field-based studies using participant-observation, case studies, qualitative interviews, field photography, and site visits. I have then had to struggle with the options for analyzing the resulting data, drawing conclusions from them, and presenting the studies before expert advisory panels or otherwise responding to peer reviews.

The career experiences underlie my attempt to have this book cover qualitative research comprehensively. The various chapters address virtually every phase of doing qualitative research, including some topics that also tend to be overlooked by other texts. For instance, nearly every qualitative study calls for presenting the meaning of social reality from the perspective of a study's participants (people whose lives are a large part of the subject of study). Yet, there are different ways of presenting their words or life histories, and this book explicitly addresses these variations (see Chapter 10). As another example, most books do not discuss the various ways of drawing conclusions from qualitative research, but this book identifies at least five such ways (see Chapter 9). Finally, contemporary qualitative research can come from brief site visits to the field that are different from the traditional ethnographic stints, and this book describes the basic site visit procedures (see Chapter 5).

THE ORGANIZATION OF THE BOOK

The Sequence of Chapters

Because books have to be presented in linear fashion, they follow a particular sequence of chapters. However, as with all of qualitative research, nothing is linear. Understanding specific topics depends on being knowledgeable about other topics that a book might not yet have presented. In a way, a reader needs to know everything at once and then to revisit specific topics recursively. As a result, readers should feel free to tamper with the sequence of chapters in the book. Readers wanting to get started with a qualitative study can jump right into the book and start at Chapter 3 or even Chapter 4. Conversely, readers wanting to understand the deeper issues in doing qualitative research might want to read Chapters 1 and 2 first. I personally wanted in my early days to understand the evidentiary basis for qualitative research, so I would have started by trying to understand the fieldwork and data collection activities in Chapters 5 and 6. You can see that the possible sequences are nearly endless.

Working Features

To stimulate a reader's active involvement with the book, the book has some additional features. First, the chapters all start with a brief abstract, overviewing the contents of each chapter. Then, the sections within each chapter all start with a *preview box*, briefly covering *what you should learn from this section*. Finally, every chapter ends with a *recap* of the terms and concepts presented in the chapter.

Second, each chapter also ends with an exercise reflecting the practices covered by the chapter. The exercises are intended to serve as out-of-class assignments that can be done on a weekly basis. As an alternative, the Appendix contains a comprehensive, semester- or year-long project that can be done in lieu of (or even in addition to) the individual exercises.

Third, to save you a little bit of trouble, the book includes a brief glossary of special terms used in qualitative research. Also at the back of the book, the editors at The Guilford Press permitted one discretionary stretching of the standard American Psychological Association format: The reference section includes the authors' first names, not just their initials. Contextually, knowing the first names clearly reduces confusion among persons who might have the same surname as well as similar initials. Such knowledge also might help readers to connect the cited authors with real-life people—who might even be teaching or have taught at one of your academic departments.

As a final goal, the book also introduces you to a variety of methodological works, whether dealing with issues of research ethics (Chapter 2), research design (Chapter 4), handling peer reviewers' comments (Chapter 11), or engaging in mixed methods studies (Chapter 12). In covering these and related topics, I have tried to create a scholarly mix of citations to classical as well as contemporary works. Likewise, the relevant concepts range from understanding the value of "thick description" to challenging the rationale for the "gold standard." At the same time, books such as the present one do not replace research readings. Textbooks cannot reproduce the rich spirit of a research field or its deeper meanings. Instead, good texts should provide two things: practical knowledge so you can pursue research, and clues in the form of citations where you can learn more about the spirit of a field. So it is with the present text.

Acknowledgments

My 30-year span of research experience covers work done at several different research and academic organizations. Within each have been key colleagues who have contributed to my understanding of the breadth of social science research, including qualitative research.

At MIT, I studied under Professor Hans-Lukas Teuber. Together, we focused on the topic of face recognition. Although the research used methods from experimental psychology, the topic—how people easily recognize and discriminate an extremely large number of faces despite their similarity according to any objective measure—still in my mind represents a qualitative question of the first order.

Later at MIT, but now in the Department of Urban Studies and Planning, I also had the pleasure of knowing Lawrence Susskind and Lloyd Rodwin, both of whom strongly encouraged my work on neighborhood development. That topic attracted a variety of research methods, ranging from the anthropological to the demographic.

Work at the New York City–Rand Institute and at the Rand Corporation's office in Washington, DC, pushed me further into the investigation of urban as well as related policy topics. Peter Szanton made his mark on my thinking, through his incessant questioning and sage advice on how to examine these topics. Similarly, a stint at American University's School of International Service, guided by Professor Nanette Levinson, led to a broader array of research on international development.

Through these years, the greatest effort has nevertheless been associated with my affiliation with COSMOS Corporation—an independent research organization devoted to the examination of a wide variety of federal and state policy issues. COSMOS's numerous clients, especially Bernice Anderson at the National Science

Foundation, have their own academic credentials and published work and created their own brand of stimulating ideas and critical feedback. The key topics of discussion, if not contention, always tended to be methodological ones.

Over the same years, I have gained a broader perspective through collaborative teaching with scholars overseas, particularly in Denmark, France, and The Netherlands. For instance, a recent assignment involves working with doctoral students being led by Professor Iben Nathan at the University of Copenhagen.

Most recently, I have spent a significant amount of time collaborating with scholars doing evaluation research at the United Nations. Together, we have had to develop rigorous but cost-conscious ways of doing qualitative research on a broad variety of international topics. At the United Nations, Sukai Prom-Jackson and Fabrizio Felloni have been primary collaborators and have sensitized me to the variety of challenges involved in doing such research.

The preparation of this book has benefited from a more immediate set of critical friends. They include seven reviewers of an earlier draft: Jessie L. Kreinert, Criminal Justice, Illinois State University (Normal); Penny Burge, Education, Virginia Tech; James A. Holstein, Social and Cultural Sciences, Marquette University; Michelle Bligh, School of Behavioral and Organizational Sciences, Claremont Graduate University; Lance Fusarelli, Education Leadership, North Carolina State University; Thalia Mulvihill, Education, Ball State University; and Susan Shepler, School of Business, American University. You reviewers all kindly offered helpful suggestions and criticisms, even helping to re-sequence and restructure chapters as well as identifying gaps that could be filled, and for this effort I will be forever grateful.

Numerous words of encouragement and advice came from a distinguished critical friend, C. Deborah Laughton, Guilford's Publisher, Methodology and Statistics, whose experience in publishing qualitative and other research methods texts probably goes farther back than she would want to acknowledge. Our longstanding acquaintance served as an invaluable presence in providing inspiration to start (and complete) this book.

Finally, my wife, Karen, and son, Andrew, had to tolerate the book's continued distraction to our family life, over a lengthy period of time. They gave their unconditional love, interspersed with compositional creativity in helping find better words and sharper sentences. The dedication of this book to them is but a small way of acknowledging their enduring support.

All of these interactions notwithstanding, none of the named institutions or individuals bears any responsibility for the final product or for the statements in this book.

Contents

PART II.   DOING QUALITATIVE RESEARCH

PART III.   PRESENTING THE RESULTS
FROM QUALITATIVE RESEARCH

CHAPTER 10. Displaying Qualitative Data   233

PART I

UNDERSTANDING QUALITATIVE RESEARCH

CHAPTER 1

What Is Qualitative Research— and Why Might You Consider Doing Such Research?

This chapter introduces qualitative research, initially illustrating it with a topically diverse group of published studies. Their breadth indicates the potential relevance and allure of qualitative research: Unlike other social science methods, virtually every real-world happening can become the subject of a qualitative study.

The chapter then discusses five features, as well as some common research practices, that together define qualitative research. (The common practices will appear in detail in the remainder of this book.) These five features and common practices notwithstanding, qualitative research remains a multifaceted field of inquiry, marked by different orientations and methodologies. Important distinctions start with whether one assumes: a singular or multiple realities, the uniqueness or potential generalizability of human events, and the need to follow a particular methodological variation of qualitative research or not. The chapter discusses all three distinctions, suggesting two mediating strategies to enable research to proceed. Most important is a final common denominator—the need for qualitative studies to demonstrate their trustworthiness and credibility, regardless of any of the three distinctions.

A. THE ALLURE OF QUALITATIVE RESEARCH: A TOPICAL PANORAMA OF STUDIES

PREVIEW—*What you should learn from this section:*
1. The broad variety of topics that can be studied through qualitative research, unlike other types of social science research.
2. The presence of qualitative research studies in many different academic disciplines and professions.

Why do qualitative research? You just might want to study a real-world setting, discover how people cope and thrive in that setting—and capture the contextual richness of people's everyday lives. Just consider the variety of topics that you might be able to study.

You could focus on a specific group of people, such as homeless women, spend many nights as a volunteer in a homeless shelter, and help others to understand how the women deal with their everyday challenges, inside and outside of the shelter (e.g., Liebow, 1993). Along the way, you might derive insights into how (and why) the women came to such a circumstance. You also might be able to illustrate these insights by tracing the life histories of many of these individual women (see "A Qualitative Study of Homeless Women," Vignette 1.1).

VIGNETTE 1.1. A QUALITATIVE STUDY OF HOMELESS WOMEN

Although a common stereotype links homelessness with men, women too can be homeless, and shelters will cater specifically to men or women. Elliot Liebow's (1993) study, in the Washington, D.C., area, covers a group of women and their shelter. To do the study, Liebow spent the better part of 4 years volunteering at the shelter, including many overnight stays.

Liebow's study depicts the culture of the shelter, involving the interactions among clients and staff striving to meet both individual and institutional needs. The women are of various ages and racially mixed, and some have had their own families. To capture this diversity, the study also includes separate life histories of about 20 of them. Throughout the book, Liebow struggles with the question of why these women are homeless, but in the process provides enough information for readers to draw their own conclusions.

Previously, Liebow completed a study of underemployed men in an urban neighborhood. This earlier work, *Talley's Corner* (1967), has for years been recognized as a classic qualitative study.

See also Vignettes 5.6 and 11.7.

Alternatively, you might want to study how government and public health officials make decisions about a threatened swine flu epidemic. In 1978, such a threat led to the mass vaccination of 40 million Americans (Neustadt & Fineberg, 1983). The officials ended the campaign prematurely when, as the flu season progressed, they realized they had overestimated the epidemic's potential—but also because they discovered that being vaccinated exposed people to a rare but deadly disease. To do this study, you might have interviewed key officials and reviewed many official documents. Your study's findings might have pointed to the difficulties and uncertainties in dealing with mass immunization campaigns—an issue, not surprisingly, still relevant in the 21st century.

At a more intimate extreme, you might want to understand and analyze the conversation and interactions between two people. You would need to be able to audio, if not videotape, their conversation because your interest would go well beyond the specific words in the conversation. Among other signs, your data also would include the way that words might have been run together or shortened, as well as the pauses, overlaps, and body language between the conversants (e.g., Drew, 2009). Your overall goal would be to unravel the power, control, and other motives each conversant might be pursuing—potentially a helpful way of understanding physician–patient, teacher–student, and peer–peer relationships in their real-world settings.

There are many other examples of qualitative research. They touch on all walks of life. Close to all of our lives, the changing role of women in American society has been the subject of a good number of studies, such as:

> - Ruth Sidel's (2006) inquiry into how single mothers confront their social and economic challenges;
> - Pamela Stone's (2007) examination of why successful career women drop out to stay at home; and
> - Kathryn Edin and Maria Kefalas's (2005) study of why women with low incomes "put motherhood before marriage."

In the three examples, the researchers conducted extended interviews with many women and their families, also visiting their homes and observing family behavior. These and other studies follow, in a way, Carol Gilligan's (1982) landmark study of a woman's place in a man's world—which argued that much of the so-called universal theories of moral and emotional development had been based exclusively on male perceptions and male experiences.

Beyond these examples, the range of topics covered by other contemporary qualitative works stretches from the rare to the commonplace, such as:

> - Unearthing surprising but still existing forms of exploitation, such as *human slavery* in Thailand, Mauritania, Brazil, Pakistan, and India (e.g., Bales, 2004);
> - Analyzing the challenges of *immigration* between other countries and the United States, whether in educational (e.g., Valenzuela, 1999) or community (e.g., Levitt, 2001) settings;
> - Studying how older people might have been admitted into a hospital or into *long-term care* in circumstances that could have been avoided (e.g., Tetley, Grant, & Davies, 2009);
> - Offering data and explanations on how a *Fortune 500 firm* in the computer business could go out of business in the 1990s (e.g., Schein, 2003);
> - Contrasting the consumer differences between *toy stores* located in middle- as opposed to working-class neighborhoods, reflecting not just the stores' practices but also the families' shopping and purchasing habits (e.g., Williams, 2006);

- Examining residential life and the differences in racial, ethnic, and class tensions in four *urban neighborhoods* (e.g., Wilson & Taub, 2006); or
- Showing the different *childhood experiences* of working- and middle-class families by making extensive observations in the homes of 12 families (e.g., Lareau, 2003).

You even can study everyday life on the streets of your city or town, such as:

- Duneier's (1999) study of sidewalk vendors;
- Lee's (2009) study of street interactions; or
- Bourgois's (2003) study of the addicts, thieves, and dealers who form part of the underground economy in some cities.

The allure of qualitative research is that it enables you to conduct in-depth studies about a broad array of topics, including your favorites, in plain and everyday terms. Moreover, qualitative research offers greater latitude in selecting topics of interest because other research methods are likely to be constrained by:

♦ the inability to establish the necessary research conditions (as in an experiment);

♦ the unavailability of sufficient data series or lack of coverage of sufficient variables (as in an economic study);

♦ the difficulty in drawing an adequate sample of respondents and obtaining a sufficiently high response rate (as in a survey); or

♦ other limitations such as being devoted to studying the past but not ongoing events (as in a history).[1]

By now, qualitative research has become an acceptable, if not mainstream, form of research in many different academic and professional fields. As a result, the large number of students and scholars who conduct qualitative studies may be part of different social science disciplines (e.g., sociology, anthropology, political science, or psychology) or different professions (e.g., education, management, nursing, urban planning, and program evaluation). In any of these fields, qualitative research represents an attractive and fruitful way of doing research.

---

[1]Oral history (Yow, 1994) is a form of more contemporary history, which may capture ongoing events. Oral history therefore falls within both the classical historical inquiry and qualitative inquiry. In a similar manner, this brief reference to other forms of social science inquiry is not intended to convey the impression of any sharp distinction among the types of research. They all can overlap in one way or another, even though they still have some core characteristics that differentiate them.

B. THE DISTINCTIVENESS OF QUALITATIVE RESEARCH

PREVIEW—*What you should learn from this section:*
1. The five features distinguishing qualitative research from other kinds of social science research.
2. How the five features point to specific ways of practicing qualitative research.

Despite the greater latitude offered by qualitative research, your colleagues may nevertheless claim that other types of social science research—for example, surveys, economic studies, experiments, quasi-experiments, and historical studies—also can address many of the same topics as the opening panorama of qualitative studies. These other types of research can be the basis for studying similar groups of people as homeless women, similar public health issues such as immunization campaigns or physician–patient relationships, similar gender and women's topics, and even topics that parallel the international and national topics of the sort also cited earlier. Your colleagues' claims therefore point to the need to confront the question of what makes qualitative research distinctive, especially in relation to other types of social science research.

Qualitative Research: A Broad Area of Inquiry

The diversity of what is called qualitative research, because of its relevance to different disciplines and professions, challenges anyone to arrive at a succinct definition. Too brief a definition will seem to exclude one discipline or another. Too broad a definition will seem uselessly global. In fact, the term *qualitative research* may be like other terms of the same genre—for example, *sociological research, psychological research*, or *education research*. Within its own particular discipline or profession, each term connotes a large body of research, embracing a variety of highly contrasting methods. Think simply, for instance, of clinical and experimental psychology. Both form vigorous parts of the same field, though the methods differ markedly.

Five Features of Qualitative Research

Instead of trying to arrive at a singular definition of qualitative research, you might consider five features, listed next and then discussed individually:

1. Studying the meaning of people's lives, under real-world conditions;
2. Representing the views and perspectives of the people (labeled throughout this book, as the *participants*[2]) in a study;

---

[2]The qualitative literature also uses the alternative label "members." However, a participant's affiliation with a qualitative study is not necessarily strong enough to warrant such a term. Most qualitative researchers also would reject another alternative, labeling a participant as a "subject" of study. Hence, use of the label "participants" seems to be the best alternative.

3. Covering the contextual conditions within which people live;
4. Contributing insights into existing or emerging concepts that may help to *explain* human social behavior; and
5. Striving to use *multiple sources of evidence* rather than relying on a single source alone.

Starting at the top of the list, qualitative research first involves studying the meaning of people's lives, under real-world conditions. People will be performing in their everyday roles or have expressed themselves through their own diaries, journals, writing, and even photography—entirely independent of any research inquiry. Social interactions will occur with minimal intrusion by artificial research procedures, and people will be saying what they want to say, not, for example, limited to responding to a researcher's preestablished questionnaire. Likewise, people will not be inhibited by the confines of a laboratory or any laboratory-like setting. And they will not be represented by such statistical averages as the average American family having 3.18 persons (as of 2006)—which at once may represent accurately an entire population but in fact by definition does not speak to any single, real-life family.

Second, qualitative research differs because of its ability to represent the views and perspectives of the participants in a study. Capturing their perspectives may be a major purpose of a qualitative study. Thus, the events and ideas emerging from qualitative research can represent the meanings given to real-life events by the people who live them, not the values, preconceptions, or meanings held by researchers.

Third, qualitative research covers contextual conditions—the social, institutional, and environmental conditions within which people's lives take place. In many ways, these contextual conditions may strongly influence all human events. However, the other social science methods (except for history) have difficulty in addressing these conditions.

Experiments, for instance, "control out" these conditions (hence the artificiality of laboratory experiments). Quasi-experiments admit such conditions but by design nevertheless focus only on a limited set of "variables," which may or may not fully appreciate the contextual conditions. Similarly, surveys are constrained by the need to manage carefully the degrees of freedom required to analyze the responses to a set of survey questions; surveys are therefore limited in the number of questions devoted to any contextual conditions. History does address contextual conditions, but in its conventional form studies the "dead past," not ongoing events as in qualitative research (refer again to footnote 1 about oral history).

Fourth, qualitative research is not just a diary or chronicle of everyday life. Such a function would be a rather mundane version of real-world events. On the contrary, qualitative research is driven by a desire to explain these events, through existing or emerging concepts. For instance, one existing concept is Goffman's

(1963) stigma management. In his original work, stigma management largely pertained to adaptations by individual people. However, a contemporary qualitative study applied his typology and framework to a collective group, thereby offering new insights into how the actions of nation-states also might try to overcome their

---

VIGNETTE 1.2. USING QUALITATIVE RESEARCH TO PRODUCE NEW INSIGHTS

Lauren Rivera's (2008) study examines how the Croatian government "altered representations of the region's history and culture through international tourism in the wake of the violent wars of Yugoslav secession" (p. 614). The government's goal was to create a vigorous tourism industry, attracting foreign travelers. To do this required "directing attention away from the war and repositioning the country as being identical to its Western European neighbors" (p. 614).

Data from a variety of field-based sources show how Croatia managed the difficulties of the past by "cultural reframing rather than public acknowledgment" (Rivera, 2008, p. 613). These findings are then discussed in light of Erving Goffman's (1963) classic work on *stigma and stigma management*. His typology of stigma management, usually applied to the study of individuals with mental or physical disabilities, is found to provide an insightful framework when applied to conditions in Croatia, a nation-state. By broadening the reach of Goffman's ideas, to understand "processes of historical and cultural representation" (p. 615), Rivera's study ably demonstrates the value of linking qualitative research with insightful social processes.

---

own historically stigmatizing events (see "Using Qualitative Research to Produce New Insights," Vignette 1.2).

Similarly, qualitative research can be the occasion for developing new concepts. The concepts might attempt to explain social processes, such as the schooling of American students. An illustrative concept offered by a qualitative study is the notion of *subtractive schooling* (see "Using an Overarching Concept to Organize a Qualitative Study," Vignette 1.3), used to provide potentially useful explanations and to form a platform for new inquiries. In fact, studies devoid of concepts, whether existing or new, or devoid of any interpretations at all, would resemble diaries or chronicles but not qualitative research.

Fifth, qualitative research strives to collect, integrate, and present data from a variety of sources of evidence as part of any given study. The variety will likely follow from your having to study a real-world setting and its participants. The complexity of the field setting and the diversity of its participants are likely to warrant the use of interviews and observations and even the inspection of documents and artifacts. The study's conclusions are likely to be based on triangulating the data from the different sources. This convergence will add to the study's credibility and trustworthiness (see more about this goal at the end of this chapter).

VIGNETTE 1.3.   USING AN OVERARCHING CONCEPT TO ORGANIZE A QUALITATIVE STUDY

Valenzuela's (1999) study of a high school in Houston shows how an overarching concept can drive the organization of an entire study. The concept is of *subtractive schooling*, an experience arising from the way that English as a second language (ESL) programs are imposed on immigrant students.

   The author spent 3 years as a participant-observer in the school, also collecting a wealth of interview and documentary data. Valenzuela notes that most studies of ESL programs had focused on how students learn, rather than on how they are schooled, leaving a gap in the literature. In brief, her study shows how the schooling experience assumes a subtractive nature because Spanish fluency, rather than being a strength on which to build, is a "barrier that needs to be overcome" (1999, p. 262). "Abandoning one's original culture" then becomes part of an alienating process (p. 264). The findings show how subtractive schooling also extends to divisions among the different groups of students.

   See also Vignette 4.5.

Common Practices

Articulating how these five distinctive features convert into actual research practice becomes the task of the remainder of this entire book. Though a formal qualitative research "methodology" may not exist, the offerings capture the methodological practices that follow directly from the five features. Several practices are briefly listed next. However, you will have to turn to the referenced chapters for details on how these and other practices can work for you:

1. The use of flexible rather than fixed research designs, covering eight choices, such as strengthening a study's validity, selecting the samples to be studied, and being concerned with generalizing (see Chapter 4);

2. The collection of "field-based" data—appropriately trying to capture contextual conditions as well as participants' perspectives—resulting from your own fieldwork and by examining the diaries, journals, writings, photographs, or other artifacts associated with the participants themselves (see Chapters 5 and 6);

3. The analysis of non-numeric data—including choices about whether to use various types of computer software in the process (see Chapter 8); and

4. The interpretation of the findings from a qualitative study, which can involve challenging conventional generalizations and social stereotypes (see Chapter 9).

   The book's other chapters cover more general issues, such as how to equip yourself to do qualitative research (Chapter 2), how to start a qualitative study (Chapter 3), how to record data properly (Chapter 7), and how to present qualitative data through written and visual forms and to create a final composition (Chapters 10 and 11). The final chapter introduces a major contemporary trend directly related to qualitative research—the increased attention devoted to *mixed methods research* (Chapter 12). Some important topics—such as maintaining awareness of how your role as a researcher can influence a study (*reflexivity*)—tend to occur throughout the book (also see Chapter 11's discussion on how to present one's "reflexive self" as part of a completed qualitative study).

C. THE MULTIFACETED WORLD OF QUALITATIVE RESEARCH

PREVIEW—*What you should learn from this section:*
1. How human events may reflect multiple realities.
2. How the study of such events, despite their uniqueness, can still follow common data collection and analysis techniques.
3. The multiple methodological variations within qualitative research.
4. Two strategies for proceeding to do a qualitative study ("mediating strategies") in light of the rich mosaic of qualitative research.

The breadth of what is called qualitative research embraces a mosaic of orientations as well as methodological choices. Taking advantage of the richness of the mosaic offers an opportunity to customize a qualitative study.

Three conditions in particular contribute to the mosaic: the potential multiplicity of interpretations of the human events being studied; the potential uniqueness of these events; and the methodological variations available within qualitative research. Each condition can involve extreme choices, often involving philosophical and not just methodological considerations. However, between the extremes lies a broad range of acceptable positions. The three conditions together therefore create much of the multifaceted world of qualitative research.

Multiple Interpretations of the Same Events?

The initial condition derives from qualitative research's desire to capture the meaning of real-world events from the perspective of a study's participants. Such an objective cannot ignore the fact that the participants' meanings, if studied and reported by a researcher, also unavoidably subsume a second set of meanings of the same events—those of the researcher.

Two complementary terms—*emic* and *etic*—though now somewhat outdated, clarify the potential duality, if not multiplicity, of meanings. An emic perspective attempts to capture participants' indigenous meanings of real-world events. In contrast, an etic perspective represents the same set of real-world events, but from an external perspective—typically that of the researcher. The two terms borrow from a linguistic parallel, whereby *phonemics* represents sounds based on their internal function within a language and *phonetics* represents the acoustic or more external properties of words (e.g., Emerson, 2001, p. 31).

The emic and etic perspectives will usually differ—owing to differences in observers' value systems, their predispositions, and their gender, age, and race and ethnicity. For instance, in a study involving "naturalistic ethnography," the investigators noted that a fieldworker entering a natural setting was an anthropological stranger who had to "remain careful not to disturb the ecology of [the participants'] social world by introducing [her] own subjectivity, beliefs, or interests as a white, middle-class, academic researcher" (Roman & Apple, 1990, p. 45). An additional challenge to researchers is "to hold in abeyance any of her or his prior political assumptions and theoretical commitments" (p. 46).

The differences in value systems permeate our very thought processes. In turn, these differences will affect the way that qualitative research will be conducted and reported. Operationally, these will show up even (and especially) when describing a set of real-world events. Thus, the apparently straightforward task of making a description becomes an interpretive matter (Lawrence-Lightfoot & Davis, 1997), if only because of an inevitable selection process (Emerson, 2001, p. 28; Wolfinger, 2002). The descriptive process cannot fully cover all the possible events that could have been observed at a field setting. Even the use of video or tape recordings of social behavior, while seemingly providing a comprehensive reach, have their basic parameters—where, when, and what to record—defined by the researcher.

Selectivity also can arise because of an investigator's preconceived categories for assigning meaning to events and their features (e.g., Becker, 1998, pp. 76–85). As stated by Robert Emerson (2001, p. 48):

> The writer decides not only which particular events are significant, which are merely worthy of inclusion, which are absolutely essential, and how to order these events, but also what is counted as an "event" in the first place.

The appeal to creating "thick description"—a term commonly associated with the work of Clifford Geertz (1973) but in fact credited by him (pp. 6–7) to Gilbert Ryle (1949)—is one way of trying to reveal or at least increase one's awareness of the selectivity and the preconceived categories (Becker, 1998). The thicker the description, the more that selectivity might be said to have been reduced.

Beyond producing a thick description, other desirable field practices include "confront[ing] ourselves with just those things that would jar us out of the conventional categories, the conventional statement of the problem, the conventional solution" (Becker, 1998, p. 85), and "identify[ing] the case that is likely to upset your thinking and [to] look for it" (p. 87).

Nevertheless, no matter how successful these confrontations might be, researchers cannot in the final analysis avoid their own research lenses in rendering reality. Thus, the goal is to acknowledge that multiple interpretations may exist and to be sure that as much as possible is done to prevent a researcher from inadvertently imposing her or his own (*etic*) interpretation onto a participant's (*emic*) interpretation.

In this sense, fieldwork descriptions are "constructed" (Guba, 1990). Even a field "setting" is not a "pre-given natural entity" but is something that is constructed

(Emerson, 2001, p. 43). When studying the culture of a people or of a place, the researcher's descriptions may be considered second- or third-order interpretations because they represent the researcher's "constructions of [participants'] constructions of what they and their compatriots are up to" (Geertz, 1973, pp. 9, 15).

Following such logic, the field researcher in effect serves as the main research instrument for collecting data in a qualitative study (see Chapter 5, Section D, for more details). No physical measuring instrument, experimental procedure, or questionnaire prevails—although all might be used as part of a qualitative study. In most situations, the researcher unavoidably serves as a research instrument because important real-world phenomena—such as the very "culture" that is a frequent topic of qualitative studies—cannot be measured by external instruments but only can be revealed by making inferences about observed behaviors and by talking to people (Spradley, 1979, p. 7).

Moreover, the researcher has a human personality and cannot perform as "a faceless robot or a machinelike recorder of human events" (Powdermaker, 1966, p. 19). This personality "is not formed in the field but has many years of conditioning behind it," including "the choice of problems and of methods, even the choice of [an academic] discipline itself" (p. 19).

People who do qualitative research view the *emic–etic* distinction and the possibility of multiple interpretations of the same events as an opportunity, not a constraint. In fact, a common theme underlying many qualitative studies is to demonstrate how participants' perspectives may diverge dramatically from those held by outsiders.

For instance, *multicultural research* aims to describe the participants' perspectives in accurate and valid but also sympathetic ways. Thus, common topics of study have been those groups "that have historically experienced racism, discrimination, and exclusion" (Banks, 2006, p. 775). In a similar manner, Edin and Kefalas's (2005) study of why the participants in their study put motherhood before marriage was an attempt to explain the worthiness of holding such a belief even though it did not represent a conventional middle-class view.

Whether adopting a multicultural orientation or not, acknowledging the possibility of multiple interpretations of similar events can cast qualitative research as a *relativist* (multiple realities and observer dependent) rather than *realist* (single reality and set of "facts," independent of any observer) type of inquiry. Most qualitative studies will position themselves along a continuum between these two philosophical extremes. For instance, your own study might signal a leaning toward the acceptance of multiple realities by highlighting participants' differing perspectives and not forcing them to converge on a single reality. You also might want to include a strong self-reflexive presentation, acknowledging the important facets of your research lens, as discussed in Chapter 11 of this book.

Alternatively, your own study might signal a leaning toward accepting a single reality by triangulating across different sources of data and seeking to establish a common set of facts. Your goal might be to define a certain reality, and within this reality you would be trying to minimize the contamination between your own interpretations and those of the participants.

The Uniqueness of Human Events?

A second condition further enriches the mosaic: Human events may be considered as either being entirely unique or having some properties that are relevant and potentially applicable to other situations. Either stance, again with a broad swath of positions in between, can be taken in studying nearly every social topic. For instance, consider a qualitative study in psychology, covering the love relationship between two people. Likewise, consider a qualitative study in sociology, covering the gentrification of a particular urban neighborhood at a particular period of time—or a qualitative study in management, covering the merger between two firms. You can imagine all of these situations to be totally unique. In contrast, you also can imagine studying the same situations and striving to identify their implications for other (presumably parallel) situations.

Within qualitative research, *phenomenological* studies, emphasizing *hermeneutic* or interpretive analyses, are most strongly devoted to capturing the uniqueness of events. As an example, as part of a psychological study, you might immerse yourself in the lives of persons being trained to practice family medicine. In carrying out such an inquiry, you might follow them during their initial years of residency, share their particular struggles, contradictions, and conflicts, and attempt to derive a deep understanding of what it has been like for those persons to undergo such a training experience (see "An Immersion Study of Physicians' Training," Vignette 1.4).

VIGNETTE 1.4. AN IMMERSION STUDY OF PHYSICIANS' TRAINING

Richard Addison (1992) used a grounded hermeneutic approach to study nine people in their first year of residency. He chose a university-affiliated family practice residency program, focusing on the first-year experiences of the new residents.

Addison started by immersing himself in the residents' everyday world, developing his own experiential understanding of their practices. He not only went around with these residents but also interviewed their spouses and others in the same educational setting as well as reading "an enormous volume of memos, schedules, and documentation" (1992, p. 115).

As part of a "hermeneutically circular process," Addison then incorporated his fuller understanding into further observations and immersion (1992, p. 116). At various stages, he also presented his emerging work to his own colleagues, a process that helped him to "stand back, reflect on, and question [his] understanding" (p. 119).

Addison's analysis constantly returned him to his main research question: how individuals become family physicians. His main findings dealt with the importance of "surviving" as a unifying theme, embedded in "a background of conflicts and contradictions in the fabric of the residency" (1992, pp. 122–123).

Phenomenological studies attend not only to the events being studied but also to their political, historical, and sociocultural contexts (e.g., Miller & Crabtree,

1992, p. 25). The studies strive to be as faithful as possible to the lived experiences, especially as might be described by the participants' own words. In education, a simple example would be asking people to describe situations in which they have learned or not learned, instead of trying to create a specific laboratory situation to test how they learn (Giorgi & Giorgi, 2009). In such inquiries, phenomenological studies resist "any use of concepts, categories, taxonomies, or reflections about the experiences" (Van Manen, 1990, p. 9). Related to this objective, Chapter 3 of this book discusses a "fieldwork first" choice that can precede identifying any research questions as part of the process of starting a new qualitative study.

Included among the features to be resisted in phenomenological studies is any interest in developing generalizations because they may distort the desired focus on the uniqueness of the events (Van Manen, 1990, p. 22). A corollary concern would be the use of any predetermined research methods whose fixed procedures might artificially constrain a rendition of the event by "rule-governing the research project" (p. 29). To this extent, the conduct of a phenomenological study might want to avoid most or all of the design choices—including the one regarding any concern with generalizing a study's findings—presented in Chapter 4 of this book.

Nevertheless, and despite taking such a stance, the uniqueness of the events being studied does not preclude a phenomenological study from using the same kind of data collection procedures as in a nonphenomenological study. The procedures include obtaining experiential descriptions from a variety of key people, doing interviews, making observations, and collecting information about lived experiences from other sources such as diaries, journals, and logs (e.g., Van Manen, 1990, pp. 53–76). These procedures would directly resemble the data collection practices presented in Chapter 6 of this book.

In like manner, phenomenological studies are likely to use the same kind of data analysis procedures as in a nonphenomenological study. For instance, the emphasis by phenomenological studies on capturing and interpreting participants' words and language readily leads to the arraying of participants' original words side by side with a researcher's interpretations and even transformations of these words (Giorgi & Giorgi, 2009, p. 44), as well as the potential need for some kind of thematic analysis (Van Manen, 1990, pp. 77–109). These procedures are not unlike the coding of textual information in other qualitative studies, or the practices presented later in Chapter 8 of this book.

In other words, many common research procedures still underlie qualitative studies that may in other respects differ strongly in their philosophical orientation and research design.

Whether to Emulate One of Qualitative Research's Variants

A third condition contributing to the overall mosaic points to the large number of formally recognized methodologies within qualitative research. In defining your own qualitative research, you may want to emulate one of the variations. You may have been recommended to do so by an adviser, or you may have a compelling need to respond to the question "what type of qualitative research are you doing?"[3] No formal typology or inventory exists, but the specialized guidance found in many articles and books (e.g., Denzin & Lincoln, 2005)provides ample models of the variations that can be followed in your own research.

For instance, consider the 10 variations depicted in Exhibit 1.1. All tend to be among the commonly accepted forms of qualitative research. They do not group into any orderly categories. As a result, the variations can overlap, such as: doing a case study based on participant-observation; or conducting a life history as part of a narrative inquiry; or doing action research and adopting a grounded theory approach in collecting and analyzing the data.

You need to be sensitive to these variations, but you do not need to choose among them if you do not wish to. Your sensitivity mainly needs to acknowledge their numerosity. For instance, in addition to the 10 varieties listed in Exhibit 1.1, others include autoethnography (e.g., Jones, 2005); conversation analysis (e.g., Drew, 2009); discourse analysis (e.g., Bloome & Clark, 2006; Willig, 2009); performance ethnography (e.g., Denzin, 2003); and symbolic interactionism (e.g., Blumer, 1969; Mead, 1934). You should therefore appreciate and be sensitive to the likelihood that articles retrieved from different qualitative research journals—such as *Action Research, Narrative Inquiry* (formerly the *Journal of Narrative and Life History*), and the *Journal of Contemporary Ethnography*, just to name a few—tend to favor different variations and hence will differ in their research orientations. Some scholars (e.g., Grbich, 2007; Rex, Steadman, & Graciano, 2006) also have identified different analytic preferences to accompany the different variations.

Despite these variations, the common qualities that distinguish qualitative research across all of its variations also have persisted and become better recognized. Regardless of any particular variation, virtually all qualitative research appears to follow most, if not all, of the five features of qualitative research described earlier. Indeed, strong, if not exemplary, studies can be conducted under the general label "qualitative research" or "field-based study," without resorting to any of the variations.

Interestingly, this kind of generalized qualitative research appears with regularity in the top academic journals and university presses. For instance, two leading journals in sociology cover all strands of sociological research. Both of them have devoted considerable space to a variety of qualitative studies (e.g., Auyero & Swistun, 2008; Cable, Shriver, & Mix, 2008; Davis & Robinson, 2009; Madsen, 2009; Moore, 2008; Read & Oselin, 2008; Rivera, 2008).

Similar citations can be found in other academic disciplines and professions—whose top journals also cater to all types of research, not just qualitative research (as but two examples, see Sauder, 2008, in the management sciences, and Sack,

---

[3]Creswell (2007, p. 5), for instance, poses this question and gives it as a major rationale for guiding people to doing studies that emphasize one of five variations of qualitative research: narrative research, phenomenology, grounded theory, ethnography, and case study. He admits to being unable to address other variations, such as action research (p. 11).

EXHIBIT 1.1. ILLUSTRATIVE VARIATIONS IN QUALITATIVE RESEARCH

Illustrative variation	Relevant works	Brief description
Action research	Lewin (1946); Small (1995); Greenwood & Levin (1998); Reason & Riley (2009)	Emphasizes the researcher's adoption of an action role or an active collaboration with study participants.
Case study	Platt (1992); Yin (2009); Yin (in press)	Studies a phenomenon (the "case") in its real-world context.
Ethnography	Powdermaker (1966); Geertz (1973); Wolcott (1999); Anderson-Levitt (2006)	Involves a field-based study lengthy enough to surface people's everyday norms, rituals, and routines in detail.
Ethnomethodology	Garfinkel (1967); Cicourel (1971); Holstein & Gubrium (2005)	Seeks to understand how people learn and know the social rituals, mannerisms, and symbols in their everyday life and culture.
Feminist research	Fine (1992); Olesen (2005); Hesse-Biber & Leavy (2007)	Embraces the perspective that methodological and other relationships embed oft-ignored power relations that can affect research findings.
Grounded theory	Glaser & Strauss (1967); Charmaz (2005); Corbin & Strauss (2007)	Assumes that the natural occurrence of social behavior within real-world contexts is best analyzed by deriving "bottom-up" grounded categories and concepts.
Life history	Lewis (1961, 1965); Langness (1965); Bertaux (1981)	Collects and narrates a person's life story, capturing its turning points and important themes.
Narrative inquiry	Riessman (1993, 2008); Chase (2005); Connelly & Clandinin (2006); Murray (2009)	Constructs a narrative rendition of the findings from a real-world setting and participants, to accentuate a sense of "being there."
Participant-observer study	Becker (1958); Spradley (1980); Tedlock (1991)	Conducts field-based research based on the researcher locating in the real-world setting being studied.
Phenomenological study	Husserl (1970); Schutz (1970); Van Manen (1990); Moustakas (1994); Giorgi & Giorgi (2009)	Studies human events as they are immediately experienced in real-world settings, resisting prior categories and concepts that might distort the experiential basis for understanding the events.

2008, in teacher education). Likewise, university presses publish many qualitative studies that assume the more general characteristics of qualitative research and that do not fall within any particular variant.

Therefore, rather than feeling forced to single out one of the variations as the basis for a qualitative study, you can exercise a viable option by conducting qualitative research in a generalized form. You can simply state—as in the articles in the leading journals just cited—that you are presenting a qualitative research study, without reference to any of the variants. Note that following the generalized form of qualitative research does not imply a rigid methodology. The design of your study (see Chapter 4), the particular data collection methods (see Chapter 6), and such analytic alternatives as whether to "code" your data or not (see Chapter 8), all still involve a set of choices that are yours to make.

Mediating Strategies

You can mediate within the mosaic of orientations and methodologies in either of two ways. Both ways help you to proceed with a qualitative study, whether you plan to follow one of the variations or to conduct a generalized form of qualitative research.

Pursuing the first way, you can explicitly recognize any methodological choices ahead of time and then indicate your sensitivity about their opportunities, constraints, and philosophical underpinnings. The process would resemble what Grbich (2007, p. 17) has described as acknowledging the *epistemological location* of your research—that is, the philosophical assumptions you make about the ways of knowing what you know. Your epistemological location could be at one of the extremes created by choosing from a combination of relativist–realist and unique–not unique dimensions. However, the location also could be anywhere in the middle, representing the "viable middle ground" as recognized by Gubrium and Holstein (1998).

> • For instance, you can express and defend your intention to do a case study because it represents a unique case, deserving to be studied on its own right. Though covering a particular situation, the case still may produce unusual insights warranting its study. Robert Stake (1995, p. 8; 2005) has called these *intrinsic case studies*.[4]
>
> Alternatively, you can assert that your case study not only presents a particular situation but is intended to inform other situations or cases, and Stake calls these *instrumental case studies* (p. 3).

Having stated your epistemological location, you would then indicate how the design of your study and the selection of your research procedures reflected the stated location—in part by citing other studies that had made similar choices and had expressed the appropriate precautions. You even might adopt different narrative "voices" in reporting your work, again noting ahead of time why you chose the particular voice.

---

[4]Rolls (2005), whose book consists of a compilation of 16 famous case studies in psychology (e.g., the case about multiple personality disorder known as *The Three Faces of Eve*), states the same point in the following way: "But do we always have to find out universal truths of behavior? Sometimes, surely, it's enough to explore the life of a unique individual" (p. 2). In history, the conduct of biographies follows a similar motive.

- For instance, John van Maanen (1988; also see Vignette 11.3) distinguishes among a dispassionate, third-person voice (*realist tale*), a participatory first-person voice that openly recognizes the researcher's role in the field (*confessional tales*), and a narration striving to place the reader in the midst of a fieldwork situation, as if to relive it (*impressionist tale*).

The different voices would accommodate and complement your chosen epistemological location.

Pursuing a second mediating strategy, an alternative and equally viable way of dealing with the mosaic is to assume that "all types of inquiry, insofar as the goal is to reach credible conclusions, [have] an underlying *epistemological similarity*" (Phillips, 1990b, p. 35, emphasis added). Such similarity may underlie all of qualitative research, regardless of the choices, variants, or customizing within the mosaic. The main goal—doing trustworthy and credible qualitative research—represents the common endeavor, and so the entirety of the next section is devoted to this second alternative.

D. BUILDING TRUSTWORTHINESS AND CREDIBILITY INTO QUALITATIVE RESEARCH

PREVIEW—*What you should learn from this section:*
Three objectives for building the trustworthiness and credibility of a qualitative study.

Transparency

The first objective for building trustworthiness and credibility is that qualitative research be done in a publicly accessible manner. To use a term that rose in popularity in the 21st century, the research procedures should be *transparent*.

This first objective means that you must describe and document your qualitative research procedures so that other people can review and try to understand them. All data need to be available for inspection, too. The general idea is that others should be able to scrutinize your work and the evidence used to support your findings and conclusions. The scrutiny can result in criticism, support, or refinement. Moreover, any person, whether a peer, a colleague, or a participant in your qualitative research study, should be able to undertake such an examination. In this manner, the final study should be able to withstand close scrutiny by others (e.g., Yardley, 2009, pp. 243–250).

Methodic-ness

A second craft objective is to do qualitative research methodically. There needs to be adequate room for discovery and allowance for unanticipated events. However, being methodic means following some orderly set of research procedures and minimizing whimsical or careless work—whether a study is based on an explicitly defined research design or on a more informal but nonetheless rigorous field routine. Being methodic also includes avoiding unexplained bias or deliberate distortion in carrying out research. Finally, being methodic also means bringing a sense of completeness to a research effort, as well as cross-checking a study's procedures and data.

Eisenhart (2006) has discussed related ways that can be used to serve the methodic-ness objective. For instance, she notes that fieldwork descriptions should show that a researcher was "really and fully present—physically, cognitively, and emotionally—in the scenes of action under study" (Eisenhart, 2006, p. 574). Her objectives pertain to qualitative research, but they may have counterparts in other types of social science research. One counterpart in experimental research might be the quality control exercised as part of the experimenter's data collection procedures, especially addressing the threat of "experimenter effects" (Rosenthal, 1966).

Eisenhart also urges qualitative researchers to demonstrate that the data and interpretations are accurate *from some point of view* [emphasis added], which leads in particular to a sensitivity about the need to report, in a self-reflexive manner, the presumed interplay between the researcher's positioning (as a research instrument) and the events and participants in the field (pp. 575–579). Especially relevant in recording such self-reflexivity may be a researcher's journal, which "will contain a record of experiences, ideas, fears, mistakes, confusions, breakthroughs, and problems that arise" (Spradley, 1979, p. 76). To be noted again is that, as a counterpart, exemplary researchers doing nonqualitative research also keep such journals, usually taking the form of a formally organized notebook.

Adherence to Evidence

A final objective is that qualitative research be based on an explicit set of evidence. For many studies, especially those where the goal is to have participants describe their own decision-making processes, the evidence will consist of participants' actual language as well as the context in which the language is expressed (Van Manen, 1990, p. 38; Willig, 2009, p. 162). In these situations, the language is valued as the representation of reality. Such a function differs from many other situations, emphasized throughout this book, in which studies are dominantly concerned with people's behavior. Under this latter circumstance, participants' words are viewed as "self-reports" about their behavior. The words cannot be literally accepted but require further corroboration, for instance, to determine whether or not the behavior actually occurred.

Regardless of the kind of data being collected, a study's conclusions should be drawn in reference to those data. If there are multiple perspectives, Anderson-Levitt (2006, p. 289) notes that analysis may mean making sense from each perspective and also testing the evidence for consistency across different sources—with deliberate efforts made to seek out contrary cases to strengthen the findings even more.

The evidentiary objective is pursued throughout this book. The objective is reflected by use of the term *empirical research*, also found throughout the book.[5] The goal is to base conclusions on data that have been collected and analyzed fairly.

Also used throughout this book are numerous illustrations of already published qualitative studies, taking the form of vignettes or short inserts within the text. The specific works include relevant methodological works, not only individual studies, especially on such subjects as composing and presenting qualitative research (see Chapters 10 and 11). The book is therefore built on an *inductive* platform, deriving much of the preferred research practices from the ways that qualitative research already has been successfully practiced. In a sense, the illustrative studies represent the "data" for the book, and so the book engages in its own evidentiary quest.

Illustrative Studies Offered by the Remainder of This Book

The inductive platform seems to match well the spirit of the entire qualitative research enterprise. The valuable ideas produced by qualitative research tend to follow a "bottom-up" approach, wherein specific processes or events drive the development of broader concepts, not the reverse.

In addition to the vignettes and inserts, four specific arrays or discussions further illustrate the inductive platform. The first directs attention to the value of creating a "study bank" (Chapter 3, Section A). The second lists a large number of qualitative studies along with their main topics and levels of data collection units (Chapter 4, Choice 3). The third dissects the tables of contents of individual studies to show their broad analytic structures (Chapter 9, Section B). And the fourth occurs through the use of two specific examples: Sample Study 1 runs across a most difficult part of qualitative research—analyzing qualitative data—in Chapters 8 and 9; and Sample Study 2 illustrates mixed methods research in Chapter 12.

The inductive approach helps to display another aspect of the mosaic of qualitative research—its diversity in representing numerous academic disciplines and professions. The vignettes and illustrative examples come from such fields as sociology, anthropology, psychology, political science, management science, social work, public health, education, and program evaluation. Regardless of academic discipline, the studies also can address major questions of U.S. public policy (see "Qualitative Research Addressing a Major U.S. Policy Shift," Vignette 1.5).

---

[5]However, use of this term should not be confused with a like-sounding similar term, an *empiricist* view of how all human knowledge is created. The latter is part of a much older philosophical debate, emanating from the writings of John Locke and Immanuel Kant, over whether such knowledge only results from learned experiences, or whether humans also start with some innate knowledge, such as the ability to perceive and produce language. The evidence-based objective pursued in this book refers to the conduct of a research study, not the (empiricist or innate) processes whereby human beings accrue knowledge.

VIGNETTE 1.5. QUALITATIVE RESEARCH ADDRESSING A MAJOR U.S. POLICY SHIFT

During the latter part of the 20th century, no domestic issue attracted more attention than the large number of people supported by public welfare. After years of controversy, the U.S. government passed "welfare reform" legislation in 1996.

Because the large number of persons on welfare makes the topic amenable to statistical analysis, quantitative studies have dominated welfare research. In contrast, Sharon Hays (2003) shows how qualitative research can contribute deep insights into the worlds of welfare recipients and welfare service workers.

Her study focuses on welfare offices in two towns, and she presents extensive field data revealing how recipients fell into their situations and how they were treated by the welfare system. Most important, her interview data present the trajectory of people's lives (before, during, and after welfare)—a story that only qualitative research can tell.

Hayes also presents her methodological practices in an alternative way. The book has no separate methods section. Instead, methodological procedures and caveats appear at various places in the text and occasionally among an extensive set of footnotes (e.g., pp. 140–141, 244–245, and 251).

Excluded from consideration were many studies conducted by professional writers or by journalists. Although their works frequently present themselves in a qualitative manner and cover salient topics, most do not include any discussion of their methodologies, either as separate sections of text or in footnotes. Whether these works in fact tried to emulate the research practices emphasized by the present book is unclear, and for this reason the studies are not included among the book's vignettes or examples.

The purpose of the book is therefore not only to present a full array of procedures for practicing qualitative research but also to give you immediate access to specific examples for your further reference. To take best advantage of this opportunity, the book assumes that readers may vary from highly to less experienced researchers, but that none are novices. In other words, you may be doing qualitative research for the first time, but you already should have a foundation in knowing how social science research works and in bringing a critical eye to the reading of published research studies.

As a final note, the research practices covered in the remainder of this book are presented from the standpoint that you indeed have found good reasons for doing qualitative research—in response to the first sentence of this chapter. Therefore, the practical guidance continually assumes the existence of a planned or ongoing hypothetical study. The study might be part of a long-term affair (e.g., see "Fifteen Years of Ethnography in the Ticuanense Community," Vignette 1.6), but it also might be completed within a year's period of time. Moreover, the hope is that the guidance is relevant whether the study is being done with your own resources or as part of a sponsored research project.

Assuming that you are interested in doing qualitative research, some reminders are needed about the personal qualities and competencies that will help you to do such research well, and these are the topic of the next chapter.

VIGNETTE 1.6. FIFTEEN YEARS OF ETHNOGRAPHY IN THE TICUANENSE COMMUNITY

Sometimes, qualitative studies can take a long time. Robert Courtney Smith (2006) studied migration from Ticuani—a small county in Mexico—to New York City over a 15-year period.

Smith's fieldwork started in the summer of 1988 and then included "five- or six-week trips [to Mexico] from 1991 through 1993, while [also] doing ethnography in New York" (2006, p. 5). He kept in touch with his main informants for the ensuing 4 years, followed by a "second period of intensive fieldwork, from 1997 to 2002" (p. 5).

One benefit of conducting a study over this extended period of time was Smith's ability to study not just the first but also the second generation of immigrants. Of his research experience, Smith writes that he has been "able to gain greater insight by seeing how things turned out in the end" (2006, p. 358).

———————————

From Smith (2006).

RECAP FOR CHAPTER 1: *Terms, phrases, and concepts that you can now define*:

1. Participants in a qualitative study
2. Contextual conditions
3. Multiple sources of evidence
4. Reflexivity
5. Emic–etic
6. Naturalistic ethnography
7. Thick description
8. The construction of fieldwork descriptions
9. The field researcher as the main research instrument
10. Relativist versus realist types of inquiry
11. Phenomenological studies
12. Formally recognized variations in qualitative research
13. Epistemological location in contrast to epistemological similarity
14. Transparency
15. Methodic-ness
16. Empirical research

**EXERCISE FOR CHAPTER 1: BIOGRAPHICAL SKETCH
RELATED TO QUALITATIVE RESEARCH**

♦ ♦ ♦

Write a three-page (double-spaced) autobiographical statement, as if it will appear as a biographical sketch in some book or article you might later author. Write the entire sketch in a promotional manner—as if you are hoping to gain some small grant or fellowship to support your pursuit of qualitative research. Rewrite the entire sketch at least once, to make the text as presentable and communicative as possible.

The sketch should start by stating the extent to which you have done any kind of *empirical* research. If you have, identify the type of research (whether in the social sciences or not), the main topic studied, and the data collection method(s) used. If you have not done such research, write about the extent of your interest and motivation in doing empirical research.

In either situation (i.e., having done empirical research or not), now cite some of the key experiences (e.g., courses taken, college papers written, or inspiring teachers) that have led to your current level of accomplishment or interest in doing *qualitative* research. (Try to avoid repeating experiences that will later show up in your autobiography under the exercise for Chapters 8 and 9.) Consider acquainting yourself with some of the studies cited in Chapter 1 and using these as exemplars whose features you might want to emulate.

CHAPTER 2

Equipping Yourself to Do Qualitative Research

Certain personal competencies, including the ability to manage field-based research, will be important for doing qualitative research well. Paramount among the competencies are being able to "listen" in a multimodal manner, along with knowing how to ask good questions. This chapter reviews these and several other key competencies. It also discusses ways of practicing research procedures before they will be used in an actual study, further adding to a researcher's preparation.

As a related topic, and in doing any research, a key trait is to uphold a code of ethics. Social science professional associations have defined specific codes that will lead to the desired research integrity, and the present chapter summarizes and discusses these codes. Finally, associated with the ethics of doing research is a formal procedure whereby prospective studies need to obtain approval from an institutional review board. The chapter concludes by describing the procedure and some of its challenges when seeking approval for a qualitative research study.

Doing qualitative research is difficult. You need to have a sharp mind and maintain a consistent demeanor about your work. The topics of inquiry do not fall within neat or well-established boundaries, and there always are surprises. In addition, the role of the researcher as a primary research instrument poses critical challenges.

As a result, people doing qualitative research need to possess certain qualities in order to succeed. This chapter discusses those qualities. Even if you already have all or most of them, quickly perusing this chapter may still provide a helpful review.

A. COMPETENCIES IN DOING QUALITATIVE RESEARCH

PREVIEW—*What you should learn from this section:*
1. Six general competencies, transcending the needed technical skills, to do qualitative research well.
2. The research situations leading to the need for these competencies.

To use the research procedures described in the remainder of this book demands that you have certain technical skills. However, these are *not* the competencies covered by the present section. Rather, the section covers six general abilities that need to be part of your persona as a researcher: "listening," asking good questions, knowing about your topic of study, caring about your data, doing parallel tasks, and persevering. These abilities transcend your specific technical skills and in this sense may be more fundamental than any specific technical skills.

To some degree, you already will exhibit most or all of the six abilities. Your challenge is to set a high bar, so that you can develop and practice them to an exemplary degree. Training, self-training, and emulating esteemed researchers who can serve as mentors or models all are ways of boosting your capabilities.

"Listening"

This ability takes many forms. It goes beyond your sense of hearing and calls upon all of your senses, including your intuitions. For instance, "listening" can begin when you size up a group of people—for example, their mood and expected friendliness or aloofness as you start to meet with them. Similarly, when you converse with other people, noticing their body language and intonations may be as important as hearing the words they speak. Finally, listening to people's spoken words, as opposed to dominating conversations with your own words, can produce helpful insights into people's thoughts about what is going on.

The desired competence here is to be able to take in large amounts of information about your environment, especially about the people in your environment. The in-taking can be explicit or inferential. Everyday phrases, such as "reading between the lines" (of a document) or "listening between the lines" (of someone's spoken words), are relevant to this type of listening. Thus, fieldworkers in qualitative research always need to suspect the existence of something between the lines that may reveal participants' motives, intentions, or deeper meanings. The more that you are able to listen for these signals, the better will be your fieldwork.

"Listening" also has a specific visual mode. It takes the form of being observant. The competence starts with some sheer physical attributes. For instance, you should know the narrowness or breadth of your peripheral vision, and whether, without turning your head, you notice something going on across the street as readily as would a companion who is walking next to you. You also should know how efficiently you are able to scan a crowd in order to find a particular person or object. These physical attributes then combine with your attentiveness to visual signals—

especially those taking the form of other people's gestures, body language, and physical demeanor—and help to build your ability to be observant.

Being observant includes a skill in scanning your physical, not just social environment. The status symbols in a doctor's office, the display of students' work in a school, and the physical well-being or deterioration of a neighborhood all may convey significant information if your study covers one or more of these environments.

> • For instance, a field-based study of reading literacy found that the public environments of low-income neighborhoods had fewer public signs and written displays than those in middle-income neighborhoods (Neuman & Celano, 2001).
>
> The study claimed that, along with the absence of public libraries and the impoverished reading curricula offered in the schools of the low-income neighborhoods, the paucity of such visual information on the streets and in other public places reinforced an undesirable low-literacy environment.

You also can listen for other features of the social environment that are not entirely based on visual cues. These include the "time" or "pace" of an environment, commotions, the pitch and tone of conversations, and the general stress that seems to be in the air. You may not be able to measure these features with any degree of precision, but ignoring them might not be a good idea either.

Asking Good Questions

Although much research data will come from listening, a lot also will come as a result of asking good questions. Without good questions, you risk collecting a lot of extraneous information while simultaneously missing some critical information. Thus, even though you want to be a good listener, this does not mean presenting yourself as a completely passive person in any given setting. It also does not mean that you should expect to say nothing but a repeated "uh-huh" in an interview. You need to ask good questions, too.

If you actually have a talent for asking good questions, you will note a difficulty in turning the talent off. For instance, when you are interviewing participants in the conversational mode common to qualitative research, but you also want to remain a courteous conversant, you will find yourself suppressing your urge to ask too many questions, for fear of interrupting participants or, worse, steering their remarks. However, after the interview has ended, the talent reappears when you suffer the frustration of now having recalled another line of questions that you neglected to ask earlier.

In a like manner, imagine reading a report related to your topic of study. The talent for asking good questions will be reflected by your tendency to ask yourself questions while still reading the report. The questions may pertain to the substance of the report but also may direct your attention to the accuracy and credibility of the report. As you read the report, you also may conjure questions about the relationship between the report and the other sources of information you have been consulting as part of your data collection. All these questions will lead to two kinds of note taking when you are reading: notes about the reading and notes reflecting your questions.

A querying mind shows itself among those people who ask a continuous series of questions—the responses to one set of questions quickly leading to yet other questions. In contrast, you may notice that some people spend a lot of their time talking about their own experiences and expressing their own opinions rather than asking questions. If you tend to be this latter type of person, you may have difficulty doing good qualitative research.

Knowing about Your Topic of Study

High among the expected competencies is knowledge of your own topic of research. Many people think that, in doing qualitative research, such knowledge revolves around having a sense of the field setting and participants in their study. Such persons ignore the fact that their chosen topic of study will likely already have been a topic of previous studies. In this sense, knowing about your topic of study requires you to know about the findings from previous research on the topic, not just the anticipated field setting and participants.

Having sufficient knowledge calls for you to chase down these other studies and learn about them, including their methodologies. Your goal is to avoid inadvertent repetition or reinvention. You even may learn about some research procedures that are worth emulating in your own study. Similarly, insights from the previous research also will help to reduce the possibility of your misinterpreting your own data.

Doing a selective, if not comprehensive, review of the literature (see Chapter 3, Section B) would be one way of learning about previous research. You need to retrieve the studies, read them, and become comfortable with the substantive issues related to your topic. You can bring the review closer to home by retrieving recent papers, theses, dissertations, and public presentations made by colleagues at your own university or research organization. For instance, you would want to know quickly whether a colleague in your own academic department or organization had completed a study bearing on yours just a few years earlier.

If, for fear of adopting categories and concepts prematurely, you choose not to review any literature but opt for a "fieldwork first" sequence (see Chapter 3, Section C), you can still make some preparation by gaining an initial familiarity with your anticipated field setting and its participants. Use the Internet and google the names of places, organizations, and people. Read about a broad variety of topics in Wikipedia. Talk to people about the field setting. Although this information may not be research-based, it still can acquaint you with your topic in a general way, as long as you retain an open mind by being prepared to being misled as well as becoming informed by these sources.

Caring about Your Data

Everyone has probably suffered at least once from inconveniently losing some precious personal belonging. As valued as such belongings are, your research data assume a near-priceless status when you are doing a research study. The relevant competence involves having a supersensitivity about recognizing your data and taking care of them. You will want to be protective and not casual about your notes, electronic files, and hardcopy files. You will want to handle carefully any documents or artifacts that are part of your data.

Research data, but especially field data in a qualitative study, demand special attention and security. For instance, you should not tolerate any disorganized or sloppy management of your field notes. To take such notes, you might have used different-sized paper or even had to write on both sides of the same piece of paper—which normally would be frowned upon. As soon as possible, you should put these notes in order or otherwise refine them as discussed in Chapter 7. You even might consider photocopying any irregularly sized materials, so that everything is of the same size and one-sided. Then, you should duplicate these notes and keep the copy separately from the original. Similarly, every time you save notes to an electronic file, you should create a backup file. Ideally, the file should be external to any computer (e.g., by using a flash disk or an external hard drive), so that the records are not jeopardized should your computer subsequently suffer from some hardware or software failure. When you do any tape recording, you need again to make duplicate tapes as soon as you can and store them apart from the original ones.

In handling your data, no amount of care is too much care. Some items when lost, even personal belongings, can be replaced. However, field notes cannot be replaced. You will not be able to replicate the exact conditions that produced the original set of notes. For instance, imagine trying to hold the same conversation over again with a participant. The conversation will not be the same, and the participant may think less of you after you have admitted losing track of the notes that contained the original conversation.

A similar situation arises with documentary data. You should determine at the outset whether you are going to be able to duplicate any documents. If not, or if you do not wish to have the burden of carrying a lot of papers around, you will have to take notes on the spot. These notes also should receive your greatest care. You may not gain access to the same documents again. Similarly, old or deteriorating documents might be best protected by putting them into their own properly labeled outer envelopes or file folders.

Doing Parallel Tasks

The activities in doing qualitative research do not come in a neatly tied bundle. You will be continually challenged by having to do or attend to multiple tasks, not all within your direct control, at the same time. This complex environment differs from the work of the stereotypic "bench" scientist, whose challenge (and talent) might be to concentrate intensely on a single display or set of data, trying to unlock some technical puzzle.

Some of the multiple tasks already have been pointed out. For instance, you will have to know how to make field observations and take field notes at the same time. The dual task may sound no different from taking notes at a meeting. However, you may have to keep up these tasks over a prolonged length of time. Fatigue and the need for rest can become an issue. Sometimes, just as you have started a break and put down your notes, some unexpected field event then occurs, demanding your renewed attention. When doing fieldwork, you may find that the only real break or rest occurs when you have left the field completely and are in a totally private environment.

Other kinds of multiple tasks in doing qualitative research can be equally demanding. For instance, the recursive rather than linear relationships among your study design, data collection, and data analysis are discussed fully in Chapters 4 through 9 of this book. Such relationships mean that, while you are collecting data, you will simultaneously need to be thinking about their analytic implications, in part to determine whether you need to collect additional data to confirm or augment the collected data.

One final example: At the simplest level of having to attend to multiple tasks in qualitative research, think about the following situation: listening to a participant's rendition of an important event, with all of its critical details and nuances reflecting a cultural environment different from yours—while maintaining an attentive social bearing to let the participant know you are caring about what is being said—while also taking notes—and while also thinking about the best follow-on question(s). Rest assured that you indeed will have developed a special competency after you have mastered such situations.

Persevering

This word is meant to cover a variety of personal qualities—all somehow related to an ability to stick to your quest in the face of the inevitable frustrations, uncertainties, and even unpleasantries that you can confront in doing qualitative research. Because you are studying real-world events, they assume their own natural course and may alternatively present unanticipated resistances and challenges. You also may have to deal successfully with embarrassing or difficult interpersonal situations.

The competency involves your ability to move forward with your research in spite of all these encounters. Naturally, there can come a point when you are best advised to cease doing your study, and if you get to such a point you should consult with other people, such as colleagues and advisers, before throwing in the towel. However, such a fate is not likely to occur in the vast majority of cases. In these cases, persevering and figuring out how to handle difficult situations can lead to exemplary studies, such as a study of family life completed by Annette Lareau (2003) and her research team (see "Overcoming the Challenges of Doing Intensive, Field-Based Research," Vignette 2.1).

VIGNETTE 2.1. OVERCOMING THE CHALLENGES
OF DOING INTENSIVE, FIELD-BASED RESEARCH

A study of 12 families focused on the "largely invisible but powerful ways that parents' social class impacts children's life experiences" (Lareau, 2003, p. 3). The study examined "how children spend their time when they are out of school and . . . the work it takes parents to get children through the day" (p. 263).

A researcher visited each family's home about 20 times over a year's time, at different times of the day. Gaining access to the families only came after researchers had obtained schools' permission to observe third-grade classrooms, become acquainted with the students, and interviewed many parents. Only after this phase did the author attempt to recruit families for the fieldwork—a process reported to be "very stressful" (Lareau, 2003, p. 265).

The home observations had their own challenges, such as overcoming the awkwardness of the first few visits (Lareau, 2003, p. 269). Fieldworkers also had to learn to be comfortable and to resist intervening in families "where there was yelling, drinking, emotional turmoil, and disciplining by hitting" (p. 267). The fieldwork included eating meals with the families, which occasionally meant pretending to enjoy all the food, even items "intensely disliked" (p. 268). The study describes these and other methodological topics in detail. Along with its substantive findings, the study not surprisingly has received prestigious awards and accolades in the field of sociology.

B. MANAGING FIELD-BASED RESEARCH

PREVIEW—*What you should learn from this section:*

1. The extended nature of fieldwork and the resulting need to consider it as a management, not just technical challenge.

2. The ways of preserving enough time to plan and anticipate your next steps as you do your fieldwork.

3. The different patterns and relationships when fieldwork is conducted by more than a single person.

Beyond these preceding personal qualities and competencies, the ability to do qualitative research includes equipping yourself to manage field-based research.

The kinds of field-based research vary. You may serve as a participant-observer in a real-world setting (see Chapter 5, Section D). Doing such research requires recognizing that, inherent in the nature of the "field," events are not within a researcher's control, nor would anyone wish them to be. Thus, the challenge of managing field-based research is to attain some degree of methodic-ness—but to avoid intruding into what is going on and to be able to tolerate occasionally high levels of uncertainty.

Alternatively, you may conduct a qualitative study that largely, if not solely, depends on conducting a series of open-ended interviews (see "A Qualitative Study Based Solely on Open-Ended Interviews," Vignette 2.2). Note that such interviews are likely to differ from the open-ended portions of survey studies.

VIGNETTE 2.2. A QUALITATIVE STUDY
BASED SOLELY ON OPEN-ENDED INTERVIEWS

The "field" in qualitative research need not always be the subject of a researcher's observations or personal interactions. Many qualitative studies can be based solely on a set of open-ended interviews. What makes the studies qualitative is that they are interested in the interviewees' words and ideas, not in arraying the responses numerically.

Such a study was done by Kathleen Bogle (2008), who studied "hooking up" on campus by interviewing 76 people (students and alumni) from two colleges. Each interview took from 1 to 1½ hours and was audio recorded, with appropriate assurances regarding anonymity (p. 188).

The study then presents numerous brief and selected dialogues (fashioned like movie scripts) between Bogle and the interviewees. Each dialogue illustrates an important topic, revealing both the interviewee's information and perspective about the topic. The dialogues thus form the actual data for the entire study.

See also Vignette 11.5.

In qualitative research, the interviews usually assume a conversational mode (explained more in Chapter 6, Section B). In a single interview, this mode can continue for an extended period, such as 2 hours. The goal is to encourage participants to have the time and opportunity to reconstruct their own experiences and reality in their own words. Thus, the interview cannot be based on a questionnaire created by the researcher. For many studies, the same person might be interviewed in such a manner on three separate occasions: The first interview might cover the participant's life history; the second might cover the events involved in the topic of study; and the third might cover the participant's reflections on the meaning of their experiences (Seidman, 2006, pp. 15–19).

To manage the fieldwork in such an interview study will involve your recruiting the participants and finding places to do the interviews. The desired locations are venues readily convenient to each participant (e.g., typically, a participant's home, depending on the nature of the study). Less desirable is to have the participant journey to a venue convenient to the researcher (e.g., the researcher's office).

These managerial challenges are then compounded in many qualitative studies, which can consist of doing both participant-observation and extended interviewing, not just one or the other.

Making Time to Think Ahead

To be organized under these circumstances requires a paradoxical posture. You will want to be able to follow the natural flow of events in the field, but you should also be sure that you are prepared to follow that flow.

In this regard, a noted management adviser and best-selling author, Stephen Covey, long ago defined a two-by-two matrix covering all kinds of work, not just fieldwork. However, the matrix presents insights that seem in fact to be especially helpful in understanding how to manage fieldwork. Along one dimension of the two-by-two matrix, work tasks may be considered urgent or not urgent; along the other dimension, the tasks may be considered important or not important (see Exhibit 2.1). The four resulting cells are labeled Cells I, II, III, and IV.

	EXHIBIT 2.1. STEPHEN COVEY'S (1989) TIME MANAGEMENT MATRIX (SLIGHTLY ABBREVIATED)	
	Urgent	**Not urgent**
Important	I Crises, pressing problems, deadline-driven projects	II Prevention, planning, recognizing new opportunities, relationship building
Not important	III Interruptions; some calls, e-mails, and meetings; some reports	IV Trivia, busywork, time wasters, pleasant activities

The matrix helps to understand what might happen in high-pressure jobs. Many tasks are unavoidably both urgent and important (Cell I). People can then aggravate their own situations by letting unimportant tasks become urgent, such as by ignoring known deadlines and then having to scramble to complete the unimportant task (Cell III).

Covey notes that the more that a workday is filled with urgent tasks, the greater is the need to refresh psychic, if not physical, energies by taking breaks and doing leisure activities that would then fall under Cell IV. You can imagine how such a break in the field might be reflected by having a leisurely meal and deliberately not thinking about your work.

One upshot of this pattern is to minimize and perhaps eliminate the time needed to do important but not urgent tasks (Cell II). In other words, if you permit your time in the field to be consumed by the tasks in Cells I, III, and IV, you may have lost the opportunity to plan, reassess your situation, build better relationships, or do the important tasks in Cell II. Thus, your preoccupation with the urgency of the events immediately confronting you may lead to your inability to anticipate new events or to take advantage of unexpected opportunities.

The matrix therefore illustrates how you may have to struggle to preserve sufficient time in the field to think about your next steps and to consider optional choices—in other words, to plan. Without such planning, and as in your own personal life, you will not be able to get slightly ahead of events by anticipating your next move. Instead, you will be constantly one or more steps behind, continually trying to catch up.

Managing as Part of a Field Team

In most qualitative studies, fieldwork, whether of the participant-observer or interview variety, is conducted by solo researchers. Under such conditions, the main challenge in managing the fieldwork involves self-management and the ability to control yourself.

However, some qualitative studies deliberately engage additional persons to assist with the fieldwork. The roles of these persons differ.

In the least demanding role, another person may be called upon to serve as a companion to the primary researcher—accompanying the primary researcher but not performing any formal research function. Sometimes, the need may be for personal security—as when a female researcher is to visit the homes of young adult males, to conduct evening interviews (e.g., Royster, 2003). In other situations, the need may be culturally based—as when the holding of a private interview between a researcher of one gender with a person of the other gender would appear to be socially inappropriate and jeopardize the researcher's standing in the community being studied (e.g., Menjívar, 2000, pp. 246–247).

More demanding roles require that the colleague be trained to perform research functions. Such a colleague might be engaged in order to address reflexivity threats. For instance, the primary researcher may worry that a gender, age, or race and ethnicity difference can lead to distorted interview results. Having a portion of the interviews conducted by a colleague who differs in some critical demographic dimension would then help to address such a concern (see "Desirable Teamwork for a Study Based on Open-Ended Interviews," Vignette 2.3).

VIGNETTE 2.3. DESIRABLE TEAMWORK FOR A STUDY BASED ON OPEN-ENDED INTERVIEWS

Pamela Stone (2007) conducted a study about why working women later quit their careers to stay at home and care for their families. The study was based on 54 interviews. In addition to describing the selection of the 54 interviewees, the interview settings, the interview protocol, and other procedures, the study also contains a three-page list, enumerating each of the interviewees (with pseudonyms) and providing key demographic data about each one.

Because the author herself was a working mother, and the study respondents were about mothers who had stopped working, the procedures also had to deal with reflexivity threats. While the author did 46 of the 54 interviews, a capable graduate assistant (younger, but *not* a working mother) was deliberately assigned to do the other eight. As a result, the author could compare the findings from two different types of interviewers. Stone's close examination subsequently revealed "few differences between the themes that emerged from my own interviews and those conducted by my research assistant" (2007, p. 251).

An altogether different motivation for having additional team members arises when the scope of study is too broad to be covered by a single researcher. The typical situation would be where a study has multiple field settings. To eliminate temporal or seasonal differences in collecting the data in these settings, the fieldwork might need to be conducted over the same period of time. In this situation, the primary researcher would need to fully train one or more co-investigators, each one covering a different setting (see "Doing Fieldwork with Multiple Persons Working in Multiple Settings," Vignette 2.4).

VIGNETTE 2.4. DOING FIELDWORK WITH MULTIPLE PERSONS WORKING IN MULTIPLE SETTINGS

In the classic fieldwork study, a single investigator works at a single site. This arrangement still dominates the bulk of qualitative research studies.

An alternative arrangement calls for multiple investigators to work at multiple sites, all part of the same study. This alternative was followed in a study that covered seven neighborhoods in New York City (Yin, 1982b). Different fieldworkers each spent 3 months in a different neighborhood, participating in and observing street life and its relation to urban services (e.g., fire and police protection, sanitation, and code enforcement).

The design's major benefit was the ability to cover a variety of neighborhoods, compare them, and reach conclusions about urban services from a street perspective. A major challenge of the design was the need to coordinate the fieldworkers and to train them on common procedures but also to exchange information about the conditions in each neighborhood that contextualized its distinctive street life and urban services. For example, a neighborhood with a plethora of abandoned houses produces a different environment from one with too many automobiles and chronic double-parking problems, but such conditions may be less evident if a study is limited to only a single neighborhood.

See also Vignette 11.2.

The need for such fully trained colleagues also can exist even if a study does not take place in multiple settings. Instead, the study might call for collecting an intensive amount of data about the same setting. In the most elaborate situation, an entire study team may establish a field office and locate there for a year or two (e.g., Lynd & Lynd, 1929). The relevant data may not be limited to field observations and interviews but can involve surveys as well as the retrieval and examination of archival and documentary information.

Less elaborately, an entire team might still have to work together for a prolonged period of time but not necessarily work out of a single office. The data collection would be varied as in the preceding example but also could be extensive, such as collecting life histories of 150 people (e.g., see "Organizing a Research Team to Collect Extensive Field Data," Vignette 2.5).

VIGNETTE 2.5. ORGANIZING A RESEARCH TEAM TO COLLECT EXTENSIVE FIELD DATA

Newman (1999) organized "a large group of doctoral students" (p. xvi) to undertake a 2-year study in the Harlem neighborhood of New York City. The study focused on the working poor—200 persons employed in "four large, successful fast food restaurants" (p. 36) as well as 100 "unsuccessful job-seekers who had come knocking on the door at two of those establishments during the same period" (p. 36).

All told, the research team amassed the following field data: surveys and interviews of all 300 persons plus the managers and owners of the four restaurants; life histories of 150 of these people, taking 3–4 hours to complete; and intensive data collected about 12 fast-food workers who were "shadowed . . . at close range" (1999, p. 37) for nearly a year, covering their personal and not just working lives. Finally, the team's graduate students also worked behind the counters of the fast food restaurants for 4 months.

As noted by Newman, "the rich, detailed data that poured in from all sides are the basis for this portrait of minimum-wage workers employed in the fast food industry in the historical capital of Black America" (1999, p. 37).

In any of these latter situations, where colleagues are collecting data in a coordinated fashion, either at multiple sites or at the same site, critical team management procedures emerge. First, the team will probably want to develop and use a common field protocol, to reduce unwanted variability in collecting the data (see Chapter 4, Choice 8, for a discussion of field protocols). Second, the team will need to convene regular meetings during the fieldwork period, conscientiously coordinating and collaborating its work (e.g., Lareau, 2003, p. 268). Leadership by the primary investigator(s) in assuring that these practices take place properly becomes essential.

C. PRACTICING

PREVIEW—*What you should learn from this section:*
1. The implications of research being more than just a scholarly endeavor.
2. Three ways of practicing your skills before starting an actual study.

Research may be considered a form of scholarship. At an earlier time, "doing research" might have meant sitting in a library and retrieving and manipulating information. Esteemed scholarship might have resulted from such desk work. Today, doing research also means actively collecting fresh data, whether in a laboratory or in a real-world setting. To this extent, research is not just a form of scholarship. Research also is a *practice*. Practices can be "practiced," and the more they are practiced, the better the results are likely to be. Equipping yourself to do qualitative research by practicing it is therefore the topic of this section.

Unfortunately, the best practice for doing a qualitative study is to have done one already. However, such logic does not help in understanding what to do before your first qualitative study. What you can do is to practice some of the key research procedures independently and on a trial basis.

Using the Exercises in This Book to Practice

The exercises in this book present some of these procedures. Possibly the preferred ones would be those directly related to collecting field data, which include cross-checking two different sources of data (exercise for Chapter 6).

In this situation, although the exercise only calls for you to complete a single example such as comparing a single document with an interview of a single person, you can do more. You could easily examine several documents, paired with interviewing several persons. To get the most out of practicing, you should assess your own work after each pairing and decide what changes or improvements you might make in the subsequent pairing. For interviews, for instance, you should with practice eventually become accustomed to listening, asking questions, and taking notes at the same time. Ideally, you will have developed a routine procedure that makes you comfortable.

Beyond self-assessment, having another person observe your work can provide feedback and be of great assistance.

Doing a Pilot Study

Pilot studies help to test and refine one or more aspects of a final study—for example, its design, fieldwork procedures, data collection instruments, or analysis plans. In this sense, the pilot study provides another opportunity to practice.

The information from a pilot study can range from logistical topics (e.g., learning about the field time needed to cover certain procedures) to more substantive ones (e.g., refining a study's research questions). Whatever the purpose of the pilot study, the participants in a pilot study need to know that they are participating in a pilot study. You may be surprised that they might be more than willing to participate because you can design some part of the pilot—and not necessarily a part that will be in the final study—to cater to their needs.

For instance, the participants might desire feedback from an outside observer regarding a pressing issue of theirs. The participants might even ask that you give them a brief written report about that issue after the pilot study has ended. Agreeing to do these tasks will make it easier to arrange the pilot study.

Getting Motivated

Increasing the motivations to do a qualitative study also can be practiced and is an important final way of equipping yourself. If you have trepidations before starting such a study, motivational boosts will help. Such boosts might come from a competitive posture, such as setting high expectations for performing your study. You might check related studies, see how other researchers have accomplished their work under similar circumstances, and aspire to do better.

If the competitive urge does not apply to you, an alternative way of increasing motivation might be to think about the satisfaction you will derive from doing qualitative research. Remember that qualitative research gives you the opportunity to study a real-world setting in its own terms, thereby putting a broad array of study topics at your disposal. Remind yourself of the knowledge to be gained by doing qualitative research. Recall the worthy experiences of other researchers, many of them well known in their fields, who have successfully done qualitative research.

Finally, you may still want to know more about qualitative research before committing yourself to this endeavor. To help you, you might skip to Chapter 5. That chapter focuses entirely on the fieldwork experience and how you might go about doing the fieldwork in a qualitative research study. The goal is to get beneath the glitter and initial allure of doing qualitative research, as discussed earlier (see Chapter 1, Section A), and to gain a realistic sense of what it's like to do the fieldwork in qualitative research, including the challenges others have faced and the remedies they have found.

Beyond practicing your research skills and motivating yourself before starting an actual study, discussed next is one more extremely important personal quality that will equip you to do qualitative research.

D. SETTING AND MAINTAINING ETHICAL STANDARDS OF CONDUCT

PREVIEW—*What you should learn from this section:*
1. An illustration of how an ethical challenge can arise in analyzing research data.
2. The codes of ethics upheld by the social science professions.
3. The ways of using disclosure to demonstrate your research integrity.

Throughout your entire career as a researcher, much less in conducting any single research study, you will need to uphold one critical personal trait: You will need to bring a strong sense of ethics to your research. Having such a sense is pivotal because of the numerous discretionary choices made by researchers and especially by qualitative researchers. (The ethical spirit transcends but is directly related to the specific procedures for protecting human subjects, the topic of the final section of this chapter.)

An Illustrative Ethical Challenge: Fairly Examining All of Your Data

For instance, in doing research, one of the most important choices involves deciding what data, once collected, to incorporate into an analysis. Although the first major objective for building trustworthiness and credibility, as discussed in Chapter 1, is to report research procedures and data as transparently as possible, some data will always fall outside of an analysis and also not get reported.

On the surface, this occurs because it is impossible to analyze all the data that have been collected. Similarly, the full reporting of all data is confined by the space available in a journal article. Larger works, such as books or dissertations, still have their limits. Researchers should work with all of their data—but might some researchers have ignored some of their data because the data did not support their study's main propositions?

No one blatantly excludes such negative instances. As discussed later in this book (see Chapter 4, Choice 2), such negative instances are in fact to be highly cherished as ways of buttressing a study, even if leading to modifications to its original premises. However, the possibility of excluding data can become a reality, even in experimental research—because a human subject appeared uncooperative or one of the experimental trials appeared irregular. Are the experimenter's data being ignored for procedural reasons or because of contrary results? In doing qualitative research, a similar situation can arise when ignoring an interview of an incredulous participant. Is the participant really incredulous, or is she or he simply disagreeing with the researcher's established beliefs? In other words, though not blatantly ignoring a selected set of data, a researcher might find some excuse to justify their exclusion.

To avoid this kind of bias requires a strong ethical standard. You need to start your research by setting clear rules to define the circumstances under which any data are later to be excluded. You will then need to monitor your own work and to have the willpower to follow your own rules. For instance, a decision-making framework, covering explicit criteria regarding how a particular situation sits with your intuitions, rules, principles and theory, values, and action, may be helpful (see Newman & Brown, 1996, pp. 101–113). You need to know yourself well enough to anticipate when you might be tempted to "make an exception" and to counter the temptation with an even stronger admonition regarding the dire consequences of breaking your own rules. (If anything, you should be *less* willing to make exceptions when they go *against* your preconceptions.)

Codes of Ethics

Behaving properly in this situation is considered a matter of *research integrity*. You can find actual guidance about such integrity from a number of sources. These sources offer formally stated *codes of ethics, ethical standards,* or *guiding principles* and are promoted by professional associations. Exhibit 2.2 contains selected illustrations from five professional associations whose members include those conducting qualitative research. The guidance pertains to all types of research covered by these professions, not just qualitative research.

These guides or codes apply whenever a person is doing research and representing a particular profession. Exhibit 2.2 only gives an overview of the associations' codes. To gain a complete picture, you should retrieve, read, and keep in

EXHIBIT 2.2. ILLUSTRATIVE ITEMS IN CODES OF ETHICS OF FIVE PROFESSIONAL ASSOCIATIONS (EXCLUDES ISSUES ON PROTECTION OF HUMAN SUBJECTS)

Association/year of publication	Illustrative items
American Anthropological Association (1998, Sec. III)	• Responsibility to people and animals being studied: e.g., avoid harm; respect well-being; reciprocate with participants • Responsibility to scholarship and science: e.g., expecting ethical dilemmas; avoiding misrepresentation and deception • Responsibility to the public: e.g., to be open and truthful
American Educational Research Association (2000)	• Responsibilities to the field: e.g., to conduct professional lives to avoid jeopardizing the profession; not to fabricate or falsify; to disclose qualifications and limitations when offering professional opinions; to report findings to all stakeholders; to disclose all data and procedures for other researchers to understand and interpret • Intellectual ownership: e.g., guidelines for coauthorship • Editing, reviewing, and appraising research
American Evaluation Association (2004)	• Systematic inquiry: e.g., to assure accuracy and credibility of findings • Competence: e.g., to possess abilities needed to undertake evaluation tasks • Integrity/honesty: e.g., in own behavior and entire evaluation process • Respect for people: e.g., their security, dignity, and self-worth • Responsibilities for public and general welfare: e.g., account for diversity of interests and values related to evaluation
American Sociological Association (1999)	• Professional competence: e.g., maintain awareness of current scientific and professional information • Integrity: e.g., honesty, fairness, and respect • Professional and scientific responsibility: e.g., adhere to highest standards and accept responsibility for own work • Respect for people's rights, dignity, and diversity • Social responsibility
American Political Science Association (APSA Committee, 2008)	• Grievance procedures: e.g., for human rights of scholars in other countries • Professional ethics adopted by the American Association of University Professors: e.g., to seek and state the truth; to develop and improve scholarly competence • Principles of professional conduct: e.g., freedom and integrity of research

mind at least one of these codes—or some similar example coming from some other profession relevant to your work—when doing your research.

The codes are not long documents. For instance, the code for the American Educational Research Association (AERA, 2000) contains six sets of guiding standards. Each set has a preamble followed by a number of standards. The preamble to the first set, dealing with "responsibilities to the field," represents a good example of what you will find in all of the codes:

> To maintain the integrity of research, educational researchers should warrant their conclusions adequately in a way consistent with the standards of their own theoretical and methodological perspectives.
>
> They should keep themselves well-informed in both their own and competing paradigms where those are relevant to their research, and they should continually evaluate the criteria of adequacy by which research is judged.

Note how the preamble does not presuppose any particular type of qualitative or nonqualitative research, much less any of the variations of qualitative research previously identified in Chapter 1. Rather, the preamble applies to any kind of research, pointing to the need to provide some sort of methodic support ("warrant") for one's conclusions and to maintain a professional level of competence ("keep . . . well-informed").

Research Integrity

This personal quality, prominently positioned and common to the various codes, should not be taken for granted. In its rawest form, *research integrity* means that you and your word(s) can be trusted as representing truthful positions and statements. Although research does not demand that you take an oath, as in other fields, people must know, through your actions, demeanor, and research methods, that you are striving to produce research that is truthful, including clarifying the point of view being represented. Truthful statements may include caveats or reservations, indicating uncertainties that could not be overcome. However, absent such caveats and reservations, people are entitled to think that you did in fact report truthful statements.

Research integrity carries special importance in qualitative research. Because the designs and procedures for doing qualitative research are potentially more flexible than doing most other kinds of research, people will want to know that qualitative researchers have gone to great length to conduct their research accurately and fairly. For instance, one sign of research integrity is the willingness to be proven wrong, or even to have your earlier thinking on a matter challenged.

Disclosure as One Way of Demonstrating Research Integrity

Nearly all researchers will readily claim that they have such research integrity. How to communicate it to others may be another matter.

One helpful way is to disclose the conditions that might influence the conduct of a study. For instance, everybody agrees that researchers should disclose as much as possible about the methodological conditions that might affect a study and its outcomes—such as how a field setting or its participants were selected. However, qualitative research demands disclosure about a researcher's personal roles and traits that also might affect a study and its outcomes.

Most commonly, these personal conditions include the influence of a researcher's demographic profile (gender, age, race and ethnicity, and social class). The profile might not only affect the *research lens* through which the researcher interprets events but also the ways in which participants might reflexively react to the researcher's presence, including the participants' choice of topics or responses in field conversations. Marwell's (2007) study of community organizations in Brooklyn presents an excellent example of how both the methodological and personal conditions can be disclosed. Her disclosure also includes describing how participants were given the choice of remaining anonymous or being named in her final manuscript (see "Detailing the Methodological Choices and Personal Conditions in Doing a Qualitative Study," Vignette 2.6).

VIGNETTE 2.6. DETAILING THE METHODOLOGICAL CHOICES AND PERSONAL CONDITIONS IN DOING A QUALITATIVE STUDY

Marwell's (2007) study of community organizations in Brooklyn, New York, exemplifies how the various methodological choices and personal conditions can be thoroughly described.

The study involved eight organizations, covering four organizational types in each of two neighborhoods. As a result, the author goes to considerable lengths to tell how she identified the candidates for these choices and how she made the final choices of both organizations and neighborhoods (pp. 239–248).

Marwell's participant-observation fieldwork took place over a 3-year period, and she describes her initial access to the field, the value of her working as a volunteer in these organizations, and her approach to keeping their identities anonymous or divulging them—the participants could decide for themselves after being shown the passages of text in which they appeared (2007, p. 253).

Finally, the author gives much attention to the potential effects of her own personal (race, class, ethnic, linguistic, gender, and age) characteristics on her fieldwork experiences, discussing the possible influence of each characteristic separately (2007, pp. 255–259).

The personal conditions also include any affiliation that a researcher might have with the participants being studied. For instance, researchers may study their own organizations, communities, or social groups—all of which might be considered a form of *insider research*. Quite commonly, researchers may reside in the same neighborhood in which the participants live, using a local residence to establish closer ties as well as to develop greater familiarity with cultural and other contextual conditions. However, these situations do not appear to create as strong a potential conflict as when researchers are studying the same organization of which they are a member. The latter can have complicated power and supervisory implications (e.g., Brannick & Coghlan, 2007; Karra & Phillips, 2008), all of which might need to be part of a disclosure about the affiliation.

As a final personal condition, in practicing some variants of qualitative research, a researcher may assume an advocacy position in relation to the topic being studied. Whether formally recognizing an advocacy role or simply favoring certain views, such perspectives demand to be disclosed as well. The broader concept, discussed throughout this book, deals with reporting about *reflexivity*—describing as best as possible the interactive effects between researcher and participants, including the social roles as they evolve in the field but also covering advocacy positions. Bales's (2004) study of contemporary human slavery provides an example of one way of divulging such information (see "Doing Qualitative Research and Advocating a Sociopolitical Cause," Vignette 2.7).

VIGNETTE 2.7. DOING QUALITATIVE RESEARCH AND ADVOCATING A SOCIOPOLITICAL CAUSE

Scholars doing qualitative research also can use the research to stir support for sociopolitical causes. Kevin Bales's (2004) study of slavery in five countries (Thailand, Mauritania, Brazil, Pakistan, and India) is based on extensive fieldwork. In each country, the field team visited slave sites (usually places of business relying on manual labor) and interviewed enslaved persons as well as slaveholders. The author shows how his use of an overarching conceptual framework, as well as the depth of his research, produce an academic and not merely journalistic contribution.

To combat slavery, the author, a professor of sociology, also created and leads an advocate organization, *Free the Slaves*. In his preface, the author proudly notes that the forming of the organization benefited from the first edition of the book, published in 1999. It called attention to the 27 million persons living in slavery or subjected to human trafficking, worldwide.

The preceding examples illustrate the use of disclosure as a way of conveying one's research integrity. A reader who disagrees with the disclosed positions or conditions then has the option of ignoring the reported research entirely. For this reason, you may want to follow a common practice of perusing the preface, methodological portions, biographical statements, and even the blurbs of book jackets, before reading the substance of a research report. If some disclosed conditions appear objectionable, you may dismiss the report entirely, or you may read it with a critical eye, to offset any concern that the research might have been unduly compromised.

Overall, the issues of ethical conduct and ways of demonstrating your research integrity are part of one additional preparatory activity, covered next.

E. PROTECTING HUMAN SUBJECTS: OBTAINING APPROVAL FROM AN INSTITUTIONAL REVIEW BOARD

PREVIEW—*What you should learn from this section:*
1. The role of an institutional review board (IRB).
2. The considerations for protecting human subjects.

Every study with human participants, qualitative or nonqualitative, requires prior approval from an institutional review board (IRB). Obtaining the needed approval can be an uneventful part of doing qualitative research. Obtaining approval also can be the source of much frustration, demanding more energy and attention than you might have imagined.

IRB approval is integrally related to the issues of human ethics just discussed. The relevance of such approval starts with a simple principle: All research with human participants (whether they are formally designated as human "subjects" or not) needs to be reviewed and approved from an ethical standpoint. The necessity for such review started with developments in medical and public health research, where serious risks of harming people participating in an experiment to test a new drug or other treatment, for instance, could arise. However, risks also can arise in social and behavioral science research.

For example, study participants can be threatened with psychological harm if they are deliberately misled or deceived as part of a social experiment. Such research, sometimes involving compatriots of the experimenter acting as "stooges," at one time represented nearly half of all the articles published in one of the most prominent journals in social psychology (National Research Council, 2003, p. 110).

Researchers must carefully indicate and then implement ways of protecting the people participating in their studies. The spirit of this quest should reflect the ethical principles just discussed in the previous section of this chapter. Specifically, the very beginning of an authoritative book on protecting participants in social and behavioral research states well the main underlying principle (National Research Council, 2003, p. 9):

> Progress in understanding people and society and in bettering the human condition depends on people's willingness to participate in research. In turn, involving people as research participants carries ethical obligations to respect their autonomy, minimize their risks of harm, maximize their benefits, and treat them fairly.

The review and approval procedures—and especially how they pertain to social and behavioral science research—have produced considerable public discussion over the past decade. The discussions have focused on the review of research that on the surface appears to pose "minimal risk" or no "serious risk of harm" to research participants because they are not part of any treatment but are acting in their everyday roles. However, if a study involves delicate questions about a participant's gender, religious, or cultural orientation, for instance, some risk might exist. The procedures also have been ambivalent over whether student projects, conducted for classroom assignments, also require approval. There have even been cases where written informed consent was to be required from participants who were part of a preliterate group (American Association of University Professors, 2006). Negotiations over these and similar situations can lead to inordinate delays in gaining approval.

To prepare yourself well for coping with these review and approval procedures, you will need to spend some time understanding how they are likely to apply to your own research. You can learn more about the topic from numerous websites or from prior IRB experiences at your own institution. There is even a blog site that in December 2008 actually had postings on the eve of the national holidays, reflecting the potentially highly charged nature of the IRB process.

Submitting Study Protocols for Review and Approval

This submission takes place before your research can start. A formally constituted review panel, usually called an IRB, will review your study protocol that outlines the main features of your study in relation to concerns over protecting its participants.

IRBs exist at every university and research organization. Commercial IRBs may serve multiple institutions. The IRB consists of a panel of five or more peers who volunteer on a rotating basis to conduct the needed reviews. The peers purposely represent different academic disciplines as well as community voices. Some IRBs have their own websites, listing their membership and explaining their schedules, deadlines, and procedures.

Although you will be focused on the outcome of the review of your protocol, be sensitive to the fact that IRBs can have a heavy workload. Already by 1995, the average IRB reviewed 578 protocols per year (National Research Council, 2003, p. 36). The number has undoubtedly risen substantially since then.

Each IRB will generally provide its own guidelines on the nature of the desired study protocol. Depending on the nature of the planned study, the IRB can conduct a full or expedited review, or it can exempt a submission from review. Besides approval or rejection, another common review outcome may be a request for modifications and then a resubmission. Under some circumstances, investigators may have to make multiple resubmissions, often then encountering unanticipated delays that interfere with the original schedule for the planned research (Lincoln, 2005, p. 167).

The IRBs operate under guidelines issued by the U.S. Public Health Service. Although every IRB is trying its best to exercise its responsibilities with great care, these guidelines do not represent hard-and-fast rules. IRBs at different institutions can follow slightly different procedures and may use slightly different criteria in their work. Shifts also can occur as the IRB's volunteer membership rotates. As a result, you should learn about the IRB at your institution and the recent experiences it has had in reviewing submissions to do qualitative research in general, if not other studies using methods similar to yours.

Specific Considerations in Protecting Human Subjects

The guidelines for the IRBs cover four main procedures that submissions must address (National Research Council, 2003, pp. 23–28):

1. Obtaining voluntary informed consent from participants, usually by having them sign a written statement ("informed" meaning that the participants understand the purpose and nature of the research);

2. Assessing the harms, risks, and benefits of the research, and minimizing any threat of harm (physical, psychological, social, economic, legal, and dignitary harm) to the participants;

3. Selecting participants equitably, so that no groups of people are unfairly included or excluded from the research; and

4. Assuring confidentiality about participants' identities, including those appearing in computer records and audio- and videotapes.

All of these procedures require careful consideration when they are customized for any given study. In the first procedure, obtaining consent can be represented by a signature, but IRBs can question whether the obtained consent actually will have been either voluntary or informed. The researchers need to show that there are no implicit constraints on a participant's decision to participate and that the decision is truly voluntary. Likewise, a planned study also needs to be presented in a straightforward manner so that participants can understand what they are agreeing to do and thereby are being truly informed.

Even more difficult may be implementing the second procedure, whereby an IRB must judge the potential harms, risks, and benefits of individual studies. Similarly, the researchers must demonstrate to the IRBs how their participant selection will be equitable. Finally, researchers need to demonstrate an awareness of their own process for deciding how to deal with confidentiality—not just of people's names but also the names of organizations and places—and not just the outcome of the process (e.g., Guenther, 2009).

Given these and other difficulties, the IRB reviews can become onerous and unending (e.g., Lincoln & Tierney, 2004). No less prominent a national organization than the American Association of University Professors (AAUP) has argued that the reviews even can "constitute a serious threat to academic freedom" (AAUP, 2006). Qualitative research presents greater challenges because of the belief that many IRB members have unfavorable views toward "emergent" research methods (Lincoln, 2005, p. 172), or methods whose procedures have not been rigidly cast.

Preparing for IRB Review

Some suggestions may help you to prepare for IRB review. The most important step already has been mentioned: Before starting the process, you should learn exactly how the IRB review has been working at your university or research organization. Your study is not likely to be the first of its kind to seek approval, so attend closely to earlier reviews of studies like yours. Knowing something about the individual IRB members and their own research studies and specialties would not hurt either. If your institution has indeed not experienced your kind of study, seek information about your kind of study when it has been the subject of review at other, comparable institutions.

Second, you should embed your study and research methods within the broader context of other similar or deliberately contrasting studies (see the "selective" review of the literature suggested in Chapter 3, Section B). Such embedding might indicate how your methods fall within acceptable and known parameters, already approved in previous studies and having either no untoward consequences or ones that can be easily anticipated. You also could describe how your study will augment the findings from other research (especially those from nonqualitative studies), thereby building a more important body of knowledge or benefit as a result of being conducted.

Third, until you have gained sufficient experience in obtaining IRB approval, make your study design modest in scope (it still can be innovative and imaginative). Set careful boundaries about how you will do your fieldwork and collect data. Have a knowledgeable colleague review your IRB submission in draft form.

The Informed Consent Dialogue (in the Field) as an Opportunity for Participants to Query You

Once you have gained IRB approval, don't be surprised by an additional dynamic. Your presentation of the provisions to obtain informed consent from participants also creates a logical opportunity for participants to query you. The situation may lend itself to questions about how you are planning to go about your study (not necessarily the substance of your study). Other questions may cover the purpose of your study; what you hope to accomplish by having the ensuing interview or conversation with the participant who is now querying you; how you plan to present your final study; how you will avoid embarrassing or otherwise demeaning others who are going to be the participants in the study; and similar other curiosities about your work.

As much as possible, these types of questions should have been anticipated at the time of the original IRB submission. When and if they arise in the fieldwork, the questions should be handled in a conversational and friendly manner, as opposed to a tone that is formal, legalistic, or defensive. To avoid appearing overly defensive when you are first confronted with such questions, do some preparation. Ideally, have a colleague simulate anticipated questions, permitting you to practice your responses.

In an earlier era and possibly still relevant in many contemporary field settings, responding to these and related questions at the most concrete level may be sufficient (e.g., "I am writing a book" about the *abc* [the name of the field setting]). You will then become known as the person who is writing a book. Being able to point to some previous publications will not hurt such an identity. Remarkably, as in the earlier era, people might still be flattered that their real world will appear as part of a book.

RECAP FOR CHAPTER 2: *Terms, phrases, and concepts that you should have covered*:

1. Listening, sizing up a situation, and reading between the lines
2. Handling data
3. Getting ahead of events
4. Study team
5. Pilot study
6. The pitfalls of ignoring data because of contrary results
7. Research integrity
8. Disclosure
9. Insider research
10. Human subjects
11. Voluntary informed consent
12. Confidentiality

EXERCISE FOR CHAPTER 2: CHALLENGING REAL-WORLD EVENT

Describe a real-world experience, involving yourself and other people, in which you felt highly challenged (e.g., interacting with others at a social event; interviewing for a job or for getting into college; trying out for a sports team or performing in some competitive event; solving some problem with your colleagues at work or family at home; or producing a term paper or other product under demanding conditions).

Describe the challenge you personally faced and how you dealt with it. Indicate how your ability to respond reflected a strength or weakness in your ethical values, personal competency, social skill, familial support, serendipity, or other personal circumstances.

Compare this real-world challenge to your personally most demanding experience in doing qualitative research. If you haven't had a qualitative research experience, compare your responses to the challenging real-world event with what you think will be the most personally demanding or difficult part of doing qualitative research. Whether with regard to an actual or a projected qualitative research experience, were your responses to the real-world event similar to those you had or anticipated in doing qualitative research? Are the two situations totally different, or do they bear some similarities? Can you apply lessons from your real-world experience in ways that will improve how you do qualitative research?

CHAPTER 3

How to Start a Research Study

Most people have difficulty starting an empirical study. Part of the challenge is to define a topic of interest. However, the study must use newly collected data, based on a fresh set of data collection procedures—not information from existing secondary sources. To reduce if not overcome this start-up problem, the present chapter shows how the creation of a study bank can help to identify the three needed features of every empirical study: a topic, a data collection method, and the possible sources of data.

The chapter also covers the subsequent steps in the start-up process. These include conducting a literature review and defining a study's research questions. Also considered is an alternative sequence whereby some fieldwork can be started before doing the review or even defining the research questions. The end of the chapter reminds readers that a researcher's own perceptions and background likely will have influenced the entire start-up process. Researchers need to be aware of their research lens and continually document it.

Chapters 1 and 2 of this book have given you a broad sense of qualitative research (Chapter 1) and a discussion of the personal competencies for being able to do qualitative research (Chapter 2).

The "learning by doing" orientation of this book assumes that the best way to learn further about qualitative research is when you actually conduct a qualitative research study. The remainder of this book therefore offers suggestions and guidance for completing one or more such studies.

In its simplest form, conducting an empirical study means:

◆ Defining something to investigate;
◆ Collecting relevant data;
◆ Analyzing and interpreting the results; and
◆ Drawing conclusions based on the empirical findings.

"Collecting relevant data" means dealing directly with a primary source of data, such as field observations or interviews, not secondary sources such as others' studies. The entire middle of this book, covering Chapters 4–9, is devoted to all of these and other related topics.

Nevertheless, despite the near-common understanding of how research consists of doing the preceding activities, starting any particular study seems to be a daunting task. Many people just get stuck and become frustrated because they don't know what to study or how to think about a study. As a result, they don't know what data are relevant, much less how analysis and interpretation are to proceed. How to overcome this start-up problem is therefore the goal of the present chapter.

The Challenge of Starting a Qualitative Study

The challenge is to come up with a topic of study for which you can indeed collect your own data. Surprisingly, much formal education through college may not have exposed students to such a challenge until they reach a thesis or dissertation stage. Especially in the social sciences, the curriculum has likely asked students to do term papers and other exercises that involve "doing some research." However, the research might have called for reviewing literature or searching some sources on the Internet. These earlier assignments may not have actually called for students to: collect their own data, based on their own data collection instrument; come into contact with real-life events and people and collect and record data in some systematic manner; and then draw conclusions supported by the data, not an author's opinions.

Most people (and their advisers) are aware of this challenge of starting a qualitative research study. Less readily recognized is that the challenge may pertain to the start-up of *any* empirical research, qualitative or nonqualitative, especially for people doing a study for the first time.

For instance, those doing laboratory experiments have the same problem of selecting a topic of study (*what to experiment on?*) for which they can collect their own data (*how to set up and do the experiment?*). Don't think that these are easy choices. Moreover, prospective experimenters need to avoid the larger number of logically possible experiments that will nevertheless not produce any useful information.

Although the plight of others may only be of passing interest to you, you can consider it in expanding your support network. Ask your colleagues doing nonqualitative research how they started their first experiment, survey, economic modeling, or other quantitative study that required them to collect their own data. You may be surprised at the relevance of learning about their struggles and eventual success.

Originality in Doing a Qualitative Study

The quest calls for defining (and then conducting) an original study. "Original" means that the study should be of your own making, using your own ideas, words, and data. To the best of your knowledge, including your explicit efforts to determine otherwise, you must do a study that has not been done before.[1]

---

[1]An important exception might be a replication study, deliberately designed to duplicate an earlier study, to determine whether the same results might be found. However, replication studies are not discussed in this book.

Beyond doing an original study lies a further caution. Inevitably, and especially because much of the remainder of this chapter suggests ways of reviewing and using previously published research, some aspects of any study will reflect the ideas or words in other people's publications. Under those circumstances, authors need to be sure to cite the other people and their publications, crediting them with the borrowed ideas or quoted words. To be avoided at all costs is any hint that an "original" study, in whole or in part, came from an uncited source—for example, that the study used someone else's exact words without putting them in quotation marks or block indentation. A failure to properly credit others would constitute plagiarism (Booth, Colomb, & Williams, 1995, p. 167).

The Rest of This Chapter

The remainder of this chapter discusses the start-up process. The chapter may cater more to inexperienced than to experienced researchers, who may therefore consider skipping the rest of this chapter and moving directly to Chapter 4.

At the same time, the differences between Chapters 3 and 4 also are worth noting. In the past, the contents of the present chapter might have been sufficient for knowing not only how to *start* a qualitative study, but also how to *design* it. The three ways of defining a new start-up—discussed in Section A—might have been assumed to be synonymous with the information needed to design the study. Older textbooks may not have delved into many of the design issues that have now emerged in qualitative research. In other words, qualitative research methods have advanced, and Chapter 4 provides more detail on the actual design issues.

A. STARTING A QUALITATIVE STUDY BY CONSIDERING THREE FEATURES

PREVIEW—*What you should learn from this section:*
1. The three main features of empirical studies and therefore the features needing to be defined as part of the start-up of a new qualitative study.
2. How to create a study bank.
3. The several ways that a study bank can help you to define a new qualitative study.

The start-up of every qualitative study needs to cover three essential features:

1. A topic (*what are you going to study?*),
2. A data collection method (*how are you going to collect the data?*), and
3. A source of data—in many cases a fieldwork setting (*where are you going to get the data that are to be collected?*).

As they pertain to defining a new study, the time spent considering these features will be constrained by the presumed time and resources available to do the entire study. Serendipity—the possibility of having one or more of these three features in place before even thinking about doing a qualitative study—also helps.

Parallel Processing the Start-Up Process

Because this book, as do all books, presents itself in linear fashion, the three features are discussed sequentially. However, in reality you should be prepared to juggle your consideration of all three—simultaneously and interactively (processing them in parallel)—before settling on your final choices. For instance, you may start with a topic of interest, only to find no ready source of data. You might then have identified a feasible source of data but now realize the need to go back and redefine a more compelling topic of inquiry. Similarly, you may start with a preference for certain kinds of data collection methods, and this preference will interact with the choices of topic and source of data.

Some people may want to think about all three features simultaneously. In so doing, they are assuming an ability to conduct the tasks in parallel. However, other people may find the three features too awesome to handle as an entire bundle. Thinking about them incrementally, one feature at a time, also is OK. Whichever your preference, the main goal is to move forward and not to get stalled.

Ways of Getting Started

You already may have a pressing interest and know the study you want to do. For instance, you might have worked as part of someone else's research team and have figured a new angle worth investigating, also then knowing the likely data collection method and source of data. You also may have had a preexisting interest in a topic, driving you to learn the qualitative methods for studying it. However, if you have not gotten to these or similar points, the following clues may help you to start thinking about the three features.

One alternative is to review what you've already covered in the social sciences. Recall your previous courses and readings, your knowledge of your colleagues' or professors' research, or even the numerous studies cited in this or other books on qualitative research. From any of these experiences, see if anything has caught your interest or fancy.

Another alternative is to start afresh. You may not have been especially impressed by your previous social science courses or reading; you may have had little exposure to your colleagues' or professors' research; and you may not want to settle for the works referenced in this or other books. The alternative lets you start over and do things your own way. It involves developing your own *study bank*, and this alternative may stimulate more creative thoughts. It works as follows.

Developing a Study Bank

Select some appropriate journals and peruse them for qualitative research studies. Be careful only to identify actual studies, in which an article has reported about a completed piece of research, especially presenting and interpreting a set of data. Exclude other articles also appearing in the same journals, such as articles on qualitative methodologies (but not any complete study); authors' reports of their research experiences in one or more studies (but not any complete study); and syntheses of previous research and theoretical discourses (but not any complete study). After identifying the desired studies, familiarize yourself with their topics, data collection methods, and sources of data. As an important caveat, note that the development of your study bank differs from a more formal review of the literature that you also are likely to do (discussed later in Section B of this chapter).

In developing your study bank, do not limit yourself to articles on any single topic or method. Instead, retrieve anything looking like a qualitative study in each of the journal issues you examine. You should find and appreciate that the studies collectively cover a diverse array of topics and methods. See whether the variety sparks some connection with your own interests and opportunities.

Results from Creating an Illustrative "Study Bank"

To show the ease and usefulness of creating such a study bank, I made one as part of preparing this chapter. My search was limited to journals likely to publish qualitative studies, listed in Exhibit 3.1. The idea was to identify some qualitative studies quickly, not to search exhaustively the journals in any particular discipline like sociology or anthropology, or any particular field like healthcare, community planning, or education. I further limited my search to studies published in the past 5 years or so, and I also tended to cover only a few broad areas: education, health, social work, and organizational research. Even such a superficial foray quickly produced over 50 articles that reported original qualitative studies.

EXHIBIT 3.1.   JOURNALS SEARCHED TO IDENTIFY QUALITATIVE STUDIES

Action Research	*Journal of Mixed Methods Research*
American Educational Research Journal	*Journal of Research in International Education*
Community College Review	*Journal of Transformative Education*
Education and Urban Society	*Organizational Research Methods*
Educational Policy	*Qualitative Health Research*
Ethnography	*Qualitative Inquiry*
Field Methods	*Qualitative Research*
Journal of Contemporary Ethnography	*Qualitative Social Work*
Journal of Hispanic Higher Education	*Urban Education*

The study bank appears at the end of this chapter and gives the full citations to the retrieved articles. Exhibit 3.2 lists their topics. The 50 or so articles show that qualitative studies can be easily found in readily available journals. The next question was how these studies might provide concrete suggestions to stimulate thinking about topics to study and methods to use, if not sources of data, too. (If

EXHIBIT 3.2. TOPICS COVERED BY ILLUSTRATIVE STUDIES CITED IN THE STUDY BANK AT THE END OF CHAPTER 3

1. **Education (K–12)**
   Students in two Catholic high schools
   Lives of international school students
   Students' dress in an inner-city high school
   Follow-up of high school graduates from 50 years ago
   School adjustment by Vietnamese immigrant youths
   Successful Latina/o students
   High- and low-performing middle schools compared
   School relocations in the Gaza Strip

2. **Education (Postsecondary)**
   College experience of ethnic minorities
   First-generation urban college students
   African American university students
   Engaging college students with political advertising
   Undergraduate pedagogy and student learning
   Overseas educational tours
   Change initiative in a community college
   Women's leadership in community colleges
   Introducing action research to preservice teachers
   State-funded merit aid for college
   Race-conscious affirmative action programs

3. **Organizations (Businesses and Work)**
   Networks of a construction contractor
   MIS systems in a manufacturing firm
   Organizational culture of two small manufacturers
   Retail sales work
   Western food restaurants in China
   Role of gender in table service in restaurants

4. **Health and Social Work**
   Perceived barriers to accessing healthcare
   Retention of foster parents in child welfare
   Parents with an autistic child
   Diabetes healthcare services
   Online support groups for breast cancer patients
   Family caregiving for demented-affected elders
   Adults' long-distance care for their parents
   Nursing home facilities
   Daughters' caregiving for dying parents
   Domestic violence services
   Women with gynecological cancer
   Homeless heroin injectors and crack smokers
   HIV-positive women
   Illness experiences of HIV-infected people
   Postpartum smoking among low-income women
   Women's health decisions
   Community mental health organizations
   End of car driving for older women

5. **Communities and Families**
   Low-income Mexican American communities
   Street corners in an urban neighborhood
   Street vendors in an urban scene
   Drug-dealing urban gangs
   Homeless men in two cities
   Work refusal among welfare recipients
   Adolescents after parents' divorce and separation
   Organizing broad-based community organizations
   Umbrella organizations for community development

you want a more detailed understanding of these particular studies, you can use the citations in the study bank to retrieve and examine the studies directly.)

Considering a Topic of Inquiry

For instance, an examination of the list in Exhibit 3.2 shows that these 50 articles alone covered a wide range of topics. Moreover, the recency of the articles helped to ensure that the topics would be contemporary, hopefully making it a realistic list for stimulating thoughts about a new study rather than pointing to social conditions that no longer exist (which might be candidate topics for doing a history but not a qualitative research study).

At this stage of your work, your choice of topic need not reflect any specific research questions or other study details. There will be ample time for those later. Thus, note that the topics in Exhibit 3.2 have been listed in general terms only, divided into the five categories that had been covered.

These topics alone should stimulate your thinking about a new topic. First, in education, the diverse ethnic and cultural backgrounds of students these days can quickly lead you to thinking about doing a study on some different group of students. Second, the topics in health are a reminder that good health these days is equally concerned with preventive behaviors—for example, following a nutritious diet—which means that a new study can take place either inside or outside of formal healthcare service settings. Third, the topics on work similarly suggest possible studies of the different kinds of part- and full-time working arrangements that people have adopted. Fourth, even the single article about educational tours, while focusing on an educational function, nevertheless also calls to mind potentially interesting topics regarding leisure activities.

Using this list as just an illustrative example, within each of the five categories the topics tend to highlight different focal units for study, including:

◆ Individuals (e.g., see "successful Latina/o students" in Exhibit 3.2);

◆ Groups of people (e.g., "family caregiving for demented-affected parents");

◆ Events (e.g., "women's health decisions"); and

◆ Organizations (e.g., "umbrella organizations for community development").

These examples should help you not only to think about a topic but also to articulate them one step further because your study also may need some kind of focal unit.

At the same time, the topics as listed in Exhibit 3.2 do not readily clarify the focal unit and the research orientation of each study. You will have to read each study of interest to figure them out:

> • For instance, the study listed under postsecondary education in Exhibit 3.2 ("change initiative in a community college") turns out to be a study of one community college's campuswide effort to upgrade itself—from an above-average institution to one of unquestioned excellence (Locke & Guglielmino, 2006).
>
> The study shows how the change initiative needed to deal with the different campus "subcultures" associated with different constituents (e.g., students, faculty, alumni, and campus staff). Such a research orientation connected the study to what the authors claimed were underdeveloped theoretical propositions about organizational subcultures, as found in the literature at that time. Their findings thereby covered the community college's initiative and also contributed to new knowledge about dealing with organizational subcultures.

The illustrative study therefore had a concrete focal unit (a contemporary community college), and its research orientation was about organizational subcultures.

Reviewing other studies in the study bank in a similar manner will suggest ideas for both focal units and research orientations. Moreover, the suggested focal units—such as new types of households or working conditions, new immigration patterns, the economy's global nature, and new education policies—may not yet have been overstudied. A new qualitative study would combine one of these examples with a particular research orientation.

Of course, you should not be relying on the characteristics of my study bank. You should be creating your own bank, which will permit you to increase the usefulness of the results even more. For instance, you can focus on the one or two general areas that have previously appealed to you and examine a fuller range of journals in these areas. Conversely, you can search more broadly than I did and cover more general areas. Finally, you also don't have to limit your search to the 50 articles I identified in not more than a couple of days' work. As you retrieve more articles, the depth of your bank will enhance your ability to think more deeply about a study topic.

Considering a Data Collection Method

At this stage, you need not work out any specific data collection method. Rather, you should be considering some broader personal preferences and experiences that might help to make initial choices. For instance, if you already have previously used any particular method, you may feel more comfortable by including it as part of your choice.

For starters, you might think of whether you want to limit your data collection to a single method (see the full array of data collection methods in Chapter 6). For instance, you should ask yourself whether you prefer to collect data by participating in and observing real-life events—that is, "doing fieldwork" (see the participant-observation studies throughout Chapter 5). Alternatively, you should consider whether you prefer to collect data by conducting a series of open-ended interviews (see the "interview-only" studies in Chapter 2, Section B). A study of 50 persons who became single mothers through separation, divorce, or widowhood provides an example (see "An Interview Study Leading to a Policy Agenda," Vignette 3.1).

If you lean toward open-ended interviews as a data collection method, you could further compare your interest and skill in interviewing (1) a larger number of people for a shorter period of time, versus (2) a smaller number of people for more extended periods of time. For instance, the larger group might consist of 40–50 persons interviewed once for 2–3 hours each, whereas the smaller group might consist of a handful of persons interviewed for 2–3 hours each, but on multiple occasions over an extended period of time. The latter choice would enable you to develop some life histories (e.g., see Lewis, 1961, for examples of lengthy life histories; and Appendix A in Liebow, 1993, for examples of life histories of more modest length).

VIGNETTE 3.1. AN INTERVIEW STUDY LEADING TO A POLICY AGENDA

Fifty women, each of whom became a single mother without intending to do so, were the subject of a study by Sidel (2006). Some of the women became single mothers as a result of separation, divorce, or widowhood; others were single at the time of conception but "assumed that their male partner would be available for some level of support—emotional, social, [or] financial" (p. 11), which turned out not to be the case.

The data for the study came from 1- to 2-hour interviews with each of the women, who varied by ethnic, racial, class background, and age. Despite this diversity of backgrounds, all of the women showed shared experiences, including genuine loss. Their lives also dispelled prevailing myths about such women as being lazy, unworthy, or undeserving (2006, p. 21).

The study's entire concluding chapter is therefore devoted to a discussion of desirable changes in U.S. family policy, including provisions related to teenage pregnancy, welfare and work, the minimum wage, universal health insurance, affordable child care, and single-parent families.

You also might be sufficiently experienced or ambitious to entertain using several data collection methods as part of the same study. This would increase your burden but also would strengthen your study. The methods could include some combination of the fieldwork, interviews, and life histories just described. You might use some or all of these methods as part of a single-case study of an organization or a social group. Social groups can include persons working together, such as an education, health, or business team.

Other methods also could be added, such as the collection of census data, organizational records, or other archival sources, to complement your fieldwork and interviews. If you are ambitious, such multiple data collection methods can get quite extensive. For instance, Levitt (2001) used six different methods in her study of transnational migration between the Dominican Republic and a neighborhood in Boston (see Exhibit 3.3).

Returning to the journal articles you retrieved for your own study bank, your foray might initially have been motivated by the desire to identify a topic of study, as previously discussed. However, the study bank also can be extremely helpful in stimulating your thinking about data collection methods. By reviewing the data collection methods used in each of the studies, you can obtain a good idea of the specific ways in which different methods have been used by others. You also might sensitize yourself to the data collection challenges encountered by previous researchers.

For instance, many of the studies listed in the study bank used *focus groups* as their main mode of data collection. You previously may not have given such a method much consideration (see Chapter 6, Section C), but if it now sounds more appealing or appropriate, you can examine those studies more closely to learn about their specific data collection experiences. The studies in the study bank also

	EXHIBIT 3.3. MULTIPLE SOURCES OF DATA USED BY LEVITT (2001, pp. 231–235; ALSO SEE VIGNETTE 4.10)
Data collection method	Data coverage
Interviewing	• 142 interviews with: people working at local, provincial, and national levels; participants in home-based religious practices; officials of religious organizations and political parties • Taped and transcribed about 75% of the interviews; over 80% conducted in Spanish
In-depth interviewing	• 20 return migrant families and 20 migrant families interviewed in their homes • Interviews generally included three or four individuals, with others periodically joining in
Participating	• Attended over 65 meetings, rallies, and special events in Boston and the Dominican Republic, including political party meetings and holiday celebrations and mass • Reproductions (e.g., of artwork or of others' drawings or pictures)
Reviewing documents	• Reviewed documents, including financial records, about each of the organizations in the study • Reviewed relevant newspaper and journal articles
Conducting a survey	• Surveyed 184 households consisting of 806 individuals
Using archival data	• Used data from the U.S. Census and household survey from the Current Population Survey, for multiple years and covering over 300,000 individuals

contain a good number of *mixed methods research* studies, enabling you to see how others have integrated qualitative and quantitative data.

You also can be more ambitious and include books, not just journal articles, in your study bank. Such a combination would be especially pertinent after you have narrowed your interests to a particular type of data collection, such as interviewing elementary school children. By searching for prior studies using this method, you might run across one that even listed the interview questions posed to the children and discussed the researcher's efforts to confirm some of the children's responses by interviewing their guardians and teachers (see "A Qualitative Study with Elementary School Children as the Main Sources of Data," Vignette 3.2).

Considering a Source of Data (e.g., Identifying a Field Setting)

This third feature can be more difficult to assess, especially for novice researchers. First, most journal articles do not give much detail about how authors went through the process of identifying their sources of evidence, so ideas from these articles may be limited. (Rather than articles, you may want to check those studies published in the form of books, where prefaces and methodological sections often divulge the authors' experiences in identifying their sources of evidence.) Second, gaining

> ### VIGNETTE 3.2. A QUALITATIVE STUDY WITH ELEMENTARY SCHOOL CHILDREN AS THE MAIN SOURCES OF DATA
>
> Studying children, and especially interviewing them about their schooling, can be a challenging task. Bullough (2001) conducted just such a study. He observed the classrooms of an elementary school, interviewed a total of 34 children covering grades 1–6, and also interviewed seven teachers and 17 guardians (p. 8).
>
> The first challenge was gaining permission to conduct the interviews, which required obtaining the child's permission as well as written permission from a guardian. A further challenge was to avoid putting words into the children's mouths or "to set an expectation that [a child] needed to say something in order to please me" (2001, p. 7). A final challenge was to confirm the children's words by interviewing their teachers or guardians.
>
> Overcoming these challenges, Bullough completed, recorded, and transcribed interviews with the 34 children. He also provides a copy of his three interview protocols for children, guardians, and teachers (2001, pp. 115–117), noting that "in many of the interviews I found it necessary to adjust the questions and follow the children's lead" (p. 115).

access to real-life situations for your fieldwork, or recruiting people for interviews, or even gaining permission to use certain kinds of documentary data, can be a challenge.

As with identifying a topic and method at this stage, do not try to work out the details of accessing particular sources of evidence—for example, gaining access to particular study settings. You can start thinking about your approach, using some of the fieldwork experiences presented later in Chapter 5 to give you some ideas. However, during this start-up phase of your study, you need only have some potential candidate sources.

Two cautions are nevertheless worth noting. First, less experienced researchers might try to "double up" on some sources where they already have some personal access, such as studying one's own school, family, or friends.

Such "doubling up" can create unwanted complications. You take a great risk that your study and your original affiliation will negatively affect each other, to the detriment of both (see Chapter 2, Section D, for a discussion of *insider research*). At the same time, many qualitative researchers have successfully completed studies about the organizations in which they were employed or neighborhoods in which they resided (see Chapter 5, Section B). A bottom-line suggestion is to avoid any "doubling up" if you are starting your first study but to entertain the possibility as you become more experienced—if you can manage the affiliation carefully and anticipate its possible consequences for your study.

Second, in thinking about studying people in service settings (e.g., health clinics, doctor's offices, social service agencies, and schools), you should not assume that the services will necessarily cooperate in helping you to study their students or clients (or their staff).

> • For instance, Sarroub (2005, p. 17) studied the educational experiences of six students attending the same high school. She made her initial arrangements with these students by meeting them at a community center where they were volunteering. After ascertaining their interest in participating in her study, she then obtained permission for their partici-pation from the officials at the high school.

In addition, the extent to which the people at a site or in a group welcome you into their circle can change over time (see Chapter 5, Section B). The high school in the aforementioned study by Sarroub (2005), for instance, though not initially helping to solicit their students' participation in her study, later became better acquainted with her study. As a result, the school made a mailbox in the teacher's faculty room available to her as she began her second year of fieldwork. Sarroub reports that this changed her work in a "dramatic way" because she felt progress in becoming an insider "of sorts," and she also could now receive daily bulletins and other materials routinely (p. 124).

Remembering Time and Resource Constraints

Everyone knows that research will require time and resources, and neither of these is unlimited. Furthermore, the most common advice, when starting a study, is to make sure that its scope falls within the anticipated time and resources.

The time and resource parameters are usually known. For instance, if you are doing a short study as part of a course assignment, you will need to limit your scope of inquiry as well as your data collection to something that can be investigated within a couple of months. Master's theses or doctoral dissertations will permit a multiyear period and even data that can come from multiple sites. Studies supported by funding sources external to your own personal resources will correspondingly broaden the possibilities even further. For instance, the minimum time for any formal study, going beyond a trial field exercise, appears to be an academic year. Doctoral dissertations commonly consume several years.

Unfortunately, the available guidance offers little information about the scope of study that seems to go with any given time and resource parameters. In the absence of such information, advice about having "modest" aims and choosing topics that are neither too complex nor too simple-minded seem to strike a hollow tone.

In contrast, your study bank can be of some help, especially if you also turn to books in addition to journal articles. Most books (and some journal articles) clarify the time period as well as the amount of time involved in doing a study. You also should estimate the chronological difference between the timing of the data collection—for example, most studies name the year(s) of their data collection—and the year of the publication. Granting a roughly 18- to 24-month period associated with publishing lags, the difference provides a clue regarding the amount of elapsed time consumed in collecting and analyzing data and composing a manuscript.

Readers doing qualitative research for their dissertations should note that the vignettes throughout this textbook contain many studies that were originally completed as dissertations. An even more practical estimate of the likely time and resource needs can therefore be obtained by reviewing the dissertations recently completed at your own academic department or university. These dissertations will provide better examples because they are from your own academic context.

B. REVIEWING RESEARCH LITERATURE

PREVIEW—*What you should learn from this section:*
1. The considerations in deciding whether to review the literature at the outset of a new qualitative study.
2. The differences between selective and comprehensive literature reviews, and how both differ from a study bank.
3. Desirable features in taking notes on the literature in literature reviews.
4. Cautions in accessing websites to retrieve reports and documents as a form of literature.

Given preliminary notions about the topic, method, and source of evidence for your emerging study, another start-up task might be to review the research literature. Such a review differs from the development of your study bank, which you used to help you with the preceding three study features. However, some of the study bank's articles, including articles that might originally have been excluded from the bank, might now be relevant to the newer literature review.

Whether (or Not) to Conduct a Review

Although literature reviews have served as a rather conventional step in doing most empirical research, an earlier view of doing qualitative research resisted formal literature reviews prior to the onset of collecting some field data.

The resistance stemmed from the belief that qualitative studies attempt, most of all, to capture the "meaning" of events, including their unique time, place, and distinct historical moment. Furthermore, the potentially most desirable meaning would come from those who were part of that unique time and place, not from a researcher's perspective.

Given this view, although a review of prior research could help to inform a new study, such a review also could hinder if not bias it by creating an unwanted filter or lens. For instance, if a study was on the topic of socially "wayward" people and the literature was dominated by mainstream cultures, even use of the term *wayward* could be perceived as viewing the lives of the study participants through the lens of not only a majority culture but also an inappropriately earlier era. The lens could therefore greatly lessen the value of doing a qualitative study in the first place.

In starting a new study, some experienced researchers may still assume the preceding point of view. However, its rationale is slowly eroding. The amount of qualitative research has increased greatly in the past few decades (e.g., note the youthfulness of many of the journals cited in the study bank, reflected by their low volume numbers), and the studies and the literature have become much more diverse. More and more, new investigators need to show their awareness, if not adroitness, in identifying specific lines of research—and the "meanings" uncovered under similar circumstances—that are likely to bear directly on a new study's topic, data collection methods, and source of data. If a new study is claimed to be entirely unique, a good literature review also can demonstrate a researcher's mastery over the literature as well as presenting the argument for the lacuna. Thus, conducting some type of literature review seems to be desirable.

If a researcher still wants to resist doing a literature review, even the methodological literature by now contains examples of researchers who have taken similar positions and who have later reported their experiences in published form. Reviewing their retrospective reports about their research experiences would not only show a new investigator's knowledge of the methodological nuances but also demonstrate her or his expertise in conducting a review of the literature as an important part of knowing how to do research.

In short, researchers starting a new qualitative study these days probably have little justification for not reviewing the literature prior to starting their studies. Such a need has become even greater with the requirement to submit study protocols to institutional review boards (see Chapter 2, Section E). The boards are likely to include at least one member who has specialized in nonqualitative research, and that member's understandable expectation would be to see some sort of literature review as part of an initial submission.

Role of Literature Review in Starting a Study

The needed review at this stage is a *selective*, not *comprehensive*, review of the literature (and both differ from the creation of the study bank previously discussed). The main purpose of the selective review is to sharpen your preliminary considerations regarding your topic of study, method, and data source. Rather than assuming a broader perspective and reporting what is known about a topic (which would be the subject of a comprehensive review), your goal is to review and report in greater detail about a specific array of previous studies directly related to your likely topic of study, method, and data source.

In a *selective* review, the studies that need to be targeted and reviewed are those that, on first appearance, closely resemble the one you have started to consider doing. Chances are that you will encounter other studies that focused on similar topics or used a similar data collection method. If you have chosen a school or community as your main source of evidence, you also may find studies that have used similar or perhaps even the same sources. Finding such a study or studies should not automatically discourage you from your original thinking. You should examine these studies carefully and determine whether you can cast yours in some importantly different manner.

For example, an earlier study might have left a loose end—even pointed out in the study's conclusions—that might serve as a priority for further inquiry. Your study could then build on the earlier study. As another possibility, if you closely examine the methodology and data presented by the earlier study, you may find it has overclaimed some critical finding or interpretation critical to the study's main conclusions. You may then be able to define your study to compensate for the earlier study's shortcomings (or oversight) and retest the critical finding or interpretation.

In pursuing these contrasts with specific other studies, your goal is to define a niche for your study, situating it in the array of related studies and not just showing how it will differ from one or more individual studies. The preferable niche can embrace differences in methodology and sources of data, but needs most of all to be defined substantively—that is, in terms of your topic of study (see "Defining a New Study's Contribution in Relation to Existing Literature," Vignette 3.3).

VIGNETTE 3.3. DEFINING A NEW STUDY'S CONTRIBUTION IN RELATION TO EXISTING LITERATURE

A study of Korean American high school students by Lew (2006) claimed that the prevailing literature had typically characterized Asian American students (and their educational performance) in a rather stereotypic as well as homogeneous manner.

In contrast, and to fill a perceived gap in the literature, Lew deliberately studied two contrasting groups of Korean American students. Both groups were second-generation immigrants, but one group was enrolled in an elite magnet high school. The other group consisted of high school dropouts enrolled in a community-based general educational development (GED) program. By covering the two groups, Lew's study was able to demonstrate a diverse set of educational experiences, reflecting family as well as schooling conditions. Her study attributed these differences to class, race, and schooling contexts and therefore challenged the existing stereotype of Asian Americans as a homogeneous and model minority.

The possibility always exists that you cannot identify any satisfactory way in which your study is likely to produce new knowledge beyond what the earlier studies already had contributed. In this case, you may need to return to your original choices of topic, data collection method, and sources of data and revisit them.

Turning to the topic of *comprehensive* literature reviews, there are occasions when such reviews are warranted. The reviews aim to bring together what is known on a particular topic, possibly highlighting controversial or disparate lines of thinking or even the progress over time in cumulating knowledge about a subject. The legitimate role of this type of review is indeed recognized by the existence of major journals, in nearly every social science discipline and subject area, devoted exclusively to such literature reviews.

Using a comprehensive review to help define a new study, however, may not be a good idea. In a comprehensive review, the literature may appear to be endless, with one topic leading to another in a rapidly spiraling manner and leaving the impression that nearly everything worthwhile already has been studied. Comprehensive reviews may be more suited to helping you to decide on a broad area of interest for what may turn out to be a lifetime's worth of studies—rather than in defining any particular study. Unfortunately, many novices may embark on a comprehensive review and spend an exhausting amount of time on such reviews without getting any closer to defining a new study.

Brief Summary: Different Types of Literature Reviews

To summarize the role of literature reviews a bit at this juncture, three different ones have been discussed. The first is an initial foray to build a study bank of previously completed qualitative studies, to help you consider the topic, method, and source of evidence for a new study. The second is a selective review, coming after you have tentatively decided what to study. The selective review deliberately targets other studies that appear to cover a similar ground and helps you to define your new study in a more nuanced manner, establishing a niche for your new study. The third is a comprehensive review, conducted out of a desire to summarize what is known on a given topic but that is not necessarily relevant in helping to start any particular new study.

Taking Notes about Existing Studies

Often unaddressed is exactly what you should be reviewing when you review an existing study. If you do not have a good idea, the risk is that you may have to read every study twice. For instance, I know a colleague who always had two piles of reading on her desk when she started a study. One pile consisted of new readings, some of which she then discarded after reviewing. The other pile consisted of the readings she initially reviewed and had not discarded. Only after finishing the first pile would she go through the second pile and take notes on the readings in that pile. The procedure worked. It just took a long time.

Some studies will take a long time to digest. You will return to them repeatedly as your own work progresses. However, many studies only need to be examined once—if you know what you are looking for, the first time around.

One procedure may work when reviewing empirical studies (studies containing data). Reading a study for the first time, try taking the following notes:

- ◆ The main topic of the study, including the issues/questions being addressed by the study;
- ◆ The data collection method, including the extent of the data collection (e.g., the number of people interviewed in an interview study, or the length and breadth of fieldwork in a participant-observer study);
- ◆ The study's main findings, including the specific data used to represent the findings;
- ◆ The study's main conclusions; and
- ◆ Your own comments about the strengths and weaknesses of the study—and the full bibliographic details for citing the study.

The more you capture this information, whether entered into a PC or written the old-fashioned way on sheets of paper or on index cards, the more likely you may not need to return to a study a second time. If you enter the information into a PC, a further clue is to use a smaller font (e.g., 10 point), hoping that no study takes more than a single page and making it easier to organize and array your notes.

Downloading Materials from Websites

Many of the journal articles you review may have come from websites and the Internet rather than a university library. The greater convenience of obtaining materials in this manner needs to be offset by the extra care needed to favor studies that have appeared in academic journals, and not just any type of publication or forum.

Unfortunately, there will be occasions when a relevant "report" appears outside of a journal but covered a topic or used qualitative methods that attracted your attention. In these situations, you need to interpret carefully the authorship and sponsorship of the report. Acceptable reports are produced by independent research organizations, although the quality of the research may still vary. Less acceptable reports may be produced by advocacy or marketing organizations, or even the research arms of advocacy organizations, mainly because the research may have been biased to represent a point of view. The key here is to learn something about a sponsoring organization before using its reports. Examining the author's prior publications also should broaden your understanding of how any specific work might be used.

For reports appearing outside of journals, you also may need to verify the authenticity of a retrieved document. No simple verification formula exists. Being aware that authenticity could be a problem is the beginning of the solution. Then, checking about the document from different sources and checking about the authoritativeness of the sources are both worthy procedures.

C. DETAILING A NEW QUALITATIVE STUDY

PREVIEW—*What you should learn from this section:*

1. The possible benefits from starting a bit of fieldwork before identifying a study's research questions.
2. The possible benefits from defining a study's research questions before doing any fieldwork.
3. How to find a study's research questions in published works, even though the questions may be embedded in descriptions of a study`s rationale or purpose.
4. The importance of knowing that your role as a research instrument already has revealed itself in the start-up activities suggested by the entire chapter.

A successful start-up to this point should have helped you to identify, at least in a preliminary manner, three things: a topic, a method, and a source of data. If as suggested you have progressed even further in this start-up process, you also will have identified a potential niche for your study, especially in relation to other similar studies. These broad outlines now need further detailing. You need to see how the broad outlines translate into research actions.

Qualitative research offers another interesting opportunity at this juncture. With appropriate preparation but no further detailing, you might now want to start some fieldwork. (For the purposes of this discussion, *fieldwork* is defined as any data collection activity you might undertake, such as any of the methods described in Chapter 6.) Alternatively, you might want to delay the fieldwork until you have taken one more step—defining some research questions. Again, as in doing most steps in a qualitative study, these and other opportunities are iterative and recursive—which means that you can do a little of one step and then return to an earlier step, adjusting the earlier step accordingly. You also can repeat this sequence more than once.

Starting with either fieldwork or research questions can both lead to acceptable results; a major caveat is how you will handle any hurdles posed when you seek approval for your study by the IRB—again, already covered in Chapter 2. But first, let's learn more about the two opportunities.

Starting a Bit of Fieldwork First

"Fieldwork first" makes sense because qualitative research attempts to capture real-life conditions, embracing the perspective of the people who are part of these conditions. Following this line of reasoning, a qualitative researcher would prefer that the real-life conditions and others' perspectives help to define the subsequent study questions and design. As a result, these researchers assign a high premium to doing fieldwork at some early stage in the start-up process.

At the same time, "fieldwork first" is likely to be more effectively done if you explicitly articulate what you hope to learn by doing the fieldwork. The anticipated learnings may take at least three forms.

First, they may be substantive (e.g., whether you should sharpen or re-shape your selected topic of interest). Second, they may be methodological (e.g., whether the people in the field are as accessible and informative as you had expected). Third, the fieldwork may orient you to relevant perspectives (e.g., how the people in the field think about their activities or about real-life events). Whichever the form, summarizing your anticipated learnings in writing beforehand will help you to focus even your initial fieldwork experience. So, in this sense "fieldwork first" still calls for preparation.

Unless you are a highly experienced researcher, a "fieldwork first" decision should not be taken lightly. Your initial field presence and queries, and others' initial exposure to you and your research aims, all will create indelible first impressions. In a real-life situation (whether you are directly observing events or are interviewing someone else about such events), you cannot afford to appear as if you do not know what you are doing. Other people will readily accept and may even appreciate that you want a field perspective to help refine or even challenge your original research intentions. However, people will be less tolerant and even resist cooperating further if they sense you may be wasting their (as well as your own) time because you lack direction.

Starting with Research Questions

Your colleagues who do other forms of research (including research outside of the social sciences), but not necessarily qualitative research, will be more accustomed to starting with research questions first. The questions will not only reflect what you hope to study but also should be attractively positioned relative to the existing literature. Thus, the "questions first" option is important. A common belief in research outside of qualitative studies is that good research usually only follows a good set of questions.

Eventually, even if you start with a "fieldwork first" option, you will need to develop a set of research questions. However, they can be revisited and revised as your research proceeds, so you should not think that the first set of questions will necessarily be the final questions.[2]

The challenge of what comprises good research questions has no ready formula. Your earlier foray into the literature, to create a study bank, will provide many examples of other studies' research questions. To develop a preliminary set of your own research questions, you can work with these or with the questions posed when describing your study goals to colleagues, or with some other source of your own making.

If you examine the study bank as a source, a brief review will show no explicit section where investigators routinely report their research questions. Instead, you must read a study closely, looking for phrases such as "the purpose of this study is to . . . " or "this study aims to . . . " When a study's research questions are not explicitly enumerated, its questions are usually contained within these or similar phrases.

Instead of looking literally for a set of research questions, think about finding something like a study's inquiry or rationale. You then should uncover such examples as the following (all three examples are taken from my study bank):

---

[2]You should not be led to believe that the iterative and recursive pattern is limited to doing qualitative research, much less to be considered a distinctive feature of such research. Laboratory experiments also follow a similar pattern, with investigators having to revise their research questions after running some initial trials and potentially revisiting their instrumentation or procedures. Chapter 12 discusses these and other parallels between qualitative and nonqualitative research further.

- The study considers how Vietnamese immigrant high school students negotiate the processes of cultural and gender identity formation as they transition to U.S. schooling. The study seeks to better understand the ways in which the categories of gender and cultural identity are connected to the academic and social experiences of recent immigrant students (Stritikus & Nguyen, 2007).

- The study attempts to explain differences between low- and high-performing schools by examining differences in the technical, managerial, and institutional levels of the schools' organizational health (Brown, Anfara, & Roney, 2004).

- The purpose of the study was to understand the perceptions of successful African American university students who had graduated from two large urban school districts that were now facing serious problems. The objective was to discover the in-depth thoughts, experiences, and constructed meanings of the students about their prior high school experience and their transition to college (Wasonga & Christman, 2003).

There are other occasions when the pertinent material is presented in the form of actual study questions, as in the following examples:

- What perceptions and attitudes do first-generation, urban college students have of their secondary school preparation for postsecondary education, and what were the strengths and weaknesses of their secondary school preparation? (Reid & Moore, 2008)

- How a particular university became the leader and defendant of race-conscious admissions policies; and how the university's leaders responded to the legal challenges, to defend its position on race-conscious policies (Green, 2004).

Regardless of the form these examples used in stating a study's inquiry, rationale, or questions, notice how the examples go much further, substantively, than the original topics listed in Exhibit 4.2. The assertions or questions begin to suggest the kind of data that will be collected by the study, which the original topics did not.

Not shown by these examples, but to be found if you closely review the actual studies listed in the study bank (or those in your own study bank), is another relationship: The introductions to the studies contain literature reviews that situate the study's aims or questions within the literature, arguing in favor of the study's potential significance in relation to the larger literature. (The presence of such a discussion does not mean, however, that the author reviewed the literature prior to starting any fieldwork—again an example of how the linear presentation of topics does not necessarily coincide with the order in which they were created.) In this sense, having a good set of research questions helps you to define the upcoming actions to conduct your study, such as the development of field and other data collection instruments, as well as to define your prospective study's niche in the larger literature.

Having established an initial set of research questions, you are now in a good position to articulate the design of your study even further, if desired, as discussed in Chapter 4.

Examining Your Own Background Knowledge and Perceptions in Relation to a New Study

There is, however, one more important prelude. Once you have started to articulate your topics, methods, and sources of evidence, together with any research questions, you need to take stock of all these considerations in relation to your own background.

Qualitative research will ultimately involve you as a primary research instrument (see Chapter 5, Section D). The needed stock-taking comes from a self-examination of your own knowledge and views that might affect your role as a research instrument. You should identify any particular prior knowledge or predilections that might affect your design or data collection actions.

Inevitably, and as a direct function of having chosen a topic of interest to you, some background factors will exist. Typically, people tend to bring sympathetic, antagonistic, or overly naive views to their topics of interest. Any such orientations can affect a study's lines of inquiry and hence the potential findings from the study. You would be fooling yourself if you think that you bring a totally neutral or objective stance to your study.

The start-up phase of your study therefore marks your initial efforts to identify and record what will later be described as your "research lens" (Chapter 11). This awareness and the maintaining of your introspections in some written form—for example, your own research journal—should continue throughout the conduct of your study. The final study report, as discussed in Chapter 11, should then contain a section about your research lens and its possible influence on the entire study and its findings.

RECAP FOR CHAPTER 3: *Terms, phrases, and concepts that you now can define:*

1. What constitutes an "original" study
2. "Defining" as opposed to "designing" a new study
3. Study bank
4. Study topics as usually consisting of a focal unit and a research orientation
5. "Doubling up" on field sources
6. Selective literature review
7. Comprehensive literature review
8. "Fieldwork first" compared to "research questions first"
9. Self-examination in relation to being the primary research instrument

EXERCISE FOR CHAPTER 3: CREATING YOUR OWN STUDY BANK

After reviewing the nature and purpose of a study bank as described in Chapter 3, develop your own study bank (see if you can use your university or organization's online account to access journal materials). Define a period of time (several years or more) and a group of 10–15 journals in which qualitative research appears regularly and with some frequency. Take a quick set of notes on the topics covered by each of about 30 studies (or more, if you wish). Remember that the study bank only should contain actual studies, not reviews of literature, methodological articles, theoretical essays, or other published works that do not present or analyze the actual data coming from a specific study or project.

Use your notes to create a formal word table containing the topics of each of the studies, possibly clustered into subgroups like the word table in Exhibit 3-2. Use parallel and short phrases and make the word table as presentable as possible, as if it will appear as a formal exhibit in some study of yours. For a smaller set of studies that may be on a topic of interest to you, take further notes and make a second word table, briefly describing the methods used in each of this smaller subset of studies.

ILLUSTRATIVE STUDY BANK FOR CHAPTER 3

QS, qualitative study; CS, case study; IS, interview study (including focus groups); MM, mixed methods study.

Bauer, M. J., Rottunda, S., & Adler, G. (2003). Older women and driving cessation. *Qualitative Social Work, 2,* 309–325. (CS)

Bempechat, J., Boulay, B. A., Piergross, S. C., & Wenk, K. A. (2008). Beyond the rhetoric: Understanding achievement and motivation in Catholic school students. *Education and Urban Society, 40,* 167–178. (IS)

Bourgois, P., & Schonberg, J. (2007). Intimate apartheid: Ethnic dimensions of habitus among homeless heroin injectors. *Ethnography, 8,* 7–31. (QS)

Britton, M. (2008). "My regular spot": Race and territory in urban public space. *Journal of Contemporary Ethnography, 37,* 442–468. (QS)

Brown, K. M., Anfara, V. A., Jr., & Roney, K. (2004). Student achievement in high performing suburban middle schools and low performing urban schools: Plausible explanations for the differences. *Education and Urban Society, 36,* 428–456. (CS)

Clawson, L. (2005). "Everybody knows him": Social networks in the life of a small contractor in Alabama. *Ethnography, 6,* 237–264. (QS)

Cleaveland, C. (2005). A desperate means to dignity: Work refusal amongst Philadelphia welfare recipients. *Ethnography, 6,* 35–60. (QS)

Cohen-Vogel, L., Ingle, W. K., Levine, A. A., & Spence, M. (2008). The "spread" of merit-based college aid: Politics, policy consortia, and interstate competition. *Education Policy, 22,* 339–362. (MM)

Collins, C. C., & Dressler, W. W. (2008). Cultural consensus and cultural diversity: A mixed methods investigation of human service providers' models of domestic violence. *Journal of Mixed Methods Research, 2,* 362–387. (MM)

Cristancho, S., Garces, D. M., Peters, K. E., & Mueller, B. C. (2008). Listening to rural Hispanic immigrants in the Midwest: A community-based participatory assessment of major barriers to health care access and use. *Qualitative Health Research, 18,* 633–646. (IS)

Dohan, D. (2002). Making cents in the barrios: The institutional roots of joblessness in Mexican America. *Ethnography, 3,* 177–200. (QS)

Fail, H., Thompson, J., & Walker, G. (2004). Belonging, identity, and third culture kids: Life histories of former international school students. *Journal of Research in International Education, 3,* 319–338. (IS)

Fetherston, B., & Kelly, R. (2007). Conflict resolution and transformative pedagogy: A grounded theory research project on learning in higher education. *Journal of Transformative Education, 5,* 262–285. (QS)

Garot, R., & Katz, J. (2003). Provocative looks: Gang appearance and dress codes in an inner-city alternative school. *Ethnography, 4,* 421–454. (QS)

Gowan, T. (2002). The nexus: Homelessness and incarceration in two American cities. *Ethnography, 3,* 500–534. (QS)

Green, D. O'N. (2004). Fighting the battle for racial diversity: A case study of Michigan's institutional responses to *Gratz* and *Grutter*. *Educational Policy, 18,* 733–751. (IS)

Gross, Z. (2008). Relocation in rural and urban settings: A case study of uprooted schools from the Gaza Strip. *Education and Urban Society, 40,* 269–285. (CS)

Hsu, C. L. (2005). A taste of "modernity": Working in a Western restaurant in market socialist China. *Ethnography, 6,* 543–565. (QS)

Huxham, C., & Vangen, S. (2003). Researching organizational practice through action research: Case studies and design choices. *Organizational Research Methods, 6,* 383–403. (CS)

Jones, L., Castellanos, J., & Cole, D. (2002). Examining the ethnic minority student experience at predominantly white institutions: A case study. *Journal of Hispanic Higher Education, 1,* 19–39. (CS)

Kadushin, C., Hecht, S., Sasson, T., & Saxe, L. (2008). Triangulation and mixed methods designs: Practicing what we preach in the evaluation of an Israel experience educational program. *Field Methods, 20,* 46–65. (MM)

Kitchen, J., & Stevens, D. (2008). Action research in teacher education: Two teacher-educators practice action research as they introduce action research to preservice teachers. *Action Research, 6,* 7–28. (QS)

Locke, M. G., & Guglielmino, L. (2006). The influence of subcultures on planned change in a community college. *Community College Review, 34,* 108–127. (CS)

MacGregor, T. E., Rodger, S., Cummings, A. L., & Leschied, A. W. (2006). *Qualitative Social Work, 5,* 351–368. (IS)

Markovic, M. (2006). Analyzing qualitative data: Health care experiences of women with gynecological cancer. *Field Methods, 18,* 413–429. (IS)

Mendenhall, T. J., & Doherty, W. J. (2007). Partners in diabetes: Action research in a primary care setting. *Action Research, 5,* 378–406. (QS)

Mendlinger, S., & Cwikel, J. (2008). Spiraling between qualitative and quantitative data on women's health behaviors: A double helix model for mixed methods. *Qualitative Health Research, 18,* 280–293. (MM)

Menning, C. L. (2008). "I've kept it that way on purpose": Adolescents' management of negative parental relationship traits after divorce and separation. *Journal of Contemporary Ethnography, 37,* 586–618. (IS)

Nandhakumar, J., & Jones, M. (2002). Development gain?: Participant observation in interpretive management information systems research. *Qualitative Research, 2,* 323–341. (QS)

Nichter, M., Adrian, S., Goldade, K., Tesler, L., & Muramoto, M. (2008). Smoking and harm-reduction efforts among postpartum women. *Qualitative Health Research, 18,* 1184–1194. (IS)

Ortner, S. B. (2002). "Burned like a tattoo": High school social categories and "American culture." *Ethnography, 3*, 115–148. (QS)

Parmelee, J. H., Perkins, S. C., & Sayre, J. J. (2007). "What about people our age?": Applying qualitative and quantitative methods to uncover how political ads alienate college students. *Journal of Mixed Methods Research, 1*, 183–199. (MM)

Pettinger, L. (2005). Representing shop work: A dual ethnography. *Qualitative Research, 5*, 347–364. (QS)

Read, T., & Wuest, J. (2007). Daughters caring for dying parents: A process of relinquishing. *Qualitative Health Research, 17*, 932–944. (IS)

Reid, M. J., & Moore, J. L., III. (2008). College readiness and academic preparation for postsecondary education: Oral histories of first-generation urban college students. *Urban Education, 43*, 240–261. (IS)

Roff, L. L., et al. (2007). Long distance parental caregivers' experience with siblings. *Qualitative Social Work, 6*, 315–334. (IS)

Scott, G. (2004). "It's a sucker's outfit": How urban gangs enable and impede the reintegration of ex-convicts. *Ethnography, 5*, 107–140. (QS)

Scott, S. M. (2003). The social construction of transformation. *Journal of Transformative Education, 1*, 264–284. (IS)

Stoller, P. (2002). Crossroads: Tracing African paths on New York City streets. *Ethnography, 3*, 35–62. (QS)

Stritikus, T., & Nguyen, D. (2007). Strategic transformation: Cultural and gender identity negotiation in first-generation Vietnamese youth. *American Educational Research Journal, 44*, 853–895. (QS)

Tedrow, B., & Rhoads, R. A. (1999). A qualitative study of women's experiences in community college leadership positions. *Community College Review, 27*, 1–18. (QS)

Tibbals, C. A. (2007). Doing gender as resistance: Waitresses and servers in contemporary table service. *Journal of Contemporary Ethnography, 36*, 731–751. (QS)

Tinney, J. (2008). Negotiating boundaries and roles: Challenges faced by the nursing home ethnographer. *Journal of Contemporary Ethnography, 37*, 202–225. (QS)

van Uden-Kraan, C., Drossaert, C. H. C., Taal, E., Shaw, B. R., Seydel, E. R., & van de Laar, M. (2008). Empowering processes and outcomes of participation in online support groups for patients with breast cancer, arthritis, or fibromyalgia. *Qualitative Health Research, 18*, 405–417. (IS)

Voils, C. I., Sandelowski, M., Barroso, J., & Hasselblad, V. (2008). Making sense of qualitative and quantitative findings in mixed research synthesis studies. *Field Methods, 20*, 3–25. (MM)

Wasonga, T., & Christman, D. E. (2003). Perceptions and construction of meaning of urban high school experiences among African American university students. *Education and Urban Society, 35*, 181–201. (IS)

Weitzman, P. F., & Levkoff, S. E. (2000). Combining qualitative and quantitative methods in health research with minority elders: Lessons from a study of dementia caregiving. *Field Methods, 12*, 195–208. (MM)

Westhue, A., Ochocka, J., Jacobson, N., Simich, L., Maiter, S., Janzen, R., et al. (2008). Developing theory from complexity: Reflections on a collaborative mixed method participatory action research study. *Qualitative Health Research, 18*, 701–717. (MM)

Woodgate, R. L., Ateah, C., & Secco, L. (2008). Living in a world of our own: The experience of parents who have a child with autism. *Qualitative Health Research, 18*, 1075–1083. (IS)

Yauch, C. A., & Steudel, H. J. (2003). Complementary use of qualitative and quantitative cultural assessment methods. *Organizational Research Methods, 6*, 465–481. (MM)

Zalaquett, C. P. (2005). Study of successful Latina/o students. *Journal of Hispanic Higher Education, 5*, 35–47. (IS)

Zhou, Y. R. (2008). Endangered womanhood: Women's experiences with HIV/AIDS in China. *Qualitative Health Research, 18*, 1115–1126. (IS)

PART II

DOING QUALITATIVE RESEARCH

CHAPTER 4

Choices in Designing
Qualitative Research Studies

Every research study has a design, whether implicit or explicit. Researchers seek to use strong designs to strengthen the validity of their studies and to ensure that the data to be collected properly address the research topic being studied. Qualitative research also has designs, but not any fixed types or categories of designs. As a result, the present chapter describes eight different procedures that can be considered in designing qualitative research.

Distinctive to qualitative research is the potential resistance to doing too much, if any, design work ahead of time—to avoid imposing external criteria or categories, or any fixed regimen on the real-world reality being studied. As a result, the present chapter discusses the eight procedures as "choices," with researchers free and not obligated to adopt the design procedures best suited to their specific studies. Not surprisingly, the first choice is whether to engage in design work at the beginning of a study or not.

You can create a sound platform for your study by thinking carefully about its research design. However, thoughtful design work does not mean automatically adopting a lot of rigid design procedures. Thoughtfulness means making explicit decisions about whether you want to worry about every one of those procedures in the first place. The overall result of your thoughtfulness, no matter which specific procedures are then followed, will be a higher probability of completing a sound study—one whose findings do indeed address the initial questions or topics of study.

BRIEF DEFINITION OF RESEARCH DESIGNS ♦

Research designs are *logical* blueprints. The designs serve as "logical" plans, not the "logistics" plans often referenced by others (the logistics plans are still needed but cover the management of your research, such as the scheduling and coordination of the work).

The logic involves the links among the research questions, the data to be collected, and the strategies for analyzing the data—so that a study's findings will address the intended research questions. The logic also helps to strengthen the validity of a study, including its accuracy.

> • For instance, a community study may have started with its main research question focused on the nature of residential crime prevention. However, the data collection only then covered formally created residents' organizations, ignoring a whole host of informal networks. The findings must therefore be limited to crime prevention by formal organizations, either resulting in a modified research question (which may be undesirable or unacceptable) or producing a distorted understanding of the full panoply of residential crime prevention.

By definition, all research studies have an implicit blueprint or design, whether you planned it or not. Nonetheless, it does not have to be created at the beginning of the study. In qualitative research, how much design work is done beforehand is a matter of choice. Furthermore, even as you conduct your study you may give different parts of designs differential attention—possibly even ignoring some parts. Designs also can change during the course of a study. The main design conditions, including whether to do any design work ahead of time, are the subject of the present chapter.

Design Options

The "choice" approach implied by the title of this chapter seems warranted because qualitative research has no array of fixed designs, as might appear to exist in doing experiments. In other words, because there is no clear typology of blueprints, every qualitative study is likely to vary in its design, and being offered the various choices permits you to customize your design as you see fit.

At the same time, make no mistake that your completed study will have, in retrospect, some kind of design. You may have planned only some of the features, letting the others emerge during the course of the study. The final design may turn out to be robust in spite of your lack of attention. Conversely, the design may not be what you wanted it to be, and the study may have flaws.

Let us turn now to the choices.

CHOICE 1: STARTING A RESEARCH DESIGN
AT THE BEGINNING OF A STUDY (OR NOT)

PREVIEW—*What you should learn from this section:*
1. The pros and cons of starting a research design at the beginning of a qualitative study.
2. Design as an iterative process.

Not all qualitative studies start by having a research design. For such studies, the design did not therefore serve as a plan for conducting the study but only served as a retrospective feature of the study.

Qualitative researchers have produced no clear consensus on the value of creating research designs before data collection starts. The differences of opinion again focus on the tension presented by the choices highlighted at the end of Chapter 3: defining a study's direction ahead of time (e.g., the "questions first" option) versus letting the initial field experiences (and hence early data collection) influence the study's direction (e.g., the "fieldwork first" option).

The present chapter takes no sides on the matter. Thus, whether to start a design ahead of time (or not), or to give early attention to some design features (as identified in the seven additional design choices in the remainder of this chapter) but not others, represents the first design "choice" presented by this chapter. Your own qualitative research experience, the norms you wish to follow, and the norms in place where you do your research all will dictate the extent to which you might develop a research design ahead of time.

Whether you are starting at the beginning or not, remember that the design process is a recursive one. This means that portions of the design can be put into place as a study proceeds and that these design features also can be revisited more than once as a study proceeds.

> • For instance, Joseph Maxwell, who has possibly written the most about qualitative research designs, characterizes the process as an *"inter*active" approach, whereby a qualitative study's purpose, research questions, conceptual context, methods, and concern for validity all continually interact (Maxwell, 1996, pp. 1–8).

The fact that these recursive and other discretionary choices can exist throughout the conduct of a study directs attention squarely to the issue of a research investigator's integrity (previously discussed in Chapter 2, Section D). Because qualitative research permits and in some ways encourages multiple midstream adjustments throughout the study process, investigators have an opportunity, unlike doing most other kinds of research, to influence the findings. Such influence may be purposeful or inadvertent.

If purposeful, a research investigator would have failed to meet the standards for acceptable research integrity. If inadvertent (and inadvertent influences can be a constant presence in research), the investigator has an obligation to address the ways in which such influences might have occurred and their potential effect on a study's findings. This obligation is so important that it is discussed in passages throughout this book in reference to maintaining notes to yourself (including a personal journal). The notes should deal with issues of reflexivity, the researcher as the research instrument, and the researcher's "lens," also as discussed throughout the book (see the discussion in Chapter 11, Section D, on your "reflective self").

CHOICE 2: TAKING STEPS TO STRENGTHEN THE VALIDITY OF A STUDY (OR NOT)

PREVIEW—What you should learn from this section:

1. How to strive for a valid study.
2. Two especially pervasive practices for strengthening the validity of a study.

The second choice actually involves several choices. All are concerned with ways of strengthening a qualitative study's validity. At first glance, the notion of "strengthening validity" runs counter to our understanding of *validity* as a strictly bivariate concept (it either exists or it doesn't). Instead, consider that every study contains many different claims, each of which may or may not be valid. Your goal would be to validate as many of these claims as you possibly can, thereby strengthening the validity of the overall study.

What Validity Means When Doing Research

For all kinds of research, including qualitative research, possibly the key quality control issue deals with the *validity* of a study and its findings. A valid study is one that has properly collected and interpreted its data, so that the conclusions accurately reflect and represent the real world (or laboratory) that was studied. Conversely, studies in any field are worthless if they arrive at false findings. Such an extreme outcome is unlikely to occur, but studies should nevertheless use design features that will strengthen the validity of their claims and findings.

Note that the validity issue is not limited to a study's findings. The issue even pertains to the sheer description of a field event or of a participant's views. These numerous items may be considered the facts presented by a study, and all of them require validation.

In qualitative research, it is essential not to confuse the desire for validity with a researcher's positioning along relativist-realist lines (previously described in Chapter 1, Section C). In other words, even a study that embraces a relativist stance (i.e., holding that no single reality exists) still needs to be concerned with the validity of the relativist findings. You may think of the problem in terms of whether another study, *given the same lens or orientation*, would have collected the same evidence and have drawn the same conclusions as those in your study.

Maxwell highlights the issues of validity by referring to "the correctness or credibility of a description, conclusion, explanation, interpretation, or other sort of account" (1996, p. 87). Based on his own work as well as numerous other qualitative studies, Maxwell also has compiled and summarized at least seven ways for addressing validity challenges (see "Seven Strategies for Combating Threats to Validity in Qualitative Research," Vignette 4.1). Most of the recommended practices are easy to understand and implement, and each of them represents a "choice." Thus, you should be able to integrate them into your study design if you so choose.

VIGNETTE 4.1. SEVEN STRATEGIES FOR COMBATING THREATS TO VALIDITY IN QUALITATIVE RESEARCH

Joseph Maxwell (2009, pp. 244–245) offers a seven-point checklist to be used in combating the threats to validity:

1. *Intensive long-term [field] involvement*—to produce a complete and in-depth understanding of field situations, including the opportunity to make repeated observations and interviews;
2. *"Rich" data*—to cover fully the field observations and interviews with detailed and varied data;
3. *Respondent validation*—to obtain feedback from the people studied, to lessen the misinterpretation of their self-reported behaviors and views;
4. *Search for discrepant evidence and negative cases*—to test rival or competing explanations;
5. *Triangulation*—to collect converging evidence from different sources;
6. *Quasi-statistics*—to use actual numbers instead of adjectives, such as when claiming something is "typical," "rare," or "prevalent"; and
7. *Comparison*—to compare explicitly the results across different settings, groups, or events.

Two of the seven practices, searching for "discrepant evidence and negative cases" (also known as testing rival or competing explanations) and "triangulation," need greater elaboration. The practices can be more pervasive than is usually recognized. Both raise the need for a researcher to assume a methodic orientation or demeanor throughout the conduct of a study. In this sense, both involve more than a single or specific practice. The two are therefore discussed in greater detail next.

Rival Explanations

Rival explanations are not merely alternative interpretations. True *rivals* compete directly with each other and cannot coexist. In research, think of your findings and their interpretation as combatants that can be challenged by one or more rivals. If one of the rivals turns out to be more plausible than your original interpretation, you would have to reject your original interpretation, not just footnote it. By appropriately recognizing the rival and rejecting your original interpretation, you would in fact have strengthened the validity of your research, especially if you then also thoroughly discuss the rationale for accepting or rejecting each of the rivals as part of your study (Campbell, 1975; Yin, 2000).

Researchers deliberately seek to strengthen their studies by searching for rivals throughout the study process. Rivals can exist at every turn, not just in the final interpretation of a study's findings. For instance, you will inevitably have made certain assumptions about the characteristics of your chosen field setting or field interviewees by having selected them. They were to be the source of valued information about your topic of study. A constant rival, as you collect your data, should point to the possibility that the information might be misleading or misguided and that other sources (settings or interviewees) might offer better vantage points. You should be taking steps continually during your data collection to "test" this rival.

Overall, the desired orientation to rival thinking by researchers assumes greater importance than merely stipulating one or more rival explanations at the conclusion of your study. The desired rival thinking should draw from a continual sense of *skepticism* as you conduct your study. The skepticism would involve asking yourself such questions as:

◆ Whether events and actions are as they appear to be;
◆ Whether participants are giving their most candid responses when talking with you; and
◆ Whether your own original assumptions about a topic and its features were indeed correct.

The skeptical attitude would cause you to collect more data and to do more analysis than if you were not concerned about rivals. For instance, you might do more double-checking, you might check more other sources than you would have done originally, and you might even explore some remote possibilities rather than ignoring them. In other words, every facet of your research and research methods could be subject to rival explanations. Having solid evidence to rule them out (or, alternatively, succumbing to a rival and rejecting your original assumptions) is an essential way of strengthening the validity of your study.

Moreover, your search for such "discrepant evidence" should be as vigorous as possible, as if you were trying to establish the potency of the rival rather than seeking to undermine it (Patton, 2002, p. 553; Rosenbaum, 2002, pp. 8–10). If no such evidence is found despite diligent search, you would feel more confident in your study's ultimate description, attribution, or interpretation.

In summary, all sorts of rivals are possible at every step in doing a study. Stronger research studies are those conducted with a skeptical frame of mind. They try to identify and test possible rival explanations as an integral part of the entire research process (Campbell, 2009; Yin, 2000). The rival thinking should then be part of the final research composition, including any short summaries of the research, usually taking the form of an abstract (Kelly & Yin, 2007).

Triangulation

The principle of *triangulation* comes from navigation, where the intersection of three different reference points is used to calculate the precise location of an object (Yardley, 2009, p. 239). In research, the principle pertains to the goal of seeking at least three ways of verifying or corroborating a particular event, description, or fact being reported by a study. Such corroboration serves as another way of strengthening the validity of a study.

As with rival thinking, triangulation also can be applied throughout a study, although the practice has tended to be associated with a study's data collection phase. In collecting data, the ideal triangulation would not only seek confirmation from three sources but would try to find three different kinds of sources. Thus, if you saw an event with your own eyes (a direct observation), and it was reported to you by someone else who was there (a verbal report)—and it was described in a similar manner by a later report written by yet someone else (a document)—you would have considerable confidence in your reporting of that event. If in contrast your study focused on a participant's view of the world without regard to its relationship to other sources, you still might want to triangulate by conversing with the participant on two or more occasions about her or his view, to make sure that you had correctly represented the participant's view.

Often, different kinds of sources may not be available. You might have to rely on the verbal reports from three different people (or the information in three different documents) but have no other source of corroboration. In such situations, you would need to be concerned over whether the sources actually represented three *independent* reports, forestalling the possibility that the reports were in some way linked. For instance, two of the three documents initially appearing as separate sources might simply have been drawing key information from the third document.

The search for independent reports can be especially problematic in working with Internet sources. What might appear to be three different reports on three different websites might easily all have come from the same original source. For instance, many news reports are based on the work of a well-known and highly regarded international press corps, the *Associated Press* (*AP*). Many websites will pick up an *AP* news item and report the same item but may not have attributed it to the *AP*. If you thought that three of these websites were reporting independently about the item, and hence helping you to corroborate or triangulate the item, you would be wrong.

The need to triangulate will be less important when you capture and record the actual data directly. For instance, if you can tape record an interview or photograph a visually important matter, there will be less, if any, need to corroborate the evidence. Unfortunately, taking these steps is not always feasible or desirable (see Chapter 7, Section D).

Many qualitative studies also involve dialogues in languages other than English. One invaluable practice, when presenting some of this dialogue in a final manuscript written in English, is to present the original language and its English translation side by side in the text. Readers familiar with the foreign language can then gauge the adequacy of the translation for themselves. Unfortunately, such a practice has been followed only rarely (see Valdés, 1996, for one of the few exceptions; also refer to Vignette 10.3).

CHOICE 3: CLARIFYING THE COMPLEXITY OF DATA COLLECTION UNITS (OR NOT)

PREVIEW—*What you should learn from this section:*
1. A key component in an empirical study, including its different levels.
2. The need for a clear understanding of the relationship between the component and the topic of a qualitative study.

Research designs also define the structure of a study. A major component in the structure, around which every empirical study pivots, consists of its unit of data collection.[1] How much you want to attend to this matter is a third choice.

Every study has its units of data collection. For instance, in the interview portion of a qualitative study, the data collection unit is an interviewee, and if your study collected data from 15 interviewees, that would mean it had 15 such units. Alternatively, if a study involved a series of focus groups as a source of data, each focus group would be one of the data collection units.

Nested Arrangements

Interestingly, most qualitative studies have more than one level of data collection unit. These multiple levels are likely to fall within a nested arrangement: a broader

---

[1]The term *data collection unit* is used here as a nontechnical reference, to avoid confusion with the more technical terms *unit of analysis, unit of assignment,* or *unit of allocation.* All of these latter terms raise issues of the appropriate units when doing analysis (especially statistical analyses), and although the data collection unit is usually the unit of analysis, there are complicated situations when it is not. However, these situations and the needed analytic strategies do not usually arise in qualitative research and are therefore outside the scope of the present book.

level (e.g., a field setting) that contains or embeds a narrower level (e.g., a participant in the setting). Each level also can have different numbers of units. Typically, most qualitative studies might have a single unit at the broader level (e.g., a single setting) but a number of units at the narrower level (e.g., multiple participants in the same setting).

To illustrate the units at these two levels, Exhibit 4.1 lists many of the qualitative studies that appear as vignettes in this book. The list shows two levels of data collection units as well as the main topic of each study. Note that the main topics in Exhibit 4.1 resemble the topics previously discussed in Chapter 3 as part of the process for starting a study.

Regarding the number of units at each level, Exhibit 4.1 also indicates the number of units at the broader level, as in Edin and Kefalas's (2005) study of eight Philadelphia neighborhoods, or Ericksen and Dyer's (2004) study of project teams in five different industries. (However, Exhibit 4.1 does not show the number of units at the narrower level.)

Examining Exhibit 4.1 further, you may note that the units at the broader level are usually some kind of geographic, organizational, or social entity. The units at the narrower level frequently consist of participants. However, the narrower level also can have policies, practices, or actions as units.

Importantly, the nested relationship between the broader and narrower levels is a relational, not absolute one. For instance, the unit at the narrower level also can be a community or an organization, as in Gross's (2008) study of the Israeli relocation out of the Gaza Strip, also listed in Exhibit 4.1. Moreover, the nested arrangement may not be limited to two levels. Some studies, but not shown in Exhibit 4.1, may actually have a third, yet additionally embedded (and even narrower) level.

Relationship between the Level of the Data Collection Units and the Main Topic of a Study

Clarifying the potential complexity in data collection units and their levels can be an important part of designing and conducting your study. Most critically, the units need to be an appropriate reflection of the main topic of study:

- For instance, in Exhibit 4.1, the main topic in Mead's (1928) study (female adolescent development) meant that the units at the broader level (three villages) largely fulfilled a contextual function, whereas the data for the main topic came from the units at the narrower level (the data collected from the individual females and their families).

- However, in other studies, such as Lynd and Lynd's (1929) study of an average U.S. city, the unit at the broader level (Muncie, Indiana) was the main topic of study, not the units at the narrower level (community practices).

EXHIBIT 4.1.　TOPICS AND TWO LEVELS OF DATA COLLECTION UNITS IN ILLUSTRATIVE QUALITATIVE STUDIES

Study	Main Topic	Level of Data Collection	
		Broader Level	Narrower Level
Allison & Zelikow (1999; orig. 1971)	Superpower confrontations	U.S.–Soviet Cuban missile crisis	Policies and actions
Anderson (1999)	Moral life of the inner city	A subregion of Philadelphia	Families and individuals
Bales (2004)	Modern slavery	Five countries	Slaves and slaveholders
Ball, Thames, & Phelps (2008)	Pedagogical content knowledge	A third-grade classroom	Everyday classroom behavior
Bogle (2008)	New sexual norms	Two university campuses	Individuals
Brubaker et al. (2006)	Ethnic nationalism	A town in Eastern Europe	Institutions and individuals
Bullough (2001)	Students' perspectives on their education	An elementary school	Individual students and their teachers
Carr (2003)	Informal social control	A neighborhood at the edge of Chicago	Community actions
Duneier (1999)	Interactions in public places	Sidewalks in a city	Street vendors and people
Dunn (2004)	Privatization of business	A factory in Poland	Employees
Edin & Kefalas (2005)	Motherhood and marriage	Eight neighborhoods in Philadelphia	Families and individuals
Ericksen & Dyer (2004)	Workplace teamwork	Five different industries	Project teams
Gilligan (1982)	Women's moral and emotional development	None identified	Individuals
Gross (2008)	Uprooting	The Gaza Strip	Communities and schools
Hays (2003)	Culture of poverty	Two welfare offices in two different cities	Individuals
Hochschild (2003; orig. 1989)	Women and work	A large corporation and related acquaintances	Couples, individuals, and caretakers
Irvine (2003)	Surrendering of pets	A pet store	Employees and clients
Kuglemass (2004)	Inclusive education	An elementary school	Teachers and staff
Lawrence-Lightfoot (1983)	School culture	Three public and three private high schools in the U.S.	Staff and students

(cont.)

EXHIBIT 4.1. *(cont.)*

| Study | Main Topic | Level of Data Collection | |
		Broader Level	Narrower Level
Levitt (2001)	Transnational migration	Local communities in the Dominican Republic and U.S.	Families and individuals
Lew (2006)	Asian American students	Two groups of students: working and middle class	Individuals
Lewis (1961)	Culture of poverty	A Mexican family	Individuals
Lewis (1965)	Culture of poverty	Four neighborhoods in San Juan, PR	Families
Liebow (1967)	Urban poverty	A low-income neighborhood in the Washington, DC, area	Underemployed men
Liebow (1993)	Homelessness	A homeless shelter in the Washington, DC, area	Individuals
Lynd & Lynd (1929)	Life in an average U.S. city	The city of Muncie, IN	Community practices
Marwell (2007)	Social integration and social order	Eight community organizations in two neighborhoods	Policies, practices, and people
McQueeny (2008)	Race, gender, and sexuality	Two lesbian and gay-affirming churches	Churchgoers and ministerial staffs
Mead (1928)	Female adolescent development	Three villages in Samoa	Families and individuals
Mulroy & Lauber (2004)	Evaluation of family center	A family center	Staff and clients
Napolitano (2002)	Urban neighborhood life	A neighborhood in Mexico	Individuals
Narotzky & Smith (2006)	Economic and political development	A region of eastern Spain	Institutions and families
Neustadt & Fineberg (1983)	National health crisis	National vaccination campaign	Policies and actions
Newman (1999)	Urban working poor	A neighborhood in New York	Employees and employers
Padraza (2007)	Immigration	Four waves of Cuban immigrants	Individuals
Pérez (2004)	Gender differences in transnational immigration	A sending community in Puerto Rico and a receiving community in New York	Individuals

(cont.)

EXHIBIT 4.1. *(cont.)*

Study	Main Topic	Level of Data Collection	
		Broader Level	Narrower Level
Rabinow (2007; orig. 1977)	Encounters in doing fieldwork	A community in the Middle Atlas Mountains of Morocco	Individuals
Royster (2003)	Men's school-to-work experiences	A vocational high school in the Baltimore area	Graduates of the school
Sarroub (2005)	Ethnic acculturation in U.S. schools	A high school in Dearborn, MI	Muslim students
Schein (2003)	Demise of a large firm	A large computer firm	Practices and individuals
Sharman (2006)	Mixed ethnic neighborhoods	A neighborhood in New York City	Individuals
Sidel (2006)	Impact of single motherhood	The New York metropolitan area	Individuals
Small (2004)	Poverty and social capital	A housing complex in Boston	Community events
Smith (2006)	Migration to the U.S.	A sending community in Mexico and a receiving community in New York City	Individuals and a community organization
Stack (1974)	Culture of poverty	A black community near Chicago	Families and individuals
Stone (2007)	Women and work	None identified	Individuals
Valdés (1996)	Ethnic acculturation in U.S. schools	Ten immigrant Mexican families	Families and school staffs
Valenzuela (1999)	Schooling of immigrant students	An urban high school	Students and staff
Williams (2006)	Workplace equity	Two toy stores, in an upscale and a downscale neighborhood	Individuals
Wilson & Taub (2006)	Racial, ethnic, and class tensions	Four neighborhoods in Chicago	Individuals
Yin (1982a)	Crime prevention	Citizen anticrime groups around the U.S.	Organization leaders and neighborhood police
Yin (1982b)	Urban services	Seven neighborhoods in New York City	Physical conditions and individuals

Overall, you will want a clear understanding of whether a study (including yours) has data collection units at more than a single level and, if so, their relationship. This understanding will lead to a more important insight, which is to tighten the relationship between the level of the data collection units and a study's main topic. For instance, after having collected some amount of data, you may find a mismatch between the original topic and the emerging findings. This mismatch can occur if the topic reflected one level of data collection unit, whereas your emerging findings came from the units at another level.

Having arrived at such a crossroad, you have two alternatives. One is to put more energy into collecting data from the units at the underemphasized data collection level, so that the emerging findings more closely reflect the main topic. The other possibility is to redefine your original topic. Note, however, that such redefinition also would require you to rethink your study's niche because the study would now be addressing a slightly different topic. In turn, such a transition could require you to cover a different set of previous studies in your selective literature review.

These kinds of complexities all are part of the structure of a study. Attending to them will help you to build an appreciation about (1) the need to define each of the data collection units with some care, (2) the likelihood of having data collection units at more than a single level, (3) the relationship between or among the levels (likely a nested arrangement), and (4) the relationship between the levels and the main topic of study. All these may be considered to be part of the design of a qualitative study.

CHOICE 4: ATTENDING TO SAMPLING (OR NOT)

PREVIEW—*What you should learn from this section:*
1. The two challenges in sampling.
2. Several different sampling strategies.
3. Rationales for deciding on the size of samples.

Formally defining and acknowledging your data collection units easily leads to a fourth design choice. The choice involves the selection (or sampling) of the specific units, as well as the number of them, to be included in a study. The task pertains to the units at both the broader and narrower levels, with the studies in Exhibit 4.1 again providing a rich array of illustrative examples at each level. Nearly every study has samples at both levels, one being at the broader level and the other at the narrower one.

The sampling challenge arises from needing to know which specific units to select and why, as well as the number of the units that are to be in a study. Especially challenging are those studies that might have only a single data collection unit:

> - For instance, recall Oscar Lewis's (1961) well-known autobiography of a single Mexican family. That study's sample consisted of one type of unit (a family) and one instance of that unit (one Mexican family), not unlike other "single-case" case studies (see Yin, 2009, pp. 46–53).

Justifying the choice of the data collection unit(s), even if there is only one of them, is part of the sampling challenge.

Purposive and Other Kinds of Sampling

In qualitative research, the samples are likely to be chosen in a deliberate manner known as *purposive sampling*. The goal or purpose for selecting the specific study units is to have those that will yield the most relevant and plentiful data, given your topic of study.

> - For instance, if you were studying how communities cope with natural disasters, you would learn more by collecting data from a site that recently had suffered through a disaster (and might offer opportunities for making direct observations, not just collecting interview or documentary data) than one whose disaster occurred many years ago (and that only could provide retrospective information—unless you were deliberately doing a historical study).
>   Similarly, if your study's broader level and main topic was an organization, your sample at the narrower level of data collection would need to include the top leader of the organization (even though the top leader of a large organization might not show up as part of a random sample of its employees).

Equally important, the selection of these units should seek to "obtain the broadest range of information and perspectives on the subject of study" (Kuzel, 1992, p. 37). Of high priority in this regard, these units should include those that might offer contrary evidence or views, especially given the need for testing rival explanations (pp. 37–41). For instance, when selecting participants, you should deliberately interview some people whom you suspect might hold different views related to your topic of study. Most of all, you want to avoid biasing your study—or any appearance of bias—by choosing only those sources that confirm your own preconceptions.

Purposive sampling differs from several other kinds of sampling: convenience sampling, snowball sampling, and random sampling. *Convenience sampling*—selecting data collection units simply because of their ready availability—normally is not preferred. It is likely to produce an unknown degree of incompleteness because the most readily available sources of data are not likely to be the most informative sources. Similarly, convenience samples are likely to produce an unwanted degree of bias.

Snowball sampling—selecting new data collection units as an offshoot of existing ones—can be acceptable if the snowballing is purposeful, not done out of convenience. For instance, in the course of an interview you might learn of other persons who can be interviewed. The snowballing occurs when you follow such a lead and let those new ones result in identifying yet other possible interviewees. The snowballing procedure can be followed, but only if you take the time beforehand to think about your reasons for choosing the subsequent interview(s). Distinguish between having a purposive reason (e.g., a prospective interviewee is thought to have additional information relevant to your study) from having only a convenience reason (e.g., the prospective interviewee happens to be around and has a free hour to talk with you).

Random sampling—selecting a statistically defined sample of units from a known population of units—can be done if your study intends to generalize its findings numerically to the entire population of units. Such a numerical rationale, along with the assumptions about the properties of the population, are not usually relevant in qualitative research—hence the rarity of finding random samples in qualitative studies. (A contrasting, non-numerical mode of generalizing, highly preferred for qualitative research, is discussed later in this chapter under Choice 7.)

The Number of Data Collection Units to Be Included in a Study

There is no formula for defining the desired number of instances[2] for each broader or narrower unit of data collection in a qualitative study. In general, larger numbers can be better than smaller numbers because a larger number can create greater confidence in a study's findings, in the following ways.

Broader Level

At the broader level, most studies have only a single data collection unit. The unit may be a field setting, organization, or other entity, again as illustrated earlier in Exhibit 4.1. Rationales for selecting the single unit include studying a rare, extreme, or conversely "typical" site, in relation to your topic of study. If your study intends to examine specific hypotheses, you also might select a "critical" site, where the hypotheses (and their rivals) can be effectively examined (Yin, 2009, pp. 47–49, discusses these selection criteria in relation to the selection of single-case studies).

At the same time, studies can have two or more instances of the units at the broader level. If chosen to be contrasting instances, note how the findings from a two-site study can yield greater confidence than those from a single-site study, because the data from one site should contrast in predictable ways with the data from the other site (see "Studying Inequality in the Retail Marketplace," Vignette 4.2).

---

[2]The term *instance* is used to connote the number (not the type) of units. An organization might be the broader unit, and studying three organizations would be an example of three instances of the broader unit. In nonqualitative research, the term *sample size* would refer to the same concept as *instance*, as used here, but for reasons discussed in the text, the concept of sample in the term *sample size* is not likely to be relevant in qualitative research.

VIGNETTE 4.2. STUDYING INEQUALITY IN THE RETAIL MARKETPLACE

Fieldwork in two contrasting sites—a toy store located in a modest neighborhood and another in an upscale one—enabled Christine Williams (2006) to study "the social construction of shopping and the implications of consumer choice for social inequality" (p. 13).

The contrasting vantage points provided data that highlighted "how gender, race, and social class shape the retail trade industry" (2006, p. 17). The study especially focused on the inequities suffered by retail workers. However, it also examines how adults of different social classes teach their children to become consumers and in so doing pass on important cultural values to the next generation.

The book's six chapter titles reveal how the author shapes her qualitative study: (1) a sociologist inside toy stores; (2) history of toy shopping in America; (3) the social organization of toy stores; (4) inequality on the shopping floor; (5) kids in toyland; and (6) toys and citizenship.

See also Vignette 5.4.

If chosen to reflect the presence of similar events at multiple sites but with diverse social and economic conditions, the confidence can be greater than if only a single site had been studied; any consistency in the findings from all of the sites, in spite of their diverse social and economic conditions, could increase the support for the study's main contentions (see "Six Ethnographic Accounts as Part of a Single Study," Vignette 4.3).

As a final example, the multiple units at the broader level need not consist of different settings, organizations, or entities. The units can represent different periods of time at the same geographic site, as in a study of Cuban immigration that deliberately and intensely covered four different waves of immigration occurring over a 50-year period (see "A Comparative, Four-Case Design across Time, within the Same Venue," Vignette 4.4).

VIGNETTE 4.3. SIX ETHNOGRAPHIC ACCOUNTS AS PART OF A SINGLE STUDY

Qualitative studies need not be limited to a single locale or place of study. On the contrary, studies can be designed to cover multiple cultures or institutional settings, with a study's final conclusions based on the experiences from all of them.

This kind of "multiple" account occurs in Lawrence-Lightfoot's (1983) award-winning study of six high schools. Each high school was chosen because of its stellar academic reputation and performance. Two were urban high schools, two were suburban, and two were private schools. The culture and character of each school is the subject of a separate account, appearing as separate chapters. The author then blends the observations from all of them into a composite portrait of "the good high school."

To these separate and composite works the author also brings her own distinctive style of *portraiture*. It is a data collection process whereby the researcher deals with both empirical and clinical dimensions in trying to define the essence of the persons and institutions being studied.

VIGNETTE 4.4. A COMPARATIVE, FOUR-CASE DESIGN ACROSS TIME, WITHIN THE SAME VENUE

Cuban immigration to the United States has been marked by four waves of immigrants, reflecting the shifting political conditions in Cuba. Silvia Pedraza (2007) examines each wave as a separate "case," but draws the cases together into an unusual rendition of the relationship between revolution and exodus.

The waves occur over a 50-year period (1959–1962, 1965–1974, 1980, and 1985 to the present). The study shows how people struggled within the context of each wave, thereby connecting individual behavior to cultural norms and institutions, especially church and family. Lengthy narratives are devoted to multiple life histories, but extensive survey and polling data also profile the broader population in each wave. Throughout, Pedraza makes ample use of extensive field sources (participant-observation in Cuban communities in Cuba and the United States; taped interviews of 120 people, many in their own homes and using a structured but open-ended questionnaire; documents and photos; census and survey data; and electoral data and public opinion polls).

Because all the ensuing analyses address the same broader theoretical framework, the author uses the four cases to create a much broader understanding of political disaffection and exit, claiming it to be relevant to all societies.

See also Vignettes 7.1 and 11.8.

At the same time, studying any additional instances of the broader level unit will consume more time and effort. For this reason, going beyond a single instance at the broader level may be beyond the scope of a single study. One way of handling this constraint is to complete a study even though it has but a single instance. If the findings from such a study are sufficiently promising, selecting and examining a second unit could be part of a separate follow-up study.

Narrower Level

At the narrower level, most qualitative studies will, in contrast to the broader level, have more than a single instance of the narrower unit. The number of interviewees, practices, policies, or actions included in a study can easily fall in the range of 25–50 such units:

> • One study of working women and how they and their families coped with their household and childrearing responsibilities involved interviews with 50 couples (100 persons) and 45 others—babysitters, day-care workers, and others supporting the couples (Hochschild, 1989).
>
> • Another study that became a best-selling book, translated into 16 languages with nearly a million copies sold, was based on interviews of 32 men and women (Gilligan, 1982).
>
> • Finally, a third study, about a controversial legal battle (Green, 2004), had only 26 key informants, but they included all of the people in the relevant elite positions.

At the narrower level, the general preference for larger over smaller numbers still persists. However, rather than seeking any formulaic guidance for selecting the appropriate number,[3] you need to think about the complexity of your study topic and the depth of data collection from each unit. For instance, capturing an entire life history might be considered a more complex topic, compared to focusing on a single life event such as a birth, wedding, or funeral. However, this complex topic can be covered with either a larger number of instances at a more superficial level—or a smaller number of instances examined intensely. For example, recall again Lewis's study of a single family: The data from that family filled the bulk of a 500-page book.

Having larger numbers is not the only way of boosting the confidence in a study's findings. Another essential consideration reflects the composition, not just the size, of the larger group. Again, you should deliberately seek data to protect against rival explanations or undesirable biases. For instance, although one researcher spent 3 years as a participant-observer in a large urban high school (the data collection unit at the broader level), the main study topic was about the youths in the high school (the units at the narrower level). To cover the narrower level sufficiently, the researcher collected data from several different groups of youths, not just one or two of them (see "Seeking Multiple Data Collection Units, but in a Methodic Variety of Ways," Vignette 4.5).

VIGNETTE 4.5. SEEKING MULTIPLE DATA COLLECTION UNITS, BUT IN A METHODIC VARIETY OF WAYS

A study of Mexican American students focused on their common schooling experiences, regardless of whether the students were first-, second-, or third-generation immigrants (Valenzuela, 1999). To do the study, the author spent 3 years as a participant-observer in a large urban high school. However, because the main study topic was about the youths in the high school and because of the size of the high school, the author feared that her data collection did not sufficiently cover a realistic profile of the student body.

To reduce these concerns, Valenzuela deliberately organized and then conducted a series of 25 open-ended group interviews (1999, p. 278). She further was concerned about the representativeness of the students in these groups, so she spent two summers deliberately interviewing students from the different cohorts (first-, second-, and third-generation immigrants) of interest to the study (p. 281). These efforts not only resulted in a study being based on data on a larger number of students, but also created greater confidence in the study's findings.

See also Vignette 1.3.

---

[3]The problem of adequate sample size exists in quantitative studies as well. There, however, researchers are able to conduct a formal *power analysis* to determine the needed sample size, assuming that certain prior data exist. The desired size will vary according to the presumed size of differences and variability in the population being sampled (e.g., an *effect size*—which a researcher needs to know ahead of time), as well as the level of confidence in the findings desired by the researcher (Lipsey, 1990). Quantitative researchers readily recognize that statistically significant differences also might not equate with findings of any practical significance. Thus, even in quantitative research the issue of the desirable sample size requires some discretionary choices.

CHOICE 5: INCORPORATING CONCEPTS AND THEORIES INTO A STUDY (OR NOT)

PREVIEW—*What you should learn from this section:*
1. Two ways of shifting between data and concepts.
2. Examples of how qualitative studies have incorporated concepts and theories, using both ways.

Qualitative research usually focuses on the *meaning* of real-life events, not just the occurrence of the events. Chapter 1 previously pointed out that important sets of meanings are those held by the participants in the events, and one strength of qualitative research is its ability to capture these meanings rather than being limited to the meanings imposed by a research investigator.

The search for meaning is in fact a search for *concepts*—ideas that are more abstract than the actual data in an empirical study. A collection of concepts, even a small collection, may be assembled in some logical fashion that then might represent a *theory* about the events that have been studied. The extent to which you want to develop both concepts and theories as part of your study—as well as in what sequence you want to recognize them in relation to your data collection activities—is a fifth design choice.

Worlds Devoid of Concepts?

Many people might think that the stereotypic qualitative study is devoid of concepts. The stereotype would cast qualitative research as some diary-like rendition of reality, spouting detail after detail about events or people without relying on any concepts, much less theories. The stereotype might regard qualitative studies as being similar to the chronicles of a medieval scribe, or even the dryly worded clinical details of a coroner's report.

Such a stereotype of qualitative research does not represent good qualitative research, and you should avoid emulating it. The preferred qualitative research captures the same empirical detail—but interwoven in some manner with abstract concepts if not theories. For instance, recall from Chapter 1 (Section A) that one of the common motives for doing qualitative research is the ability to study events within their real-world context—including the relevant culture of the people, organization, or groups being studied. Note quickly, however, that *culture* is an abstract concept, if not a theory about the existence of unwritten rules and norms governing the social behavior of groups of people.

Inductive versus Deductive Approaches

The desire for interweaving detailed empirical data with some set of concepts and theories returns us to the earlier introduction regarding the inductive approach in the present book (see Chapter 1, Section D). Inductive approaches contrast with deductive approaches, as the two reflect different ways of shifting between data and concepts. Inductive approaches tend to let the data lead to the emergence of concepts; deductive approaches tend to let the concepts—if only taking the form of initial "categories" (which are another common form of concepts)—lead to the definition of the relevant data that need to be collected.

Most qualitative research follows an inductive approach. However, nothing is wrong with taking a deductive approach. Examples of each are discussed next.

One study that followed a more inductive approach started with the topic of neighborhood crime prevention, in which residents themselves form anticrime groups (Yin, 1982a). At that time, many such groups existed in different varieties of neighborhoods, but little was known about such groups—or even whether they were of the same ilk. As a result, the fieldwork for a new study began without much conceptualizing or theorizing. Only after the fieldwork had been completed did there emerge a useful, fourfold typology of anticrime groups (see "How Fieldwork Can Lead to a Useful Typology," Vignette 4.6).

VIGNETTE 4.6. HOW FIELDWORK CAN LEAD TO A USEFUL TYPOLOGY

When residential crime rates rise, citizens themselves often form anticrime groups. The groups can vary from encouraging neighbors to keep their "eyes on the streets" to conducting patrol routines. Unwanted vigilantism is an occasional result.

Forming public policies to support or discourage such anticrime groups requires distinguishing among different groups. For this purpose, the present author initially collected data about 226 such groups, not having any preconceptions about how they were organized (Yin, 1982a). Later fieldwork covering 32 of them led to a fourfold typology not previously revealed by the research literature—groups that (1) patrol buildings or well-circumscribed residential compounds; (2) patrol less well-defined neighborhood areas; (3) combine crime prevention with other social services; or (4) protect residents from potential abuses by the local police. A major finding was that building patrols (type 1) can readily screen strangers, keep them off the premises, and increase residents' sense of security. In contrast, neighborhood patrols (type 2) cannot easily distinguish strangers from residents, thereby often making the neighborhood's own residents feel more uncomfortable than safe.

This type of inductive approach is entirely appropriate for qualitative research. Do not be discouraged if the relevant concepts or theories take some time to emerge:

- The concepts may be newer to the literature, such as Valenzuela's (1999) notion of "subtractive schooling" in relation to her study of immigrant students (see Vignette 4.5 and also Chapter 1, Vignette 1.3). Or,
- The concepts may fit closely with a well-developed and long-standing literature, such as Hays's (2003) revisiting of the "culture of poverty" in relation to her study of women participating under new welfare reform policies.

By comparison, the deductive approach has other merits. It can save you from suffering through a lot of uncertainty in doing your initial fieldwork because you would have started with relevant concepts rather than waiting for them to emerge. However, a major risk could be the premature loss of any fresh insights into the real-world events being studied.

A deductive approach can be extremely helpful under certain circumstances. For instance, imagine that you have access to detailed videotapes of an entire year of mathematics teaching in a third-grade public school classroom. Without some initial concepts or theories, you might spend an unending amount of time viewing these tapes, not knowing what you were looking for and desperately waiting for behavioral patterns and thus concepts to emerge. Instead, suppose you used these tapes to reexamine a concept you had clearly identified beforehand. You might then produce a distinguished study because of the widespread interest in that concept (see "Studying a Preestablished Concept: Pedagogical Content Knowledge," Vignette 4.7).

VIGNETTE 4.7. STUDYING A PREESTABLISHED CONCEPT: PEDAGOGICAL CONTENT KNOWLEDGE

The concept of *pedagogical content knowledge* points to the distinction between simply knowing the content of an academic subject and knowing how to teach it effectively to students.

The concept already had been well developed and had attracted widespread interest in the field of education, with extensive citations in 125 different journals (Ball, Thames, & Hoover, 2008, p. 392). Ball and colleagues (2008) reexamined this concept by reviewing videotapes and audiotapes covering the entire year of mathematics teaching in a third-grade public school classroom.

By reviewing and analyzing the tapes, they found that the concept, rather than assuming a singular form, consisted of two important subdomains: specialized content knowledge that teachers need to know, and common content knowledge that teachers and nonteachers need to know (2008, pp. 399–402). The authors concluded by suggesting that this delineation had important implications for future professional development programs for teachers.

The deductive approach also can help to establish the importance of a study. For instance, a study of one manufacturing firm, which otherwise might not have been considered a particularly special site, assumed greater importance because the firm was one of Eastern Europe's first state-owned enterprises to be privatized after the fall of Soviet Russia (see "Studying Privatization within Former Soviet-Bloc Countries," Vignette 4.8).

From both the inductive and deductive perspectives, the preceding examples should suggest the benefit of interweaving qualitative studies with both concepts and theories. Note that, although the concepts are abstractions, they are not neces-

> ### VIGNETTE 4.8. STUDYING PRIVATIZATION
> ### WITHIN FORMER SOVIET-BLOC COUNTRIES
>
> Elizabeth Dunn (2004) studied the transition of a Polish factory from a socialist to a capitalist system. Michigan-based Gerber Products Co. had purchased the firm, operating it as the Alima-Gerber S.A. baby food company— one of Eastern Europe's first state-owned enterprises to be privatized (p. 27).
>
> Dunn's study was based on a 16-month stint, from 1995 to 1997, as a participant-observer working in the firm. Her main focus was on the culture change among the employees. For them, the transition changed "the very foundation of what it means to be a person" (2004, p. 6). Her entire book is devoted to exploring how the employees "use experiences of socialism, Solidarity union activism, as well as Catholic, kin, and gender ideologies, to redefine themselves and negotiate work processes and relationships within the firm" (p. 8). For instance, a key tenet is that "the most important consideration in the production process is moral, not financial" (p. 170).
>
> Dunn's explorations show how a single field study can be embedded within a much broader sphere of important socioeconomic and political changes.

sarily representations of *grand theory*. As a result, the interweaving need not be an awesome task. The relevant concepts and theories should be well within the reach of your own knowledge and research.

Done on extremely rare occasions are qualitative studies that organize themselves entirely around their theoretical concepts:

> - For instance, "social capital" has been a prominent theoretical construct in recent community studies. Small (2004) organized his study's chapters according to the aspects of social capital rather than around the single housing complex that was his actual subject of study.

The merits of following such a conceptual arrangement, compared to focusing on a particular field setting and its features, need to be weighed carefully.

CHOICE 6: PLANNING AT AN EARLY STAGE (OR NOT) TO OBTAIN PARTICIPANT FEEDBACK

PREVIEW—*What you should learn from this section:*
1. The rationale for defining the feedback process as a design activity.
2. The different portions of a study that can be shared for obtaining feedback.

At a later stage of your study, you will likely share some of your study's findings or data with one or more of the participants in your study—that is, those whom you have interviewed and with whom you have collaborated—to gain their feedback.

Only at that later stage might you confront for the first time the issue of what to share with whom—a practice that many scholars have referred to as *member checks*.

Alternatively, and as an increasingly frequent practice in qualitative research, you can confront this issue earlier—during the design of your study. You can tentatively think about the topics and types of materials (e.g., field notes or early drafts of your narrative) you are later going to share and with whom. You can then incorporate your plan into your research plans as well as into your informed consent procedure. As with all plans, the actual practice may evolve and change during the conduct of the study, but at least you will have started with a plan. To this extent, thinking about the issue at this earlier stage can be treated as a design issue, similar to the other choices in this chapter.

As with all of the other design issues, the procedure of having participants provide feedback about your work can go smoothly but also can create unforeseen obstacles. And as with all of the other design issues, there is no airtight way of ensuring that everything will proceed smoothly, especially without your constant attention as well as willingness to adapt your original plan.

Feedback Choices

Locke and Velamuri (2009) have made a helpful compilation of your likely choices. For instance, they point out that the motives for sharing work with participants relate both to the corrections and changes that will increase the validity of a study (also see the reference to "respondent validation" in Vignette 4.1) and to the need to reinforce the collaborative and ethical relationships with participants (Locke & Velamuri, 2009, pp. 488–489). Similarly, they classify the choices of the findings to be shared, which range from sharing a draft summary of the final product to showing the completed notes for any particular interview to the original participant (p. 494).

A good idea is to discuss your initial thoughts about what will be shared and with whom as part of the informed consent conversation you will have with each participant. You should determine whether the participant(s) have other suggestions or preferences and work together to arrive at an acceptable procedure.

Addressing the issue at this early juncture has two benefits. First, the issue will have been raised before, possibly, it becomes an "issue." Second, as with other design choices, you will have defined the planned path in the absence of having any findings from the study. Therefore, you and the participants later cannot be accused of biasing the plan because anyone knew the nature of the findings.

Potential Influence on a Study's Later Narrative

Anticipation of the feedback process should not be permitted to influence your study's findings. However, the process will impose a degree of delicacy on your writing. Beyond striving for accuracy, you should find yourself being more sensitive to the need to avoid choices of words that can unnecessarily incite participants in a personal way.

You also cannot be oblivious to contextual conditions that may have changed from the time of your data collection to the time when you will be completing your writing. A prefatory note can clarify the timing. However, conditions might have changed dramatically—recall that the lag between data collection and final reporting might be a year or longer. In such a case, you might have to make additional adjustments, such as repeating some of the data collection and presenting the later work as an epilogue.

CHOICE 7: BEING CONCERNED WITH GENERALIZING A STUDY'S FINDINGS (OR NOT)

PREVIEW—*What you should learn from this section:*
1. The potential value of trying to generalize the findings from a qualitative study.
2. Two ways of thinking about how to develop any generalizations.

By its very nature, qualitative research is particularistic. Understanding the nuances and patterns of social behavior only results from studying specific situations and people, complemented by attending carefully to specific contextual conditions. The particularistic feature makes it difficult to consider how the findings from qualitative studies can be generalized to some broader set of conditions—beyond those in the immediate study.

Much dialogue exists regarding the relevance and nature of generalizations in qualitative research (e.g., Gomm, Hammersley, & Foster, 2000). Some would argue that generalizing has a limited role when doing qualitative research. For instance, the early roots in cultural anthropology focused heavily on the distinctiveness of exotic and distant cultures, not on generalizing from their experiences (e.g., Schofield, 1990, pp. 202–205) (also see the earlier discussion in Chapter 1, Section C, on the uniqueness of human events).

You certainly have the choice of agreeing with these limited roles, but you also may want to have the choice of trying to generalize the findings from your study. If so, the rationale for wanting to generalize the findings from a single study is the fact that any given study (qualitative or not) can only collect a limited amount of data, involving limited numbers of data collection units.

Yet, most studies can derive greater value if their findings and conclusions have implications going beyond the data collected—that is, the extent to which the findings can be "generalized" to other studies and other situations. The more that research of any kind is generalizable in this fashion, the more that the research may be valued. This is true even where a study might have only a single data collection unit, such as a single case study. How to make the actual generalizations from qualitative research is therefore another choice that deserves your closest attention.

Need for Reaching beyond *Statistical* Generalizations

For qualitative research, a major barrier in thinking about generalizing has been an unfortunate preconception. It starts with the notion that there is only one way of generalizing. Furthermore, this way of generalizing assumes that a study's findings represent a "sample," and that if the sample has been properly chosen, the findings can then generalize to the larger "population" from which the sample was drawn. This mode of generalizing characterizes most survey studies, wherein the objective is to select a representative sample of respondents and then to extrapolate the findings to the original universe of respondents.

Because the relationship between samples and their population is based on numeric estimates, this way of generalizing may be described as *statistical generalization* (Yin, 2009, pp. 15, 38–39). Such thinking has been so pervasive that even scholars who only do qualitative research continually think along these lines, asking themselves how the results from their (often single) site can be generalized to experiences at other sites, as if their study site(s) represented some sort of sample of a presumed population of sites.

For qualitative research, this kind of thinking does not work well and leads to an inevitable dilemma: No small number of data collection units, much less a single unit, can adequately represent the larger population of units, even when the larger population can be defined. For example, a study of democratic institution-building in specific countries cannot readily be generalized to other specific countries, even if the studied countries have been selected to (1) be of varying size; (2) represent different continents and economic conditions; and (3) consist of peoples of different color. The numerics don't work because countries vary along so many dimensions that the size of any sample will be inadequate to represent the population of countries.

An alternative way of generalizing requires you to relinquish any thinking about samples or populations. Your study's data collection units, at either the broad or narrow level as previously discussed, are not "sampling units," and all such considerations need to be wholly dismissed.

Making *Analytic* Generalizations

The alternative mode is commonly practiced in research but not commonly recognized. This notion starts with the observation that all research, not just qualitative research, takes place in the form of single studies. The challenge of generalizing to other conditions therefore arises with laboratory experiments, for example. How to generalize the results from a single experiment, taking place with a specific group of experimental subjects in a given place and time (and subjected to specific experimental interventions and procedures), also might seem problematic.

With both qualitative studies and laboratory experiments, the objective for generalizing the findings is the same: The findings or results from the single study are to follow a process of *analytic generalization* (Yin, 2009, p. 43). Analytic generalization may be defined as a two-step process. The first involves a conceptual claim whereby investigators show how their study's findings are likely to inform a particular set of concepts, theoretical constructs, or hypothesized sequence of events. The second involves applying the same theory to implicate other similar situations where similar concepts might be relevant.

This mode of generalizing can be found in any number of studies, including those that have been bestsellers in their academic fields (see "Generalizing the Findings from a Single-Case Study," Vignette 4.9). A similar approach pertains to the earlier example about case studies of countries pursuing democratic institution-building: Instead of trying to generalize to the population of other countries, such a study should seek to develop and then discuss how its findings might have implications for an improved understanding of particular concepts—in this case, the democratic institution-building process.

VIGNETTE 4.9. GENERALIZING THE FINDINGS FROM A SINGLE-CASE STUDY

In their famous case study of the Cuban missile crisis, Allison and Zelikow (1999) positioned their work as one that would investigate a broader theoretical domain— how superpowers confront each other (not just the specifics of the missile crisis). The case itself involved the United States and the former Soviet Union threatening each other in 1962, over offensive missiles located in Cuba that could reach the United States—a confrontation that threatened the triggering of a nuclear holocaust.

The study initially casts three different theories of superpower confrontation, as represented in the existing literature. The facts of the single case are then presented in relation to these three theories, with a major finding being that such confrontations are not driven by a "great man" pattern of leadership, which had been among the dominant theories at that time.

The authors claim that their findings can be applied to a wide variety of other superpower confrontations, including those from other eras and involving superpowers other than the United States and the Soviet Union. The study has been so well conceived and conducted that it has been a bestseller among readings in political science courses for several decades since its original publication (Allison, 1971).

- As another example bearing on a highly relevant and contemporary issue, Neustadt and Fineberg's (1983) case study of "the epidemic that never was"—a swine flu vaccination program launched by the federal government in 1976—retrospectively attracts continuing popular attention.

  Their case involved the early spread of an influenza, the mass inoculation of people, and the subsequent cancellation of the vaccine program. In the face of new threats by flu epidemics, such as the H1N1 strain of 2008–2010 in the United States and abroad, the study has been of great interest in helping to understand the quandaries of public actions and health crises.

Making analytic generalizations requires carefully constructed argument, again whether for a qualitative study or for an experiment. The argument is not likely to achieve the status of a "proof" in geometry, but the argument must be presented soundly and be resistant to logical challenge. The relevant "theory" may be no more than a series of hypotheses or even a single hypothesis. Cronbach (1975) further clarifies that the sought-after generalization is not that of a conclusion but rather more like a "working hypothesis" (also see Lincoln & Guba, 1985, pp. 122–123). Confidence in such hypotheses can then build as new studies, again as in the case of experiments, continue to produce findings in support of the hypotheses.

The argument needs to be cast in relation to existing research literature, not the specific conditions in the actual study. In other words, the goal is to pose the propositions and hypotheses at a conceptual level higher than that of the specific findings. (Typically, this higher level might have been needed to justify the research importance for studying the chosen topic in the first place.)

The study's findings should demonstrate whether and how the empirical results supported or challenged the theory. If supported, the investigators then need to show how the theoretical advances can pertain (generalize) to situations other than those examined as part of the original study (see "An Example of Analytic Generalization from a Single Qualitative Study," Vignette 4.10).

VIGNETTE 4.10. AN EXAMPLE OF ANALYTIC GENERALIZATION FROM A SINGLE QUALITATIVE STUDY

A study of recent migration between the Dominican Republic and the United States (Levitt, 2001) provides an excellent example of *analytic generalization*. The author provides evidence on how the new migratory pattern differs from the more historic migrations from European countries to the United States in the early 20th century (pp. 21–27). In contrast, the newer patterns assume a "transnational" character, with the new migrants remaining simultaneously networked to communities both in their country of origin and in the United States ("transnational villages").

The study shows how the newer migratory patterns are marked by the high proportion of the country of origin's population involved in such migration (2001, p. 16), as well as the country of origin's granting its migrants a formal, dual-citizen-like status (p. 19). Similar conditions are shown to exist with other contemporary migratory patterns (pp. 16–21). The concluding chapter discusses these other "transnational" patterns and how the findings from the Dominican–United States experience may inform (and be generalizable to) them.

See also Exhibit 4.3.

As a final note, stating and examining rival explanations, as discussed earlier in this chapter, will greatly strengthen any claimed analytic generalization. Meaningful or plausible rivals to the initial hypotheses may have been identified at the outset of the study or encountered during its conduct. Thorough examination of the rivals entails sincere efforts to collect data, during the study, *in support of* the rivals. If such data have been stringently sought but do not support the rival, the rival can be rejected. Study findings that support the main hypotheses while simultaneously rejecting plausible rivals comprise strong grounds for claiming analytic generalizations.

CHOICE 8: PREPARING A RESEARCH PROTOCOL (OR NOT)

PREVIEW—*What you should learn from this section:*
1. The topics that might be covered in a research protocol.
2. The differences between a protocol and an instrument.
3. How a protocol represents a mental framework.

This final design choice reflects another potential dilemma in doing qualitative research. Having a *research protocol* may undermine a major strength of qualitative research, which is the ability to capture real life as others live and see it, not as researchers hypothesize or expect it to be. Yet, the researcher's values, expectations, and perspective are implicitly contained in any research protocol.

Not surprisingly, many qualitative researchers resist defining any protocol ahead of time. They try to assume an open-minded attitude in doing their initial fieldwork. In like manner, early field interviews also are based on an open-ended conversational style that avoids steering interviewees as much as possible.

At the same time, if you have defined your study topic and even started to articulate some key research questions, and if you have chosen your data collection units on the expectation that they will provide certain types of needed data, some sort of protocol can help to guide your study and all of its data collection in a productive manner. You still need to retain an open mind to capture properly a field perspective and to attend to emerging and unexpected information, but a protocol can help to remind you about your original topic and questions.

The eighth design choice is the degree to which you indeed want to prepare a protocol ahead of time.[4] Your choice can vary from one extreme (no protocol) to the other (a well-articulated protocol). Most likely, you will end up somewhere in the middle, but the choice is yours.

Protocols, Not Instruments

The term *protocol* is used to imply a broader set of procedures and queries than the classic *instrument*. The most common instruments are usually well structured, with closed- and open-ended questions in survey research or numeric items and procedures in human experiments. In contrast, a highly structured protocol still

---

[4]In most cases, the research protocol would serve the needs for a *study* protocol used in obtaining IRB approval (see Chapter 2, Section E). However, and depending on the IRB's guidance, a study protocol might give more emphasis to logistical procedures and not cover substantive topics in as great detail as a *research* protocol.

only consists of a stated set of topics. These topics cover the substantive ground you need to cover as part of a line of inquiry, described in greater detail below. However, they do not "script" a spoken and specific series of questions, as an instrument would do.

For nearly all types of qualitative research, "instruments" are therefore not likely to be relevant. If you did use an instrument, even an open-ended survey instrument, you still might find yourself doing a survey rather than a qualitative study. In fact, the vast majority of the qualitative studies cited in the vignettes in this book, when based on or even limited to a set of interviews, did not have any instrument (or at least did not discuss or present one). The interview data were collected through a more conversational mode discussed in Chapter 6 (Section C), but not the predefined question-and-answer format, even of open-ended questions, that signals a survey.

Therefore, the main choice for qualitative studies appears to be about protocols, not instruments. But what is a protocol if it is not an instrument?

Protocols as Mental Frameworks

A protocol should connote a broad set of behaviors you are to undertake, rather than any tightly scripted interaction between you and any source of evidence, such as a field participant. Although a protocol may be initially prepared on and studied from a piece of paper, you do not carry a written protocol with you when doing your fieldwork. The protocol is in your head and in this sense serves as a mental framework.

An apt analogy is to the clinical queries made by medical doctors. In asking about ailments that patients might have difficulty describing, the doctors will converse casually with their patients, but the doctors also are following an established line of inquiry to check out the symptoms. While asking their questions, the doctors are entertaining the possible ailments that might be relevant. Note that in this interview process the doctors may take notes while making their queries, but the doctors are not holding any written protocol or reading questions off of any instrument.

An equally apt analogy is to doing detective work. When solving crimes, detectives' investigations occur at two levels. The first involves collecting evidence (that is, carrying out data collection), whereas the second involves simultaneously entertaining their own ideas about how and why the crimes might have occurred. The questions leading to detectives' hunches and theories about the crimes, tentative at first and later becoming firmer as more evidence is collected, may be considered the detectives' mental frameworks.

The protocol for a qualitative study has some predictable features. First, it should contain sufficient questions, central to the topic being studied, that guides one or more lines of inquiry—for example, what evidence to seek and from what sources. The broad lines of inquiry work toward revealing the issues for the entire study. Note carefully that these questions are *yours* to answer, based on evidence (including interviews) you will gather.

Because the questions are yours to answer, they are relevant to all of your sources of evidence—for example, the questions in your head as you review documents or make field observations. When you are interviewing someone as one of these sources of evidence, note that the protocol's questions do not represent any particular sequence of spoken questions, as would a questionnaire instrument. You will create the spoken questions as part of a more natural conversation with any given participant. Those spoken questions will reflect the questions in your protocol, but the actual wording and sequence of the spoken questions will be customized to the specific interview situation.

Second, keeping the protocol as a mental and thus private framework paradoxically helps both the detective and the qualitative researcher to present a neutral posture in collecting the full variety of data, whether interviewing persons, sifting through documents, making observations, or otherwise reviewing field evidence. The trick is not to permit the existence of one's mental framework to bias the data collection. On the contrary, the existence of the framework, if used properly, should point to opportunities to search for contrary as well as supporting evidence. If there were no protocol or framework, such opportunities might be overlooked. The appropriate use of a protocol therefore should encourage a fairer inquiry.

Third, the protocol questions will help you to strive for converging and triangulating evidence, as discussed earlier in this chapter (see Choice 2). Again, the fluidity of the data collection process leaves opportunities for such convergence or triangulation that may be overlooked in the absence of a protocol.

Finally, one of the important virtues of qualitative studies is the possibility of discovering new insights during data collection. The use of a research protocol should not inhibit the discovery process. Although the protocol's questions come from the original topics and questions posed by a study, you also need to maintain an open mind during the data collection process. Thus, while a protocol has the three other features just described, you also should be able to think "outside the box" (in this case, outside of the entire mental framework) when unexpected evidence is encountered.

When discovery occurs, you may need to pause in the data collection process and rethink the original protocol. You may want to alter any plans for your subsequent data collection activities in order to incorporate the newly discovered findings. One caution is that if the discovery is significant, rethinking the protocol also may lead to rethinking (or redesigning) the entire study and its original objectives. For instance, the main research questions may need to be restated, and any earlier literature reviews may need to be augmented.

Exhibits 4.2 and 4.3 contain illustrative protocols from two different qualitative studies. The protocol in Exhibit 4.2 was used to study over 40 neighborhood organizations (National Commission on Neighborhoods, 1979). Each organization was the subject of a case study. The study protocol served as a protocol for each case study and had the features just described. In this study, the protocol also helped to support the use of parallel data collection procedures across the case studies. The main topic of inquiry had to do with the role of neighborhood organizations in promoting neighborhood revitalization—a topic of great interest in the 1970s that

EXHIBIT 4.2. EXAMPLE OF FIELD PROTOCOL FOR STUDY OF NEIGHBORHOOD ORGANIZATION

Topics and Protocol Questions
(illustrative questions shown only)

A. Initiation and structure of the organization

  1. In what year did the organization come into being?
  2. What caused its creation, and who or what was the main source of support in the creation?
  3. What was the original source of funding?
  4. What was the early orientation of the organization?
  5. How has the organization changed since the early days?

(five other questions not shown)

B. Revitalization activities and their support

  6. What activities have been completed or are underway?
  7. How did the organization become involved in these activities?

(seven other questions not shown)

C. Relationship to voluntary associations and networks

  8. Is the organization part of a larger, umbrella organization?
  9. Describe the relationship between the organization and other local organizations in the same neighborhood.

(five other questions not shown)

D. Relationship to city government

  10. Does the organization have any relationship with specific officials or offices in city government?
  11. Is the relationship formal or informal?
  12. Has this relationship been productive?

(four other questions not shown)

E. Outcomes

  13. During the lifetime of the organization, has there been any tangible evidence of neighborhood improvement?
  14. Has there been any evidence of the organization having blocked or prevented some change in the physical condition of the neighborhood?
  15. Have the organization's activities resulted in increased residents' participation?
  16. Is there increased unity or fragmentation in the neighborhood since the founding of the organization?
  17. How has the organization dealt with neighborhood problems of race and poverty?

(four other questions not shown)

Source: National Commission on Neighborhoods (1979).

EXHIBIT 4.3. GENERAL INTERVIEW PROTOCOL USED TO INTERVIEW MEN

History in community

1. Ask about how long R has lived in Golden Valley, why he came if he came from somewhere else. What kinds of ties does R have in community? Is R happy here? What does R like about living in Golden Valley?
2. Has the community changed over R's lifetime? In what ways? Is life here better now than it was in the past?

Family history

1. Ask R about what parents did while growing up, how work was allocated within family, what roles each parent played in household and with regard to children. Which parent was R closer to?
2. Ask R to describe father and relationship with him. Was he a role model or someone R wanted to be like?
3. Ask R if he expected his own life to be like that of his parents. What were his expectations of himself with regard to work and family life as an adult?
4. Have R's expectations changed? Is life better or worse than what he envisioned for himself as a child?

Work history and leisure

1. Ask R about current job or struggle to find work. Is R happy with his current work situation?
2. What kinds of work has R done in past? Which were the best jobs? Has work life been affected by the mill closure?
3. If R has struggled to find work, talk about the process. How does he feel about himself when he can't find work? How does he deal with this emotion? Ask R to talk about specific instances when he lost jobs and how they affected him.
4. What does he do for money when he can't find work? Has he made sacrifices in order to stay in the community? Why does he stay if he has trouble finding work?
5. What other kinds of activities does R do with free time? What does he enjoy most? Try to find out about hunting/fishing/outdoors activities as well as socializing, drinking, etc.

Marriage and family

1. Is R married or has ever been? For how long and/or how many times? Is he happier married or single? What kind of relationship is he currently in?
2. Does R have children? How many? Who do they live with? How were custody arrangements decided?
3. Talk about relationship with children. What kind of role does R play as father? What are some of the things that he most enjoys doing with his kids? Does he feel he has been a good father to his children? What does this mean to him? What are some of the happiest moments as a father? What were some of the biggest challenges or disappointments?
4. Is R much like his own father? In what ways is he similar or different? Would he prefer to be more or less like him? What kinds of things make a good father?
5. If R has no children, does he want them? Why? Does he have any relationships with children in his life, and if so, describe his role.
6. If R has never been married, does he want to be? What kinds of relationships has he had— cohabitation, etc. What kinds of qualities is R looking for in a partner? Is he single by choice?
7. What have been some of the biggest challenges or problems in his relationships with partners? Go into depth on causes if possible. How has he dealt with these problems? If multiple relationships, what were some of the causes of the breakups? How does he feel about exes?
8. Have there been ways in which job- (or lack thereof) related stress has affected his relationships? Describe if possible.

Source: Sherman (2009, Appendix A, p. 617).

has continued to this day (e.g., Chaskin, 2001; Marwell, 2007). The protocol's questions are directed to the fieldworker, not any given participant or interviewee. The fieldworker is to write a response to each question, citing any combination of data, including interviews with officials and residents, relevant documents and archival evidence, and direct observations of neighborhood conditions.

The protocol in Exhibit 4.3 was used in a study of job loss, gender norms, and family stability in a rural community (Sherman, 2009). The community had long been dependent on a specific industry for employment, and the study focused on the aftermath among the families, following the decline of the industry. The interest in gender pertained to the consequent shift in male and female roles at work and in households. The protocol was used to conduct qualitative interviews with the male participants in the study (note how the protocol is written in a grammatical voice that directs the questions to the interviewer, not the participant).

Operational Definitions

Whether organized into a research protocol or not, one of the benefits of thinking about the data to be collected is to define the various kinds of data. For instance, you would clearly want to distinguish between an observed event and a reported (but not observed) one. Depending on the topic of study, many relevant concepts, such as community "cohesiveness," organizational "change," health "promotion," education "reform," or "poor" leadership—to name just a few—all will require some sort of operational definition.

In other types of research, these operational definitions may be embedded in the tools and instruments used in the research. In qualitative research, because you are likely to be the most important research instrument, you will need to give yourself some guidelines for recognizing a phenomenon of interest consistently. These guidelines also can be prompted by a well-designed research protocol.

RECAP FOR CHAPTER 4: *Terms, phrases, and concepts that you can now define:*

1. Research design
2. Research validity
3. Rival explanations
4. Triangulation
5. Data collection units
6. Purposive, snowball, and random samples
7. Inductive versus deductive ways of relating concepts with data
8. Member checks
9. Statistical versus analytic generalization
10. Research protocol
11. Mental framework

EXERCISE FOR CHAPTER 4: STUDY DESIGN

◆ ◆ ◆

Designing studies is possibly the most difficult part of doing research. You have to start from scratch, and you have little guidance. One way of practicing design work without becoming totally frustrated is to diagnose the design of existing studies. Thus, for the exercise for Chapter 4, select six qualitative studies from your study bank (created as the exercise for Chapter 3). Choose those that appear to have described their designs as thoroughly as possible.

Examine and summarize each of the selected studies for the following design features (for your further reference, the first feature below was described in Chapter 3; all of the remaining features appear as one of the choices in Chapter 4):

- The study's research question(s);
- Its type(s) and number of data collection unit(s);
- The way in which the study selected the sample of each type of unit;
- Whether the study indicates the use of a research protocol of any sort, and the nature of the protocol; and
- Whether the study makes any attempt to generalize the findings to other situations that were not studied.

Do not be surprised if one or more of the studies you have chosen has left gaps or missing information in relation to one or more of the preceding features. If so, note how carefully you searched through the text of the studies and why you are confident that the needed design information was truly absent.

CHAPTER 5

Doing Fieldwork

Collecting data for qualitative research usually implies interacting with real-world situations and the people in them. These all become part of the field setting for a research study. The variety of field settings adds to the numerous important and interesting human events that can become the subject of qualitative studies. At the same time, because the field settings are real-world situations, researchers need to enter and exit them with some formality, in particular obtaining the necessary permissions to do their study. Maintaining healthy field relationships then becomes a continuing challenge.

The present chapter discusses the entire range of issues associated with doing research in field settings, focusing heavily on participant-observation as the role usually filled by a researcher. The chapter also discusses site visiting as a separate but related option for collecting data from real-world settings.

For most people, doing some sort of fieldwork goes hand in hand with doing qualitative research. Field-based data—whether coming from direct field observations, interviews, or videotapes, or the review of contemporary documents such as participants' journals, daily logs, or even photographs—will form much of the evidence used in a qualitative study. For this reason, you may want to acquaint yourself with the fieldwork process as part of understanding an initial commitment to doing qualitative research. Discussed in this chapter are the ways of working in a field setting—apart from any specific data collection procedures, which are the topics of Chapter 6.

Fieldwork takes place in real-world settings, with people in their real-life roles. The settings, illustrated in greater detail later in this chapter, can be people's homes, company workplaces, streets and other public places, or services such as schools or health clinics. Fieldwork also can focus on groups of people, independent of any particular physical setting.

Working in the field requires establishing and maintaining genuine relationships with other people and being able to converse comfortably with them. Developing workable relationships may be the greatest personal challenge in doing qualitative research. Many of the needed skills come together in being able to manage the fieldwork process—and in being able to cope with the uncertainties it creates.

Because the field is a real-life environment with people carrying out their everyday routines, a most important caution is that you will be entering their space and time and social relationships. Note how the reality of a field setting in qualitative research contrasts strongly with the artificiality of the settings for doing other kinds of research. Compared to these other settings, you will not have the luxury of defining your working conditions, as in scheduling to your convenience the hours for administering a series of questionnaires in a survey or for "running subjects" in a laboratory experiment—or even for quietly searching for archival information in a library or on the Internet.

Not surprisingly, the first encounters in the field have simultaneously been among the most exciting and nerve-racking. To a great extent, doing fieldwork initially may involve "going with the flow." Only with more extended time in a setting will fieldworkers identify the best opportunities for choosing when and where to position themselves in the field. Even experienced qualitative researchers cannot predict their initial encounters in the field when they are starting a new study (nor would many of these researchers want to). Every field situation is unique.

You nevertheless would want to prepare properly for your fieldwork. A lot of information already is likely to be available about the field setting you might consider studying. Relevant media coverage, online information, as well as previous research studies all are likely to be available. You should consult this information ahead of time. Thus, and as an extremely important caution for doing fieldwork in these 21st-century times, "going with the flow" means being adaptive and flexible when you actually start your fieldwork, but not overlooking the need to prepare carefully for the fieldwork in the first place.

Furthermore, the procedure for assuring the protection of human subjects will require its own preview of many of the expected fieldwork issues. An institutional review board (IRB) (see Chapter 2, Section E) will have to review and approve your assurances.

To get you better acquainted with the challenges of doing fieldwork, the present chapter discusses how other scholars have experienced their days in the field, including how they gained and maintained access to the field. The chapter's first three sections highlight working in the field and the initiation and nurturing of field relationships. These issues are likely to be relevant regardless of your specific fieldwork methodology. The two subsequent sections then describe two of the main ways whereby fieldwork methods have been formally recognized: *participant-observation* and *site visiting*.

A. WORKING IN THE FIELD

PREVIEW—*What you should learn from this section:*
1. The different ways of defining field settings for a qualitative study.
2. Variations in working in field settings, both in relation to their public or private nature and in the amount of time to be spent in the field.

Variety of Field Settings

One way of thinking about fieldwork is to think about its diverse settings. In anthropology and sociology, the earliest and classic field settings were both remote (the early anthropological studies of native tribes in New Guinea or the Trobriand Islands—Malinowski, 1922) and proximal (the sociological studies of gangs— Thrasher, 1927; settlement houses—Addams & Messinger, 1919; and other neighborhood groups studied by the scholars at the University of Chicago—the "Chicago school"—in the early 20th century, e.g., Burgess & Bogue, 1967; Park, Burgess, & McKenzie, 1925; Shaw, 1930; Thomas & Znaniecki, 1927; Zorbaugh, 1929). Whether remote or nearby, the settings represented cultures and lifestyles that were socially distant from those of the researchers and their (dominantly) middle-class counterparts. These early studies were therefore valued because they offered revelations about everyday life from the perspective of different cultures.

At the same time, other settings were deliberately chosen to be "average," such as the Lynds' original and follow-up studies of Muncie, Indiana, chosen because it represented a demographically average American city at that time (Lynd & Lynd, 1929, 1937). Though not culturally distant, information about these "average" settings also contributed to a deeper understanding of the social and institutional relationships at a time when these were still not frequent topics of study.

Field settings can be defined in many ways (Anderson-Levitt, 2006). First, they can include small groups of people who share a common bond, such as a gang or a work group. Second, they can cover residents of the same small geographic area. Both of these first two types were the topics of many urban studies that prevailed in the mid-20th century, especially focusing on people who lived in inner-city urban areas (e.g., Gans, 1962; Hannerz, 1969; Liebow, 1967; Molotch, 1969; Suttles, 1968; Vidich et al., 1964; Whyte, 1955, 1984, 1989, 1992). Attention to these kinds of groups also has continued to the present (e.g., Anderson, 1999; Liebow, 1993; Wilson & Taub, 2006).

Third, field settings can focus on institutional scenes. Everyday life in many different kinds of institutions, such as clinical settings or schools, can be the topics of study:

> • For instance, a study of long-term care focused on older people's decision-making processes and used three community centers as settings for making observations and doing interviews (e.g., Tetley, Grant, & Davies, 2009).

There can be a full variety of potential institutional and everyday settings offering real-world experiences worthy of qualitative study (see "Examples of 'Everyday' Settings," Vignette 5.1).

VIGNETTE 5.1. EXAMPLES OF "EVERYDAY" SETTINGS

Qualitative research can produce insights into social settings not fully appreciated by most people. The result can be a fuller understanding of our own society as well as emergent theories on how society works in these settings.

Some of the settings (and clues to the emergent theories as illustrated by the titles used by researchers who have studied the settings) are captured in a collection of readings by Glenn Jacobs (1970). Although the settings come from an earlier era, they may still suggest counterparts that contemporary students and scholars might study: ghetto capitalism (Black enterprises), street addicts (the needle scene), a tenants' grievance committee (birth of a mini-movement), a mental institution (the gilded asylum), street culture (time and cool people), a martial arts studio (urban samurai), collegiate gambling groups (poker and pop), a neighborhood cocktail lounge (home territory bar), waitering at a summer resort (the "shlockhaus" waiter), hustling in the poolroom (the hustler), welfare workers and clients (life in the colonies), and unemployed neighborhood men.

Fourth, field settings may be defined as unrelated groups of people. They may share some common condition, such as a similar health problem or medical ailment, but they do not interact as a group, reside in geographically proximal areas, or serve as members of similar institutional settings. This fourth definition has been prominent in grounded theory research (e.g., Charmaz, 1999, 2002; Glaser & Strauss, 1967; Strauss & Corbin, 1998). The participants of interest also can share some common characteristic, such as being learners of English as a second language (e.g., Duff, 2008). In these situations, qualitative research in psychology might engage in careful *discourse analysis*, emphasizing the participants' use of language as a way of their constructing social reality (e.g., Coyle, 2007).

The term *field settings* as used throughout the remainder of this chapter pertains to all of the preceding types of situations. All offer qualitative researchers the opportunity to portray cultures, social organizations, and lifestyles, in order to gain potentially important insights into how people interact, cope, and thrive. All offer excellent opportunities to study topics that may have been overlooked by previous research. The insights and discoveries from these studies can lead to new ideas that in turn may have important implications well beyond the particular culture, social organization, lifestyle, or psychological condition that was the original subject of study. The contributions of qualitative research thus can assume a twofold nature: new information about something that was previously little known, combined with concepts and insights that have implications for broader interpretations of human affairs.

You would want to seek a similar combination when doing your own qualitative research. The field setting can be exotic or average. But remember that what might at first appear to be just another setting can become something more special by highlighting some key concepts and using them to derive new insights.

Differing Rules and Expectations for Public or Private Places as Field Settings

Some field settings will require permission to be studied. For instance, note how, among the settings enumerated in Vignette 5.1, you would not necessarily need the same permission to locate yourself, talk to others, or even take pictures in the field settings that are public (e.g., the streets) compared to those that are private places (e.g., the martial arts studio).

However, the boundaries between public and private places will not always be clear. For instance, "public" schools are "private" in the sense that you will need permission from school officials to conduct research as well as permission from those officials and parents if you want to converse with or take pictures of any of the students. Houses of worship, retail stores, "public" libraries, and the like present the same dualism—welcoming all people as if they were public places but considering themselves private if you want to do a research study on their premises. A recommended rule of thumb is to ask whether and from whom you might have to request permission if you were to do a study of a particular setting or about a particular group of people.

Varying the Amount of Time in the Field

Fieldworkers can consume several years or spend only several days in the field, depending on their theoretical interests as well as their resources. The classical studies tended to involve extended field time because of the desire to study the fuller complexities of the culture or social structure of a place or people. Such deeper inquiries called for examining how human events and interactions might have been repeated or have changed over a lengthy period of time—for example, recall the 15 years presented earlier in Vignette 1.6—and across a variety of people and groups.

You may not want or need to invest such a lengthy period of time in your fieldwork. However, be aware that at a minimum, many types of lifestyles that might be the subject of your qualitative research do tend to vary according to the four seasons. A one-year period of fieldwork would therefore make sense as a logical period of fieldwork time. If such seasonal variation does not appear relevant, shorter fieldwork periods might be acceptable.

Less classical but still worthy qualitative studies tend to focus on specific practices—for example, how mathematics is taught in the fourth grade; how communities plan for their response to disasters; how private enterprises diversify their businesses; or how individuals cope with the psychological loss of significant others.

The fieldwork in these instances might extend over a period of several months, and the fieldworker might only be present sporadically and not constantly throughout this period.

The most limited amount of time in the field—2 or 3 days—is nevertheless justifiable if the topic of inquiry is correspondingly limited. Such studies might be aimed at determining whether a particular action has taken or is taking place. Examples deliberately mimicking those in the preceding paragraph but with greater focus might be the ways in which teachers are using a particular instructional method in their classrooms; the nature of a community's specific disaster response plan (and the awareness of this plan by local officials and residents); the evidence that a business has become diversified (or not); and the immediate coping behavior upon the initial loss of a significant other. The shorter periods of time also may suit those studies involving multiple settings (see the discussion on "making site visits," in Section E).

If your resources or motivations for doing fieldwork (or for collecting any kind of research data) are limited, the lesson here is to identify a limited topic of inquiry. Conversely, if your intellectual ambitions are great, and you have the resources to support them, you will benefit from spending a lot of time in the field.

B.   GAINING AND MAINTAINING ACCESS TO THE FIELD

PREVIEW—*What you should learn from this section:*
1. The dynamic conditions involved in gaining and maintaining access to field settings.
2. The relationship between the nature of the initial field contacts and the subsequent course of a qualitative study.

Real-life settings belong to those in real life, not the researchers intruding into these settings. Doing research in these settings requires special attention to the way you might gain permission to study them and your subsequent access to them. To accomplish these tasks, fieldworkers often get assistance from others who may know more about the setting than they do. For instance, if earlier research or personal relationships have not produced a close acquaintance with the setting that is to be studied, a collaborator highly familiar with that setting will be extremely valuable. The ideal collaborator can help identify and get a fieldworker in touch with the key persons in the setting.

Gaining Access to a Field Setting: A Process, Not an Event

Less experienced researchers may think about "access" as an event, much like applying for admissions into college or graduate school. However, in those situations, an admitted student stays admitted, usually having no further contact with the admissions office. The admissions procedure was an event that has now passed. Students may later get expelled or suspended, but the actions leading to such sanctions are well defined ahead of time and become a separate set of events. Moreover, a drastic action such as expulsion occurs rarely.

Any admissions-like image vastly oversimplifies the fieldwork situation. Having access may be more of a process than a one-time event (e.g., Maginn, 2007). Throughout any fieldwork, the threat of losing access (not the same as being expelled) always exists. Fieldworkers must therefore manage access throughout their time in the field. Once having gained access, the experienced ones do not take it for granted. They avoid behavior that may appear as "wearing out their welcome." Access can either be lost completely or limited, as hosts may deliberately exclude fieldworkers from certain activities (see "Access Gained and Then Restricted," Vignette 5.2). Participants even can raise objections to a study that has been ongoing for some time. For instance, Kugelmass (2004) reported such challenges to her study after having gained the appropriate permissions and after having completed 2 years of fieldwork at a school (see "Questions of Continuation Raised in the Third Year of Fieldwork," Vignette 5.3).

VIGNETTE 5.2. ACCESS GAINED AND THEN RESTRICTED

As part of his textbook on the participant-observer method, Danny Jorgensen (1989) cited his own study of the occult to illustrate various methodological techniques and lessons (see pp. 63, 71, 89, and 92).

Early on in the study, Jorgensen had developed close relationships with several people and was able to collect much data, which included interviews and documents. Only late in the research, however, did he become aware of the rival groups within the occult community. He then neglected to attend a psychic fair sponsored by one of the groups. The group's leader already had started to identify Jorgensen with its rival and used the absence to challenge the researcher's commitment to occultism. Consequently, Jorgensen was unable to interact with the offended group and was denied access to their activities. The author reports that the "episode was personally traumatizing and extremely problematic. It nevertheless was invaluable in confirming the emergent picture . . . of networks, segments, and politics in this community of occultists" (1989, p. 79).

How the Process Can Influence the Substance of a Study

For most field settings, and especially those with readily acknowledged organizational or social networks, a fieldworker's main access appropriately comes from an official of the institution or the leader of the network. Such a person is commonly regarded as a "gatekeeper." However, this manner of gaining access may result in others at the institution or in the network believing that a research study represents the interests of the gatekeeper. Such a perception will affect the fieldworker's reception by the other members in the field setting. For instance, the gatekeeper may have represented one faction at a site, and a researcher may then be seen by the other factions as representing the interests of the gatekeeper's faction. Similarly, in an institutional setting, employees may respond differently if they believe

---

VIGNETTE 5.3. QUESTIONS OF CONTINUATION RAISED IN THE THIRD YEAR OF FIELDWORK

A study of a single elementary school by Judy Kugelmass (2004) eventually involved 5 years of fieldwork. The study focused on teachers' efforts to create inclusive classrooms—intending to celebrate diversity in its broadest sense, not limited to students with disabilities or special needs.

Although Kugelmass had received permission to conduct the research from all relevant quarters, after 2 years of fieldwork two teachers "began to express fears about how [her research] might be perceived by the 'outside world'. They, along with one parent, did not want [her research] to continue" (2004, p. 20).

The concerns reflected "growing tensions between the school and the larger school system" over a tightening of accountability rules and the possibility that the research findings could "be misinterpreted outside the context of the school's culture" (2004, p. 20). After extended discussions, the study did continue, along with an agreement to maintain the anonymity of the school and of the individual participants.

---

that a study has been sanctioned by their employer (see "Working as a Store Clerk," Vignette 5.4).

The implicit associations created by any of these situations cannot always be avoided. The main goal should be to bring a sensitivity to the implications of how a site has been accessed, and how the initial contacts might affect a study and its findings.

A somewhat different situation arises when access to a field setting occurs as part of a more natural process because the fieldworker already was located at a site or was a member of a social group prior to starting the study. In fact, being part of the site or the social group may have been the main rationale for considering the study in the first place.

VIGNETTE 5.4. WORKING AS A STORE CLERK

Christine Williams (2006) met the challenge of being a participant-observer by interviewing for and then being hired to work as a clerk in two toy stores (located in a modest and an upscale neighborhood, respectively). She worked for about 6 weeks of 8-hour shifts in each store.

Williams "did not seek official approval from management to conduct a formal study . . . [because] workers are often suspicious of researchers who have managerial approval, treating them like corporate spies" (2006, p. 18). Despite this condition, she "was never undercover. When I was working . . . I really was a salesclerk" (p. 18). She also notes that no one asked about her background because most workers do not make such inquiries about each other, and she was not the only worker with an advanced degree.

See also Vignette 4.2.

The literature contains many studies in which the investigator happened to live in a foreign country, work in a particular organization, or be acquainted with a certain group of people, and in which these situations all became the settings for subsequent field studies. In one of these studies, a researcher and his spouse moved into a neighborhood and tried to start a nonprofit arts organization there. The neighborhood and its residents subsequently became the subject of an ethnographic study (see "Residing and Working in a Transitioning Urban Neighborhood," Vignette 5.5). In like manner, two researchers studied 162 women in eight neighborhoods, each researcher residing in one of the neighborhoods, and each doing volunteer work there (Edin & Kefalas, 2005).

In these situations, gaining access assumes a slightly different meaning. You would be less likely to need permission to be present at a scene, but you would still need to gain permission to speak with or interview the specific persons who are

---

VIGNETTE 5.5. RESIDING AND WORKING IN A TRANSITIONING URBAN NEIGHBORHOOD

Russell Leigh Sharman (2006) studied an ethnically mixed New York City neighborhood after moving into it and starting a nonprofit, arts education organization. From that vantage point, he became closely acquainted with many neighborhood residents, some of whom became the subjects of the life histories that dominate his book. The life histories occupy separate chapters, each chapter calling attention to the neighborhood's extreme ethnic mix: Italians, Puerto Ricans, African Americans, Mexicans, West Africans, and Chinese.

The arts organization did not survive after several years, as the neighborhood was undergoing an expensive upgrading process commonly called gentrification. However, Sharman deliberately stays away from letting any theoretical perspective introduce or otherwise cloud the presentation of the life histories. In what he himself says is "an unusual style of ethnography" (2006, p. xiii), the life histories are his way of "allowing ethnography to do the work of theoretical abstraction" (p. xiii).

---

part of the scene. In these situations, the fact that a study is being conducted should not be disguised, much less hidden. People should know when they are conversing with you that it is either part of a study or not, an issue that should have been explicitly covered as part of the procedure for protecting human subjects.

The longer that a fieldworker is in a field setting, the more complicated the social relationships can become. The complications may arise from having more intense relationships with individual people. Even more difficult to anticipate, others will talk with each other and exchange information about you and your work, potentially coloring their subsequent responses to your queries.

The most complicated situation arises when a fieldworker appears to become a full-fledged member of the setting or group being studied, with possibly little realization that a loss of the appropriate research perspective also is occurring.

Fieldworkers under these circumstances risk being accused of "going native," with a negative connotation attached to their research findings.

A frequently recommended antidote to all these complications is, while doing your fieldwork, to dialogue frequently during off hours with a trusted colleague who is not part of the field setting or of the study. Debriefing colleagues and alerting them to watch for unwanted complications or your unknowing immersion into a field setting's affairs is one way of keeping the needed research perspective.

C. NURTURING FIELD RELATIONSHIPS

PREVIEW—*What you should learn from this section:*

The role you will assume in doing fieldwork, including your identity, relationships with the participants in the field, and coping behavior.

Gaining and maintaining access are but part of a larger undertaking in doing fieldwork. You also need to manage an ongoing set of human relationships. Some of these relationships may have predated your fieldwork, but the bulk will have been formed during the fieldwork. And some relationships may linger (whether by design or not) after you have completed your fieldwork.

The task is not as daunting as you might imagine. But there will be surprises, and there are risks.

Portraying Your Authentic Self

This is the safest and sanest way of presenting the identity for building field relationships. The identity includes a primary function (that of doing a study) as well as a personality (your own). It is the preferred identity because you will represent most faithfully the original motive for being in the field in the first place, and you will be able to maintain a consistent posture and demeanor in interacting with others.

Presenting yourself as doing a research study can be attractive because the identity connotes a serious and professional commitment rather than a casual curiosity into other people's lives. At the same time, because so many studies have been done on so many topics, some of the people who will participate in a new study already may have their own views about such studies. They may believe that studies can become obtrusive and betray trusts, when shared experiences are exposed in writing. Early on, you therefore should be prepared (1) to define the kind of writing (report or book) that will result; (2) whether and how you will share this writing with the people you have studied; and (3) the degree of anonymity with which the information will be presented (also see Chapter 4, Choice 6).

Presenting yourself in some other function depends on the authenticity of the chosen alternative and its relationship to your research. As mentioned previously regarding the process of gaining access to the field, you might have a job, serve as a volunteer, or be an actual resident at the setting being studied. Such vantage points can provide a sound basis for participating in field activities, but if you know you are doing a study you also need to inform people that you are doing one. In this regard, Elliot Liebow was one of the most forthright persons I have had the privilege of knowing. In his study of homeless women (1993), he poignantly touches on all of the issues regarding his presentation of self in forming field relationships (see "The Fieldworker in Action," Vignette 5.6).

VIGNETTE 5.6. THE FIELDWORKER IN ACTION

In his study of homeless women, Elliot Liebow (1993) discusses how he positioned himself as a fieldworker, fully acknowledging his function as a research instrument. Three issues illustrate his discussion.

First, Liebow comments on his own background and "prejudices" because "everything reported about the women in this study has been selected by me and filtered through me" (1993, p. vii).

Second, believing that relationships be "as symmetrical as possible," Liebow encouraged visits by his wife and (adult) daughters to the homeless shelter, following a "quid pro quo" principle: "the women needed to know as much about me as I knew about them" (1993, p. xii). They also could then ask more vividly how his family was doing when discussing their families and child-rearing experiences.

Third, Liebow discusses his ethical standards—"what to do when learning about the women's shoplifting," for instance. There, he tried "to bring the same ethics to fieldwork that I bring to any other part of my life" (1993, p. 327).

See also Vignettes 1.1 and 11.7.

Importance of Personal Demeanor

Typical demeanors include being respectful and not condescending, friendly but not ingratiating, and attentive to others but not pandering to them. Fieldworkers should be intent on "listening" (with all modalities) to what is taking place, but they cannot become totally passive personalities. Conversely, fieldworkers who overtly assert their own views or opinions, besides leading to possibly overbearing demeanors, also create a critical methodological risk. The views and opinions may heavily influence the reactions of others as well as shape events in the field. In this way a study will fail to capture the meaning of the very real-world conditions that were to be the subject of inquiry.

Overall, through your choice of dress and personal accessories, your goal is to be genuine but not to call undue attention to yourself. Remember that others are the subject of study, not you. Note, too, that any subtle signs that you emit can be as important as what you might state overtly. Again, remember that in real-life conditions you are not just observing other people—they are simultaneously "reading" you, and some of these people may have a great knack for reading. Your body language, pauses and hesitations, and facial and verbal expressions all convey information. For instance, any and all of these gestures can lead to others perceiving you as being directive when you might have thought you were being properly nondirective.

Doing Favors for Participants: Part of the Relationship or Not?

Although being in the field means being part of a real-world setting, the fieldworkers' role is still somewhat artificial because the reason for being present is that a study is being conducted. A common dilemma is whether the role includes doing favors, and if so, the limit of those favors.

Small favors can range from small loans ($10 to $20) to watching after a child, pet, or elderly relative while a participant has gone shopping, carried out an errand, or become otherwise preoccupied, to doing relational favors such as talking to another person on behalf of the one who is asking for the favor. Larger favors may involve higher stakes.

All fieldworkers must decide for themselves what feels most comfortable and is acceptable. A few rules of thumb might be (1) to avoid larger favors at all; (2) to do smaller favors only on a rare occasion, making it clear to others that it is a rare occasion; and (3) to maintain a principled enough demeanor that no one would even ask you to do a favor bordering on anything illegal or resulting in physically or psychologically harming another person.

Coping with Unexpected Events

The most startling event may be a simple one: Though you are focused on asking questions related to your research, others also may ask questions of you. Their questions can be about your study, about your personal background and views, or about nearly any other subject matter. Although you cannot anticipate all of these questions, thinking ahead of time about where you might want to draw some lines—such as how much you are willing to divulge about your personal life—would be an advisable exercise.

Other unexpected events range from being invited to participate in certain activities (including being invited into personal relationships) to becoming aware of illegal or otherwise undesirable activities. These situations have no easy solutions. Many years ago, Florence Kluckhohn (1940) already described how a field participant presented himself as a male suitor trying to arrange a date with her. She did not feel entirely comfortable in her field relations until, due to a later set of congenial circumstances, he apologized directly and disavowed any further efforts along the same lines.

A final type of unexpected event may involve threats or hazards to yourself and your livelihood (e.g., Howell, 1990). Be aware of (and study) the contemporary economic, political, and social conditions in your field setting as they might affect the people and setting you are studying. Your preparation should keep in mind that the focus of your work is others' real-life routines. The context for those routines belongs to the world you are studying, not your world. If the context involves physical violence such as studying law enforcement work (e.g., Punch, 1989) or group hostilities of any sort, be conservative and expect adverse rather than congenial reactions in doing your fieldwork.

Planning How to Exit, Not Just Enter, the Field

Much attention is properly aimed at how you will introduce yourself and enter the field. Less is given to the equally important phase of exiting. For instance, are you planning to return to a field setting once your writing has been completed?

In most cases, you probably will not return, and exiting would mean arriving at mutual understandings with the people whom you have been studying. You may indicate how or whether you will be sharing some of your later writing with them. You also may want to "stay in touch," even though you are not planning to return to the setting per se. Some relationships are best left to linger rather than ending in a firmly established "goodbye." You even may want to leave open the opportunity of returning to the field setting someday, to do a follow-up study.

No single exiting strategy fits all situations. Aside from any commitments you may have made (and should keep) when first offering human subjects protection or in your early interactions with participants, the situations are dominated by unique human relationships. You are in the best position to decide which strategy to pursue, so give the matter some thought before the exiting process really begins.

D. DOING PARTICIPANT-OBSERVATION

PREVIEW—*What you should learn from this section:*
1. How doing participant-observation accentuates the role of the researcher as the research instrument in a qualitative study.
2. How to give the events in the field an influential role, compared to preconceptions held prior to the fieldwork.

From a methodological standpoint, fieldwork roles can vary. The common methodology associated with doing fieldwork has been *participant-observation* (Anderson-Levitt, 2006; Jacobs, 1970; Jorgensen, 1989; Kidder & Judd, 1986; Kluckhohn, 1940; McCall & Simmons, 1969; Platt, 1992; Spradley, 1980).

Participant-observation of one form or another has been practiced for over 100 years in anthropology and for nearly that long in sociology:

> • In anthropology (Emerson, 2001, pp. 4–7), the early work includes studies by Franz Boas and later by other notable scholars who were his students (e.g., Ruth Benedict, Margaret Mead, Robert Lowie, and Alfred Kroeber) and by Bronislaw Malinowski and later by others who were his students (e.g., Evans-Pritchard, Raymond Firth, and Hortense Powdermaker).

> • In sociology, the early contributors were Robert E. Park and the "Chicago School" of sociology (Platt, 1992, pp. 37–38), which also includes a renowned collection of scholars (e.g., W. I. Thomas, R. C. Angell, and C. R. Shaw).

In these participant-observation works, the topic of studies varied from whole societies to groups of people to individual people.

According to Bruyn (1966), the term *participant-observation* was probably first coined by Eduard Lindeman, and the first detailed statements about the method were written by Lohman (1937) and Kluckhohn (1940). By the 1950s, the term had become nearly synonymous with doing field research (Emerson, 2001, p. 13; Platt, 1992, pp. 39–43).

The method was then used to study the urban neighborhoods described earlier in this chapter as well as many social groups such as medical students (e.g., Becker, Geer, Hughes, & Strauss, 1961). For latter-day researchers and especially those practicing ethnography, participant-observation emphasizes close, intimate, and active involvement, strongly linked with the goal of studying others' cultures (Emerson, 2001, pp. 17–18).

The relative emphasis between "participating" and "observing" can produce four variants: (1) being a participant only, (2) being a participant who also observes, (3) being an observer who also participates, and (4) being an observer only (Gold, 1958; Schwartz & Schwartz, 1955). (A fifth, logical combination would be a nonparticipant who also does not observe—but no fieldwork would take place under this combination.) The essence of being a participant-observer calls for emulating the middle two of the four variants—that is, having some participation and some observation, and not neglecting either one entirely.

The Researcher as the "Research Instrument"

Think about a research instrument as a tool for collecting data. Common examples from schoolwork might be a ruler, compass, protractor, or thermometer. Common examples from psychology or sociology might be an audiometer (to test people's hearing) or a closed-ended questionnaire (to collect verbal responses). In all of these instances, human beings use the tool and can create undesirable "measurement error," but each tool has its own metric, whereby a measurement can be expressed and recorded.

No such tool exists in working as a participant-observer. You may have a questionnaire as part of your fieldwork, but unless you are doing an interview-only study, you also will be directly observing and recording the actions, events, and conversations that occur in the field. You will be taking notes (discussed in Chapter 7, Section B), but they only record what you have yourself "measured." Even if you video- or audiotape events, these records do not in themselves provide any metric—for instance, to distinguish important from unimportant events or the meaning of interviewees' insights.

In other words, real-life encounters dominate fieldwork. In these situations, your five senses will be the main modalities for measuring and assessing information from the field. You also will be constrained by your ability to recall and remember actions, and you will be exercising your own discretion in deciding what to record. All these functions mean that you will be serving as the main research instrument (see "Doing Fieldwork in Two Houses of Worship," Vignette 5.7).

VIGNETTE 5.7. DOING FIELDWORK IN TWO HOUSES OF WORSHIP

Two lesbian- and gay-affirming churches—one "predominantly black, working class, lesbian, and evangelical, and the other mostly white, middle class, heterosexual, and liberal" (p. 151)— served as the venues for a well-executed field study by Krista McQueeney (2009).

The fieldwork included 200 hours of participant-observation involving worship services, Bible studies, holy unions, social events, and regional conferences; 25 semi-structured interviews (including all four pastors of the two churches) that were tape-recorded and fully transcribed; and reviews of newsletters, local news articles, and other related publications.

McQueeney readily acknowledges her own "perspective and privilege as a white, lesbian graduate student fieldworker," and she "routinely reflected and wrote analytic memos about how [her] expectations, biases, and interactions with participants shaped [her] analysis" (2009, p. 154). The thoroughness of the work and good writing also show how such a study can be presented within the space limitations of an article in a contemporary academic journal.

Being the prime research instrument requires fieldworkers to be aware of the instrument's (i.e., your) potential biases and idiosyncrasies. These include conditions arising from your personal background, your motives for doing the research, and your categories or filters that might influence your understanding of field events and actions.

Prominent among these personal attributes is the match between the race or ethnicity of a researcher and those of the participants in a study. There are well-known examples of contrasting situations, including white researchers who studied Black family or social life (e.g., Hannerz, 1969; Liebow, 1967; Stack, 1974), as well as studies by those with closely matched identities also involving non-English-speaking matches (e.g., Brubaker et al., 2006; Padraza, 2007; Rivera, 2008; Sarroub, 2005; Valenzuela, 1999). One team of researchers, by dint of its multiracial composition and its focus on a multiple set of neighborhoods with different racial compositions, was actually able to study the apparent differences and similarities of matched and nonmatched conditions (see "Racial and Ethnic Congruencies," Vignette 5.8). Another diverse team studied the lives of 12 diverse families and therefore had the same opportunity (Lareau, 2003).

VIGNETTE 5.8. RACIAL AND ETHNIC CONGRUENCIES

Two professors and nine graduate students immersed themselves in four urban neighborhoods for over 30 months, roughly two persons per neighborhood (Wilson & Taub, 2006). The teams mapped the neighborhoods and collected census and other historical data about them. For the bulk of the time, the fieldworkers participated in neighborhood activities, attended church, school, and other meetings, talked to knowledgeable informants, and served as volunteers in jobs with neighborhood organizations.

The multisite and multiteam arrangement enabled the authors to comment on the advantages of having researchers with racial or ethnic backgrounds that either differ from or are the same as those of the neighborhood residents. The authors feel that congruent relationships are likely to be more sensitive to cultural signals and to engender more trust. Noncongruent relationships are likely to bring fresh eyes to the scene; the social distance also may increase access to information that would not be shared with friends or those with congruent characteristics (pp. 192–193).

See also Vignette 8.4.

Taking an Inductive Stance Even If a Study Started with Some Propositions

Anthropologists commonly use fieldwork as a means of trying to depict the culture of a group or place. Such a quest requires the ability to capture and then put together the meaning of rituals, symbols, roles, and social practices. These all vary, making fieldwork hard to do. However, to do it well requires that a fieldworker bring a minimum of preconceptions into the field.

Whether you are studying a culture or not, you should adhere to the same goal. The preconceptions to be minimized come not only from your personal beliefs but from the initial theoretical propositions that might have led to your study. Important in both realms are hypothetical constructs called categories (e.g., Becker, 1998, pp. 76–85), previously discussed in Chapter 1 (Section C). Everyone uses categories everyday to sort experiences into meaningful patterns. However, when initially starting your fieldwork, you should try not to "categorize" events and occurrences prematurely.

The successful *inductive* stance permits the events in the field to drive the later development of categories, propositions, and eventually "meaning," based on the actions in the field and not preconceptions. Starting a study with preconceptions, prior to doing fieldwork, would be considered a *deductive* procedure.

Now comes a critical paradox. Earlier, Chapter 4 discussed how qualitative research could start with a range of designs, including those based on preconceived theoretical propositions (see Chapter 4, Choice 5). Even if a study starts with such a design, the fieldwork will be most beneficial if the initial propositions are ignored temporarily. In other words, do your best to let the field tell the story first, in its own way. Later, you always will have time to compare that story with your earlier propositions.

The paradoxical situation is not unlike a clinical or medical setting where a doctor starts talking to a patient by asking "How do you feel?" The good clinician is trained first to make the patient comfortable enough to share her or his innermost feelings, and then to listen carefully, and finally to let the patient's responses lead to additional queries or probes.

The good clinician is "sizing up" the situation. However, that doesn't mean that the clinician was devoid of any knowledge (i.e., propositions) to begin with. In this day and age, the clinician is likely to be a specialist and will assume that the patient came because of a belief that the ailment was related to the specialization (otherwise, the patient would have gone to some other specialist). Some (possibly most) clinicians are nevertheless good enough to suspend their preconceptions and to recognize when a patient has incorrectly guessed about an ailment and should really be going to another specialist. Other clinicians will stick to their specialized knowledge and might undesirably divert the patient's reports toward that specialty.

Training yourself to be a fieldworker who emulates the former and not the latter kind of clinician takes time and patience. A participant-observer's creed might be as follows:

- ◆ Start fieldwork by listening carefully to what's going on;
- ◆ Make a good mental record of what's going on;
- ◆ Avoid comparing an initial field experience with your earlier (field or nonfield) experiences;
- ◆ Make as few initial assumptions as possible;
- ◆ Have confidence that patterns will emerge without artificial prompting;
- ◆ Have additional confidence that, if a study started with some propositions, the field experiences and those propositions will eventually interact in some productive way, including the discovery that the initial propositions need to be discarded, enhanced, or redefined in some interesting way.

E. MAKING SITE VISITS

PREVIEW—*What you should learn from this section:*

1. The situations for which site visits are well suited.
2. The major advantages and disadvantages in doing site visits, compared to participant-observation.

Making site visits is another formally recognized way of doing fieldwork. In fact, the term *fieldwork* in most policy, organizational, and evaluation studies refers to making site visits. Moreover, in these situations the site visits directly connote the qualitative research portion of a study, sometimes serving as a study's only method but in other instances used as part of a mixed methods research study.

Few specialists in other scientific disciplines recognize that they even may perform site visits routinely. Such site visits occur whenever visiting committees review the work of university departments and programs. In doing these site visits, and by collecting and analyzing data about a university department or program, these specialists are actually doing qualitative research.

Most texts do not discuss either the preceding application or other forms of site visits as a formal procedure. Yet, the data from site visits can be as worthy as data from participant-observation. Major differences also exist, of course. First, the typical site visit spans but several days. Second, site visit fieldwork may be deliberately designed to involve two or more fieldworkers in doing a site visit. The additional person(s) can help to offset the lack of overall time in the field, as the team members may divide responsibilities and separately cover different events or interviews.

A few highlights of the site visit process are as follows.

Studying a Large Number of Field Settings

Although site visiting offers a shallower experience for any single field setting than doing participant-observation, a major advantage of using site visits as a fieldwork procedure is the ability to collect data from many field settings as part of the same study. Whereas participant-observation is likely to be limited to one or two field settings, the use of site visits can easily cover a dozen or more settings. The data from any single setting may be more limited than those in a participant-observer study, but site visit data from multiple settings can support meaningful cross-site findings and patterns. Site visit fieldwork therefore suits situations where cross-site patterns are the main objective of research.

Conversely, the preferred field settings are likely to be smaller or more self-contained than those involved in participant-observation. Frequent site visit settings include classrooms, clinics, offices, and working environments such as industrial plants and service outlets. Doing site visits for these kinds of settings can produce the needed information when cross-site patterns serve as the main research questions. Part of the pattern also can call for site visiting the same settings two or more times, to gain a time as well as cross-site perspective. If the topic of study happens to involve extensive documentary evidence, field reviews of any earlier documentation can extend the time perspective even further.

Adhering to Formal Schedules and Plans

Site visiting is likely to be more rigid than participant-observation. Because of the limited field time, site visiting usually follows a preestablished schedule, as well as an agenda while in the field. Both will increase the likelihood of interviewing or conversing with the necessary participants or of observing the desired events in the field. Once into a scheduled interview or observation, the data collection and recording procedures for site visits may not appear to differ strongly from those followed in participant-observation. However, the context may be entirely different—with the scheduled interview or observation taking place under more artificial conditions than when doing participant-observation.

You should not underestimate the potential influence of these contextual conditions. For instance, members of a field setting that is being site-visited may have helped to arrange the schedule, thereby manipulating it to their advantage. Moreover, those in the field also will know the schedule ahead of time and can prepare for your site visit, again manipulating it to their advantage. In these situations, the activities and responses during your site visit may not represent what normally occurs at that field setting. The activities may have an idealized flavor, and the responses may bear greater resemblance to what the participants think you want to hear than what they normally would profess.

Being "Hosted" during a Site Visit

A further complication arises when a site visitor is accompanied by her or his host, either when observing field activities or when interviewing the others in the field. The host may have two different motives. One is to monitor the site visitor. The other is to see or hear what the site visitor appears to be learning. For instance, when organizations are the setting for field research, the site visitor may have access to a higher official who might not normally give such access to the host.

The presence of the host during any field activities makes the issue of reflexivity even more complicated. The other participants may not only respond artificially to the site visitor but also may alter their entire demeanor due to the presence of the host. Thus, site visitors need to decide when they would prefer not to be accompanied by the host and discuss this matter with the host ahead of time. Such preparation will avoid embarrassing situations from arising in the middle of a site visit.

Building Teamwork

Site visit research involving multiple persons per field team (or even multiple teams covering different sites) calls for additional team-building efforts. For instance, common training and preparation are needed to increase the consistency of fieldwork. Team members also must communicate with each other to build a chemistry that includes understanding how to avoid interrupting each other when they are jointly interviewing a participant and following a line of inquiry.

The team-building efforts require a degree of collaboration and planning that go beyond what you have to do if you were conducting a "solo" study. However, team research offers offsetting benefits, such as creating the opportunity to strengthen the validity and reliability of a study and giving greater attention to the triangulation objectives discussed in Chapter 6 (Section C). Essentially, having multiple site visitors means having the opportunity to use multiple research instruments in the field, compared to the limitations of solo participant-observers.

RECAP FOR CHAPTER 5: *Terms, phrases, and concepts that you now can define*:
1. Field setting
2. Field access
3. Gatekeeper
4. "Going native"

5. Entering and exiting a field setting
6. Participant-observation
7. The identity of the research instrument in doing participant-observation
8. "Letting the field tell the story first"
9. Site visiting
10. Being "hosted" in a field setting

EXERCISE FOR CHAPTER 5: MAKING FIELD OBSERVATIONS (JOB SHADOWING EXERCISE)

Make a job-shadowing arrangement with a university official (e.g., an administrator in a dean's office, an official in the food services or campus services departments, a person at one of the university's affiliated research centers, or some other person who has a "desk job" but who has many visitors or who moves around to various campus locations in some daily manner). During a two-week period, choose 3 (or more) days to accompany (shadow) this person and observe her or his actions, including her or his conversations and interactions with other people. If possible, choose 3 days when your host's calendar looks busy rather than days when she or he will simply be sitting at her or his desk. Be prepared to explain the reasons for your presence to any of the other people (having previously agreed upon the explanation with your host) and make sure they have no objections to it.

Prior to the fieldwork, hypothesize what difficulties you may encounter in making good observations while also taking good field notes, without the aid of a tape or video recorder. The product for this exercise should be your responses to the following four questions (the notes themselves will later be used to create the products for the exercises associated with Chapters 10, 11, and 12):

1. Are conversations always easy to render accurately?
2. How easy was it to describe nuances in meaning, body language, or details in the physical environment, and were these an important part of the events being observed?
3. Were there any unanticipated occurrences when you were brought into a conversation or became part of the events being observed in some way?
4. What did you do with your note-taking procedure then?

[Alternative field settings when job shadowing cannot be arranged: Audit several different classes or courses where the instructor has had a reputation for engaging students in class discussions; or attend several different but lengthy meetings where you can be an observer—a good opportunity would be some type of public meeting, such as the meeting of an elected city council or school board, which should be open to the public.]

CHAPTER 6

Data Collection Methods

Data serve as the foundation for a research study. In qualitative research, the relevant data derive from four field-based activities: interviewing, observing, collecting and examining (materials), and feeling. The present chapter describes these activities in detail. In doing interviews, the contrast between structured and qualitative interviews draws special attention. Regarding observations, important choices involve determining "what, when, and where" to observe. On collecting materials, artifacts, many different types of objects can be usefully collected while doing fieldwork. Feelings—as represented by multiple senses not limited to the sense of touch—can involve the noise, temporal pace, and warmth/coldness of a field setting, as well as conjectures about the social relationships among participants. Across all four types of field-based activities, the chapter discusses five desirable practices, including distinguishing among first-, second-, and thirdhand evidence.

To do empirical research, you need to collect data. Different kinds of social science research favor different kinds of data collection procedures, and data collection for qualitative research likewise has distinctive characteristics and challenges.

A. WHAT ARE DATA?

To collect qualitative data properly, you might first ask whether you know what data are. An initial observation is that the word "data" appears as both a plural and singular noun. Both usages are acceptable, although most researchers might prefer the plural form, as used in this book. But *what are data*? Who and where are they? Would you know them if you encountered them, and if not, how could you be expected to collect them?

Wikipedia seemed like a reasonable source for a relevant definition, especially because its definition did not differ substantially from those in more conventional dictionaries. According to *Wikipedia*,

"Data" refers to a collection of organized information, usually the result of experience, observation, experiment. . . . This may consist of numbers, words, or images, particularly as measurements or observations of a set of variables.

To provide additional insight, *Wikipedia* gives the following example, which distinguishes among *data, information*, and *knowledge*. The example defines the height of Mount Everest as "data," a book on Mount Everest's geological features as "information," and a report containing practical information on the best way to reach Mount Everest's peak as "knowledge." From this example, it should be evident that "data" are the smallest or lowest entities or recorded elements resulting from some experience, observation, experiment, or other similar situation.

Note that all these situations appear to be external to a researcher. Thus, in nonqualitative research, a researcher's role in collecting data may be to take a reading with some mechanical instrument, such as a meter. However, and as a reminder, in qualitative research you the researcher are the main research instrument (see Chapter 5, Section D). Thus, although the original events being measured may be external, what you report and how you report them are filtered through your own thinking and the meaning you impute into your data collection. In this sense, the data cannot be completely external.

B. INTRODUCTION TO FOUR TYPES OF DATA COLLECTION ACTIVITIES

PREVIEW—*What you should learn from this section:*
1. The relationship between participant-observation and the different types of data collection activities.
2. The likely types of data produced by each of the data collection activities.

Some type of participant-observation, ranging from the most active to the most passive orientations (also previously described in Chapter 5, Section D), is likely to be the way you position yourself when doing qualitative research. However, participant-observation is not in itself a data collection method. As a participant-observer, you still must undertake some specific activity to collect data.

From this perspective, as well as when you position yourself in ways other than being a participant-observer but want to collect data for qualitative research, the potential data collection activities are:

- ♦ Interviewing;
- ♦ Observing;
- ♦ Collecting and examining; and
- ♦ Feeling.

At first blush, these four activities may sound too informal to be considered research activities. However, if desired, you could implement each of the activities by using (1) a formal instrument and (2) a rigorously defined data collection procedure.

For instance, "interviewing" could rely on a fixed questionnaire with explicit interview protocols. "Observing" could rely on photographing unobtrusive signs such as the fronts of vacant houses as part of a neighborhood study. "Collecting" could occur as a result of a formal search and retrieval procedure that uses electronic bibliographic searches as a tool. Some type of mechanical instrument even could be used to assess certain types of "feelings," such as feeling warm or cold (which could be supported by the use of an instrument such as a thermometer), perceiving the passage of time (which could be supported by your watch), or interpreting the noisiness of a place (which could be measured by an audiometer).

Similarly, you could follow formal sampling procedures for selecting the specific occasions upon which you would undertake these data collecting activities. In this way, for instance, researchers have conducted studies using *systematic observations*, in which strict time intervals trigger the relevant sample of observations. The observational procedures have been followed in studies ranging from children's behavior in watching television (e.g., Palmer, 1973) to police officers' behavior while on law enforcement patrol (e.g., Reiss, 1971).

Nonetheless, qualitative research does not generally involve the use of such fixed instruments, procedures, or samples. Although you might adopt a mechanical instrument to aid the data collection process, you are likely to remain as the main research instrument.

Each of the four data collection activities also produces a different kind of data (see Exhibit 6.1). The array shown in the exhibit should sensitize you to the varieties of data that are potentially relevant to doing qualitative research. Each type of data collection also has its limitations.

EXHIBIT 6.1. DATA COLLECTION METHODS AND TYPES OF DATA FOR QUALITATIVE RESEARCH

Data collection method	Illustrative types of data	Specific examples of data
Interviewing and conversing	Language (verbal and body)	Another person's explanation of some behavior or action; a recollection
Observing	People's gestures; social interactions; actions; scenes and the physical environment	Amount and nature of coordination between two people; spatial arrangements
Collecting	*Contents of:* personal documents, other printed materials, graphics, archival records, and physical artifacts	Titles, texts, dates, and chronologies; other written words; entries in an archival record
Feeling	Sensations	Coldness or warmth of a place; perceived time; interpretation of other people's comfort or discomfort

For instance, if your data collection only consists of interviewing and conversing and your main interest is in knowing how people actually behaved in a given situation, your data will be limited to your interactions with a set of participants and their *self-reported* behavior, beliefs, and perceptions. Depending on your study, these self-reports and how they are worded may reveal extremely important insights into how the participants may be thinking about or derive their own understanding of some behavior. However, you would be foolish to regard these self-reports as representing totally accurate renditions of the real-life behavior and how it actually transpired.

You also may interview and converse with participants because, as in many qualitative psychology studies, you value the reality of what people say (e.g., Willig, 2009). In this case, you would analyze the spoken words and phrases and not necessarily try to relate them to any specific behavior. To do a complete analysis of a conversational interaction, you could go beyond analyzing the spoken words and examine the nonverbal portions of the conversation between two (or more) people, including people's tone of voice, pauses, interruptions of each other, and other mannerisms (e.g., Drew, 2009).

As another example and from the opposite perspective, if you enter a field setting but only observe and do not interview or converse with the participants, your data will consist of observations of human actions and the physical environment at the site, but you will not derive any self-reported insights from those whom you are observing. You also will not know the meaning that the participants impute onto the events.

To gain more detailed insights into these limitations as well as to use the four data collection activities in your own research, the remainder of this chapter discusses them in greater depth, in two ways. The first presents each type of data collection activity separately, to appreciate their characteristics and associated procedures. The second then points to some desirable data collection practices that pertain to all of the different kinds of activities as a group.

C. INTERVIEWING

PREVIEW—*What you should learn from this section:*
1. The differences between structured and qualitative interviews.
2. Hints at conversing successfully as part of a qualitative interview.
3. The usefulness of probes and follow-up questions and other desirable interactions in a qualitative interview.
4. Procedures for conducting group interviews

Interviews can take many forms, but for the sake of argument you may consider all of the forms to fall into either of two types: *structured interviews* and *qualitative interviews.*[1] The following discussion deliberately stereotypes the two, to provide a clear contrast between them. (Experienced researchers may have devised their own ways of mixing the two types, but such combinations are usually highly customized and are beyond the scope of the present text.)

Structured Interviews

All interviews involve an interaction between an interviewer and a participant (or interviewee). Structured interviews carefully script this interaction. First, the researcher will use a formal questionnaire that lists every question to be asked. Second, the researcher will formally adopt the role of an interviewer, trying to elicit responses from an interviewee. Third, the researcher as interviewer will try to adopt the same consistent behavior and demeanor when interviewing every participant. The interviewer's behavior and demeanor are therefore also scripted, usually the result of some earlier and study-specific training aimed at conducting the data collection as uniformly as possible.

When people use the term *interviewing*, they usually refer to structured interviews. People think of interviews as being part of some sort of survey or poll. These studies also call for drawing a representative sample of participants or interviewees, closely attending to the definition and drawing of the sample to make it as precise as possible. Appropriate statistical tests then assess the link between a study's findings and the sample's larger population.

Given all these conditions, if a study only uses structured interviews, the study is most likely to be a survey or poll, not a qualitative study. If you emulate completely the methods used in conducting structured interviews but also use qualitative methods to collect and analyze additional kinds of data, you are likely to be doing a *mixed methods research* study, discussed further in Chapter 12.

Aside from having a distinctive set of procedures, structured interviews also tend to favor certain kinds of questions—namely, questions where interviewees are limited to a set of responses predefined by the researcher, otherwise known as *closed-ended questions*. Whether a survey takes the form of telephone interviews, face-to-face interviews, or "intercept" interviews in shopping malls and public places, the procedure is designed to ask all of the interviewees the same set of questions, each having a limited set of response categories (Fontana & Frey, 2005).

Many survey researchers believe that these closed-ended questions lead to more accurate data and a more definitive analysis. For instance, two noted survey researchers observe that "the answers are probably more reliable and valid when a list is provided than when the question is asked in open form" (Fowler & Cosenza,

---

[1]The term *qualitative interviewing* was preferred over alternatives such as *unstructured interviewing*, *intensive interviewing*, and *in-depth interviewing*, because qualitative interviewing has become sufficiently diverse that, under different circumstances, it may include any of the variants in some combination. See the discussion in Robert Weiss's brief Appendix A, "Other Names for Qualitative Interviewing" (1994).

2009, p. 398). Overall, survey research has had a long history of dealing with this and other issues of questionnaire design (e.g., Sudman & Bradburn, 1982).

Qualitative Interviews

Doing qualitative interviews is likely to be the overwhelmingly dominant mode of interviewing in qualitative research. This type of interview differs in key ways from structured interviews.

First, the relationship between the researcher and the participant is not strictly scripted. There is no questionnaire containing the complete list of the questions to be posed to a participant. The researcher will have a mental framework of study questions, but the specifically verbalized questions as posed to any given participant will differ according to the context and setting of the interview.

Second, the qualitative researcher does not try to adopt any uniform behavior or demeanor for every interview. Rather, the qualitative interview follows a conversational mode, and the interview itself will lead to a social relationship of sorts, with the quality of the relationship individualized to every participant (see "Qualitative Interviewing as a Social Relationship," Vignette 6.1).

VIGNETTE 6.1. QUALITATIVE INTERVIEWING AS A SOCIAL RELATIONSHIP

Entire textbooks have been devoted to qualitative interviewing. One of them, by Irving Seidman (2006), neatly discusses the procedures and underlying philosophies in doing such interviews.

Among the book's many features is a helpful chapter on "interviewing as a relationship" (2006, pp. 95–111). For instance, the chapter suggests that the relationship needs to be friendly but is not a friendship. The chapter also notes the challenge of "saying enough . . . to be . . . responsive but little enough to preserve the autonomy of the participant's words" (p. 96).

Another part of Seidman's book advises against certain kinds of interviews that have an unwanted influence on the interview relationship, such as supervisors interviewing people whom they supervise, teachers interviewing their own students, and fieldworkers interviewing their acquaintances and friends (2006, pp. 41–42). All these situations produce mixed and unclear interview relationships.

Overall, the book helps readers to understand the basic objective of qualitative interviewing—that is, to pursue "an interest in understanding the lived experience of other people and the meaning they make of that experience" (2006, p. 9).

This conversational mode, compared to structured interviews, presents the opportunity for two-way interactions, in which a participant even may query the researcher. In addition, qualitative interviews can take place between the researcher and a group of persons rather than a single person only.

In the conversational mode, participants may vary in the directness of their words, being candid at some points but coy at others, and the researcher will need to know how to distinguish the two. As a result, "qualitative interviewing requires intense listening . . . and a systematic effort to really hear and understand what people tell you" (Rubin & Rubin, 1995, p. 17). The listening is "to hear the meaning of what is being said" (p. 7).

Third, the more important questions in a qualitative interview will be *open-* rather than *closed*-ended questions. Having participants limit their responses to single-word answers would be a qualitative researcher's last wish. On the contrary, the researcher tries to have participants use their own words, not those predefined by the researcher, to discuss topics.

These three surface distinctions reflect a much deeper difference between structured and qualitative interviews. Structured interviews follow directly the word usage, phrases, and hence meaning of the researchers, whereas qualitative interviews aim at understanding participants "on their own terms and how they make meaning of their own lives, experiences, and cognitive processes" (Brenner, 2006, p. 357). This aim suits one of the fundamental objectives of qualitative research, which is to depict a complex social world from a participant's perspective.

Structured interviews also are limited in their ability to appreciate trends and contextual conditions across a participant's lifetime, whereas qualitative interviews may dwell on these trends and conditions. Such coverage is made possible in part because qualitative interviews may be much longer than structured ones and may involve a series of interviews with the same participant. For instance, the same participant may be interviewed three times, each for 90 minutes, over a period of days if not weeks. The first of the three interviews may establish the context of a participant's experience, typically by covering the participant's personal background; the second interview may have the participant reconstruct the details of the experience that is the topic of study; and a third interview may ask the participant to reflect on the meaning of the experience (Seidman, 2006, pp. 16–19).

In addition, structured and qualitative interviews have two contrasting impacts on those conducting the interviews. When doing structured interviews, a researcher tries to repeat the same set of questions and to present the same personal demeanor with every interviewee. A researcher who does a lot of interviews in this manner on the same day may feel *physically* exhausted at the end of the day but may still have a surplus of *mental energy*.

In contrast, when doing qualitative interviews, a researcher tries to understand a participant's world, which is likely to include concentrated efforts at mastering the meanings of the participant's words and phrases. The line of questioning is not controlled by a questionnaire but requires the researcher to exert continual mental energy. A researcher who does a lot of interviews in this manner on the same day will feel *mentally* exhausted at the end of the day but may still have a surplus of *physical energy*.

Doing Qualitative Interviews

The conversational mode in qualitative interviews resembles the conversing that is a natural part of everyone's routine spoken communications. For this very reason, it is *not* easy to do as a research procedure. Paradoxically, the challenge can be even more difficult when a researcher and participant speak in the same tongue. The participant may use special or everyday words with meanings unfamiliar to researchers, who in turn may inadvertently presume that they know the meanings. Such difficulties arise especially when a qualitative study focuses on cultural matters, as in societal cultures but also in examining the culture of places, such as institutions (Spradley, 1979).

To converse successfully as part of a qualitative interview requires practice. You must "learn from people" rather than study them (Spradley, 1979, p. 3). A few hints follow.

1. *Speaking in modest amounts.* One important practice is to try to speak less than the other person—much less. You need to find ways of querying others that will lead to extended dialogues on their part. The opposite and undesirable situation arises when you pose a lengthy question that is essentially a "yes/no" question, to which the other person can satisfactorily respond by giving a one-word answer, namely, "yes" or "no."

You also need to avoid asking multiple questions that are embedded in the same sentence, or alternatively asking multiple questions on top of each other without giving the other person a chance to respond to the first question. Remember that conversing does not mean interrogating, and your relatively fewer words still need to be sufficient (1) to keep a healthy conversation going; (2) to demonstrate your sincere interest in the other person's responses; and (3) to resemble, in all other respects, a normal conversation.

One key to keeping a conversation going with a minimum of your own words is to master the use of probes and follow-up questions. After a participant has made an insightful comment but one that is possibly shorter than desired, judicious use of probes and follow-up questions can stimulate the participant to expand upon the original comment. As a conversing tactic, probes need not appear in the same form as they do in closed-ended questionnaires. The conversing probes may take the form of brief utterances, such as: *uh-huh, say more, why?, how come?, say that another way,* or remarkably, a silent but deliberate pause. However, be careful not to overuse such probes. To the participant, you still must be an active and intelligent conversant. You cannot start to sound like someone who has been programmed like a robot.

2. *Being nondirective.* A second important practice is to be as nondirective as possible. Your goal is to let participants vocalize their own priorities as part of their own way of describing the world as they perceive it. To take but a simple example, among the alternative perspectives even may be the sequence of topics discussed by a participant. The sequence may differ from the one that you had planned to follow. However, by giving participants an opportunity to follow their own sequences, later analyses might reveal an important part of the participants' perspectives.

As a result of trying to avoid being directive, which includes signalling any sequence of topics, how you open a qualitative interview, with an initial query or statement, becomes critical. You need to set the boundaries for the conversation but nevertheless permit the participant to color it—as well as giving the participant an opportunity to move outside of the boundaries when needed. To deal with these conditions, researchers have identified *grand tour* questions as one feasible way of starting their conversing (Spradley, 1979, pp. 86–88). A grand tour question establishes a broad topic or scene but does not bias the conversation by presenting a specific item of interest, much less any particular sequence of topics (see "Using 'Grand Tour' Questions to Start Your Conversing," Vignette 6.2).

VIGNETTE 6.2. USING "GRAND TOUR" QUESTIONS TO START YOUR CONVERSING

The initial question in an open-ended interview or conversation is not easy to identify. Several motives are in play at the same time: to give the interview a sufficiently rich start so that the interviewee can respond expansively (and comfortably) rather than with a short answer; to get the interview started on a topic relevant to the research study; and to direct the interviewee in as minimal way as possible.

Researchers like Mary Brenner (2006) commonly refer to "grand tour" questions as satisfying these motives most of the time. She credits Spradley (1979) with having first described the format. In education, potential grand tour questions might cover recent events at a school (e.g., "What have been the main developments at the school this year?") or the role of the person being interviewed (e.g., "What are your responsibilities as principal of this school?"). Once started, the interviewer can then ask follow-up questions on more specific aspects of the "grand tour," eventually getting to the desired level of detail.

Beyond the initial opening, remaining nondirective throughout a qualitative interview also is important. This is especially true if your inquiry is trying to get at the salience of some topic in participants' worlds by using their own words. You may want to infer the importance a participant assigns to a topic by listening for its first mention. In such a case, if instead you happen to make the first mention, assessing the salience will be impossible (see "Nondirectively Interviewing People about the Key Topic of Study," Vignette 6.3).

3. *Staying neutral.* This third practice is part of being nondirective but serves as a reminder that your entire presentation of self during the conversing process— your body language and your expressions, as well as your words—needs to be carefully cast in a neutral manner. You need to be sure that the content and mannerisms of your responses to the participant's words or queries do not convey your own biases or preferences that in turn will affect the participant's subsequent retort. The least desirable conversation occurs where participants try to please or otherwise cater to you—as opposed to expressing their candid views. The catering is more likely to occur when your tone of voice, mannerisms, or other interpersonal signals contain an approving or disapproving intimation.

VIGNETTE 6.3. NONDIRECTIVELY INTERVIEWING PEOPLE ABOUT THE KEY TOPIC OF STUDY

Nationalist Politics and Everyday Ethnicity in a Transylvanian Town (Brubaker et al., 2006) deals with an extremely abstract subject: "ethnicity and nationhood as they are represented and contested in the political sphere" (p. xiii). The study focuses on everyday life in a Romanian town as the setting for fieldwork between 1995 and 2001. All of the authors spoke Romanian and Hungarian. They recorded well over 100 interviews, held numerous group discussions (also transcribed), and made sustained observations as participant-observers. The resulting book, also building on a scholarly collection of historical literature, combines a compelling historical perspective with an enormous amount of contemporary field evidence.

The fieldwork highlights the role of ethnicity and the mix of Romanian and Hungarian presences in the town of Cluj. To reduce bias, Brubaker and colleagues exercised extreme care in their interviews, avoiding direct reference to ethnicity because it "is all too easy to find if one goes looking for it" (2006, p. 381). Instead, interviews began with topics "with no prima facie connection to ethnicity," covering everyday events and then allowing "ethnicity to emerge spontaneously, if at all, in the course of discussion" (p. 383). The book's preface, introductory chapter, and appended "note on data" give further details about how the authors pursued this task as well as their other field strategies.

See also Vignette 11.5.

Philosophically, experienced qualitative researchers recognize that true neutrality may not exist. Qualitative interviews are interpersonal activities or social encounters that occur in natural settings (e.g., Fontana & Frey, 2005); under these conditions, you will inevitably bring a point of view to all of your conversations, producing a *negotiated text* (pp. 716–717). The desired remedy is to avoid blatant biases but also to be sensitive to those that remain. Later, you should do your best to reveal and discuss how they might affect your findings (see "Presenting Your *Reflective* Self," in Chapter 11, Section D).

4. *Maintaining rapport.* A fourth practice is interpersonal. You need to maintain good rapport with the participant. Because you have created the particular research situation, you also have a special responsibility to avoid conversations that might do harm to the other person—for example, using words that lead to hateful thoughts, the divulgence of totally private if not criminal topics, or undue unhappiness on the part of the participant.

In summary, these first four practices are not easy to follow. All your interviews will have their own context and situation that will govern how you specifically follow each practice. As described by one writer, the goal is to get to the heart of the matter, or what might be called "accelerated intimacy" (Wilkerson, 2007):

> I do everything I can to make my subjects feel comfortable enough to talk with me. I still ask questions—lots of them. I try to be a great audience. I nod; I look straight into their eyes; I laugh at their jokes, whether I think they're funny or not. I am serious when they are serious.

5. *Using an interview protocol.* This additional practice can guide you in your interviews. The protocol should substantively reflect the broader study protocol that might exist (see Chapter 5, Choice 7), but the interview protocol itself will be modest in size.

The interview protocol usually contains a small subset of topics—those that are considered relevant to a given interview. Each topic might be followed by some brief probes and follow-up queries, but the interview protocol should in no sense be considered a questionnaire. Thus, the protocol again represents your *mental framework* (see Chapter 5, Choice 8) and is not a list of the actual questions to be verbalized to a participant.

When used properly, an interview protocol therefore produces a "guided conversation," with the protocol serving as a conversational guide (Rubin & Rubin, 1995, pp. 145, 161–164). Moreover, if desired, you can retain a guide in its written form and hold it as a "prop" during an interview. Such use can have a surprising benefit. For instance, seeing you hold the guide and being able to glance at its topics, participants may feel that they are part of a more formal inquiry and may be more self-revealing on controversial issues (Rubin & Rubin, 1995, p. 164). However, if you raised such issues as part of a completely casual conversation, without showing my formal guide as a "prop," a participant might not take you as seriously and might be inclined to ignore your query.

6. *Analyzing when interviewing.* As a final reminder, and as with any other data collection in qualitative research, data collection is constantly accompanied by analysis. You will be deciding when to probe for more detail, when to shift topics, and when to modify your original protocol or agenda to accommodate new revelations. These all are analytic choices, and you need to make them sensitively, so that the other person is neither surprised nor lost by your part of the conversation.

"Entering" and "Exiting" Qualitative Interviews

Your grand tour or other initial question represents your initial substantive question. However, this is not where your conversing likely began. You more likely would have exchanged some initial pleasantries with the other person, possibly part of a more formal introduction to your interview-to-be that also reflects the provisions for informed consent (see Chapter 2, Section E).

Similarly, when your conversation has ended, the final interchange of words is not likely to be a substantive one but again will conclude with some sort of interpersonal flourish calling attention to the ending of the conversation. Polite "thank-you's" and well-wishes for the remainder of the day are typical.

How you start and end your conversation are largely matters of courtesy and culture. Possibly for this reason most textbooks do not call attention to these two phases of a conversation and therefore of qualitative interviews. Nevertheless, the entrances and exits are among my favorites in suggesting how conversing can proceed in doing qualitative research.

First, you should know two things about entrances and exits. The "entering" can clearly set an interpersonal tone that will carry into the substantive conversation, so you should prepare your "entering" dialogue and not just wander into it. Think about how you want to approach each person you interview and the topics you want to cover *before* starting any new conversations. Think about the possibility that "entering" a conversation may not differ from the broader challenge in doing fieldwork of "entering" the field.

The "exiting" can be even more important. Two famous television detectives, now considerably out-of-date to contemporary viewers (one, a man named "Columbo" and played by the actor Peter Falk, and the other a woman named "Jessica Fletcher" and played by Angela Lansbury) chronically used the "exit" mode as the opportunity to ask additional substantive questions. Typically, the person being interviewed thought the conversation was in its exiting phase and had in some way let down her or his guard. The detective, having put on a coat and even appearing to walk away, then turns and says, "Oh, by the way . . . " and appears to get an important piece of information while in the (presumed) exiting mode.

Another comment about exiting: You may have noticed that professional conversations with your colleagues in everyday life occasionally can become unexpectedly prolonged—far beyond the time that was either intended or available. Sometimes, this is because you and your colleague (unknowingly) both need to have the "last word." Every time one of you says something, the other person needs to say something back, and so on. Be sure that you do not let this happen in your data collecting conversations. The remedy is to harness your ego and let the other person have the last word.

Interviewing Groups of People

There will be occasions, planned or unplanned, when you have the opportunity to interview a *group* of people. The group may be small (2 to 3 persons) or of moderate size (7 to 10 persons). These opportunities call for careful preparation and responses on your part.

You might treat very small groups (2 to 3 persons) as adjuncts of interviewing individuals. You may direct your attention to one of these persons while still being appropriately respectful to the others and not making them feel like they only have subsidiary roles.

Once your group exceeds a very small size, however, you need to direct your attention to the entire group, not any single individual. This is a difficult challenge, and you should avoid interviewing the moderately sized groups until you first have had some practice and experience with such groups, independent of your ongoing qualitative study. If you have not had such practice, set up some opportunities within your academic or personal groups.

Focus Group Interviewing as a Method of Collecting Qualitative Data

The research literature considers "focus groups" as the main type of moderately sized groups, and many texts and articles cover this type of data collection (e.g., Stewart, Shamdasani, & Rook, 2009). The groups are "focused" because you have gathered individuals who previously have had some common experience or presumably share some common views (see "A Distinguished 'Manual' for Collecting Focus Group Data," Vignette 6.4). When conversing with such groups, you would serve as what has been defined as a *moderator*. Moderators try to induce all the members of a group to express their opinions but with minimum, if any, direction.

VIGNETTE 6.4. A DISTINGUISHED "MANUAL" FOR COLLECTING FOCUS GROUP DATA

The Focused Interview: A Manual of Problems and Procedures, by Robert K. Merton, Marjorie Fiske, and Patricia L. Kendall, is among the numerous books and guidances on how to collect focus group data. First published in 1956, the second edition was issued in 1990 and contains detailed and helpful hints on how to organize focus groups, develop opening questions, and serve as a successful moderator. The book reviews focus group dynamics and gives concrete suggestions (e.g., seating the groups in a circular or semicircular arrangement so the moderator can be part of the group), and it presents important cautions still highly relevant today.

Unlike many latter-day guidances, Merton et al.'s book comes from an age when qualitative and quantitative research were genuinely complementary endeavors, as in conducting studies of mass communications. Merton and his colleagues were eminent sociologists and part of a renowned scholarly group at Columbia University's Bureau of Applied Social Research that also blazed the frontier for conducting sample surveys and conducting statistical analyses.

- For instance, a study engaged the caregivers of older family members in a series of focus groups. The goal was to gain the caregivers' perspectives on the institutionalization and diagnosis of these older members, rather than assuming that the researchers already had this knowledge, as well as to avoid permitting the researchers' predispositions on these topics to influence an initial line of questions (Morgan, 1992, p. 206).

Focus groups originally began as a way of collecting data about how sample audiences might have perceived a particular radio program or other types of mass

communications (Merton, Fiske, & Kendall, 1990). One obvious trade-off compared to interviewing individuals is the gain in efficiency (speaking with several
people at the same time) but a loss in depth (gaining less information from any
single participant). However, a major rationale for conducting group interviews
does not have to do with this trade-off. Rather, group interviews are desirable when
you suspect that people (e.g., youngsters and children) may more readily express
themselves when they are part of a group than when they are the target of a solo
interview with you. Conversely, if a participant appears silent in a group setting, you
still may try to have a brief solo interview with that person at the end of the group
session.

Focus groups have their own dynamics that you will need to manage. Successfully moderating a focus group is a skill that you are likely to develop only with
experience. For instance, there is high risk that one or two persons will dominate a
group's discussion. You will have to have an appropriately polite but firm style that
controls the overtalkative persons and stimulates the reticent ones—all without
influencing and hence biasing the group's discussion. Similarly, there may come
a point when the entire group is silent. You will need to find the words to restart
the group's conversation, again without biasing its direction. Finally, one or more
members of the group may start to ask questions of you or the others. On the spot,
you will immediately have to decide whether their questions help or hinder your
agenda—and you will have to behave accordingly, in real time.

As a further variation, you may collect data from a number of focus groups,
not just a single group. If you can successfully master the procedures, and if the
focus groups provide a sufficient amount of data, the multiple focus groups even
may provide the bulk of your field data (see "Using Focus Groups as the Only Data
from the 'Field,'" Vignette 6.5).

VIGNETTE 6.5. USING FOCUS GROUPS AS THE ONLY DATA FROM THE "FIELD"

Sometimes an important topic does not lend itself to traditional fieldwork. Such has
been the case with an important issue in public education, where advocates want
students to have a greater ability to select the school they are to attend (most public
school systems assign students to a particular school). Across the country, "school
choice" arrangements therefore have continued to be tested.

To understand how school choice has worked from the standpoint of the students and their families, a research team organized a series of focus groups. The
team carefully selected the participants, held the focus groups, and recorded and
transcribed the discussions. The data served as the main evidence for an entire qualitative study.

The "consumer"-oriented data have been highly valued. However, carrying out
conventional fieldwork would have been difficult and not very revealing. Unless one
follows a particular student around (highly obtrusive and likely to produce strong
"researcher" effects), there is not much to experience or "see" in a school choice setting because the arrangements do not involve new educational practices.

D. OBSERVING

PREVIEW—*What you should learn from this section:*
1. Ways of dealing with bias and potential lack of representativeness in making field observations.
2. The variety of items that can be the subject of observations.

"Observing" can be an invaluable way of collecting data because what you see with your own eyes and perceive with your own senses is not filtered by what others might have (self-) reported to you or what the author of some document might have seen. In this sense, your observations are a form of *primary data*, to be highly cherished. Not surprisingly, strictly observational studies have been a long-standing part of the research methods in social psychology (e.g., Weick, 1968). There, the researcher is completely passive.

Doing "Systematic Observation" as the Basis for an Entire Qualitative Study

In qualitative research, you also may assume a totally passive role, although you are more likely also to engage in some participatory activity. Regardless of the degree of passivity, the most formal observational methods will typically include a formal (observational) instrument and the identification of a specific set of occasions for making the observations (see "Systematic Observations in School Classrooms," Vignette 6.6).

VIGNETTE 6.6. SYSTEMATIC OBSERVATIONS IN SCHOOL CLASSROOMS

School classrooms present a common opportunity for making systematic observations. Such observations were conducted by Borman et al. (2005) as part of a larger study of mathematics and science education in four public school systems across the country.

The researchers observed nearly 200 classrooms at all grade levels, using a formal observational instrument provided as part of a methodological appendix (2005, pp. 225–227). Such instruments typically ask observers to make qualitative judgments—for example, whether an instructional practice appears to be teacher-centered, subject-centered, or student-centered—and then to rate the extent of such practices during a classroom period. The ratings can produce quantitative evidence about the behavior being observed. Borman et al. followed this procedure, presenting a tally of the observations and then discussing the patterns found (pp. 96–103). One such pattern reported by the authors was that "roughly one-quarter of the teachers we observed were engaged in lessons that involved reviewing material previously presented to the class" (p. 103).

Such systematic observational studies may be an excellent example of the complementarity of qualitative and quantitative research methods. One way is illustrated by having a sufficiently large sample that will permit data to be tallied. Another way would be to use a quasi-experimental design that deliberately identifies two different groups that happen to differ by having some type of "treatment" or "no treatment" condition (e.g., smokers versus nonsmokers) but who otherwise have similar characteristics. (The paradigm is "quasi"-experimental because it does not manipulate the treatment and no-treatment conditions; if it did, the paradigm would be "experimental.")

Thus, do not be surprised to find that the term *observational studies*, as you search the methodological literature review, can refer to heavily statistical and quasi-experimental works, typically in the field of social psychology (see "'Observational Studies' Also Refer to Research Defined by Statistical Principles and Methods," Vignette 6.7). Despite the statistics, these observational studies still share some common features with qualitative research, such as highlighting the importance of rival explanations.

VIGNETTE 6.7. "OBSERVATIONAL STUDIES" ALSO REFER TO RESEARCH DEFINED BY STATISTICAL PRINCIPLES AND METHODS

Although observations are a common method of collecting qualitative data, observational studies also can refer to statistical studies. These studies resemble experimental studies because a "treatment" is the subject of study, but the researcher cannot manipulate the treatment.

Statistics aside, the studies share important common principles with those in doing qualitative research. Paul Rosenbaum's *Observational Studies* (2002) shows how to apply these principles, which include the helpfulness of starting with *elaborate* theories; the need to avoid *hidden* bias; and the importance of entertaining rival explanations. For case study research, two other principles include: selecting cases whose outcomes already are known; and assessing multiple outcomes within the same case. You can decide whether these and other common principles begin to demonstrate the unity rather than fragmentation of the social sciences.

Deciding When and Where to Observe

Most qualitative research will not be based solely on your making observations at a single, fixed location. In acting as a participant-observer, you are likely to locate yourself in some field setting that is fluid in time and space. Such fluidity will require you to make explicit decisions about your observational procedures.

For instance, whether you use a formal instrument or not, the fluidity means that you cannot be at all places at all times. If a scene is sufficiently complex, you also cannot watch everything that is going on. The resulting selectivity, regarding "when" and "where" to observe, needs to be an explicit part of your data collection procedure. You may not have a strict rationale for making your decisions, but you need to be aware of their consequences: What you observe and record will not necessarily be either the most important events taking place or representative of all that is occurring in the field setting.

The first way of giving this matter your careful attention is simply to record your observational times and locations, which would include noting the participants present in the field setting when you were doing your observations. You also would make a summary notation of the type of event (or nonevent) that seems to be taking place.

Another way of reducing bias and lack of representativeness is to make your observations on multiple occasions. If possible, you could initially "size up" your site and later schedule your observational opportunities to cover different times of day (if not different days or even seasons); slightly different locations within the same field setting; and occasions when different people are present. (Of course, such scheduling would not be relevant if your observations focused on a unique situation or event.)

Notwithstanding how you make your choices, a final way of buttressing your observational data collection is to discuss your choices and their possible consequences as part of your personal journal (see Chapter 7, Section E). You should conjecture how your decisions might have affected your findings and conclusions. From these, you should express any caveats or cautions (or distinctive strengths) about your work.

Deciding What to Observe

Many items can be the subject of your observations. The salience of these items depends on the topic of your qualitative research. The relevant categories can include:

◆ The characteristics of individual people, including their dress, gestures, and nonverbal behavior;

◆ The interactions between or among people;

◆ The "actions" taking place, whether human or mechanical; and

◆ The physical surroundings, including visual and audio cues.

Part of the last category covers what might be called *props* (Murphy, 1980), which include the wall hangings, posters, plaques, books on bookshelves, and other objects associated with a specific person or that person's organization. The props can provide clues about earlier events that might have been meaningful to an individual or an organization; at a minimum, the props can serve as a point of departure in starting a qualitative interview.

Taking Advantage of Unobtrusive Measures

The issue of reflexivity, discussed throughout this book, readily arises when you observe any human being or human activity. Your presence will have an unknown influence on the other persons. Conversely, their activity may directly influence the way you do your observations. Such reflexivity is unavoidable and again deserves some comment in your final methodological report.

The chances of reflexivity are minimized, if not eliminated, when you observe features in the physical world that nevertheless can be highly revealing about some prior human activity. Physical traces of human activity, such as the turned corners of the pages in a book that has been read by someone else, as well as photographs and recordings made by others as part of their everyday lives, all can be considered the source of what have been called *unobtrusive measures* (Webb et al., 1966, 1981). The main value of these measures is that they involve "nonreactive" situations, where you as a researcher cannot have influenced the participants' behavior that produced the physical traces (see "'Unobtrusive Measures' As the Subject of Observations," Vignette 6.8).

VIGNETTE 6.8. "UNOBTRUSIVE MEASURES" AS THE SUBJECT OF OBSERVATIONS

Unobtrusive measures record aspects of the social and physical environment already in place, not manipulated by researchers or affected by their presence. The useful features of such measures—also called *nonreactive measures*—were extensively reported by a group of notable nonqualitative as well as qualitative scholars (Webb et al., 1981).

Physical traces, such as a worn pathway across a campus lawn showing where people actually walk from building to building, are prime examples of such measures. As another example, archives can include photographic and videotaped materials homemade during everyday routines and therefore *not* recorded by the researcher (Webb et al., 1981, p. 247). Whereas nonqualitative studies might count unobtrusive measures in some manner, qualitative studies might try to discern their meaning.

Because of their nonreactivity, unobtrusive measures readily complement other measures, such as the use of interviews and questionnaires, which can suffer from the reactivity effects when researchers are the primary research instrument (Webb et al., 1981, p. 241). In this sense, unobtrusive measures can be an integral part of qualitative studies.

The collection of unobtrusive measures alone will not likely produce sufficient evidence to support a qualitative study fully. However, you can use the measures to complement the collection of interview or other data within the same qualitative study. Because these other data are susceptible to a researcher's influence, having some data that are based on a nonreactive source can greatly strengthen your study. Whether one or more unobtrusive measures might be relevant to your study therefore deserves your careful consideration.

Deriving Meaning from Observations, and Triangulating Observational Evidence with Other Sources

Even if you are dealing with unobtrusive measures, what makes observing difficult is that you will not simply want to record observations as if you were a mechanical device. Your qualitative study is likely to be concerned with broader concepts regarding people's social behavior, such as their routines, rituals, and interactions with other people. You need to make and record your observations so that you will have the opportunity, if not at the time of your observations at least in your later analytic procedures, to define these more meaningful concepts.

The meanings you derive from your observations will be inferences of a sort—for example, whether a particular interaction between two people represented the disapproval of one person by the other, or whether the office trappings of an official reflect a person of high status in an organization. You can strengthen these inferences by collecting other data, such as interview data, to corroborate or challenge your inferences. Doing so would be an example of "triangulating" that is an essential part of qualitative data collection and that is discussed more fully later in this chapter.

E. COLLECTING AND EXAMINING

PREVIEW—*What you should learn from this section:*
1. The variety of objects that can be collected and examined.
2. Two ways of keeping the collection of objects within reasonable limits regarding the time and effort you spend in your fieldwork.

"Collecting" refers to the compiling or accumulating of objects (documents, artifacts, and archival records) related to your study topic. Most of the collecting will occur while you are in the field, but you also can collect objects from other sources, including libraries, historical archives, and electronically based sources (see "Intertwining Historical and Field Evidence," Vignette 6.9). Sometimes, you will not be able to take an object away with you. In these situations, you may want to spend time examining it. This subsection's reference to "collecting" is intended to include such examining.

Any of the collected (or examined) objects can produce a variety of verbal, numeric, graphic, and pictorial data. The data can be about the physical and social environment (e.g., existing pictures of a field setting and its members) but also can yield invaluable data about things not directly observable (e.g., abstract topics such as an organization's policies and procedures, as represented in documents), human relationships (e.g., an exchange of letters between two people), and more historical information (e.g., trends revealed by archival records). In addition, collected objects can include those produced directly by participants, such as their journals and photographs, whose use might complement the information obtained from interviews with the participants (e.g., Murray, 2009, p. 118).

VIGNETTE 6.9. INTERTWINING HISTORICAL AND FIELD EVIDENCE

Qualitative research can combine fieldwork with the extensive examination of historical archives. This is what Circe Sturm did in her study (2002) of the Cherokee Nation, the nation's largest tribe and one that "has a large and diverse multiracial population" (p. 2).

The fieldwork took place over a three-year period in the Cherokee Nation and its communities in northeastern Oklahoma, emphasizing interviews with numerous individuals. The historical work involved access to university and special archives as well as the collections of the Cherokee National Historical Society and an attorney's personal papers on Cherokee freedmen legal cases.

The author compiled the information from these sources into a book that traces Cherokee identity politics and self-identities—and their basis in blood quantum (ranging from full to 1/2,048 degree Cherokee blood), color, and race—through three centuries. The voices of those interviewed are sprinkled throughout a largely historical narrative. The result is the creation of a literally living history.

See also Vignette 10.3.

Collecting Objects (e.g., Documents, Artifacts, and Archival Records) in the Field: Invaluable but Also Time-Consuming

Because these objects generally represent another form of primary evidence, they can be invaluable to your qualitative study. Computer printouts of students' work, for instance, can go a long way toward helping you to understand the content of the education occurring in a classroom. Similarly, an artifact such as a personal letter, a piece of art, or a personal memento also can be highly revealing. Finally, archival records such as population statistics, municipal service records on housing or crime, school records, or newspaper or magazine articles can provide important contextual information to complement your own fieldwork.

All these types of objects are likely to exist in great abundance, regardless of the topic of your study. As a result, collecting documents and records, even if they are already in electronic form, can be time-consuming. (Just think about the possibility of having to collect and review other people's e-mail records.) You therefore need to exert great care in deciding which objects deserve your attention and the amount of time you will devote to their collection.

Two tactics can help you to make such collection productive. First, get an initial idea of the full array of any type of object to be collected, such as the numerosity and scope of the available documents, or the size and range of an archive of statistical data. Also get an idea of the difficulty you will have in accessing and retrieving these objects. Then, decide whether you need to collect the entire array or whether a sample will do. If a sample is sufficient, define the sample carefully in order to minimize any unwanted bias.

Second, after doing some preliminary collecting, immediately review the resulting data. Consider how the collected material is likely to fit the rest of your study. Speculate whether the material will be central and useful to your study, in comparison to the other data you have or will be collecting. You may then decide to invest less (or even more) time in the collection effort. This second tactic also deserves repeating at some midpoint juncture, to test again how well you are spending your time.

Using Documents to Complement Field Interviews and Conversations

Many documents can be useful simply by the nature of the details they contain. These include the spelling of names, titles, and organizations, the affixing of specific dates to events, and the specific language used in mottos, slogans, mission statements, and other communications.

Prior to important interviews, you may have had the good fortune of reviewing many documents and knowing their contents, which will then keep you from having to interrupt an otherwise healthy flow of conversation by asking a participant, for instance, how to spell a name or title. You also might know ahead of time about the availability of various documents. Then, even if you have not reviewed them by the time of an important interview, you might guess that the documents will clarify details such as the spelling of names, so that you again will not have to interrupt your interviews to verify such information.

"Surfing" and "Googling" for Related Information

For most topics covered by qualitative research, these days you should probably spend some time checking for relevant Web-based information. The massive amount of available information is likely to have a few if not many useful clues for your research.

One of the most relevant searches will uncover other studies or literature on your topic of study. You even might have already searched for such material when you were defining your topic, as in amassing a study bank (see Chapter 3, Section A). Whether the search can provide the information needed for completing a literature review that will be needed as part of your research will depend on the access you have to the websites of various journals and bibliographic search engines—most of which require membership or fees of some sort. Again, you should be alert to the potentially time-consuming nature of this form of data collection, and you need to exercise the cautions previously discussed.

Of high priority in using Web-based information is to note, understand, and fully cite (in your study) the source of the information. Your understanding should include learning about any widely recognized biases associated with the source.

For instance, newspaper articles can be very helpful, but you should know something about the newspaper's reputation or political stance before accepting its news accounts at face value. You might find that metropolitan dailies and community papers differ substantially in their coverage of community events, especially racially charged ones (e.g., Jacobs, 1996). "Official" government reports may exclude unwanted information (see Chapter 12, Section B). Worse, blogs and personal postings can be entirely biased in their selection of the material to be available and their intended slant. Finally, press releases and other forms of overt publicity usually have some underlying motive that you must take into account before citing.

Collecting or Examining Objects as a Complementary Part of Your Data Collection

The collected objects can reduce the problems and challenges of *reflexivity*. These objects were created for some reason other than your inquiry and cannot be said to have been influenced by your inquiry.

In contrast, qualitative interviews can be reflexive in two directions: your influence on a participant but also the participant's influence on you. "Observing" can have a one-way reflexive effect—your influence on those being observed, regardless of the relative unobtrusiveness of your observing procedures. Collected documents, artifacts, and archival records suffer from neither type of reflexivity but must still be used with care. Although they were produced for some reason not related to reflexivity, you should still pay attention to their motive and hence potential slant.

F. FEELINGS

PREVIEW—*What you should learn from this section:*
The way that "feelings" can cover a variety of useful and important features in field settings.

Reference to "feelings" as a form of data is not intended to reignite the earlier discussion about the differences between assuming singular and multiple realities (see Chapter 1, Section C). Nor is the term *feelings* only used here to represent the results accompanying one's sense of touch. You need to think about feelings as covering a variety of traits within yourself that are potentially important in your research and that you should not ignore.

"Feelings" Take Different Forms

As an initial foray into this mode of data, realize that certain feelings represent explicit data about the environment (e.g., warmth/coldness, noisiness/quiet, or the temporal pace of a place). If you needed to, you could probably use a mechanical instrument to measure these aspects of the environment, but your "feelings" will usually be an acceptable substitute, even if they are not as precise.

Other feelings represent data about other people (e.g., feeling that someone is dependent/rebellious in a work setting, that two people are distant/close, or that a group works congenially/disruptively). These are more difficult to measure and do not necessarily align with the others' self-report in an interview or conversation— although if you have a chance you should always ask other people what they think about their own conditions. You should nevertheless not ignore your own feelings, which present another situation demanding corroboration or rejection by triangulating with other data.

Finally, yet other feelings are even more complex and may represent your intuitions or "gut feelings" about a situation. Such feelings are not limited to any single sensation and cannot always be explained. The intuitions can nevertheless provide important clues for interpreting what is transpiring in a given situation. You should again treat such feelings as needing to be corroborated (or challenged) by other data.

Documenting and Recording Feelings

The data here are your feelings. You should write these feelings down as carefully as possible, noting when and where they occurred. Along with the stated feeling, you also should describe as best as possible the event, behavior, or condition that seemed to have accounted for the feelings. These records may later give you greater insights when you collect other data about the same event, behavior, or condition.

G. DESIRABLE PRACTICES PERTINENT TO ALL MODES OF DATA COLLECTION

PREVIEW—*What you should learn from this section:*
Five important practices for doing good fieldwork.

Across all these forms of data collection, you should consider certain practices that will strengthen your work. At least five are important.

1. *Being a good "listener."* As previously discussed (see Chapter 2, Section B), the term *listening* refers to its figurative, not literal, meaning, and therefore to a desired way of attending to your surroundings. Thus, when observing, an equivalent trait would be your ability to be observant.

The social world that has presumably attracted you to qualitative research in the first place offers a complex and nuanced environment. Being a good listener ranges from letting others do more of the talking to being able to "listen between the lines" during a conversation. You also might have to "read between the lines" when interpreting a document or written message. When collecting qualitative data, you would not be exhibiting a desirable trait if you had what people call a "deaf ear" or were totally unaware of the possibility of subtextual meanings.

2. *Being inquisitive.* Being a good "listener" but also being inquisitive at the same time may at first appear to be conflicting postures. Without delving into cog-

nitive psychology, you can and should do both. The apparent conflict only arises if you associate being "inquisitive" with taking over a conversation and leading it—thereby diminishing the opportunity to "listen."

Instead, think of "being inquisitive" as a state of your mind. As you listen or observe, you also should be thinking about the meaning of what you hear or see, and this should lead to additional questions. You do not need to verbalize those questions at that very moment but can keep a mental note to make some later inquiry, even outside of the immediate interview or observational situation.

3. *Being sensitive in managing others' time—and yours, too.* The preceding sections have continually pointed to the likelihood that data collection can take a lot of time. If you are interviewing others, you are spending others' time and not just yours.

Participants have their own priorities and needs, and they do not have an endless amount of time to devote to your research inquiries. Find ways of learning about others' time restrictions or preferences and cater to them. Respecting these time restrictions or preferences will further reinforce a healthy relationship between you and the participants who are part of your study.

Similarly, be sensitive to your own time restrictions or preferences. Respecting them will make you happier with yourself—not a low-priority outcome either.

4. *Distinguishing between firsthand, secondhand, and thirdhand evidence.* This is an expanded version of distinguishing between primary and secondary evidence. The relevant dimension being depicted is one of filtering or being remote, with "primary" or "firsthand" evidence being data produced by a situation without being recorded by someone other than yourself. What you hear with your own ears or see with your own eyes are examples of firsthand evidence. Assuming that you have been sufficiently sensitive to the influence of reflexivity mentioned throughout this chapter, and all other things being equal, you would give your greatest credibility to your primary evidence.

The potential filtering by others begins with secondary or secondhand evidence. A historian's writing about events would be secondary evidence about those events. Similarly, what a participant tells you about something that has happened also is "secondhand" evidence about what happened (although the fact that you heard directly from a participant is still the firsthand evidence of what the participant said).

"Thirdhand" evidence is the most remote and occurs when there are two filters: Someone tells you (first filter) what she or he has heard another person say (second filter) about some event (the actual behavior you are wanting to learn about). If you cite a news article that is quoting another person speaking about an event, you are using thirdhand evidence (the journalist's writing being the first filter and the quoted person being the second filter).

Distinguishing among these three types of evidence does not mean you should ignore secondhand or thirdhand evidence. You are not likely to be able to complete a qualitative study by collecting only first-hand evidence.

The earlier discussion on "observing," for instance, pointed out how you can only be at one place at a time, even though important events may be happening elsewhere or at some other times. You will likely be using secondhand and third-hand evidence to cover a fuller range of events that you are unable to observe directly, and you should consider the second- or thirdhand evidence as containing valuable insights into your subject of study. The main point is that you should not rely solely on second- and thirdhand evidence without trying to obtain corroborating information from some other source—which leads to the next practice.

5. *Triangulating evidence from multiple sources.* This practice is discussed last because it may be extremely important to all forms of empirical research, not just qualitative research. The idea, previously introduced as an important way of strengthening the validity of a study (see Chapter 4, Choice 2), is to determine whether data from two or more sources converge or lead to the same finding. One example of convergence occurs when you observe an event or hear a person say something in a conversation, and your field colleague who is present also observes or hears the same thing, and you both draw the same conclusion after checking with each other. (The typical conversation between you, after leaving the event or conversation with the other person, begins with one of you saying "Did you see what I saw?" or "Did you hear what I heard?")

The more that you can show such convergence, especially on key findings, the stronger your evidence. Use of the term *triangulating* points to the ideal situation when evidence from three different sources converge. For instance, you saw something, someone else also at the scene saw the same thing, and a news article later reported the same thing.

As a final example, education research often focuses on the instructional practices that occur in a classroom. Separate evidence might result from your own observation inside the classroom (firsthand), your interviewing the teacher but not seeing the practice yourself (secondhand), or your interviewing the principal about what she or he thought was going on in a classroom without having been in it, either (thirdhand). You would feel better about your evidence if all three sources dealt with the same classroom events and agreed. You would be on thin ice if you relied solely on what the principal said, to define your rendition of the instructional practice that had taken place.

The role of triangulation carries great importance in doing qualitative research. Triangulating even may be thought of as a frame of mind rather than as a methodological technique—something that helps to keep your eyes and ears open for corroborating or conflicting ideas or data, whatever you are doing.

RECAP FOR CHAPTER 6: *Terms, phrases, and concepts that you can now define:*

1. Structured interviews

2. Qualitative interviews

3. Closed-ended and open-ended questions

4. Adhering to a strict script between researcher and participant

5. Being nondirective

6. Grand tour questions

7. Focus groups

8. Systematic observations and observational studies

9. Unobtrusive measures

10. Being inquisitive as a state of mind

11. First-, second-, and thirdhand evidence

EXERCISE FOR CHAPTER 6: CROSS-CHECKING TWO DIFFERENT SOURCES OF DATA (DOCUMENT REVIEW AND INTERVIEW)

Select a topic related to the operations of your university or workplace. The topic should cover important issues readily familiar to most people at your university or workplace (e.g., some recent institutional accomplishment, event, or ongoing dialogue). Retrieve some detailed documentation (i.e., not just a pamphlet) on the same topic, possibly finding a lengthy news article or other substantive document, possibly on the university's or workplace's website.

Prepare a brief protocol to guide you in conducting an open-ended interview with someone at your university or workplace, such as a peer, staff person, or faculty member on the same topic (because this is an exercise, a friend at your university or workplace also will be acceptable). Take field notes during the interview but do not formalize the notes until you do the exercise for Chapter 7.

Instead, focus your attention on your queries, which should be directed at comparing what the person reports to you with what appears in the document. For this exercise, you can create your own queries to suit your own interests, but you also can use the following as a suggested set (but note that the queries are directed at *you*, not the person you interviewed):

1. What are the major discrepancies, if any, between the person's awareness of the topic and its presentation in the document, and why might the discrepancies exist?

2. If there were few or no discrepancies, how did the person derive such a good understanding of the topic (i.e., did the person gain the understanding from the document you retrieved or from other sources, and if so, what sources)?

3. How does the person's depth of understanding of the underlying issues compare to what is presented in the documentation?

4. Regardless of the person's level of awareness or knowledge, in what ways, if any, might the person agree or disagree with the issues stated in the document?

CHAPTER 7

Recording Data

Deciding what to record is an integral part of collecting qualitative data. Moreover, to improve their completeness and accuracy, the initial notes taken during the actual fieldwork need to be reviewed and refined on a nightly basis. At such times, researchers will find that their original notes have gaps and uninterpretable jottings that can still be fixed. This chapter covers all of these note-taking practices, including the desire to capture words verbatim in the first place. The chapter also discusses the use of other types of recording devices, such as audio- and video-tapes, in addition to taking notes. Such recordings can be a qualitative study's main data collection technique and therefore deserve careful handling, including the need to obtain permission to use the devices and further permission to share their recordings. A final record needed in qualitative research is the keeping of a researcher's own journal.

You did say that you've been taking notes while reading or studying this book, didn't you? If you were actually doing a qualitative research study (and not just reading this book), you might have started taking notes for your study throughout the start-up and design procedures covered in Chapters 3 and 4, much less the actual data collection procedures as portrayed in Chapter 6. You also might have started a separate journal containing your private comments about your research experiences (see Section E).

Some people think that, in order to excel at qualitative research, taking notes and keeping journals are so essential that they need to be an integral part of one's persona. Those people may not be far wrong. Consider the words of one well-known writer who has completed bestselling books based on qualitative methods (Kidder, 1990):

> I usually take more than ten thousand pages of steno notes for a book. . . . I fill another set of notebooks with library research and standard office interviews. Once I have it all, I have to organize it. (Kidder, 2007, p. 52)

A separate but related observation involves the adjective "copious." Everyone knows what the word means and how to use it, but somehow it is rarely used outside of the phrase "copious notes."

This chapter discusses different forms of recording, not just writing notes. Nevertheless, note taking (and later reworking your field notes) is likely to be the dominant mode of recording when doing qualitative research. The note-taking mode therefore receives the most attention. The peculiar challenge is that you will have to take notes (or otherwise record your field data) while being an active participant in the field, as well as observing and listening to what is going on. You will not have the luxury of the laboratory or the classroom, where you can quietly take notes at a desk.

The virtual simultaneity of doing fieldwork and taking notes, hour after hour and day after day, means that the notes and other records do not just come after doing fieldwork, as in a strictly linear sequence. Your fieldwork clearly influences your recording procedures. Less appreciated, perhaps, is that the recording procedures, and especially note taking, can lead to helpful hints for the ongoing fieldwork—following a recursive rather than strictly linear relationship that is highly typical of qualitative research.

This book's discussion of these topics—data collection and recording— nevertheless must be presented linearly. For instance, Chapter 7 had to follow Chapter 6 even though some note taking could precede, accompany, and follow your data collection activities. Thus, in real life the activities in both chapters might overlap.

With regard to Chapter 7's focus on note taking and other modes of recording, let's start with the information you should be recording (Section A) and then discuss various recording practices (Sections B, C, D, and E).

A. WHAT TO RECORD

PREVIEW—*What you should learn from this section:*
1. Taking notes about actions and vivid images.
2. Capturing words verbatim.
3. Handling and taking notes about written materials collected at the field setting.

Trying to Record "Everything" versus Being Too Selective

Every researcher confronts this dilemma. Recording "everything" is impossible, but some people nevertheless take too many notes, well beyond the needs of their study. The burden of this effort is often transferred to participants, who must be asked either to speak more slowly or to pause while the researcher catches up with the note taking. The word of advice here is to learn how to record what you need without disrupting a participant's rhythm or pace. As with the way you dress and present yourself in the field, the note-taking process should be another silent partner and not call attention to itself. Even the physical movement used in taking notes should be as unobtrusive as possible.

The other extreme presents even greater problems. Record too little and you risk being inaccurate or not having enough information to analyze. You might not even have a study.

Between these extremes lies a golden mean. With experience in doing and completing several studies, every researcher finds her or his own comfort level. The goal is to take sufficient notes to support the later analytic and compositional needs, but not so many notes that much of your material will go unused. Also, having too many notes can sometimes paralyze you at the analytic stage because you won't know where to start sorting all of it.

Experience helps people to anticipate the most useful level of volume ahead of time. The golden mean then becomes synonymous with any given researcher's "style." Some researchers may be known to covet rich descriptive passages that emulate for the reader the experience of "being there," while other researchers may be known to provide compelling evidence for highly focused research questions. Yet other researchers may be known for repeatedly discovering something new and fascinating that was not part of the original study plan.

Highlighting Actions and Capturing Words Verbatim

Most people are likely to find their first day in the field to be overwhelming, even if they have done fieldwork before. What to record will be a challenge for experienced and novice researchers alike, but, for novices especially, some guidance can come from two strategies: highlighting the *actions* in the field and capturing words *verbatim*.

The "first day" may be a full-fledged observational opportunity or may simply be represented by the first field interview. In either situation, you may be confronted by too much unfamiliar territory. You will have little idea of the meaning of many observations, including identifying who is who. In the interview situation, you will have little familiarity with the context for your interviewee's remarks as well as the identity of the others who might be referenced in those remarks.

The note taking under these circumstances can be more tentative and even fragmentary. Your goal is to gain your own understanding of the new environment and participants rather than to take copious notes. "Listening" may be more important than "doing" and should be done with an open mind. In this process, an early challenge is to avoid premature stereotyping on your part, in either the observational or the interview situation.

In the observational situation, focusing on *actions* that take place in the field, as opposed to describing a person or a scene, is one way of noting what is going on while minimizing the stereotyping. The aim is to record a "vivid image" rather than a "visual stereotype" (Emerson, Fretz, & Shaw, 1995, pp. 70–71). The vivid images can involve the activities of a single person, of groups of persons, or of a participant-observer experience (see "Different Examples of 'Vivid Images,'" Vignette 7.1).

VIGNETTE 7.1. DIFFERENT EXAMPLES OF "VIVID IMAGES"

Three highly different studies show how qualitative researchers can vividly portray their fieldwork.

First, Anderson (1999) uses his concluding chapter to present the street life of "Robert." The bulk of the chapter describes Robert's adjustments after being released from prison. Highlighted are numerous street events and scenes, reflecting Robert's new relationships, attitude, and work, and providing readers with concrete images of Robert's new life.

Second, Pedraza (2007) devotes separate chapters to the four waves of Cuban immigrants who were the main subject of her fieldwork. She labels the waves distinctively, further attracting the reader's interest: the 1959–1962 exodus of Cuba's "elite," following Castro's initial rise; the 1965–1974 relocations involving the country's "petite bourgeoisie;" the "chaotic flotilla exodus" of young males from the harbor of Mariel in 1980, who became known as *los Marielitos*; and the 1985–1993 exodus of the *balseros*, based on the term *balsas* (rafts, tires, and makeshift vessels) and how the people risked starvation, dehydration, drowning, and sharks.

Third, Van Maanen (1988) describes his participant-observer fieldwork with an urban police department, including a seven-page tale of his riding with an officer during a wild chase through the city's streets, entitled "one with a gun, one with a dog, and one with the shivers."

See also Vignettes 9.3, 11.3, 11.5, and 11.8.

In the interview situation, focusing on words *verbatim* serves a similar purpose. If the notes from your first interview (or two) contain nothing else, they should have the specific terms, labels, words, and phrases used by the interviewee, not your paraphrasing and hence stereotyping of them.

The desirability of capturing the exact words and phrases—as well as gestures and expressions (e.g., Emerson, Fretz, & Shaw, 1995, pp. 30–32)—goes well beyond the first few interviews. The more you are studying the culture of a place or group of people, the more important it is to capture their language. As noted by Spradley (1995, pp. 7–8),

> Culture, the knowledge that people have learned as members of a group, cannot be observed directly. . . . If we want to find out what people know, we must get inside their heads.

Spradley then observes that fieldworkers, from the very beginning, must cope with the problem of using a particular language in their notes. Throughout your field interviews, a continuing focus on capturing words verbatim eventually helps to give you insight into the meaning of the interviewees' thoughts, rather than your inferred meaning (see "The Verbatim Principle," Vignette 7.2).

In both the observing and interviewing situations, and especially during the early fieldwork, your notes should avoid using not only your own paraphrasing but, more subtly, your own "categories" for describing reality. Examples would be your depiction of a classroom scene by using the term *didactic instruction* rather than

---

VIGNETTE 7.2. THE VERBATIM PRINCIPLE

Most experienced fieldworkers understand the importance of taking verbatim notes—that is, capturing the exact terminology, colloquialisms, and labels used by those being interviewed. James Spradley (1979, p. 73) has called this the "verbatim principle."

In applying the principle, fieldworkers must first recognize that the "field" may have multiple languages, even if everyone speaks in the same tongue. As examples, Spradley cites the fieldworker's language as "observer's terms" and the field members' language as "native terms." He further points out that different field members' roles, such as service providers and service clients, may have their own languages.

Spradley echoes the insights of many qualitative researchers who know that language is a direct reflection of the culture being studied. Fieldworkers therefore need to be highly sensitive to differences in language, and Spradley regards the taking of verbatim notes as among the "first steps along the path to discovering the inner meaning of another culture" (1979, p. 73).

---

recording the lack of interchange between teacher and students; or noting that a person was dressed "sloppily" rather than describing the actual dress.

Your data collection practices already should have alerted you to this issue of avoiding premature categorization and stereotyping. The point here is that, if you are not careful, your notes can inadvertently take a regressive step in this direction. The risks include lapsing into an ethnocentric or other self-centered perspective whereby (1) unfamiliar expressions are associated with an alien connotation; (2) interpretations carry with them the unstated assumption that a single view is "true"; or (3) descriptions are framed in terms of "what is supposed to be" (Emerson, Fretz, & Shaw, 1995, pp. 110–111).

Remembering Your Research Questions

This is another strategy for knowing what to record, besides highlighting actions or capturing words verbatim.

Whether you developed a formal research protocol or not, your study started with some questions or main points of interest. You identified those points, as well as selected your field setting, only after careful consideration. Thus, you also can give these same points your initial note-taking (and question-asking) priority by giving more attention to those actions and verbatim words that appear to be related to your research questions.

Taking Notes about Written Studies, Reports, and Documents Found in the Field

Besides observing and interviewing, a third common source of field notes comes from written materials. You already will have taken such notes in reviewing the literature as part of the preparation for designing your qualitative research study.

However, unless you are studying a preliterate social group, you are likely to encounter additional written materials as part of your fieldwork.

For these materials, the note taking should not differ from your interview notes, with an emphasis again on capturing the exact words and phrases in the written material. Have a clear way of distinguishing between use of the exact words (quotation marks are fine) and paraphrasing, so that if you reuse these materials you will cite them properly and cannot be accused in any way of plagiarizing the intellectual property.

Even though the written materials can be voluminous, as in doing field research about an organization, the note taking should be as complete as possible. It should be undertaken with the intention of avoiding having to retrieve again the same material at some later date, just to complete the notes as opposed to corroborating some new finding. Thus, make sure that you attend not only to the contents of the document but also to the details you will need to cite it—for example, the specific dates and the formal names and associated organizational titles needed to cite the document formally.

Treat the opportunity to review the written material as if it were your only opportunity to access and read the document (which it may very well be). By doing so, you will reduce later frustrations by having to return to the document. You also will minimize inconveniencing any people who may have had to retrieve the materials for you. Alternatively, and while still in the field, you may think about making duplicate copies of the material—but this procedure has at least one important pro and con as described next.

Duplicating Copies of Documents and Written Materials While in the Field

Some fieldwork colleagues commonly find and then use commercial copying services during their time in the field. This way, they can duplicate fully any written materials they have encountered. However, the colleagues may be postponing a headache that will come later.

After completing their fieldwork, the colleagues then confront the duplicated materials, which still assume their raw form. The relevance of some of the materials to the overall qualitative study may now be questioned or, worse yet, forgotten. The importance of particular portions of these materials also may no longer be evident. If both of these conditions prevail, the materials become part of the fieldwork recordings that will now fall outside of any useful analysis.

At the same time, the materials may remain an invaluable part of your study. So, duplicate them if the opportunities arise. But—while still in the field—attend to these materials sufficiently, usually by taking notes about their contents or by marking up the copies, so that you know what to look for and what to quote when you have returned from the field. Make yourself a note saying how and why the material appeared to be relevant to you at the time (many fieldworkers use "Post-it" notes for this purpose).

A final topic: In the special case when the written materials include research studies, their usefulness may be accentuated if you focus on their evidence and conclusions. You should consider xeroxing a key table, graphic, or other presentation of data so that there is no chance that you have made a "copy" error on some critical piece of evidence. By focusing on the evidence and conclusions, you also may again minimize the need for returning to the material and having to spend more time with it. Finally, unlike the observing and interviewing in the field, the note taking for written materials may take place in a quieter environment where the notes can be taken on a computer.

B. NOTE-TAKING PRACTICES WHEN DOING FIELDWORK

PREVIEW—*What you should learn from this section:*
1. Formatting your notes.
2. Using your own notations and transcribing language.

Being Prepared

Like the classic photographer who always carries a camera just in case a photo opportunity arises, when you are doing your research you always should be prepared to write something down. You therefore should always be carrying some kind of writing instrument. Similarly, having a small pad (which could fit into a purse or a side pocket) or even a clean scrap of paper to write on also will prepare you for taking notes at a moment's notice (Scanlan, 2000, p. 28). Over time, once you become comfortable with a particular type of writing instrument (e.g., pen or pencil) and pad (e.g., classroom size or small enough to fit into a pocket or purse), think about stockpiling these items for future studies.

Given the small size of today's technology, the preparatory steps also can include carrying a pocket-sized audio recorder and a cell phone with photographic capabilities. You will then be prepared to record events in multiple modalities (however, see Section D for suggestions and caveats about using mechanical recording devices).

Setting Up Your Notes

In spite of their seeming informality, your "jottings" (Emerson, Fretz, & Shaw, 1995, pp. 19–35) or initial field notes still should follow a certain format. This format can resemble your classroom (lecture) notes, so everyone already has some formatting style that also will work in taking field notes. For setting up your notes when doing fieldwork, three general reminders may be helpful.

First, you need to decide whether you are most comfortable taking notes on standard-sized notebook paper, in a bound notebook, on stenographic or journalistic-sized pads, or on index cards. If the fieldwork will involve a lot of movement, for example, into and out of cars, or otherwise involves environments with little or no writing surfaces, you will prefer a paper or pad with some cardboard backing. The same fieldwork conditions will probably preclude your using a laptop or small computer to take notes, as you may not find a stable surface on which to set the computer (the convenience of your lap disappears when most of your fieldwork involves walking or standing). You also will have difficulty viewing a computer screen when working outdoors.

Second, the general formatting style also includes making a habit out of writing the date (if not time) of the note, briefly identifying the person or scene covered by the note, and numbering all of your pages. Writing on one side of a page (except when writing in a notebook) also is advisable because of the later difficulty of finding specific passages when you are desperately rifling through your notes looking for some phrase or fragment that happens to be written on the back of a page.

A third formatting feature is deliberately to leave empty spaces on each page (see Exhibit 7.1). The notes in Exhibit 7.1 come from a group conversation with several participants, with the underlined initials or names at the left indicating the speakers, followed by their comments. These comments were purposely written to occupy only the left side of the note paper, with the right side being a place to put the fieldworker's comments (or to add another related comment—see the initials "JH" in the right column). The space in between these two columns permits the use of arrows, brackets, and parentheses where the fieldworker wants to hypothesize some relationship either that will lead to an immediate follow-up question or that will be examined later.

In your own notes, you may leave wide margins, write down one column, leave a second column open on every page, or use any other pattern that pleases you. Just don't fill up every page. You will find the empty space useful if you later happen to remember an item that belongs on the original notes and can then add it (with a different-colored writing instrument), or even later when you are reviewing your notes and want to insert your own comment or mark next to specific passages (again with a different color or notation style).

Developing Your Own Transcribing Language

Remember that, when taking field notes, you will be listening, watching, and assimilating real-life events at the same time. On top of all this, the verbatim principle and the richness of what is occurring in the field or during an unstructured interview will pose even greater demands on your ability to do parallel tasks. Finally, you have to take sufficient notes that you will only minimally have to trust your memory (which is likely to be overloaded, not to speak of the distortions that could occur).

All of these conditions behoove you to think about your note taking as requiring and involving its own separate transcribing language. The language needs most of all to have shortcuts that nevertheless preserve accuracy and precision. However, the language may differ sharply from your regular writing.

EXHIBIT 7.1.   SAMPLE OF FIELD NOTES

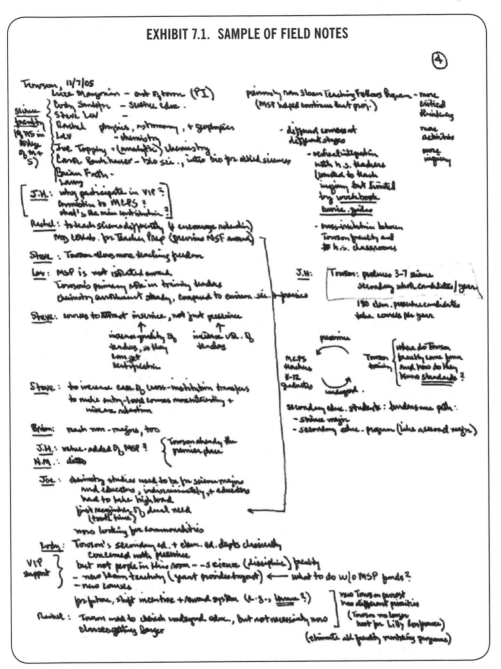

For instance, knowing formal shorthand does not hurt, but most people are not interested in mastering that language. Some concoction of your own, similar to text-messaging or instant-messaging languages, will do—as long as you can read and interpret your own writing. Using abbreviations and acronyms is a must, but again be careful that you do not errantly use the same abbreviations or acronyms for two or more different concepts. Along the same vein, if you fall behind when taking notes, one suggestion is not to try to complete every sentence, but to start a new sentence even if you did not complete the previous one (Scanlan, 2000, p. 32). If you try to complete the previous one, you are not likely to hear the new one.

To overcome having too many incomplete sentences or too much fragmentation (if not confusion) in your notes, you should try to find some time to make quick fixes while you are still in the field. Find a quiet place between interviews or observations or during a break from the fieldwork and look for those incomplete sentences or other fragments. Any fixes that you can make at this intermediate juncture will be much better than waiting until the end of the day.

Recommended, too, is to write small. You can get more words on a page—and you also can write faster—than if you emulate the elementary student's broad-sized script with wrist and arm movements rather than only finger movements. Similarly, for nearly everyone, script is faster than printing.

A critical characteristic of the desired transcribing language is to be able to distinguish (1) notes about others and external events from (2) notes to yourself. You will want to be able to make a brief note about what you have just heard or observed, but you need to separate your own comments clearly from the other notes. Using brackets or backslashes (and saving parentheses for true parenthetical remarks), or reserving the marginal space for your comments alone, all will work. Other punctuation also can matter, especially in using quotation marks when you are able to quote directly what someone has said. As a result, as with abbreviations and acronyms, decide ahead of time the meaning of any of the punctuation or other marks (e.g., checkmarks or x-marks) that you plan to use. Making a personal glossary for each of your studies would not hurt, either.

Like everything else, you need to practice your transcribing language. The main test will be whether you thought you took down everything that you wanted to and later, when you find out whether your notes are completely readable to yourself.

Creating Drawings and Sketches as Part of the Notes

Field notes also can include your own drawings or sketches. Such renditions are highly desirable supplements to your writing because the drawings will help you to keep track of certain relationships while you are still in the field, as well as to recall these relationships after you have completed your fieldwork.

The most obvious type of drawing would capture the spatial layouts of particular scenes. Moreover, creating such drawings does not require "language facility or a great deal of rapport with informants," so the drawings can be rendered early during the fieldwork period (Pelto & Pelto, 1978, pp. 193–194).

The spatial scenes might include the spatial relationships between or among participants and not just the physical features of a landscape. Although you may have some artistic talent, do not become preoccupied with that talent. The idea is to sketch something quickly and to capture the scene, not to perfect a still-life drawing at the risk of neglecting the ongoing activities or discussions. For instance, you can quickly note and number the positions of participants at a group meeting, with the decoding to take place at some later time (see Exhibit 7.2).

EXHIBIT 7.2. SKETCHES IN FIELD NOTES

Field scenes may include group discussions or meetings. The group may be seated at a conference table (see below) or gathered informally. The fieldworker may not be introduced to the individuals; or, if introduced, may not remember all of their names. Then, conversations may begin (and notes need to be taken) before the fieldworker has had a chance to get fully oriented.

A quick way of getting this recorded is to mark the seating positions and to assign numbers to each position. Later, as the discussion progresses or as a result of separate queries, the fieldworker can decode the seating positions with the names of the appropriate person. As an added benefit, the sketch also captures the relationships among the seating positions, which may reflect implicit social hierarchies or interpersonal relationships that could later turn out to be important.

As with your written notes as discussed in Section C, the only requirement for the clarity of the sketch is that you can later understand it yourself. (At that later time, if you are still enthralled with your artistic talent, you can expand the original sketch into a full-blown drawing.)

Besides rendering the physical and sociophysical features of particular scenes, drawings also can be helpful in capturing social relationships as represented by family trees and organizational charts. When the relationships are complex or numerous, the drawings can serve a useful orienting purpose while you are still in the field.

C. CONVERTING FIELD NOTES INTO FULLER NOTES

PREVIEW—*What you should learn from this section:*
1. Using the time to convert notes as an opportunity to assess the progress you are making in your study.
2. Expanding on ideas when converting notes.
3. Reviewing notes for hints at verification needs.

The preceding note-taking practices pertain to notes taken during fieldwork or when actually doing an interview. These field notes will have been constrained by a shortness of time and attention because the main attention will have been devoted to doing the fieldwork or conducting the interview. As a result, these notes, sometimes considered "jottings," can be fragmentary, incomplete, or cryptic. The field notes therefore need to be revised and converted into a more formal set of notes that will eventually become part of your qualitative research study's database.

Converting Field Notes Quickly

The main objective is to convert the field notes to fuller notes as soon after every field event as possible. On most occasions, the opportunity will arise at the end of every day, so at a minimum you should set aside a time slot to do the task. However, be ready to take advantage of opportunities that may arise during the middle of the day.

Although such a daily routine may at first appear to be highly demanding, most qualitative researchers have found that they enthusiastically look forward to it because the time also provides a chance to "collect one's thoughts" and to reflect on what happened during the day. When pursuing interesting research questions, the reflections include potential discoveries and revelations that in some cases can be quite exciting.

If nothing else, the nightly reflections also present opportunities to think (or rethink) about the fieldwork plans for the next day. As previously discussed in Chapter 5 (Section A), fieldwork schedules and agendas for qualitative research are not likely to be tightly defined (as in doing the fieldwork for a survey), so each day may present some flexibility in arrangements. As a result, your nightly reflections can lead to new ideas about modifying your priorities for the next day.

Especially difficult in making such choices is whether you think you are getting anywhere in your study. You may feel that a given fieldwork day, upon later reflection, did not provide much useful information. Whether you should modify the priorities for the next day or stick to your original plans will always be a difficult call. On the one hand, you may indeed be wasting your time unless you make some change in direction; on the other hand, relevant social or institutional patterns in the field may not emerge until after several days of repetitive exposure. Patience being a virtue, you probably should not make hasty judgments and only consider altering your routine after some (unproductive) repetition already has taken place.

Minimum Requirement for the Daily Conversion of the Original Field Notes

There are many ways of converting the original field notes during the nightly routine. One essential step needs to be taken even if you do not have the time to make any other enhancements: You must write out any fragments, abbreviations, or other cryptic comments that you may not later understand. This requirement includes expanding or correcting sentences whose meanings are not absolutely clear. You also may have deliberately left question marks around certain portions of your original field notes because you knew you would try to interpret the meaning of the notes during this nightly routine.

No one should underestimate the importance of this minimum requirement. If you have taken a lot of class notes your whole life, you already will have suffered the embarrassing experience, as we all do, of not being able to decipher your own writing or (worse) of not being able to understand your own phrases or sentences that were written down at some earlier time. Moreover, the field experience is likely to have consisted of unfamiliar customs, language, and actions in comparison to your regular life, so the risk of later being unable to understand your own notes will be greater.

Four Additional Ways of Enhancing the Original Field Notes

Beyond the minimum requirement, you can enhance your original field notes in four other ways. First, reading your notes may stimulate you to recall additional details about the events observed or interviews conducted during the day. Feel free to add such embellishments, but put them down with a different writing instrument or separate symbolic code, so that you can later differentiate between the original notes and the embellishments.

Second, you may have your own conjectures, interpretations, or comments about particular portions of the original field notes. Some of the comments may only be "loose end" reminders to yourself—that certain topics need to be examined more closely during your later field opportunities, for example. Such reminders do not need to be literally written onto the original notes but may be kept on a separate list that is then appended to the original notes.

Third, your review of the notes for the preceding day may suggest some emerging themes, categories, or even tentative solutions and answers related to your research questions. These ideas are clearly worth recording and can be connected to the specific portions or items in your notes that stimulated the ideas. By so doing, you also could be starting to anticipate some of the "codes" that will be used in your later analysis of your data (see Chapter 8, Section B).

Fourth, you should add the day's notes, in some organized fashion, to your other field notes. The organized fashion should attempt to create some filing categories that go beyond simply keeping the notes in chronological order. The goal is to avoid having all of your notes, possibly from fieldwork as well as from the documents you have read, merely becoming part of an increasingly large "pile." If you let your notes pile up, you are leaving yourself open to a highly frustrating experience at the end of your fieldwork.

Deepening Your Understanding of Your Fieldwork

This nightly period for expanding your original field notes offers great substantive opportunities and value. You should be clarifying your own understanding of what is going on in the field. The clarification can involve a wide range of items, from particular details to new conjectures related to your original research questions. Such advantages will be lost if you only think of the task as a transcription task of "remembering and getting it down" (Emerson, Fretz, & Shaw, 1995, p. 63).

Any clarifying thoughts can have a pragmatic value: identifying loose ends that need additional fieldwork. Exhibit 7.3 contains a sample of such loose ends from a study of school "reform"—efforts to improve schools in some fundamental way by simultaneously reorganizing curricula, daily schedules, the recruitment and training of teachers, and family and parent involvement—so that students will learn more effectively. Each example in the exhibit shows how some portion of the notes revealed the need to collect additional evidence in the ongoing fieldwork.

Verifying Field Notes

The nightly reviews of field notes also give you an opportunity to cover a methodologically important step occasionally overlooked in doing qualitative research: verifying the data being collected. Examining the notes and records from this perspective, while fieldwork is still ongoing, provides opportunities to tighten your data collection (see " 'Checking Stuff,' " Vignette 7.3). In addition, from another perspective, the verification activities may be considered to be the beginning of analyzing your data.

Many types of verification will be relevant. For instance, key points in your notes that you think may lead to important findings deserve to be rechecked, possibly repeatedly (Pelto & Pelto, 1978, p. 194). As another example, the credibility of every interviewee should not be assumed but also deserves some verification effort

EXHIBIT 7.3. SAMPLE ITEMS NEEDING FURTHER FIELD CLARIFICATION, AS REVEALED DURING NIGHTLY REVIEW OF FIELD NOTES

Sample item	Illustrative example from a study of school reform
Factual details about key informants	Notes suggest that interviewee had not served as a teacher before becoming a district superintendent; need to confirm this biographical item, as it may explain some insensitivities in the superintendent's new reform policies.
Co-location of an elementary and a middle school	Field visit had been to an elementary school, but school building seemed also to contain older-looking students; need to check whether building also contains a middle school, which could complicate reform activities.
Salience of reform vision	Rereading of notes suggests that most of the school interviewees participated in reform activities but were unaware of the broader vision that encompassed the activities; need to check whether interviewees think they are a part of a broader reform effort.
Attendance in teachers' workshops	School is dominated by Hispanic students and has a good proportion of Spanish-speaking teachers, but major reform activity involving teachers' workshops only appears to be offered in English; need to ask whether all teachers attend workshops, or whether Spanish-speaking teachers tend not to attend because workshops do not offer enough Spanish to help them work with their students.

VIGNETTE 7.3. "CHECKING STUFF"

Doing empirical research means working with evidence and making sure, almost obsessively, about its accuracy. Duneier (1999) called this practice "checking stuff" in his study of sidewalk vendors in New York City. He points out several kinds of checks as part of an extensive methodological appendix—itself another sign of sound research procedures.

First, Duneier felt more confident when the same events were told to him "over and over again in the context of different individual lives" (1999, p. 345). Second, he made deliberate attempts to obtain physical evidence to corroborate people's stories—for example, seeing their welfare cards or written notices if they claimed to be on welfare (p. 346). In other cases, he deliberately sought out other people, such as family members, to confirm a person's story.

All of this checking took time, and the relevant incidents only "occurred over a period of years [that] were chiefly a consequence of [his] being there over time" (1999, p. 346). Duneier's approach reinforces the usefulness of conducting fieldwork over an extended period of time but also shows how "checking stuff" needs to be a routine part of that fieldwork.

See also Vignette 10.6.

(Becker, 1958). At a minimum, you would like to know that an interviewee actually was present at the time and place pertinent to her or his direct observations, rather than risking the possibility that the interviewee passed on to you others' hearsay about those events.

Most important among the possible verifications, you may want to start comparing information from the different sources of evidence that became available during your fieldwork, to see whether you have been accumulating conflicting or complementary renditions of the same real-life happenings. Exhibit 7.4 contains different examples of such verifications. Each example illustrates the verifications arising from a different combination of sources. Although the examples come from a study of a community partnership, they should readily evoke parallel instances for qualitative studies on other topics.

The examples in Exhibit 7.4 were deliberately chosen to represent completed verifications and to show how different sources can point to the same conclusion. However, an additional benefit of taking such a proactive stance with your notes and recordings at this early stage is that you again are likely to be in the midst of your fieldwork and data collection activities. You therefore have an opportunity to do some additional cross-checking if needed. You may not have such an opportunity at a later date.

EXHIBIT 7.4. ILLUSTRATIVE TYPES OF VERIFICATIONS BETWEEN DIFFERENT SOURCES OF FIELD EVIDENCE

Sample combination of sources	Illustrative example from a study of a community partnership
Between interviews with different people	Interviewees at one of the partnering organizations indicate the difficulty of relationships with another of the partnering organizations; interviewees at the other organization independently cite the same difficulties
Between interview and documentary evidence	Interviewees all say that the partnership began in 1995, and key documents also show the partnership forming at that time, with no trace of any partnership at an earlier date
Between interviews and observational data	The partnership appears to be supported by an outside organization that is not part of the partnership; field observations at the partnership's office reveal signage and a directory confirming the existence of this other organization, and interviews confirm the overlapping of officers between the partnership and this organization
Between different documentary sources	A local news article under a reporter's by-line uses independent data to assess one of the partnership's major initiatives and its apparent benefits; the conclusions appear to agree with those from a totally separate study by a local university professor
Between two fieldworkers (if the study involves a research team)	Fieldworkers query each other about having heard a common interviewee admit to wanting to move on to another job; each fieldworker remembers the same words having been said

D. RECORDING DATA THROUGH MODES OTHER THAN WRITING

PREVIEW—_What you should learn from this section:_

1. The advantages and disadvantages of using other modes of recording field events, besides note taking.
2. Permissions to record and permissions to show recordings, when using other modes of recording.
3. Types of qualitative studies using other modes of recording as their main data collection technique.

Written notes, including associated sketches, have dominated the discussion thus far. Yet, field events can be recorded through multiple modes, not just in what is written down. The prominent modes primarily make use of recording devices and include audiotaping, videotaping, and taking pictures.

These devices can create invaluable by-products because they represent literal replicas of field events, given the obvious caveat regarding the selectivity in deciding when, where, and what to record (Fetterman, 2009, pp. 564–572). At the same time, using these devices can entail major complications that can outweigh the value of the products.

Every researcher needs to make her or his own decision about the appropriate balance between the complications and the added value. One possible practice, followed by many experienced researchers, is to rely mainly on written notes and only to use recording devices under special circumstances. Thus, rather than audiotaping every interview, these researchers might consider audiotaping only a specific interview that is likely to be lengthy or critical. However, in other situations, such as the videotaping of classroom behavior discussed at the end of this section, using a recording device is intrinsic to the entire data collection process.

Nevertheless, the potential complications are sufficiently strong that you need to proceed with caution. These complications are discussed next.

Obtaining Permission to Record

To begin with, using recording devices of any sort requires you to obtain the permission of those who are to be recorded. The simplest request might occur when audiotaping. Just before an interview starts, many researchers note that they say something like, "do you mind if I record this conversation?" If the participant has no objection and the researcher is adept at using the recording device, it is placed at an appropriate spot and turned on. The interview proceeds, and the intrusiveness of the device can be minimal.

Making visual recordings, either with a videotape or a camera, presents a slightly different situation. Even if the recording does not focus on any particular participant or conversation—as in recording people at work or school children at play—some sort of permission is still required. A person in authority needs to approve, and in some situations the approval may have to be obtained in writing.

A golden rule is to understand that, regardless of the situation, all researchers should make sure that they have secured permission from some relevant person to make any specific recording. Without gaining such permission, trouble is bound to arise later. The topic also should have been part of the human subjects approval procedure discussed previously in Chapter 2, Section E.

Mastering Recording Devices before Using Them

Nothing is more distracting than the interruption caused when a recording device malfunctions while in use. For instance, such malfunctions of an audio recorder can potentially offset the cherished rapport you might have established with a participant. The participant may even (silently) question whether you know what you are doing—possibly extending this doubt into your substantive questions (the logic is as follows: If you didn't prepare sufficiently to know how your own recording device functions or might malfunction, how much preparation went into the questions you are posing?).

Everyone is aware of the typical embarrassments suffered when travelers report being at a historic scene or experiencing a precious moment—and a recording device malfunctioned, often for want of a charged battery. Beyond such malfunctions, sloppy handling of recording devices can call undesirable attention to use of the device, diverting attention away from the substance of a discussion or observation.

The essential familiarity with a device also means knowing that it will work properly and produce the expected output. In too many instances researchers have thought they had successfully made audio- or videotapes, only to find later that the quality of the tapes was too poor, making the tapes unusable. Typically, an audiotape's recording may turn out to be too faint, or pertinent conversations are later found to have been drowned out by some unnoticed background noise. Similarly, videotapes and photos may later be discovered to be out of focus, to have insufficient lighting, or to suffer from some backlight that was ignored during the photo opportunity.

A final point about using recording devices pertains to those devices that are not part of your study. Be sure that these other devices, such as a cell phone or a beeper, are turned off when you are doing your fieldwork. At least one field researcher has reported how his beeper buzzed just at a critical point in a field interview, thereby changing the mood of the entire interview (Rowe, 1999, p. 9).

Sharing the Recordings and Maintaining Their Security

Once a recording device has been successfully used, the resulting tape or photo raises new questions. Displaying any of this material publicly again requires written permission from the persons or owners of the properties that were in the tape or photo. Participants also may ask to have their own copy of your material, and you will have to decide the conditions for granting or denying them your permission.

Given the public's ready use of Internet media for sharing recorded or taped information, the issues can become quite sticky quite fast.

Beyond deciding how the materials are to be shared is the question of how they will be stored and how their security will be maintained. Given the desired protection of human subjects, a major threat would result from any improper divulgence of the identities of the people or places in your fieldwork. As a result, you may have to have a plan for deleting such information before storing your records. This task is made more difficult by the information automatically stored as part of today's digital photos and records.

Being Prepared to Spend Time Reviewing and Editing the Recordings

The successful recordings will help you to increase the precision of your fieldwork. They even may stimulate your own reminiscences of other happenings in the field that did not become part of the record, such as the facial expression or body language of an interviewee who had only been audiotaped.

Taking full advantage of these recordings will require their dedicated and systematic review. Such review may take a lot of time because recordings produce massive amounts of information. Moreover, unless you are skilled at randomly accessing various portions of audio- or videotapes, you will need to conduct your review linearly, potentially making the process a tedious rather than stimulating one. Investing the needed time in this review process can have valuable payoffs. Make sure, however, that you intelligently anticipate the needed time before finally deciding whether to use any recording device in the first place.

When Electronic Recordings Are the Main Data Collection Technique

Notwithstanding all of the preceding complications, some qualitative research depends heavily on the use of recording devices. Major examples are studies of classroom behavior or work situations, where videotaping is the primary mode of data collection. The tapes capture both the actions and sounds of the classroom or work environments, enabling researchers to study instructional practices (in the classroom) or workers' actions and interactions (in the workplace). As another example, a qualitative study might deal with the interactions between physicians and patients (e.g., Stewart, 1992).

Under these and similar circumstances where the recording device actually becomes the main data collection instrument, the fieldwork is likely to become formalized in at least two ways. First, specially skilled persons will be needed to make the recordings in the first place, to ensure their quality and later utility.

Second, analysis of the products is likely to require formal protocols to be used when later viewing the tapes (Erickson, 2006). For instance, studies based on *conversation analysis* are interested in going beyond the spoken words. Such studies need to develop a detailed set of symbols for coding conversants' mannerisms such as pauses, pacing, intonations, and interruptions (Drew, 2009). The protocols also should cover the procedures for conducting reliability checks—for example, by having two or more viewers make their own coding or scoring of the tapes (e.g., Hall, 2000). The videotapes can be paused at specific frames, so that the research can hone in on the finest details. At the same time, a video camera has many limitations compared to the human eye, and the camera will not capture what human observers actually see (Roschelle, 2000).

Interestingly, the lead researchers in these studies may still take their own written notes, while the action is taking place and being recorded. Now the written notes assume a more casual role because the recording device is producing the actual data.

Producing Finished Products

Many people, yourself included, may think of using the outputs from the recording devices (e.g., a photo or a segment of a videotape or audiotape) as part of their professional presentations. Photos also can appear in final manuscripts and publications (e.g., Brubaker, Feischmidt, Fox, & Grancea, 2006; Pedraza, 2007), as also discussed in Chapter 10, Section B.

When you are considering such presentations, you might also heed a word of caution. Because nearly everyone has been exposed to high-quality visual media, the audience is likely not to appreciate a visual (or audio) product that only has a "homemade" quality. Poor visual products might even detract from what otherwise might be an excellent study. An obvious response to this problem is to reference and encourage the use of increasingly easy-to-use digital editing software (e.g., Fetterman, 2009, p. 571). Such software can substantially improve your product. Highly polished visual images are especially found in education studies, where researchers commonly present visual images of the interactions between a teacher and a student, or among students or teachers alone.

The caution is this: Overediting the visual or audio images potentially distorts the images in their representation as qualitative data. As a result, especially when the editing has produced a genuinely high-quality product, the risk is that the "scene" will be interpreted as not fully representing a fully spontaneous or authentic rendition. Overediting also can lead to other suspicions. For instance, audiences might not simply accept that editing was the only intervention; they might now wonder whether the depicted teachers or students were coached to look into (or to look away from) a camera, to make the final product more appealing.

Given these possibilities, you may want to consider not doing any editing and clearly stating the absence of such editing, when (especially digital) images are presented. To make the images as attractive as possible, the challenge then would be to do the original recording with skillful techniques, so that the final product is presentable without any editing. From a photographer's perspective, the goal would be to produce a high-quality but still candid image of the reality being studied.

E. KEEPING A PERSONAL JOURNAL   ◆

All the energy and attention devoted to note taking and other recordings may deplete your remaining capacity for any further writing. However, there is one other writing activity that parallels the data collection (and other) processes in a research study. The activity involves keeping a personal journal or diary, capturing your own feelings and reflections on your research work.

The entries in such a journal do not need to be lengthy or even contain complete sentences. As with your field notes, the entries also can use your own personal abbreviations and acronyms—as long as you will later know what they mean.

In qualitative research, such a journal can play more than a private role. Because you the researcher are likely to be the main research instrument, any introspections and insights into your own reactions or feelings about ongoing fieldwork (or the study as a whole) may later reveal unwanted biases. Keeping a journal also can surface your own methodological or personal tendencies over time. You may not have been aware of such tendencies, but acknowledging them may lead to useful thoughts about how to approach your later analysis.

Chapter 11 (Section D) will suggest that the final reporting of your work should include coverage of your *reflexive self*. Any journal or diary would naturally be a good source of information for this aspect of the final reporting.

RECAP FOR CHAPTER 7: *Terms, phrases, and concepts that you can now define*:

1. Vivid images rather than visual stereotypes
2. The verbatim principle
3. Jottings
4. Verifications between different sources of evidence
5. Permissions to record and permissions to show recordings, when using mechanical devices
6. Conversation analysis
7. Overediting visual recordings

EXERCISE FOR CHAPTER 7: "WRITING UP" AN INTERVIEW

Return to your notes from the interview in the Chapter 6 exercise and now create a formal rendition of the interview. At a minimum, the rendition should include your own reactions to different portions of the interview while also strengthening the sentence structure and clarity of the original notes. Feel free to add footnotes, citations, and references to your original interview.

CHAPTER 8

Analyzing Qualitative Data, I

Compiling, Disassembling, and Reassembling

The analysis of qualitative data usually moves through five phases, the first three of which are covered in the present chapter. The first analytic phase, *compiling* data into a formal database, calls for the careful and methodic organizing of the original data. The second phase, *disassembling* the data in the database, can involve a formal coding procedure but does not need to. The third phase, *reassembling*, is less mechanical and benefits from a researcher's insightfulness in seeing emerging patterns. Various ways of creating data arrays can help to reveal such patterns in this third phase.

Constantly improving computer software is available to assist in the entire analysis process. However, whether researchers decide to use such software or not, all of the analytic decisions must be made by the researcher. One risk in using software is the added attention needed to follow the software's procedures and terminology. Such attention may detract from the desired analytic thinking, energy, and decisions that are needed to carry out a strong analysis.

OK, so now comes that magical moment. Somehow, you are going to amass and sort all of your qualitative data in some efficient manner. You are going to follow some instructional cookbook that makes your procedure rigorous. And this analytic process will lead directly to your ability to draw the needed conclusions for your study and to write them up.

The preceding scenario can produce two opposing reactions. First, some people wish that the scenario were true. They even may believe that, by using computer software specially designed to analyze qualitative data, they will find the needed sanctuary. Second, other people know that the scenario is not true. However, they revel at the opportunity presented by qualitative research and the freedom *not* to be encumbered by some fixed methodology.

Whichever view you embrace, and however you end up analyzing your data, the most important part of the scenario is the part about rigor. The rigor derives by exercising three precautions:

1. Checking and rechecking the accuracy of your data;
2. Making your analysis as thorough and complete as possible rather than cutting corners; and
3. Continually acknowledging the unwanted biases imposed by your own values when you are analyzing your data.

These and other related items are even better monitored if you also create and maintain a set of methodological notes (sometimes referred to as *memos*—see "Memo Writing" in Section C) for your own continued reference.

Specific techniques, discussed later in this chapter, also help and should be fully utilized, such as making *constant comparisons*, being especially alert to *negative instances*, developing *rival explanations*, and continually *posing questions* about your data and to yourself as you proceed analytically. Keeping, organizing, and reviewing methodological notes or memos about the analytic process at frequent times also is a strongly recommended practice. All of these procedures are important because the analysis of qualitative research does not have a universally accepted routine.

A. OVERVIEW OF THE ANALYTIC PHASES

PREVIEW—*What you should learn from this section:*
1. The full cycle of phases for analyzing qualitative data.
2. The potential role of computer software to support the analytic functions.

At the same time, although analyzing qualitative research does not follow any cookbook, neither is it totally undisciplined. In fact, practical experience in doing qualitative research as well as the analytic styles portrayed in numerous texts suggest that most qualitative analysis—regardless of the particular qualitative orientation being adopted—follows a general, five-phased cycle. The rest of this chapter is therefore structured around this cycle, briefly described next.

Introduction to a Five-Phased Cycle: (1) Compiling, (2) Disassembling, (3) Reassembling (and Arraying), (4) Interpreting, and (5) Concluding

Exhibit 8.1 depicts the complete cycle and its five phases, with the arrows showing the sequencing among the five phases. The two-way arrows imply that you can go back and forth between two phases. As a result, the entire exhibit suggests how analysis is likely to occur in a nonlinear fashion. The following introduction to the

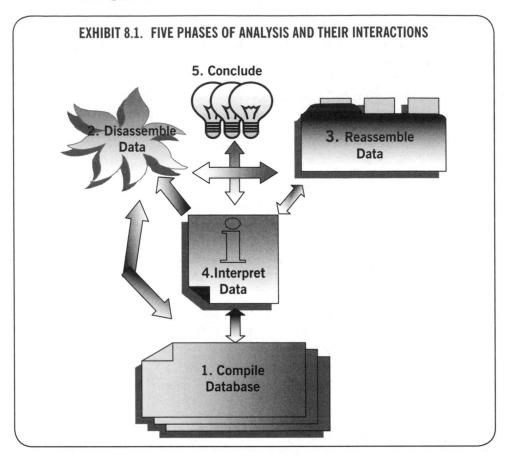

EXHIBIT 8.1. FIVE PHASES OF ANALYSIS AND THEIR INTERACTIONS

cycle quickly defines each phase, after which the remainder of Chapter 8 as well as the entirety of Chapter 9 discuss how each phase works.

Analysis "begins"[1] by *Compiling* and sorting the field notes amassed from your fieldwork and other data collection. You would have refined these notes nightly, as previously described in Chapter 7 (Section C), and you might have separately amassed notes from archival sources. But neither set would necessarily have been put in any order other than the order in which they had been created. The first phase—*Compiling*—therefore means putting them in some order. The finished compilation might be considered a database.

The second phase calls for breaking down the compiled data into smaller fragments or pieces, which may be considered a *Disassembling* procedure. The procedure may (but does not have to) be accompanied by your assigning new labels, or "codes," to the fragments or pieces. The disassembling procedure may be repeated many times as part of a trial-and-error process of testing codes, accounting for the two-way arrow between these first two phases.

---

[1] "Begins" is used for convenience only. A distinguishing characteristic of qualitative research, as pointed out throughout this book, is the need to do analysis during the earlier phases of a research study, especially during data collection.

The second phase is then followed by using substantive themes (or even codes or clusters of codes) to reorganize the disassembled fragments or pieces into different groupings and sequences than might have been in the original notes. This third phase may be considered a *Reassembling* procedure. The rearrangements and recombinations may be facilitated by depicting the data graphically or by arraying them in lists and other tabular forms. Again, the two-way arrow in Exhibit 8.1 suggests how the assembling and disassembling phases may be repeated several or more times in alternating fashion.

The fourth phase involves using the reassembled material to create a new narrative, with accompanying tables and graphics where relevant, that will become the key analytic portion of your draft manuscript. The fourth phase may be considered one of *Interpreting* the reassembled data. Initial interpretations may lead to the desire to recompile the database in some fresh way, or to disassemble or reassemble the data differently, all of these sequences represented by the respective one-way and two-way arrows.

The fifth and final phase may be considered one of *Concluding*. It calls for drawing the conclusions from your entire study. Such conclusions should be related to the interpretation in the fourth phase and through it to all of the other phases of the cycle.

Overall, you now should have a preliminary understanding of the five phases. You also should now see how they do not fall into a linear sequence, but have *recursive* and *iterative* relationships. The entire analytic process should occur over an extended period of time—weeks, if not months. During this time, your exposure to other experiences unrelated to your study might serendipitously affect your thinking about one or more of these five phases.

Not all qualitative researchers attend equally to the five phases. More experienced researchers may be able to move quickly through all of the first three phases and reach the *Interpretation* phase sooner rather than later. Less experienced researchers may give too much attention to the *Disassembling* phase and then struggle with the *Reassembling* phase, delaying *Interpreting* and *Concluding* beyond original deadlines or their own patience.

Because the five phases will take space to explain, this book somewhat arbitrarily divides them so that the present chapter covers the first three phases, whereas Chapter 9 covers the fourth and fifth phases. Adding to the concreteness of the material will be vignettes and examples but also a single **Sample Study 1**, also split between Chapters 8 and 9 (the study's first three phases are presented at the end of this chapter, and the final two are presented at the end of Chapter 9).

Using Computer Software to Assist in Analyzing Qualitative Data

This chapter will refer intermittently to the use of computer software specifically designed to assist in analyzing qualitative data. There are many such software programs. Each comes from a different vendor, and the prices for any given program can exceed $1,000. Each vendor also issues updated versions periodically. Widely used programs appear to be *ATLAS-ti5, NVivo7,* and *MAXqda2* (Lewins & Silver, 2007). Other programs include *HyperRESEARCH6, QDA Miner 2.0, Qualrus,* and *Transana 2.*

The various software programs fall under a generic label known as "Computer Assisted Qualitative Data AnalysiS" (or CAQDAS, pronounced "cactus") software (e.g., Fielding & Lee, 1998). Because this book takes no position in favoring the use of one program over any other, the discussion will refer only to CAQDAS as the generic software and to the general analytic procedures for using such software.

The reference to CAQDAS also is intended to cover the use of less specialized but nevertheless highly useful and more common software programs, such as *Word, Excel,* and *Access.* Nearly everyone knows how to use these common programs, and they can support nearly the entire process of analyzing qualitative data:

> For instance, Christopher Hahn (2008) gives step-by-step guidance for using the three software programs, with separate chapters devoted to the functions of *Word, Access,* and *Excel.* As an illustrative function, *Word's* tables and index tools are sufficient to organize and array textual data and even to assign initial codes to such data (Chap. 6 of Hahn's text). Likewise, the two spreadsheet/database programs can support higher level coding (i.e., creation of categories) and an ability to retrieve, manipulate, and tally the materials in a highly efficient manner (Chaps. 7 and 8).

Whether to contemplate using any CAQDAS or common software in the first place is another matter. Older cohorts of researchers may have become accustomed to their own manual techniques for analyzing qualitative data. Such researchers might consider the adoption of computer-based techniques to be troublesome and somewhat bound by the software's own inevitable limitations, if not rigidity. Younger cohorts of researchers may have never seen, much less used, a typewriter. They may be accustomed to using computer software for a full variety of daily functions. These younger researchers may have to rely on CAQDAS software to be an integral if not essential part of their qualitative research.

Over the years, CAQDAS software has improved considerably. Its functionality mimics the most essential steps in doing analysis, although with each new function also comes more complicated computer-based procedures and navigation rules. Nevertheless, the main caution in using such software still remains: *You have to do all of the analytic thinking.* You will have to instruct the software every step of the way. To do this will require an added burden because you will have to use the software's language while also keeping track of your own (substantive) analytic path.

Possibly inappropriate and inflated expectations about the capability of CAQDAS software come from what most people know about computer-assisted *quantitative* analysis. In that situation, computer routines commonly perform complex mathematical operations, ranging from computing a structural equation model to testing two- and three-level hierarchical linear models to building and testing latent growth models. In these quantitative situations, the analyst provides a set of input data, and the computer arrives at the result. However, the analyst does not have to know the formulas underlying the mathematical operations, much less how to derive the formulas. (A good bet would be that most quantitative analysts do not themselves know how to derive even a chi-square formula, much less the ones used in the more complex models.)

The challenge presented by qualitative analysis is that there are no such formulas. You as the analyst still need to provide a set of input data, usually taking the form of text, not numbers. More importantly, you cannot call upon a preset formula as in quantitative research but must yourself develop the entire underlying substantive procedure, such as sorting, coding, combining, and recombining portions of the text. You also must give the computer step-by-step instructions to carry out the procedure.

Later, you must defend the logic and validity of the entire operation. You cannot hide behind a statement as used in quantitative research, where investigators can simply cite their having used a particular version of a particular statistical model from a particular software program. In this sense, the computer capabilities for quantitative and qualitative analyses differ markedly.

Given this understanding, you can nevertheless consider using CAQDAS software, especially if you can readily configure software and instruct computers, and especially if you have a large amount of data. If you do use CAQDAS software, you also should not rely entirely on the documentation that accompanies any particular CAQDAS software but also would want to have one or more special books on the topic at your side (see "A Helpful Guide for Using CAQDAS Software," Vignette 8.1). Moreover, examining such texts before selecting a software program may help you to take into account the different factors related to the selection process. For instance, the softwares differ in their user-friendliness as well as in their strengths. Whether your needs tend toward text retrieving, textbase management, coding and retrieving, code-based theory building, or network building, you might then favor different packages (e.g., Weitzman, 1999, pp. 1246–1248).

VIGNETTE 8.1. A HELPFUL GUIDE FOR USING CAQDAS SOFTWARE

Computer Assisted Qualitative Data AnalysiS (CAQDAS) tools can help to analyze qualitative data. However, the tools also can consume a lot of a researcher's time and energy and then still produce disappointing results.

One approach is to move gingerly and incrementally in using any software, and Lewins and Silver's (2007) book provides just that kind of guidance. The book is filled with specific computer-based procedures, discussed generically at first but then showing how the procedures work with regard to three leading CAQDAS packages discussed individually: *ATLAS.ti5, MAXqda2,* and *NVivo7.*

The authors are not unabashed advocates of CAQDAS. Their book therefore contains repeated caveats about how not to expect the software to do the actual analytic work, as well as repeated reminders about the value of downloading computer output and handling and marking hardcopy materials directly. Whether derived from their book or others like it, having access to such external advice for using CAQDAS software seems highly prudent.

B. COMPILING AN ORDERLY SET OF DATA

PREVIEW—*What you should learn from this section:*
1. How to think of your data as needing to be organized into a formal database.
2. How to use the process to refamiliarize yourself with the data, not just compile them.
3. The importance of being consistent throughout the organizing process.

The first phase in the analytic cycle is an essential prelude to the analysis of any qualitative data. The phase may be likened to one of creating a "database"— a term that does not customarily appear in qualitative research textbooks.[2] Most of the textbooks nevertheless seem to assume that researchers will have compiled their field notes and other notes and evidentiary materials in some orderly fashion.

The importance of this assumption leads to the need to recognize the desired end-result more formally. For this reason the suggestion to compile an orderly set of records or "database" seems appropriate. The objective is to organize your qualitative data in a systematic fashion before formal analysis starts, not unlike straightening your desk and organizing your files before starting on an assignment. More orderly data will lead to stronger analyses and ultimately to more rigorous qualitative research.

At a minimum, such organizing helps researchers to find and access their own field notes and materials. More beneficially, such organizing helps with data analysis. Although not everyone uses a formal label such as a "database," anyone who has successfully completed a qualitative research study will likely have undertaken some kind of organizing effort and will have created a usable database.

Once organized and therefore compiled, the data may be considered your database. The useful ways of organizing the data are discussed next.

Parallel to Quantitative Research?

In quantitative research, a database usually consists of an electronic file containing discrete records. Each record has a uniform set of *fields*, with data entered into each field. A *data dictionary* then contains the definition of each field and precisely defines its possible entries. Before the database can be used, the data need to be "cleaned" and "verified" by checking the logic, consistency, and accuracy of the entries or data in each record.

Qualitative research may rely on analogous functions and nearly parallel procedures, whether the qualitative database is to be electronic or nonelectronic. The main difference, compared to quantitative analysis, is likely to be that textual (rather than numeric) data are to be ordered in some systematic manner. In quali-

---

[2]For case study research, this author has advocated the compiling of a "case study database" since 1984 in the various editions of the text on *Case Study Research: Design and Methods* (2009).

tative analysis, a *glossary* can help to define the important terminology found in the qualitative text, assuring their consistent use. The glossary's role may be similar to the use of a "data dictionary" in quantitative analysis.

Precisely how formal you make your compiled set of qualitative data depends on your own preferences and style of work. You may load your data into an electronic set of records, also grouping the records according to a meaningful set of files. You also may store your data in a nonelectronic medium, reorganizing them into a set of old-fashioned index cards. More important than its formality or format is the attention and care with which you compile your data.

Rereading and Relistening: Getting to "Know" Your Field Notes

The first function served by the *Compiling* phase is to familiarize you with your own field notes. You should be continually reviewing the field notes and other recordings discussed in Chapter 7. The rereading should remind you of your field observations and interviews, as well as your earlier reading of any documents or use of other sources of evidence.

To the extent that you tape recorded your interviews but may not have transcribed them, relistening rather than rereading will be the relevant activity. You will want to check the recordings repeatedly, again to familiarize yourself with the data you have collected. If you already had transcribed the recordings verbatim, you will want to reread the transcripts. (If you have not yet transcribed the recordings, you may want to consider transcribing some portion of them at this time.)

During your review of your field notes and materials, however, you are no longer doing fieldwork. You can therefore assimilate the information more thoughtfully and at a more measured pace. The reviewing should be highly analytic and might take a long time (weeks or months may not be too short, depending on the extent of the fieldwork and scope of the research). You should be asking yourself such questions as:

◆ What are the distinctive features of your study?;
◆ How might the collected data relate to the original research questions?; or
◆ Are there potentially new insights that have emerged?

Continually asking yourself these and similar questions should mark the entire analytic process.

Putting Everything into a Consistent Form

The orderly data or database will differ from your earlier notes because you will start to organize the earlier notes into a consistent form. Key to the form will be your attending carefully to potentially inconsistent usages of different words and terms. For instance, as you review your earlier notes and consider how to rearrange them into a more orderly fashion, you may find that you used the same terminology in two entirely different, if not contradictory, ways in your notes because they covered two different field interviews or observations. Such disparate, even inconsistent, usage may create analysis problems later and should therefore be cleared up at this point.

At the same time, the process must be done delicately. Some interviewees may have used a particular set of words that bear important meaning, and these words should not be obliterated just because you are trying to establish a consistent vocabulary across your data. Deciding what can be relabeled and what should be left alone will be another judgment call. Building a *glossary* to keep track of your deliberations will be very helpful, whether you decide to change some terms or retain their original usage.

Equally important, putting your data into consistent form also means separating the data into some set of records. What constitutes a *record* will vary from study to study. The appropriate unit may be a source, such as an interview or a document. Thus, if a study had 57 interviews and information from 13 documents, there might then be 70 records, even if there had been multiple interviews of the same person. Alternatively, each record can represent a different day in the field. Finally, a record can reflect one of the known focuses of a study. For instance, if a study was focused on interpersonal relationships, each record could represent an interaction between two or more people that were part of the study.

For experienced researchers, the record already may be a conceptual category of information, with each category compiling the information from the earlier field notes. In this case, the researcher can risk creating records that do not fairly or even fully represent all of the field notes, but the conceptual categories have quickly moved the researcher into the third (*Reassembling* and arraying) phase of an analysis.

The content of the data also should not be limited to text or narrative information. Your earlier notes may have contained tables, graphs, or other visual materials, and these also need to be organized and to become part of the database. If your research involved videotapes, the same attention needs to be given to the creation of edited tapes that follow some consistent form (Erickson, 2006).

Using Computer Software to Compile Your Records

Use of any CAQDAS software or the common software previously mentioned can help at this stage. Most of the different types of software are organized around separate records of one sort or another. Each record may become a separate file or "case." Some CAQDAS software also readily accepts non-narrative forms of materials, including videotapes, as records that will be an integral part of your database.

The software will help you to compile your data more formally. For instance, if you create a different file for each record, the software will then require a file name, a date, and other possible identifiers for each file. The software also will reinforce the use of a glossary to ensure consistent use of your terminology; remind you to mark your data with specific identifiers assigned to different people in your interviews; and permit you to add new electronic notes or marks, such as might be part of your own memos, onto each record.

Deciding whether to use some CAQDAS software to help you to create a formal database again depends on your own preference. If you are going to use such software to assist with the disassembling phase described next, you will have to organize your data into such records anyway.

You also may consider using the software in a limited way, to assist in your *Compiling* phase only. Recognizing the time needed to learn how to use the software, you should proceed cautiously before adopting this more limited application of the software, also comparing the process with the use of other more commonly used software tools.

Whether you are using electronic or nonelectronic formats, expect the compiling of your notes into an orderly set of data to be a demanding and time-consuming procedure. Remember that in the process, you will be gaining thorough familiarity with your original data, which is essential to doing acceptable qualitative research. In general, the newly compiled data should retain as much of the original detail from your earlier notes as possible. Thus, expect that the creation of the needed database will require much effort and patience on your part, not to speak of the care with which you will be doing this work.

Generally, the creation of a database will be one of the most important parts of your research. As a result, you should set high standards for being thorough and complete and should resist cutting any corners. Tracking your procedures as part of your personal journal also is desirable.

> As an example, the compiled database in a study of 40 community organizations consisted of 40 separate reports. Each report covered the data collected in response to 49 questions in a field protocol (the protocol was previously shown in Exhibit 4.2). The reports were then organized according to the field team's responses to the same 49 questions, which essentially served as a common outline, but with the information addressing each question differing from report to report (see Yin, 2003, pp. 31–52, for a complete example containing the questions and responses for one of the reports).

C. DISASSEMBLING DATA

PREVIEW—*What you should learn from this section:*
1. How to disassemble data by formally coding them.
2. How to disassemble data without formally coding them.
3. Who does the coding when computer software is used to code data.

Assuming that you have now properly organized your data, you are ready to start the second phase in the five-phase cycle, which calls for *Disassembling*[3] your data in some manner. Remember again that the phases can be recursive, which means that while you are in one phase you may go backward or forward at the same time—backward by returning to alter something done in an earlier phase, and forward by previewing or surfacing an idea for an upcoming phase.

Memo Writing

Similarly, expect the *Disassembling* phase itself to contain iterative steps. You will continually go back and forth between your initial ideas about how to disassemble the data and the actual data, potentially leading to modifications to your initial ideas. These kinds of thoughts should themselves be recorded as part of a series of *memos* kept throughout your analysis. Good memos can preserve what at first appear to be "half-baked" ideas that later may become invaluable as well as reduce the frustration of being uncertain of whether you already had considered and then rejected a certain idea. Most researchers experienced at doing qualitative analysis would say that this memo writing is imperative. In the words of one of them, "whenever *anything* related to and significant about the coding or analysis of the data comes to mind, stop whatever you're doing and write a memo about it immediately" (Saldaña, 2009, p. 33, original emphasis).

To Code or Not to Code

You can disassemble your data in many ways. Some ways are discussed here, but you also can devise your own peculiar disassembling process because there is no fixed routine.[4]

---

[3]Use of the term *disassemble* was preferred over two other terms frequently found in the literature. Some texts and methodologies refer to *fracturing* the data. This usage was resisted because of the connotation from the everyday meaning of *fracturing*—that the result may be harmful to the data, or that the data may be broken in some undesirable way. Scholars also have referred to the disassembling process as one of *data reduction* (because, for instance, many words in an original record are being coded into a shorter version). This second term also was resisted because disassembling data may not always result in reducing the data, nor should data reduction be the overarching goal for the disassembling process.

[4]Depending on the amount of textual data you have collected, a preliminary step may be to make the disassembling procedure more manageable by analyzing only that portion of the text that appears related to the specific topic of your study (e.g., Auerbach & Silverstein, 2003, p. 37). Although you should want to omit text that is totally irrelevant, nevertheless note that reducing it to manageable proportions always entails the risk of ignoring some potentially insightful information because it just did not seem relevant to you at the time.

The various ways, including everyone's home-grown versions, will nevertheless boil down to one critical choice: whether to code portions of the data—that is, by assigning new labels or codes to selected words, phrases, or other chunks of data in a database—or not. Supporters of the *grounded theory* approach to qualitative research have been at the forefront of describing how such coding might work (see "Guidance for Coding Qualitative Data," Vignette 8.2). However, deciding whether you should code or not code is not quite an "either–or" proposition. You can code your data for some topics in your study but not others, and you can therefore use both approaches. Each choice is discussed in turn.

VIGNETTE 8.2. GUIDANCE FOR CODING QUALITATIVE DATA

For over 40 years, the originators and supporters of grounded theory have provided much guidance on different approaches for coding qualitative data. The guidance is relevant to all scholars who want to consider coding their data, not just people practicing grounded theory.

Grounded theorists have defined three types of coding. In *open coding*, which is used at the outset, "the analyst is concerned with generating categories and their properties"; in *axial coding*, "categories are systematically developed and linked with subcategories"; and in *selective coding* analysts are concerned with "the process of integrating and refining categories" (Strauss & Corbin, 1998, p. 143). These three types of coding may be accompanied by *process coding*, helping to describe "a series of evolving sequences of action/interaction that occur over time and space" (p. 165).

The authors give detailed attention to these coding practices. The practices are discussed comprehensively, and they roughly align with two of the present book's five analytic phases: Disassembling (*open coding*) and Reassembling (*axial coding*, *selective coding*, and *process coding*).

Coding Data

In most qualitative research, the original text in a set of field notes and therefore in your organized database will consist of specific items, such as field actions and events, objects, and specific opinions, explanations, and other views expressed by field interviewees. Associated with these items will have been highly contextualized details, such as the time of day, the place, and the people involved in the item. Each item will therefore be unique.

The purpose of trying to code these items is to begin moving methodically to a slightly higher conceptual level. The uniqueness of the original field actions is not to be ignored, but items that seem to be essentially similar will be assigned the same code. This higher conceptual level will enable you later to sort the items from different records in different ways, such as into similar and dissimilar groups. Once sorted, you can examine the related features of these groups and gain insight into them.

The nature of the initial codes, which can be referred to as Level 1 codes or open codes (e.g., Hahn, 2008, pp. 6–8), can vary. These codes can stick closely to the original items, even reusing the exact words in the original item, sometimes referred to as *in vivo* codes (e.g., Saldaña, 2009, p. 3). As you progress in doing this first level of coding, you may start to think of ways that some of the Level 1 codes relate to each other, and your next goal is to move incrementally to an even higher conceptual level by recognizing the categories within which the Level 1 codes may fall. Your coding therefore proceeds to a second and higher set of codes, which can be referred to as Level 2 or category codes.

The Collaborative Homework Problem, I

Exhibit 8.2 illustrates these first two levels in an oversimplified manner. The samples of text come from a fieldworker's hypothetical set of notes. The study involved home observations and family interviews about a student who was having difficulty getting her parent to collaborate with her in doing homework (such collaboration was part of the curriculum promoted by the student's school).

Column 1 in Exhibit 8.2 has the original text, column 2 shows the Level 1 code assigned to each portion of text, and column 3 shows the Level 2 codes that were then assigned.

Assuming that these samples of text were the only data available in this oversimplified example, the disassembling process has produced four Level 2 categories: "barriers," "positive expectations," "relevant parental expertise," and "additional external support."

(Bringing these categories together would then become a task of the next phase of *Reassembling* the data. But let's first turn to the other *Disassembling* option.)

(to be continued)

Disassembling Data without Coding Them

Especially given the oversimplified nature of the homework example, you also could have disassembled the data without coding them. The process may be more discretionary and less routine, but in the hands of a seasoned researcher, it has the potential benefit of being more thoughtful and insightful. This is because coding routines can produce their own distractions—for example, having to attend to the mechanics of the coding process rather than struggling to think about the data. When not coding the data, however, the process can lead to nonsystematic and inconsistent judgments, so a researcher who decides not to code the data needs to take the precautions related to maintaining a rigorous analytic procedure, including the three precautions described at the outset of this chapter.

When not coding your data, your disassembling process will likely involve identifying text from the original database and creating a new set of your own substantive (not methodological) notes. In these new substantive notes, you will essentially be taking notes about your original data, but your new notes can cover the data in some different order or under different concepts and ideas. You might put these

EXHIBIT 8.2.   EXAMPLES OF LEVEL 1 AND LEVEL 2 CODING

Illustrative words from original field notes	Initial code (Level 1)	Category code (Level 2)
1. "Samantha brought homework home, but she did not always have the right assignment."	Student oversight	Barrier for getting homework done
2. "Whenever Samantha asked her mother to collaborate in doing the homework, her mother was usually busy."	Parent unavailability	Barrier for getting homework done
3. "When her mother was available, she would frequently allow herself to be interrupted and not return to work with Samantha."	External interruption	Barrier for getting homework done
4. "Samantha's teacher reported that Samantha seemed to be exceedingly talented, and the teacher did not readily understand why the homework assignments were such a problem."	Positive teacher's views	Positive expectations (for getting homework done)
5. "Samantha expressed enjoyment in doing schoolwork and looked forward to her homework assignments."	Positive student's views	Positive expectations (for getting homework done)
6. "Samantha's mother also thought that Samantha was sufficiently skilled to perform well at school."	Positive mother's views	Positive expectations (for getting homework done)
7. "Samantha's mother seemed to be familiar with the concepts covered by the homework."	Positive mother background	Relevant parental expertise
8. "Samantha's mother had at least one productive meeting with the teacher and no other apparently negative interactions."	Positive home–school collaboration	Additional external support

new notes on index cards or separate sheets of typed paper, to facilitate your ability to test different arrangements—part of the upcoming *Reassembling* phase.

Creating useful and helpful substantive notes will not be a necessarily efficient process. You may initially write some notes only to find later that they do not provide sufficient clues about what to do with the data. For instance, you may start with a new topic, extract relevant items from the original notes, and then find that the items do not fit well under the new topic. You might then modify the topic. Returning to your database with the modified topic in mind, you might then find that it leads to the selection of additional items to be extracted. You may later find that even the modified topic was not very useful after all and start the process all over again. Overall, there may be days of great uncertainty that you will need to learn how to tolerate.

In spite of the uncertainty, many researchers prefer to disassemble their data without formal coding because creative ideas seem to move faster and better. To overcome the inevitable pitfalls of inconsistency and inaccuracy that might occur, these researchers will then return to their original data many times and make sure that their disassembled topics are as faithful to the original data as possible.

Using Computer Software to Assist in Disassembling Data

CAQDAS or other software can definitely help in the disassembling process, especially if your database is large and warrants formal coding. Once you have assigned codes to the text, the software offers many advantages in checking and rechecking the coded materials, in retrieving and manipulating them, and in later assigning them to the next level of category codes.

When you use the software to support the coding process, again be prepared for the software's routines to demand their own attention. You will likely have to learn additional software terminology and worry about properly performing the software's routines. Such attention comes at the potential cost of having less time to think about the substantive patterns and themes in your data. These latter ruminations are the beginning of the third and fourth phases of the analytic cycle, and by having your attention diverted to the software's operations, you risk losing sight of some initial ruminations that can turn out to be invaluable.

Remember also that the software does not actually do the coding. *You do*. The software then conveniently records your codes and the coded items, making later retrieval much easier than had you worked manually only. You also can more easily recode items and change codes, even repeatedly. The efficiency of making these revisions as well as of the later retrieval and further analytic manipulation of the coded items is a major strength of the software, especially when you have a large database.

D. REASSEMBLING DATA

PREVIEW—*What you should learn from this section:*
1. The importance of emerging patterns in the reassembly process.
2. Different ways of arraying the data as a prelude to further analysis.
3. Three procedures to minimize or reveal biases in the reassembly process.
4. The challenge of bringing a qualitative and not a numeric orientation, if using computer software to assist in reassembling the data.

Looking for Patterns

During the *Disassembling* phase (i.e., either when coding and sorting or when reviewing your own new substantive notes if you are not formally coding), you may have become aware of potentially broader patterns in the data. The meticulousness of the disassembling process should not have kept you from thinking about the broader meaning of the data—for example, how they might inform the original study questions or reveal some important new insights into the original study topic. Noting any such patterns is the beginning of the third phase in the analysis cycle, that of *Reassembling* the data.

If you continue to use a formal coding process, the reassembling will take the form of bringing your Level 1 and Level 2 codes onto an even higher conceptual plane, whereby themes or even theoretical concepts start to emerge and may be considered Level 3 and Level 4 codes (e.g., Hahn, 2008, pp. 6–8).

Regardless of whether you are following the coding or noncoding option, during the reassembling process you should constantly be querying yourself (and the data). The querying process is intrinsic to doing analysis. More important than the specific answers to the queries may be that you are proactively sifting and sorting your ideas, searching for patterns. Typical questions might be: Do the emerging patterns make sense? Are they moving you to a substantively important plane? How do the patterns relate to the concepts and hypotheses entertained at the outset of your study? Do the patterns (desirably) become more complicated or expansive when you review additional items from your database (e.g., Nespor, 2006, pp. 298–302)?

Using Arrays to Help Reassemble Data

The reassembling process can involve "playing with the data," which means considering them under different arrangements and themes and then altering and re-altering the arrangements and themes until something emerges that seems satisfactory to you. For instance, with CAQDAS software you can use Boolean logic to examine different combinations of codes. Alternatively, if your new set of substantive notes is on index cards and in manual form, you can manipulate the cards into different combinations. The manipulations might follow one or more of the following patterns (Nespor, 2006, pp. 298–302): tracking how the same individual is represented at different times and places; examining the structure of actions in terms of the people, things, or ideas involved; or comparing some patterns with those found by others.

Besides using your own intuitions (or in the absence of any intuitions), one specific way of "playing with the data" is to array them in an organized fashion, as in the following three examples, discussed in the next several sections:

◆ Creating hierarchical arrays,
◆ Designing matrices as arrays, and
◆ Working with other types of arrays.

Creating Hierarchical Arrays

One common way is to build hierarchies, with the most concrete database item at one end of the hierarchy, a more abstract concept representing the concrete items at a higher level, and so on. Most often, each level of the hierarchy helps to pull together a larger group of similar items at the next level below. By reassembling the data so that similar data fall under similar concepts and dissimilar data fall under separate concepts, the hierarchy can point to different groupings (i.e., potential "classes" or "typologies" of things). The hierarchy also can suggest associations across groupings (i.e., the relationships across the "classes" or "typologies"). For the coding option, the hierarchy can simply be seen as an arraying of Level 1 to Level 4 codes and concepts; for the noncoding option, a similar hierarchy can be developed—probably in a more conceptual than literal manner—from the new set of substantive notes taken during the *Disassembling* phase.

In this manner, you can create more than a single hierarchy. One or more of them can then become the basis for structuring the data to organize your entire study, with the ensuing analysis focusing on the groupings and their relationships. Additional detail could then be added at each level of the hierarchy, to ensure that your eventual report contained as rich a rendition of the original data as desired.

The Collaborative Homework Problem, II (*continued*)

Returning now to the illustrative example of the student's homework, the emerging Level 3 themes (from using either the coding or noncoding options) might have been the same: to improve the desired student–parent collaboration, the household needed to address the original barriers because the expectations, parent's expertise, and home–school conditions all seemed to be supportive. Such an emerging theme fits well with the education literature that suggests that parents are often too busy to collaborate with their children in doing homework—often because the parents work full time or need to attend to other children or loved ones at home.

To go one hypothetical step further, and under either the coding or noncoding options, the fieldworker in this example was not entirely convinced of this reassembly. Other loose ends had revealed themselves—in particular, a seeming willingness by the mother to *allow herself to be interrupted* (see item 3, Exhibit 8.2) in spite of being familiar with the concepts in the homework (item 7, Exhibit 8.2).

The skepticism caused the fieldworker to revisit background data that had been collected but that had not been part of either the original coding or noncoding option. The data revealed that the study had taken place in a community with a decades-long declining economy and population.

Although such background information did not originally appear relevant, the fieldworker then recalled that the adults in the community were concerned about their children leaving it to start new lives outside of the community. This led the fieldworker to speculate that the parent was not too busy or distracted to collaborate on the homework but in fact might have feared that her child's excelling in school would increase the chances of her eventually leaving the community—a theme less often pointed out by the education literature. The possibility of this broader theme now became the topic of a follow-up inquiry by the fieldworker.

Equally pertinent to the present chapter, note that the fieldworker's skepticism in the collaborative homework problem was the important attribute, regardless of whether the *Disassembling* and *Reassembling* phases had involved formal coding or not. Thus, and to repeat earlier cautions, the researcher and not any computer routine bear the brunt of doing the entirety of the analytic work.

Designing Matrices as Arrays

A second common way of arraying the data takes the form of some kind of matrix (see "Creating Matrices to Reassemble Qualitative Data," Vignette 8.3). The simplest matrix is essentially a table of rows and columns. The rows represent one dimension and the columns represent another.

VIGNETTE 8.3. CREATING MATRICES TO REASSEMBLE QUALITATIVE DATA

Creating a matrix—in its simplest form a two-dimensional array of rows and columns—is one of the most common devices for reassembling qualitative data.

Miles and Huberman (1994) present numerous types of matrices. For instance, they discuss matrices that are time-ordered (e.g., chronological), role-ordered (e.g., according to people's roles), and conceptually ordered (e.g., a set of categories arrayed against another set) (pp. 110–142). They also offer sound advice regarding the contents of a matrix—that is, the data to be entered into each cell of a matrix—and although their matrices are dominantly two-dimensional, the authors clearly note that matrices can have more than two dimensions (p. 241). Their text serves as a good source of illustrative examples of matrices and instruction on how matrices work.

If you do not have at least two dimensions that are of immediate interest, you can start with some of the most common dimensions that are likely to pertain to nearly every qualitative study. For instance, qualitative data usually capture actions and events taking place over a period of time. One dimension can therefore be a chronological one, with each row representing a different chronological period. You then might have studied several individual people and their experiences or statuses over time, so the experiences or statuses for each person may appear in a separate column. The resulting matrix then asks that you place the relevant items from your original data in each cell, indicating the specific experience or status of each individual person at each chronological period.

Alternatively, you might have studied several groups, organizations, or neighborhoods over time. You can reassemble all of your data according to these situations and eventually develop a full narrative about each (see "Studying Neighborhood Change," Vignette 8.4). To get started in this process, a chronological matrix would enable you to search for patterns of change. For instance, in a study of 30 schools, 15 had adopted some type of new curriculum or instructional practice with federal support, whereas the other 15 had not received any award. The chronological patterns were placed in a multipage matrix for all 30 schools, to compare the two groups (see Exhibit 8.3 for a sample page, showing 5 of the 30 schools).

VIGNETTE 8.4. STUDYING NEIGHBORHOOD CHANGE

Neighborhood change was the topic of a study of four neighborhoods in the same city (Wilson & Taub, 2006). The study focused on the ethnic and racial segregation and turnover in the neighborhoods, examining Albert O. Hirschman's well-known theory of *Exit, Voice, and Loyalty* (1970)—that is, the extent to which residents leave or remain in neighborhoods as new residents enter the neighborhoods.

The study discusses each neighborhood in a separate chapter, tracing the changes in each over a 20-year period. Of the four neighborhoods, one maintained a persistent white majority, the second showed large-scale shifts from white to Hispanic residents, a third was a transient Hispanic neighborhood with upwardly mobile residents leaving as soon as they had the resources to do so, and the fourth had a stable and large lower-middle-class black population.

The study used its fieldwork data to explain why the population changes occurred or did not occur in these four neighborhoods, largely supporting Hirschman's theory. The book also concluded that urban neighborhoods are likely to remain divided, racially and culturally.

See also Vignette 5.8.

Besides having rows and columns, all matrices also have another component— their cells. For reassembling the data, the goal is to place some data into each cell (including noting when no data exist for that cell). A completed matrix then permits you to scan your actual data across the rows and columns.

The amount and nature of the data that you place in each cell can help or hinder the scanning process. First, the entries should be your actual data, whether represented directly or by the codes assigned in the disassembling process.

Second, and especially when not using codes, transferring the data from your database into the cells may make the cells too large or crowded. The matrix may then also become too large and clumsy, slowing the desired scanning into a piecemeal and disjointed rather than smooth process. In this situation, you may need to do some judicious abbreviating, so that only the essence of the data appears in each cell. However, the abbreviated version should be footnoted to refer back to the original data in your database, enabling you to revisit the relationship between the abbreviated and original versions of the data. You should revisit the relationship frequently enough to make sure that the abbreviated version faithfully represents the original.

Third, the content of the cells should not contain your own opinions or conclusions. The desired matrix is to be a *data* matrix, permitting you to examine your data and only then to start drawing conclusions (note the content of the cells in Exhibit 8.3). In other words, at this stage in your analysis, the main goal is to reassemble your data, and the desired matrix should be considered a form of documentation only, not a device for communicating with your later readers. As with other types of documentation, the desired matrix might then appear, if at all, in an appendix to a report. (From this documentation, and for the body of the text of your study, you may later create more simplified and attractive tables, graphics, and other ways of presenting your study data (see Chapter 10, Section B).

EXHIBIT 8.3. ILLUSTRATIVE CHRONOLOGY MATRIX

	School A (grades 6–8)	School U (grades preK–5)	School Q (grades preK–5)	School G (grades preK–8)	School K (grades 10–12)
1995–1996			State starts "adequate-yearly-progress" (AYP) process		
1996–1997				Designated as Title I school; starts schoolwide improvement committee, and starts *Four Blocks of Literacy* in all grades	
1997–1998	Restructures to serve grades 6–8		Student population shifting over next 2 years, from 60 to 95% eligible for free- and reduced-price lunch	Starts district-led *Literacy Groups* initiative for grades 1–2	
1998–1999					
1999–2000			Required by state to develop annual school improvement plan (SIP)	Selected as *Reading Recovery* training site; also selected by state as a lighthouse school for *Four Blocks of Literacy*	
2000–2001	Staff introduced to *Turning Points* (TP) and comprehensive school reform (CSR) at a state conference; 83% of faculty vote to adopt TP prior to CSR application (Apr.)		Fails to meet AYP (fall)	Adds preschool and full-day kindergarten	Conducts needs assessment, indicating achievement and dropout problems; establishes leadership team to study school reform, with principal as key member
2001–2002	Receives CSR funding (Jan.); starts TP training (spring)	Designated as failing to meet AYP (fall); attends state CSR fair with method developers (Jan.); votes to adopt *Learning Focused Schools* (LFS) and applies for CSR (May)	Is in school identified for improvement status for second year; teachers attend methods fairs; faculty votes 100% to adopt *Co-nect*; submits CSR application (SIP is foundation)		Faculty votes to begin readiness activities for *Urban Learning Communities* (ULC) (Jan.); receive orientation and establish four committees to implement *ULC*; starts school of technology as first academy
2002–2003	Begins *TP*, with external coach visiting first-days/month	Receives CSR award (Aug.) and starts *LFS*	Receives CSR award (Aug.), but all methods suspended by district for 2002–2003, so that *Open Court* can be used by all schools, to align with state's curriculum framework	Starts CSR award, closely aligned with Title I Schoolwide plan	Receives CSR funds and contracts with *ULC* for services; plans second academy (in health careers)
2003–2004		Initially fails AYP but successfully appeals, based on changes in state assessment	Suspension lifted by district; school begins *Co-nect* (and first-year CSR) and continues *Open Court* (and other methods)		

Source: COSMOS Corporation

In sum, matrices, like hierarchies, are a central form of qualitative analysis.[5] The disassembled data now have been reassembled in some orderly and conceptually meaningful fashion. You may find that one or more of your matrices now leads to broader conceptual themes relevant to your study. In turn, these broader themes can start to become the basis for interpreting and then composing the narrative for your entire study. Alternatively, one of your matrices can itself serve as the entire empirical basis for the narrative.

Working with Other Types of Arrays

Hierarchies and matrices are but two ways of arraying your data. The methodological literature has many other illustrative arrays, which include the use of more graphic displays, such as flowcharts and logic models (e.g., Yin, 2009, pp. 149–156), organization charts, concept maps (e.g., Kane & Trochim, 2007), and diagrams more generally.

More complex arrays also need not be two-dimensional. You can readily conceptualize how a third dimension could be added to a two-dimensional matrix, although graphically depicting the three dimensions might be more difficult. Harder to imagine would be additional dimensions, but the only limit is your imagination and the relevance of such multiple dimensions to your study's goals.

Summarizing the Arraying Process

The formality of pursuing the arraying process again varies according to a researcher's own style and preferences. There is no single right way or recommended set of arrays. Some researchers even can skip the need to array their data and be able to move quickly to the fourth phase in the analytic cycle as later covered in Chapter 9 (Section A)—the *Interpreting* phase. Other researchers may be able to conceptualize the relevant arrays by creating yet a new set of substantive notes or expanding their earlier notes, but without spending time to construct any arrays formally.

Still other researchers work best if they lay out the various possibilities in formally constructed arrays. If they do so manually and put their arrays on large sheets of paper, the arrays may fill a large portion of wall or floor space, depending on whether the sheets of paper are hung on the wall or allowed to spread across a floor.

Important Procedures during the Reassembling Process

The reassembling process inevitably involves an increasing number of discretionary choices. Each choice—for example, about what to retrieve from the database, as well as how to build hierarchical relationships and to design matrices—involves your own judgments. Your emerging analysis is therefore vulnerable to unknown biases. You need to take as many precautions to minimize or at least reveal such biases, and three procedures can help: making constant comparisons, watching for negative cases, and engaging in rival thinking.

---

[5]Matrices may be a central form of *quantitative* analysis, as well. For more on this possibility, see the discussion in Chapter 12.

As a preliminary comment, note that the suggestion to engage in these three procedures, such as rival thinking, again does not imply that you have assumed a positivist orientation (e.g., Eisenhart, 2006; Rex et al., 2006). You may have been exercising an interpretivist and not positivist view (or some other perspective) throughout your research. If so, your use of the three procedures can embrace the same view—that is, how comparisons, negative cases, and rivals might be conjectured *given* your particular research lens.

The first procedure is to make *constant comparisons*—for example, watching for similarities and dissimilarities among the items in your data—and questioning why you might have regarded the items as being similar or dissimilar in the reassembling of your data:

> For instance, your fieldwork had focused on organizational leadership, and during the *Reassembling* phase you realized you were considering "leadership" to cover situations with more participatory opportunities along with other situations with no such opportunities. By making this and other *constant comparisons* you might now question whether your emerging theme really embraces both kinds of situations or whether you should broaden your initial thinking about the theme.

The second procedure is to watch for *negative instances*—for example, uncovering items that on the surface might have seemed similar but on closer examination appeared to be misfits. The negative instances might therefore challenge the robustness of the code or label:

> For instance, your fieldwork involved work with several different community groups, and you are trying to build a theme related to group "solidarity." All of the groups but one appeared to work together as a whole. The one group consisted of subgroups that worked well together.
>
> Your goal would not be to ignore this seemingly nuanced difference but to investigate the last group's other features more carefully as a *negative instance* because its decentralized manner of working might not in fact represent group solidarity.

The third procedure is to engage constantly in *rival thinking*—for example, searching for alternative explanations for your initial observations:

> For instance, you might be studying how an innovative practice was being implemented in a healthcare clinic. When implementation faltered, your initial thinking during the *Reassembling* phase might have been that particular workers resisted using the practice. However, before finalizing this interpretation, you should examine your data carefully for any plausible *rival explanations*. You would then want your analysis to show explicitly the (lack of) evidence for any competing explanations before concluding that resistance indeed was the main explanation for the faltering.

In summary, because the reassembling process remains a keenly analytic process, you should again avoid any purely mechanistic approach. You can increase the accuracy and robustness of your work by giving close attention to constant comparisons, to negative or contrary cases, and to rival thinking.

Using Computer Software to Assist in Reassembling Data

Computer software can be of great assistance in trying different ways to reassemble data. For instance, building hierarchies is inherent in nearly every type of CAQDAS software. An added benefit is that the software can then present the resulting hierarchy graphically. Some of the software also can reassemble and present the data according to the other types of arrays, including matrices and concept maps.

There is one important caution in using CAQDAS software to create arrays in some situations and with some CAQDAS software: If you are not aware of the type of array you will desire ahead of time, you may need to revise your original codes or categories upon finding an array that is of interest to you. For instance, the categories used to build a hierarchy may not be exactly the same kinds of categories needed to build matrices.

The software also may not be able to support the development of more creative arrays. In this situation, you can consider a combination of computer-based and manual operations. The main goal is to have the flexibility to think analytically—that is, to think "outside the box"—and not to be limited to doing what the preprogrammed software is limited to doing.

Another general but critical caution in using CAQDAS software is to resist using it to count the frequency of occurrence of words as the main reassembling strategy, except for possibly three situations:

1. Your study had specifically hypothesized some frequency as part of its original research questions (but such a question would not be a very interesting *qualitative* question);

2. Open-ended survey items as part of your broader qualitative study (not just as part of a survey study) were specifically designed to be coded and counted, as in trying to establish the frequency of different kinds of reasons or explanations that respondents gave for a previous closed-ended question (e.g., the sequence in a poll represented by a closed-ended "Whom did you vote for?" followed by an open-ended "Why?"); or

3. The frequency of word usage was considered an important part of a content analysis study (e.g., Grbich, 2007).

These three situations notwithstanding, reassembling data by counting frequencies is not an analytic strategy that will result in especially insightful qualitative research. Yet, the danger is great, both because of a predilection to think of research as a "counting" activity and because the software programs will do such counting so easily. You risk greatly disappointing your qualitative audience by following such a path (and you might not have shown your mastery over qualitative research in this manner).

Put another way, the main challenge in using CAQDAS software successfully will be your ability to bring a *qualitative* orientation to the task, even though a computer's natural inclination may be to engage in counting as a conventional but quantitative strategy. The challenge may be likened to several other situations that pit your creativity against some preprogrammed way of thinking, such as searching the stacks of a library directly rather than relying solely on using a card catalog; or putting together an individualized profile of a new student without being biased by the most common formats that seem relevant; or, finally, solving a detective case by piecing together the unique elements of a crime.

Final Words on Reassembling

Successful reassembling, along with satisfactory arrays (whether graphically rendered or not), means that you should be seeing the broader themes or outline of your entire analysis. If such themes have not emerged, you need to stick with additional iterations between the *Disassembling* and the *Reassembling* phases. If the broader themes or outline have indeed emerged, you are ready for *Interpreting* and then *Concluding*, which are the fourth and fifth phases of the analytic cycle covered by the next chapter.

RECAP FOR CHAPTER 8: *Terms, phrases, and concepts that you can now define*:

1. Compiling, disassembling, and reassembling
2. Computer software to support data analysis
3. A data record and its fields
4. The advantages and disadvantages of coding data versus not coding them
5. Grounded theory
6. Literal codes and category codes
7. Playing with the data
8. Hierarchies, matrices, chronologies, and graphic depictions as data arrays
9. Constant comparisons
10. Negative instances
11. Rival thinking

EXERCISE FOR CHAPTERS 8 AND 9: DISASSEMBLING, REASSEMBLING, AND INTERPRETING AUTOBIOGRAPHICAL DATA

♦ ♦ ♦

Portion Related to Chapter 8

Write a short autobiography, organizing it in *chronological* fashion (starting with where and when you were born and bringing it into the present) [do not duplicate the material in the exercise for Chapter 1].

You don't have to try to recall every important experience, but for the experiences you do write down, make sure that you describe the situations so others can feel that they might have been there—for example, covering such details as the geographic location, other people who were involved and your relationship to them, the institutional setting for the experience, and any objects or relevant features of the physical environment. The short autobiography should be about five pages (double-space) in length. Let this version represent the *Compilation* phase, or your compiled database.

After you have finished, return to the entire text and manually code the details. Have at least 8–10 codes, choosing them in either of two ways: (1) Let an item suggest a "higher" conceptual category (*inductive*), or (2) start with concepts you already think might be important and then find items in the text that illustrate these concepts (*deductive*). Write the codes near the relevant text of the autobiography.

Now examine the codes. Decide which ones might be related to each other, totally unrelated, or related in some more complex manner. Add category codes to suit these situations and write them next to the original codes. Let this version represent the *Disassembling* phase of your analysis.

Array the codes and categories in some manner that starts to make sense of your autobiography (e.g., in a hierarchy, matrix, or flow diagram). Let one of the arrays represent the *Reassembling* phase of your analysis.

Portion Related to Chapter 9

Given what you have reassembled, think of broader interpretations about your autobiography and address issues of interest to you (you also can use the following as a suggested set):

1. In 1–2 pages, and citing specific portions of your arrays (from the exercise in Chapter 8), discuss how the experiences you selected share anything in common, or whether they fall under a few major topics (and if so, what are they?). If the experiences do not share anything in common or fall under no major topics, discuss why the experiences tend to be disconnected or unrelated to each other.

2. Continuing your interpretation for another 1–2 pages, cite specific coded materials or arrays to support your claim about what the autobiography might tell a reader about: "The important people in my life" and "Enduring relationships with different kinds of institutions or organizations."

3. In a final page, discuss the extent to which your autobiography is totally unique, compared to one that might provide a basis for generalizing to other people's experiences.

SAMPLE STUDY 1: STUDY OF UNIVERSITY–SCHOOL PARTNERSHIPS AS AN EXAMPLE FOR CHAPTERS 8 AND 9 (CHAPTER 8 PORTION)

Introduction to the Sample Study

This example is a study of partnerships between universities and K–12 schools. Because the subject is about the schooling everyone has had or is still having, the example may be readily understandable to nearly all readers of this book. The context and issues should be evident to nonspecialists.

More specifically, the example covers 48 partnerships. In each partnership, faculty in a university mathematics or science department collaborated with K–12 schools to improve K–12 mathematics and science education. The main research question involved these partnerships' prospects for becoming self-sustaining after initial external funds from the federal government expire. (The example and its research question are part of a broader evaluation covering many facets of these partnerships—see Moyer-Packenham et al., 2009; Wong et al., 2008.) The issue of sustainability has been a common issue in public policy, but these kinds of math–science partnerships had not in the past shown much sustainability in the absence of finding new sources of external funds.

The study involved extensive fieldwork, including interviews, observations, and reviews of documents. The study therefore used qualitative methods and illustrates the analytic techniques discussed in relation to the five-phased cycle.

The study will be referred to hereafter as **Sample Study 1**. The *Compiling, Disassembling,* and *Reassembling* phases of the study are described next; the *Interpreting* and *Concluding* phases are discussed at the end of Chapter 9.

Database Compiled for Sample Study 1

The study of 48 partnerships had a rather straightforward database that nevertheless took time to compile. Each partnership was located in a different place around the country, and each had been the subject of separate fieldwork and also separate searches for archival material.

The research team compiled all of these field notes and notes from archival materials into a separate report about each partnership (each report constituted a separate record). The reports were mainly written in narrative form, although they contained occasional numeric tables and graphs as well as diagrams. However, the reports were composed so that they all followed the exact same broad outline of topics (which appeared as the headings in each report), and the reports all used a similar terminology (see Exhibit 8.4 for the outline and an abbreviated version of the glossary that was used). The 48 separate reports, not part of any CAQDAS software, then became the database to be used for analysis.

EXHIBIT 8.4. HEADINGS AND SAMPLE GLOSSARY FOR A SINGLE RECORD IN SAMPLE STUDY 1

a. Topical Headings Used to Organize Text for
   Each of 48 Separate Reports:

   - Sec. 1. Overview of Logic Model (How the Partnership Is Organized to Improve K–12 Mathematics and Science Education)
   - Sec. 2. Sample of Partnership's Data Collection and Other Evaluation Activities
   - Sec. 3. Teacher Quality, Quantity, and Diversity
   - Sec. 4. Challenging Courses and Curricula
   - Sec. 5. Role of University Discipline Faculty
   - Sec. 6. Rival Explanations
   - Sec. 7. Evolving Innovations and Discoveries
   - Sec. 8. Sources and References

b. Sample Glossary Items:

   - *Preservice education*: education for prospective K–12 teachers
   - *Inservice education*: training or education for existing K–12 teachers
   - *Challenging curricula*: K–12 curricula selected to meet state standards (not the curricula used in preservice or inservice education)
   - *Discipline faculty*: university faculty with science, technology, engineering, or mathematics as their field of research, usually being located in a discipline-based academic department in a school of arts and sciences
   - *Rival explanations*: alternative explanations, other than the work of the partnership, that might account for changes in K–12 mathematics and science education
   - *Sustainability*: the ability of the partnership to continue its activities beyond the period of its original grant award from the federal government

---

Disassembling Procedure in Sample Study 1

For the purpose of keeping the example simple for its use in this book, the disassembling procedure focused on a single topic: the role of university faculty in conducting activities related to K–12 mathematics and science education. The coding took place in two steps and was done manually.

First, the database was reviewed thoroughly for any mention of a university or university faculty. Many such mentions were found, and brackets were placed around each one. Second, if a bracketed mention involved an activity between the university faculty and any aspect of K–12 education, the activity was given a Level 1 code (or a label). (If the bracketed mention did not involve such an activity, no code was assigned.) The codes deliberately pointed to the aspect of K–12 education that appeared to be involved, and eight (Level 2) categories of activities emerged (see Exhibit 8.5).

EXHIBIT 8.5. EIGHT ACTIVITIES EMERGING FROM REVIEW OF DATABASE, THEN USED AS CODES IN SAMPLE STUDY 1

Variety of Activities Involving University Faculty in K–12 Education Activities

1. *Preservice Education*: Faculty offer courses and programs in mathematics and science departments, for enrollment by students who may become K–12 teachers.
2. *Inservice Training for Existing K–12 Teachers*: Faculty offer ad hoc workshops, summer institutes, and mentoring support to existing mathematics and science teachers.
3. *University Courses for Existing K–12 Teachers*: Faculty design new undergraduate or graduate courses offered by their departments to strengthen existing teachers' opportunities for obtaining certification or advanced degrees.
4. *Assistance to School Districts*: Faculty help districts to define curriculum frameworks, pacing guides, or classroom assessments in mathematics and science.
5. *Direct Contact with K–12 Students*: Faculty instruct K–12 students as part of informal science program (e.g., at a science center), as interns working in university research laboratories, in judging science fairs, or in some similar capacity.
6. *Community Education*: Faculty participate in meetings attended by families of K–12 students, as in family mathematics nights sponsored by local schools.
7. *Research*: Faculty conduct their own research focusing on K–12 educational topics, such as K–12 curricula or instructional methods.
8. *University Instruction*: Faculty modify their own courses, adopting new instructional methods learned as a result of being exposed to K–12 pedagogical principles (e.g., use of inquiry-based science or mathematics).

All labels and categories were then handwritten in the margin of the report alongside the bracketed item, together with a unique identifying number. These numbered items served as the (Level 3) codes that were used in the later phase of the analysis.

The manual procedure had the benefit of creating a hardcopy text whereby the bracketed items and their labels could be reviewed and re-reviewed, for consistency of labeling or for any other purpose. Use of CAQDAS software would have provided the same benefit but also more—for instance, the software would have permitted quicker scanning as well as the ability to search more easily for specific items. Nevertheless, the study team in **Sample Study 1** did not deem the amount of records large enough to warrant the effort involved in using the software and converting the materials into computer form—illustrating a decision that will confront every researcher at a comparable stage of work.

Example of Reassembling Array Used in Sample Study 1

The coded data were reassembled according to a two-dimensional matrix (however, this large matrix has not been reproduced as part of the present text). One dimension (the rows) represented each of the eight activities previously defined in Exhibit 8.5. The second dimension (the columns) represented the 48 partnerships in the study. Within each cell of the matrix was placed the actual item from the database that had been coded as one of the eight activities, along with its unique identifying number, creating a matrix with 8 × 48 cells. Essentially, the matrix helped the researchers to organize systematically the original data, according to the eight specific types of K–12 education activities being conducted by the university faculty in each of the 48 partnerships.

CHAPTER 9

Analyzing Qualitative Data, II

Interpreting and Concluding

Research studies do not end with the sheer analysis of their data or the literal presentation of their empirical findings. Good studies must go two further steps— trying to interpret the findings and then drawing some overall conclusion(s) from the study in its entirety. Unfortunately, the ability to make these two additional steps is often taken for granted. For instance, many empirical studies (not just in qualitative research) conclude by repeating or rewording their findings. To strengthen the ability in doing qualitative research, the present chapter presents an array of choices and examples for both of the two steps. Clearly identified and discussed in detail are three ways of making interpretations and five ways of drawing conclusions.

There's no snappy introduction to this chapter. It continues the five-phased analytic cycle introduced in Chapter 8 by covering the fourth phase, *Interpreting*, and the fifth phase, *Concluding*. Yet, absent any snappy introduction, these phases of qualitative analysis are the most intriguing of all social science research. The phases challenge you to put your findings into order, to create the right words and concepts, and to tell the world the significance of your research.

A continuing reminder is the recursive relationship among all of the analytic phases. Exhibit 9.1 truncates the original five phases (shown earlier in Exhibit 8.1) by focusing only on the last four. This focus highlights the critical role of the interpretive phase.

As suggested by the two-way arrows in Exhibit 9.1, your initial interpretations can cause you to return to the *Reassembling* phase—for example, to revise the relevant data arrays. You might go back and forth between these two phases more than once or twice. Exhibit 9.1 also suggests that the *Interpreting* phase even might cause you to revisit the *Disassembling* phase, possibly to recode some items. The recoded items would then produce new themes in the *Reassembling* phase. Likewise, the *Interpreting* and *Concluding* phases also can have a recursive relationship.

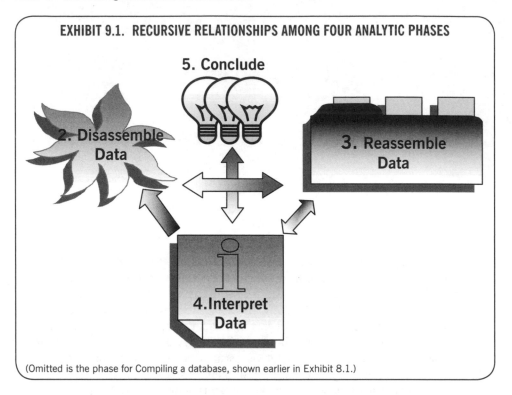

EXHIBIT 9.1. RECURSIVE RELATIONSHIPS AMONG FOUR ANALYTIC PHASES

5. Conclude

2. Disassemble Data

3. Reassemble Data

4. Interpret Data

(Omitted is the phase for Compiling a database, shown earlier in Exhibit 8.1.)

By starting the *Interpreting* phase, you should have developed some data arrays or other ways of reassembling your data. You should have in your mind how an empirically based interpretation of your data has emerged. Use of the term *interpreting* deliberately signals the possibility that others might interpret the same data differently. If you are ambitious, you may want to strive for an interpretation that anticipates the main alternatives and addresses why those may be less compelling.

By starting the fifth or *Concluding* phase, you should have a firm if still preliminary version of your interpretation. You should have given some thought to the conclusions to be made from your research. Compelling conclusions bring unity to the entire rest of a study. If yours has not achieved such status, you may want to rework your interpretation, so that it builds more strongly toward an anticipated conclusion. Continuing the illustrative example that started at the end of Chapter 8, the end of this chapter shows how **Sample Study 1** dealt with both its interpreting and concluding phases.

One final clarification: This chapter has a different objective from Chapter 11, although on the surface the two chapters may appear to cover similar topics. The later chapter assumes you have put your interpretation and conclusion together and suggests ways of presenting them as forcefully but sensitively as possible. This chapter aims to help you to put them together in the first place.

A. INTERPRETING

PREVIEW—*What you should learn from this section:*
1. The objective of having interpretations embraces an entire study, not just a single table or set of data.
2. Five attributes of a comprehensive or desirable interpretation.

Interpreting may be considered the craft of giving your own meaning to your reassembled data and data arrays. This phase brings your entire analysis together and stands at its pinnacle.

This fourth phase in your analysis calls for a wide-ranging use of your interpretive skills, covering the critical portions—if not the bulk—of your data as well as your deepest meanings. In other words, the reference here to "interpreting" is not a narrow one, such as interpreting the data in a specific table. Rather, the goal is to develop a comprehensive interpretation, still encompassing specific data, but whose main themes will become the basis for understanding your entire study.

What constitutes a comprehensive or good interpretation has no firm definition. You may want to consider striving for as many of the following attributes as possible:

◆ *Completeness* (Does your interpretation have a beginning, middle, and end?)

◆ *Fairness* (Given your interpretive stance, would others with the same stance arrive at the same interpretation?)

◆ *Empirical accuracy* (Does your interpretation fairly represent your data?)

◆ *Value-added* (Is the interpretation new, or is it mainly a repetition of your topic's literature?)

◆ *Credibility* (Independent of its creativity, how would the most esteemed peers in your field critique or accept your interpretation?)

Seasoned qualitative researchers already will have a strong sense of the conditions that meet these five criteria. Newcomers to qualitative research will still be searching. The best advice is to obtain continued feedback from colleagues, even as you develop your interpretation.

Data do not "speak for themselves." The closest occasion might be when everyone's interpretation of the same set of data is likely to coincide. However, such convergence of opinions may not occur except under rare circumstances.[1] Thus, the quality of your interpretation can make a difference in how your entire study is viewed. The desired interpretation and the strength of your data also go hand in hand. To be avoided are either of two extremes: having a lot of data but a superfi-

---

[1]Those who might consider this to be mainly a limitation of qualitative data would do well to remember the lack of consensus and starkly different interpretations emanating from a field dominated by quantitative data—economics.

cial interpretation that does not fully "mine" the data, or having a pressing interpretation that overreaches the quality of the data. The golden mean again cannot
be readily defined, but you should strive for it.

B. MODES OF INTERPRETING

PREVIEW—*What you should learn from this section:*
1. Three modes of interpreting a qualitative study.
2. How to associate a descriptive interpretation with the organization of a study's chapters.
3. How the subtitles of qualitative studies frequently summarize a study's main descriptive topic.
4. The variety of substantive topics, such as the diversity of people or social groups, that can be covered by qualitative studies.
5. How to place a study's interpretation within the context of weak to strong literatures already covering the same topic.

There is no typology of interpretations. In crafting an interpretation, you will
be treading on common but still rather uncharted territory. Nevertheless, an inductive approach may serve a helpful purpose: to determine whether some common
lessons can be derived by reviewing the interpretations found in existing qualitative studies.

Such a review, to be undertaken momentarily, suggests a short and simple list
of the potential modes of interpretation (separately, you may want to conduct your
own review of some of your favorite qualitative studies and see whether you can
augment or modify these modes):

◆ Description;
◆ Description plus a call for action; and
◆ Explanation.

At first glance, the list may appear trivial. For instance, everyone knows that qualitative data provide a strong basis for the first mode, "description," so referring to it
does not seem very insightful.

To produce good description, however, is not necessarily easy. Coming up with
a mundane description that wanders all over the place with no apparent aim is one
of the potential traps in qualitative analyses. So, let's see if we can develop some
usable ideas to help make your descriptions more riveting renditions of social science. Also discussed are the two other modes, "description plus call for action" and
"explanation."

"Description" as a Major Type of Interpretation

Our inductive strategy starts by reviewing two classic qualitative studies: *Middletown* (Lynd & Lynd, 1929) and *Coming of Age in Samoa* (Mead, 1928). These works are deliberately drawn from the two disciplines that have contributed most to qualitative research—sociology and anthropology. Remarkably, the publication dates are nearly identical, and both are approaching 100 years in age. During this time, both studies have been the subject of repeated new editions, demonstrating their classic and now presumably timeless status. Both works have established an esteemed position in their respective disciplines.[2]

The interpretations in both works are mainly *descriptive* interpretations. *Middletown* describes everyday life in an "average" small town in middle America during the early 20th century. The scope of its description appears extremely straightforward, capturing the potentially universal aspects of family and community life that might be found in any society, as reflected by the study's six chapter headings:

Chapter I. Getting a Living
Chapter II. Making a Home
Chapter III. Training the Young
Chapter IV. Using Leisure
Chapter V. Engaging in Religious Practices
Chapter VI. Engaging in Community Activities

The distinctiveness of the work may stem from two characteristics. First, few social scientists had previously collected a wide array of field data about life in an average American town. The study team, consisting of two leaders as well as other team members, opened a local office in the town they were studying. The team spent 2 years participating in local life, also compiling local statistics, using questionnaires to conduct interviews, and examining numerous documentary materials. Second, the particular historic period being studied captured a way of American life in an age when an agricultural economy still dominated such an average town, and before the full emergence of an industrial economy had occurred, thereby covering a significant era in American history.[3]

---

[2]As with any other long-standing research works (whether in the social or natural sciences), the original studies often come under renewed scrutiny. In the case of Mead's *Coming of Age in Samoa*, later researchers have found Samoan life to be dramatically different—more sexually constrained—than that depicted by Mead (e.g., Gardner, 1993, The great Samoan hoax, *Skeptical Inquirer, 17*, 131–135, as reported in Reichardt & Rallis, 1994b, p. 7). The suspicion by the latter-day researchers is that Mead's limited knowledge of the local language made her vulnerable to being misled by her informants, who thought that Mead's line of inquiry suggested that she was searching for a sexually promiscuous society, and the informants therefore told Mead what they thought she wanted to hear (Reichardt & Rallis, 1994b, p. 7).

[3]The transition from the agricultural to industrial economy is more directly studied in a sequel to *Middletown* (see *Middletown in Transition* by Lynd & Lynd, 1937).

Coming of Age in Samoa deals with an entirely different world. The book focuses on the developmental cycle of adolescent girls. The study collected data from all 68 girls, aged 9–20, who lived in three villages on one coast of a Samoan island, where the author spent 6 months collecting data. Interviews were conducted in the Samoan language, including a makeshift intelligence test given in Samoan, and the study also made a detailed examination of the social structure of the families in the three villages.

The chapters in the book are organized according to the life of an adolescent:

I. Introduction	IX. The Attitude towards Personality
II. A Day in Samoa	X. The Experience and Individuality of the Average Girl
III. The Education of the Samoan Child	
IV. The Samoan Household	XI. The Girl in Conflict
V. The Girl and Her Age Group	XII. Maturity and Old Age
VI. The Girl in the Community	XIII. Our Educational Problems in the Light of Samoan Contrasts
VII. Formal Sex Relations	
VIII. The Role of the Dance	XIV. Education for Choice

Like *Middletown*, the distinctiveness of *Coming of Age in Samoa* also stems from the richness of its data, in this case about a then-unknown corner of the world. However, and also like *Middletown*, the study addresses a much broader topic, trying to gain insight into the "symptoms of conflict and stress" that appear to exist with American girls but apparently absent among Samoan girls (p. 136). One of the study's main objectives was to determine whether "these difficulties are due to being an adolescent or to being adolescent in America" (p. 6), and the study used the Samoan situation as a way of gaining insight into the American one. This broader objective is the subject of the introductory as well as the final two chapters of Mead's book.

In both works, the descriptions are intense and revealing, especially because the subjects of study had not previously been so systematically examined by earlier social scientists. But in addition, both works also demonstrate how their descriptions aim at reaching conclusions about much broader issues—a generalizing type of conclusion illustrating the fifth phase of the analytic cycle and discussed later in this chapter. For the moment, however, let us explore further the nature of description as a mode of interpretation.

Continuing our review, the nature of *description* as a major type of qualitative interpretation is further disclosed by examining some contemporary works. These works provide insight into the substance of the descriptions. You therefore should examine these or other works closely, by obtaining and reading or skimming them.

For the purpose of the discussion in this book, however, one way of gaining an overview of these descriptions is to attend to the subtitles of existing studies. Exhibit 9.2 cites nine of the studies according to their exact subtitles (not their titles). Remarkably, and in spite of their brevity, the subtitles as shown at the top of

EXHIBIT 9.2. DESCRIPTION AS INTERPRETATION: AUTHORS, SUBTITLES, AND CHAPTER HEADINGS OF ILLUSTRATIVE STUDIES

	1 Liebow (1993)	2 Anderson (1999)	3 Sharman (2006)
Author			
Subtitle of study	The lives of homeless women	Decency, violence, and the moral life of the inner city	The tenants of East Harlem
Introduction	n.a.	Down Germantown Avenue	n.a.
Chapter 1	Day by Day	Decent and Street Families	East Harlem
Chapter 2	Work and Jobs	Campaigning for Respect	Pleasant Avenue: The Italians
Chapter 3	Family	Drugs, Violence, and Street Crime	106th Street: The Puerto Ricans
Chapter 4	The Servers and the Served	The Mating Game	125th Street: The African Americans
Chapter 5	My Friends, My God, and Myself	The Decent Daddy	116th Street: The Mexicans
Chapter 6	Making It Together	The Black Inner-City Grandmother in Transition	Third Avenue: The West Africans
Chapter 7	Some Thoughts on Homelessness	John Turner's Story	Second Avenue: The Chinese
Chapter 8	n.a.	n.a.	Urban Renewal and the Final Migration
Conclusion	n.a.	The Conversion of a Role Model: Looking for Mr. Johnson	n.a.

	4 Napolitano (2002)	5 McQueeney (2009)	6 Pérez (2004)
Author			
Subtitle of study	Living in urban Mexico	Race, gender, and sexuality in lesbian and gay-affirming congregations	Migration, displacement, and Puerto Rican families
Introduction	Prisms of Belonging and Alternative Modernities	n.a.	n.a.
Chapter 1	Internationalizing Region, Expanding City, Neighborhoods in Transition	Research Method	Introduction: A Gendered Tale of Two Barrios
Chapter 2	Migration, Space, and Belonging	Settings: Faith Church and Unity Church	Fleeing the Cane and the Origins of Displacement
Chapter 3	Religious Discourses and the Politics of Modernity	The Homosexual/Christian Conflict	Know Your Fellow American Citizen from Puerto Rico
Chapter 4	Medical Pluralism	Minimizing, Normalizing, and Moralizing Sexuality	Los de Afuera, Transnationalism, and the Cultural Politics of Identity
Chapter 5	Becoming a Mujercita	n.a.	Gentrification, Intrametropolitan Migration, and the Politics of Place
Chapter 6	Neither Married, Widowed, Single, or Divorced: Gender Negotiation, Compliance, Resistance	n.a.	Transnational Lives, Kin Work, and Strategies of Survival
Conclusion	n.a.	Conclusion	Conclusion: Revisiting the Gender, Poverty, and Migration Debate

(cont.)

EXHIBIT 9.2. *(cont.)*

Author	7 Hays (2003)	8 Bogle (2008)	9 Padraza (2007)
Subtitle of study	Women in the age of welfare reform	Sex, dating, and relationships on college campuses	Political disaffection in Cuba's revolution and exodus
Introduction	n.a.	n.a.	n.a.
Chapter 1	Money and Morality	Introduction	False Hopes
Chapter 2	Enforcing the Work Ethic	From Dating to Hooking Up	The Revolution Defines Itself
Chapter 3	Promoting Family Values	The Hookup	The Revolution Deepens
Chapter 4	Fear, Hope, and Resignation in the Welfare Office	The Hookup Scene	The Revolution Redefines Itself
Chapter 5	Pyramids of Inequality	The Campus as a Sexual Arena	The Revolution Consolidated
Chapter 6	Invisibility and Inclusion	Men, Women, and the Sexual Double Standard	*Los Marielitos* of 1980
Chapter 7	Cultures of Poverty	Life after College: A Return to Dating	After the Soviet Collapse
Chapter 8	The Success of Welfare Reform	Hooking Up and Dating: A Comparison	The Last Wave
Chapter 9	n.a.	n.a.	The Church and Civil Society
Chapter 10	n.a.	n.a.	Democratization and Migration
Chapter 11	n.a.	n.a.	The Impossible Triangle
Conclusion	n.a.	n.a.	n.a.

n.a., not applicable to illustrative work

each cited work in Exhibit 9.2 usually capture the broad theme and scope of the entire study.

Exhibit 9.2 then lists the chapter headings of each study. These headings yield clues about the structure of the ensuing description. (For qualitative research published in journal article format, the subheadings in the article may serve a similar function to the chapter headings for qualitative studies that have appeared as books.)

Some studies typically cover the everyday lives of people within a social group or within a geographical area. One structure for these descriptions evolves by presenting *the routine functions in coping with everyday life*, including:

- Liebow's (1993) study of the lives of homeless women; and
- Anderson's (1999) study of street life in an inner-city neighborhood.

(See Items 1 and 2, Exhibit 9.2.)

Alternatively, the description can be based on the *diversity of people or social groups* in a geographical area, such as:

> - Sharman's (2006) study of the residents of East Harlem, a well-known mixed neighborhood in New York City.
>
> (See Item 3, Exhibit 9.2.)

Other studies, while also covering the everyday lives of people, may be more concerned with the nature of social institutions. In these situations, the descriptions are structured according to *institutional structures, functions*, or *topics*, including:

> - Napolitano's (2002) study of urban life in Mexico;
> - McQueeney's (2009) study of the moral dilemmas faced by two Christian churches;
> - Pérez's (2004) study of Puerto Rican migration; and
> - Hays's (2003) study of women's lives after new welfare reform policies were adopted in the United States.
>
> (See Items 4, 5, 6, and 7, Exhibit 9.2.)

Studies that examine *processes over time* can organize their descriptions in a temporal sequence, which when following a *narrative inquiry* variant of qualitative research can include ventures into the past and even distant past (e.g., Connelly & Clandinin, 2006). The descriptive structures can vary widely, from:

> - Bogle's (2008) study of sex on college campuses, which follows a dating–hookup–dating sequence; to
> - Padraza's (2007) sweeping coverage of three waves of Cuban immigration over several decades.
>
> (See Items 8 and 9, Exhibit 9.2.)

All of the preceding descriptive structures can serve as templates for analyzing and interpreting your own data. Furthermore, the descriptions can be presented with varying levels of detail. *Thick description* (Geertz, 1973, 1983), or highly detailed accounts, enable readers to appreciate and ultimately to derive a deep understanding of the social conditions being studied. When successful, the thickness of the description moves the interpretation away from researcher-centric perspectives, portraying instead the people, events, and actions within their locally meaningful contexts. Regardless of whether they contain highly detailed descriptions, a key feature is that most studies then seek to represent some broader social theme, relative to the prevailing research literature.

The best descriptions embrace a study's data. These data can be highly diverse, including profiles of individual people based on the study's interviews, historic data based on searches of documents, and numeric data culled from archival sources. As a reminder, phase three of your data analysis would have included some minimum attempt to reassemble these data. However, the reassembling also can continue as you build your descriptive interpretation.

Description plus a Call for Action

A somewhat separate type of description occurs when a study also tries to promote some subsequent action—typically calling for changes in public policy or in policy agendas—following the presentation of an otherwise descriptive interpretation (see the subtitles and chapter headings for three additional studies in Exhibit 9.3). Some of these studies might have been undertaken with an explicit advocacy motive from their outset. Thus, by design, *action research* openly engages the researcher and participants in a collaborative mode from the start of a study (e.g.,

---

EXHIBIT 9.3. DESCRIPTION-PLUS-CALL-FOR-ACTION AS INTERPRETATION: AUTHORS, SUBTITLES, AND CHAPTER HEADINGS OF ILLUSTRATIVE STUDIES

	1	2	3
Author	Bales (2004)	Sidel (2006)	Newman (1999)
Subtitle of study	New slavery in the global economy	Single mothers and the American dream	The working poor in the inner city
Introduction	n.a.	Introduction	n.a.
Chapter 1	The New Slavery	Moving Beyond Stigma	Working Lives
Chapter 2	Thailand: Because She Looks Like a Child	Genuine Family Values	The Invisible Poor
Chapter 3	Mauritania: Old Times There Are Not Forgotten	Loss	Getting a Job in the Inner City
Chapter 4	Brazil: Life on the Edge	Resilience, Strength, and Perseverance	No Shame in (This) Game
Chapter 5	Pakistan: When Is a Slave not a Slave?	Everybody Knows My Grandma: Extended Families and Other Support Networks	School and Skill in the Low-Wage World
Chapter 6	India: The Ploughman's Lunch	I Have to Do Something with My Life: Derailed Dreams	Getting Stuck, Moving Up
Chapter 7	What Can Be Done?	I Really, Really Believed He Would Stick Around: Conflicting Conceptions of Commitment	Family Values
Chapter 8	n.a.	An Agenda for the Twenty-first Century: Caring for All Our Families	Who's In, Who's Out?
Chapter 9	n.a.	n.a.	What We Can Do for the Working Poor
Conclusion	CODA: Three Things You Can Do to Stop Slavery	n.a.	n.a.

Reason & Riley, 2009). As yet another example, *autoethnographic* inquiries place the researcher directly in the midst of the setting being studied (Johns, 2005).

Conversely, the call for action might not have been considered beforehand, and its relevance might only have emerged as a result of a study's findings. Regardless of the sequence, the studies differ from the mainstream type of description just described, in the following manner.

First, the call for action is likely to dominate the study's conclusions. Observing the chapter headings again provides clues about how this is done, such as:

> • Bales's (2004) study of the "new slavery" in the global economy; and
> • Sidel's (2006) study of single mothers and the American dream.
>
> (See Items 1 and 2, Exhibit 9.3.)

Second, the call for action can result in readers re-inspecting the study's data with a different type of scrutiny. Even when the data are largely presented in a descriptive mode, there is now the possibility that the presentation is strongly skewed in some way, to support the call for action. The possible skew comes in addition to the concern over reflexivity and selection bias normally associated with qualitative research: hence, the stronger the call, the greater the scrutiny.

Third, the call for action may cover highly complex and controversial public policy topics. In contemporary U.S. politics, the illustrative topics might include raising the minimum wage, providing universal healthcare, expanding day-care programs, and the like. These topics have an extensive (qualitative and nonqualitative) literature and are deserving of book-length treatment on their own right; the needed depth exceeds what can be provided in a single chapter. Thus, by including a call for action, a qualitative researcher risks presenting a naive rendering of the policy topics. In turn, this again may backwash into skepticism about the quality of the empirical portion of the study.

Many scholars believe that an acceptable role of social science research is to collect and present evidence to support or challenge policy positions. Other scholars extend the argument even further—that the selection of topics and methods in any research study implicitly reflects a cultural value system that has its own biases. For instance, as discussed later in this book (see Chapter 12, Section B), the postmodernist stance posits that even natural scientists may unknowingly impose their own personal values into their research, such as in their definition and therefore selection of the topics worthy of being studied (e.g., Butler, 2002). Given all these circumstances, having a call for action may not be as objectionable as might first appear.

Nonetheless, an alert to you is that if you want to include some kind of call for action as part of your study, do so with scholarly care. Present any policy topics or substantive advocacy issues in the context of their own research literature, possibly adding a lengthy appendix to your study to indicate your mastery of the topic. Alternatively, you may include extensive and detailed footnotes discussing the policy issues in greater depth and citing relevant policy literature, as done in one example[4]:

> • Newman's (1999) study of the "working poor" in the inner city.
>
> (See Item 3, Exhibit 9.3.)

In this manner, the inclusion of the call for action should raise fewer challenges to the credibility of the empirical portion of your research.

"Explanation" as a Type of Interpretation

Explanation always can occur as part of a descriptive interpretation. For instance, in her study of entry-level employees in fast-food restaurants, Newman (1999), as just cited in Exhibit 9.3, included an effort to explain how the employees overcame the peer stigma of working in such jobs, but this effort was only one part of the broader descriptive study.

The difference emphasized here is that some entire interpretations are devoted to unraveling the events that have been studied. The whole interpretation is dedicated to *explaining how or why events came about*, or alternatively *how or why people were able to pursue particular courses of action*. In this situation, the interpretive framework assumes an explanatory mode, illustrated by the subtitles and chapter headings of five more studies, listed in Exhibit 9.4.

When a study is preoccupied with an overarching explanation, the explanation drives the structure of the entire study, not just part of it. Some explanatory interpretations begin, either in the introductory or initial chapter, with a statement about a human condition in need of explanation. More often than not in qualitative research, the human condition of interest is a normative one—such as the existence of social inequality:

> • Royster's (2003) study of the exclusion of black men from blue-collar jobs; and
> • Williams's (2006) study of inequality in the retail marketplace.
>
> (See Items 1 and 2, Exhibit 9.4.)

Other studies can begin with a statement about some social preference as the theme in need of explanation, as in:

---

[4]Newman's book is 376 pages long, not including its index. Of these pages, 65 are devoted to a lengthy set of detailed footnotes, most of which are about the policy agenda and not the qualitative research. In this manner, the author appears to have done extensive research on the policy topics, conveying a strong sense of mastery over her call for action.

EXHIBIT 9.4. EXPLANATION AS INTERPRETATION: AUTHORS, SUBTITLES, AND CHAPTER HEADINGS OF ILLUSTRATIVE STUDIES

	1	2	3
Author	Royster (2003)	Williams (2006)	Edin & Kefalas (2005)
Subtitle of study	How white networks exclude black men from blue-collar jobs	Working, shopping, and inequality	Why poor women put motherhood before marriage
Introduction	n.a.	n.a.	Introduction
Chapter 1	Introduction	A Sociologist Inside Toy Stores	Before We Had a Baby . . .
Chapter 2	Invisible and Visible Hands	History of Toy Shopping in America	When I Got Pregnant . . .
Chapter 3	From School to Work . . . in Black and White	The Social Organization of Toy Stores	How Does the Dream Die?
Chapter 4	Getting a Job, Not Getting a Job	Inequality on the Shopping Floor	What Marriage Means
Chapter 5	Evaluating Market Explanations	Kids in Toyland	Labor of Love
Chapter 6	Embedded Transitions	Toys and Citizenship	How Motherhood Changed My Life
Chapter 7	Networks of Inclusion, Networks of Exclusion	n.a.	n.a.
Chapter 8	White Privilege and Black Accommodation	n.a.	n.a.
Conclusion	n.a.	n.a.	Conclusion: Making Sense of Single Motherhood

	4	5
Author(s)	Allison & Zelikow (1999)	Neustadt & Fineberg (1983)
Main theme	Explaining the Cuban missile crisis	The epidemic that never was
Introduction	Introduction	Introduction
Chapter 1	Model I: The Rational Actor	The New Flu
Chapter 2	The Cuban Missile Crisis: A First Cut	Sencer Decides
Chapter 3	Model II: Organizational Behavior	Cooper Endorses
Chapter 4	The Cuban Missile Crisis: A Second Cut	Ford Announces
Chapter 5	Model III: Government Politics	Organizing
Chapter 6	The Cuban Missile Crisis: A Third Cut	Field Trials
Chapter 7	n.a.	Liability
Chapter 8	n.a.	Legislation
Chapter 9	n.a.	Starting and Stopping
Chapter 10	n.a.	Califano Comes In
Chapter 11	n.a.	Legacies
Chapter 12	n.a.	Reflections
Chapter 13	n.a.	Technical Afterword
Conclusion	Conclusion	n.a.

- Edin and Kefalas's (2005) study of why poor women put motherhood before marriage.

(See Item 3, Exhibit 9.4.)

As yet another example, in political science, qualitative studies can be driven by an overarching need to explain some critical geopolitical event. The condition of interest is usually an event with some national if not international significance, such as:

- Allison and Zelikow's (1999) effort to explain the Cuban missile crisis; and
- Neustadt and Fineberg's (1983) study of a near-influenza-epidemic in the late 1970s in the United States.

(See Items 4 and 5, Exhibit 9.4.)

Whatever the human, social, or political events of interest, the ensuing chapters then permit the author to build the desired explanation. Each chapter adds a piece of the explanation or adds information about contextually relevant conditions. Along the way, the most effective explanation also attends to alternative or rival explanations.

The consideration of *rival explanations* throughout your methodological procedures, as discussed earlier in Chapter 4 (Choice 2), is one of the important ways of improving the technical quality of your analysis. When reaching the interpretation phase of your analysis, and when the interpretation is based on an explanatory framework, the relevance of rival explanations is doubly compelling. You should formulate and present evidence related to realistic or plausible rivals, seeking to show how the evidence might *favor* the rival, as if it were your primary explanation. Ideally, the compiled evidence should of its own weight then dispel the rival, without your having to make any strong expository argument. The overall result should be the presentation of a sound and plausible explanation for your findings.

An excellent qualitative study in the field of management had an unusual way of presenting its rival explanations (Schein, 2003). The entire study was organized around an explanation for the demise of a major computer company that had been among the country's top 50 corporations in size. Although the author presented ample interview and documentary evidence in support of his own explanation, he also included supplemental chapters at the end of the book. Each supplemental chapter gave a key executive of the former firm the opportunity to present his own rival explanation.

Building a good explanation is not easy. You therefore are unlikely to do it without help. The main help will come from informed colleagues and peers—those who know something about the subject matter or the design of your study.

The desired relationship with these colleagues and peers includes a continuing dialogue during the explanation-building process as well as reviews of your preliminary drafts.

The external perspectives of your colleagues can reveal gaps or oddities in your explanatory framework that you may want to remedy. Thus, this is not the stage of your research to go into a cocoon. Talk with friends and colleagues and start telling the story of your research. The more you interact with others, the more likely you will create some insightful interpretive framework for your study.

Creating Insightful and Usable Interpretations

Cheer yourself by knowing that the analytic possibilities are limitless, as long as they are empirically grounded. Only your inattention to your own data or lack of creativity stand in the way of finding a good interpretive framework. The ideal interpretations will connect the ideas of interest—reflected, for instance, by the relevant literature—with your reassembled data.

You can start the interpretation in several ways. First, you already may know the main theme of your research, reflected as we have found, by stating a possible subtitle for a qualitative study. Second, you may have analytically observed important, new, and persistent patterns in your research data—for example, across different individuals or events. The noteworthy patterns go beyond any single set of data—for example, permeating a good portion of all your data. These newly found patterns can become the pillars for creating an innovative interpretation. Third, you should always be able to start an interpretation with your original research questions and build around them.

You also need not think about *interpreting* as only being part of a linear sequence—that is, waiting until the fourth analytic phase before attempting to do any interpreting. Some qualitative studies reveal and then present their interpretations well ahead of time. For instance, Adrian (2003) weaves her interpretation throughout the presentation of her study (see "An Interpretive Theme That Appears throughout a Qualitative Study," Vignette 9.1). Such a strategy entails risks regarding possible selectivity in choosing the data to be presented. However (and as in the example of Adrian's study), the presentation of ample detailed data, covering a range of relevant topics in separate chapters, can help to offset these risks.

In retrospect, what also may make any and all of these alternatives work is a thorough knowledge of the relevant literature. If the literature is weak (i.e., has few previous studies on your topic or an unclear thematic and theoretical base), show how the interpretation of your study will build new strength for subsequent studies. If the literature is strong (i.e., has many previous studies reflecting a rather crowded topic), develop an interpretation pointing to a niche that may still have been left uncovered. If the literature is in the middle, stretch the conventional boundaries and develop an interpretation that demonstrates "outside-of-the-box" thinking.

> ### VIGNETTE 9.1. AN INTERPRETIVE THEME THAT APPEARS THROUGHOUT A QUALITATIVE STUDY
>
> One way of confronting the inevitable challenge of interpreting the findings from a qualitative research study is to embed a study within a broader theme from the very outset.
>
> Bonnie Adrian's (2003) study starts with a specific incident—observing her Taiwanese friend's three-foot-high wedding portrait in the family bedroom and her possession of a huge album of 15-inch-high wedding photos as a keepsake (pp. 1–2). The photos reflect a broader change in Taiwanese society, spurred by a highly competitive industry of bridal photography salons and the packaging and promotion of bridal beauty.
>
> At the same time, Adrian quickly introduces what will become the main interpretation of her study—*the globalization of a consuming society*—permitting her to conclude with a discussion of how "Taiwanese bridal photography is not merely a response to Taiwan's rapid globalization but is itself part of the . . . process" (2003, p. 244). Throughout the study, the particulars of wedding ceremonies and marriage rituals in Taiwan are continually contextualized within the globalization theme.

C. CONCLUDING

PREVIEW—*What you should learn from this section:*

1. How a conclusion captures the "significance" of a study (not necessarily meaning that the study's findings need to be generalizable).
2. Examples of five types of conclusions.

Beyond the *Interpreting* phase lies this fifth analytic phase, *Concluding*. Completed empirical studies, whether based on qualitative research or not, all should have one or more conclusions. The preferred logic is that the conclusion(s) be connected both to the preceding interpretive phase and to a study's main data or empirical findings. In this sense, drawing conclusions still may be considered as part of a study's analysis, and it therefore serves as the fifth phase.

In a way, every study's conclusions can be highly specific, possibly even unique. For this reason, little discourse would at first seem relevant. However, noting the kinds of conclusions that have been drawn by others again may yield suggestions on how to think about the conclusions for your own research.

A conclusion is some kind of overarching statement or series of statements that raises the findings of a study to a higher conceptual level or broader set of ideas. In one sense, the conclusion captures the broader "significance" of a study. The spirit of a conclusion lies in such concepts as "lessons learned" and "implications of the research," as well as more pragmatic slogans such as "practical implications" (but none of these concepts or slogans should necessarily appear as actual phrases in your conclusion). Your discretionary freedom, more so than for any other part of a research study, permits you to make inferences from the research as a whole. Not desired are conclusions that only restate the findings by saying them another way.

The following paragraphs give five examples of conclusions. You can emulate them singly or in any combination. Or you can concoct your own conclusion that is entirely different from any of the five examples.

Concluding by Calling for New Research

A rich research tradition, possibly born out of basic research, calls for studies to conclude by showing how a study's findings (e.g., original propositions found to be supported or not supported) now point to new research in need of being conducted. The main conclusion lies along the lines of "what we still don't know."

In this situation, the conclusion(s) typically take the form of question(s) to be addressed by future research. The questions may even be accompanied by suggestions for the needed research methods. The most complete conclusion of this sort would therefore start to resemble the design of a new study.

Qualitative researchers can follow this tradition but also have more attractive choices that can be used in lieu of or in addition to pointing to topics for new research.

Concluding by Challenging Conventional Generalizations and Social Stereotypes

A second kind of conclusion, commonly found among qualitative studies, derives from the fact that qualitative research usually focuses on a concrete and particular set of circumstances. To draw conclusions, a new qualitative study may begin by using previously published research as a point of departure. The previous research, often based on methods other than qualitative methods, may have produced a large body of evidence, in some way depicting or even stereotyping human behavior, its rituals, or its organization. In contrast, the newly completed qualitative study might have shown different and unexpected patterns of behavior, and these can form the basis for the study's conclusions.

For instance, one of the most common conventional generalizations pertains to the depiction of people living in poverty—that they are victims of their own dysfunctional behavior, lack the perseverance needed to do an honest day's work, and create disorganized and unhealthy neighborhoods and living environments. Furthermore, through "broken" family structures, these people perpetuate their condition to future generations.

The resulting generalizations regarding the lives of people living in poverty have been enhanced over the years by numerous qualitative studies. Among the earliest were the well-known anthropological studies by Oscar Lewis (1959, 1961, 1965). He advanced the concept of people living in a "culture of poverty" as presenting a potential barrier to efforts to overcome important social problems (1965, pp. xlii–lii).

More contemporary works have striven to challenge the basic premise of the generalization—the depiction of social disorganization and individual dysfunction among lower-income people in the first place. For instance, Pérez (2004) used her study of first- and second-generation Puerto Rican migrants (see Exhibit 9.2, Item 6) to challenge an "underclass stereotype" (see "Conclusions That Challenge Conventional Generalizations," Vignette 9.2). Similarly, Hays's (2003, pp. 180–181) study of mothers under U.S. welfare reform also concluded by challenging the stereotype of the typical welfare mother as an inept or unwilling wage earner (Exhibit 9.2, Item 7). Finally, Bourgois (2003) studied drug dealers and others in an underground urban economy and concluded by arguing "how history, culture and political-economic structures constrain the lives of individuals" (p. 16).

VIGNETTE 9.2. CONCLUSIONS THAT CHALLENGE CONVENTIONAL GENERALIZATIONS

The lives of first- and second-generation Puerto Rican migrants were the subject of a "dual-site research project" (p. 20) by Gina Pérez (2004). She conducted ethnographic research in Chicago, Illinois, and San Sebastián, Puerto Rico, and analyzed numerous documents in the archives of historical societies.

The study was conducted from both a gender and a transnational perspective. For instance, migration experiences are "extremely gendered, . . . making some things possible and others not" (p. 17). From a transnational perspective, the study's findings "challenge earlier work suggesting that circular migration is commonplace" (Pérez, 2004, p. 198). The Puerto Ricans in the study displayed a sense of transnationalism, but it was not based on the circular pattern. The study therefore challenges the underclass stereotype often linked to the pattern—that migration contributes to a social disorganization transmitted intergenerationally, reproducing a cycle of poverty (p. 199).

In like manner, findings from qualitative studies have challenged many other prevailing generalizations regarding such topics as the role of women at work and in the home; the role of men at work and in the home; adversarial relationships between employees and employers based on presumably contrasting economic interests; conflicts among different ethnic or racial groups; and any number of other major stereotypes among human societies.

In addressing all these stereotypes, a typical contribution of qualitative research has been to reveal the existence of more diverse conditions than have been recognized by previous research because qualitative research offers the chance to deal with nonmainstream cultures and social conditions. Such research typically focuses on social groups that have historically experienced racism, discrimination, and exclusion (Banks, 2006, p. 775). Thus, qualitative research can add a richness and depth of understanding to the profiles such as that of "the (statistically) average family," which may fail to connote the full diversity and complexity of actual family composition or behavior.

Qualitative research also can go beyond challenging conventional generalizations by suggesting how they might be altered, adapted, or enriched. For instance:

> • Carr's (2003) study of a suburban neighborhood led to his challenging previous research that had supported the importance of dense social ties as a successful deterrent for thwarting youth-related crime. The neighborhood studied by Carr was successful, even though it had no such internal network or social ties. Carr therefore concluded by suggesting a revised theory of informal social control to account for suburban neighborhoods' dealing with youth-related crime.

Concluding with New Concepts, Theories, and Even "Discoveries" about Human Social Behavior

Whether challenging conventional wisdom or not, the conclusions from qualitative research can point to the need for and usefulness of new concepts and theories. These might be considered a third kind of conclusion found in qualitative studies.

Among the illustrative studies in this chapter, Anderson's (1999) "code of the street" (Exhibit 9.2, Item 2) stands out as a culminating concept that the author promotes as providing insight into the lives of inner-city residents (see "Using Qualitative Research to Create and Test a Theoretical Construct: 'The Code of the Street,'" Vignette 9.3). On a totally different topic, Allison and Zelikow's (1999) work on the Cuban missile crisis (Exhibit 9.4, Item 4) concludes by pointing to the importance of understanding complex organizational behavior, rather than solo actions by single political leaders, as underlying significant international decisions.

VIGNETTE 9.3. USING QUALITATIVE RESEARCH TO CREATE AND TEST A THEORETICAL CONSTRUCT: "THE CODE OF THE STREET"

Elijah Anderson's (1999) study is about a particular place at a particular time (Philadelphia in the 1990s). The author's interest is nevertheless in having his study make a broader statement about an important aspect of urban culture—"the social consequences of persistent urban poverty and joblessness," and how these forces "coalesce into acute alienation from mainstream society and institutions, especially among the young" (p. 323).

Anderson claims that "the most public manifestation of this alienation is the 'code of the street,' a kind of adaptation to a lost sense of security of the local inner-city neighborhood and . . . a profound lack of faith in the police and the judicial system" (1999, p. 323). His study describes neighborhood features and events, and it presents the lives of youths and families as they cope with everyday confrontations with drugs, crime, and the law. These data provide concrete evidence of the "code of the street" and enable the reader to appreciate this new theoretical construct as a contribution to an understanding of urban culture.

See also Vignettes 7.1 and 11.5.

Conclusions also may suggest new ways of thinking that have broad disciplinary implications. For instance, at the end of her study of neighborhood transition (Exhibit 9.2, Item 4), Napolitano (2002) raises the possibility that such neighborhoods might be better studied from the perspective of "culture as an open-ended and unfinished process" rather than by depicting "the standard anthropology of a barrio" (see "Studying Neighborhood Transition in Urban Mexico," Vignette 9.4).

VIGNETTE 9.4. STUDYING NEIGHBORHOOD TRANSITION IN URBAN MEXICO

Over the years, much qualitative research has focused on "transitioning" neighborhoods. These neighborhoods experience residential turnover and economic abandonment (and decline) or development (and "gentrification"). Most of the studies have been about U.S. cities and neighborhoods, but similar phenomena can obviously occur in other settings.

Valentina Napolitano (2002) studied a neighborhood in Guadalajara, the largest urban center in Western Mexico, with a population exceeding 3 million in 1990. Her fieldwork stretched over 10 years, with 6 months in 1989 and 2 years in 1990–1992, and then month-long visits in 1997, 1998, and 1999. Her "Italian-ness" placed her in a position of an "exotic outsider" but also opened doors that "would otherwise have remained closed" (p. xvi).

Napolitano's study pulls together the everyday life of the neighborhood as its economy was undergoing internationalization and "renewed crisis for the low -income population" (2002, p. 22). The study also embeds its data within a rich anthropological framework that highlights "culture as an open-ended and unfinished process" rather than presenting a "standard anthropology of a barrio" (p. 2).

As for "discoveries," one classic mixed methods (quantitative and qualitative) study, based on large-scale surveys as well as extensive fieldwork, stands out. The study was produced in five volumes and focused on the social class structure of a small city in New England. The main discovery is covered in the first of the five volumes. One part of the discovery was showing how a person's class designation was independent of her or his economic condition. A second part of the discovery was the emergence of evidence for a highly differentiated structure of six classes. With their data, the researchers were able to estimate the percentage of the total population within each of the classes, also developing a terminology that has survived to this day (Warner & Lunt, 1941, pp. 81–91):

◆ "Upper-upper class" (1.4%),

◆ "Lower-upper class" (1.6%),

◆ "Upper-middle class" (10.2%),

◆ "Lower-middle class" (28.1%),

◆ "Upper-lower class" (32.6%), and

◆ "Lower-lower class" (25.2%).

One result of this landmark study was to call attention to the subtleties of social stratification within communities, a topic that has received continuing research attention since the study was completed.

Concluding by Making Substantive (not Methodological) Propositions

Yet a fourth kind of conclusion takes a stronger posture. The author can wrap up a study with one or more propositions. The proposition(s) can attempt to explain the key facet of a study or even to make a prediction. For instance, Liebow's (1993, p. 223) study of homeless women (Exhibit 9.2, Item 1) concludes with a proposition that he admits sounds tautological at first: "Homeless people are homeless because they do not have a place to live." However, he goes on to contrast and discuss this proposition in light of other more frequent claims, that homelessness is a result of homeless people's physical or mental conditions or lack of employment.

Showing how a proposition can take the form of a prediction, Wilson and Taub (2006), after studying multiple neighborhoods having residents with different mixes of racial and ethnic backgrounds, conclude with the prediction that "neighborhoods in urban America . . . are likely to remain divided, racially and culturally" (p. 161). The insights from the study do not derive simply from this prediction. The main insights come from the study's explanations regarding residents' sensitivity in preferring neighborhoods in which they feel comfortable in some economic or cultural sense.

Concluding by Generalizing to a Broader Set of Situations

A fifth and final kind of conclusion comes from prevailing research practices that consider a study's conclusions to be the occasion for generalizing its findings to situations other than the one(s) that was (were) part of the study.

Chapter 4 (Choice 6) previously previewed this type of conclusion by describing a process of *analytic generalization* that follows a two-step process. Defining a particular set of concepts, theoretical constructs, or hypothesized sequence of events serves as a key to this process. Given such constructs as the vehicle, the first of the two steps connects the findings of a qualitative study to the constructs, and the second then argues how the constructs apply to new situations other than the one(s) studied. As previously referenced in this and other chapters of this book, the two steps are illustrated by generalizing from:

- A single missile crisis to the manner of confrontation between two world powers under other conditions (Allison & Zelikow, 1999);

- The experience of Mexican youth immigrants to the "subtractive schooling" experience of other limited English-speaking students (Valenzuela, 1999); or

- The bridal industry to "the globalization of a consuming society" (Adrian, 2006).

"World power confrontation," "subtractive schooling," and "globalization" all represent examples of the needed constructs.

Less desirable for qualitative studies are two other kinds of generalization common to nonqualitative studies. The first comes from survey methods. It assumes that a study has deliberately focused on some numerically known sample of people, sites, or events. If so, the generalizing conclusions will infer that the study's findings apply to the full population or universe of such people, sites, or events. This manner of concluding, called *statistical generalization* and also discussed earlier in Chapter 4 (Choice 6), only makes a numeric and not any conceptual contribution regarding the larger significance of a study. Qualitative studies can try to apply this type of generalizing, but even where a sample of people, sites, or events has been carefully selected to be representative of some larger group, the number of people, sites, or events in a qualitative study will likely be too small to warrant any statistical generalization.

The second type of less desirable generalization comes from experimental methods. It assumes that the results from an experiment may be sufficiently replicated in similar situations that the findings may be generalized to other similar situations. In the experimental methodology, this second way of generalizing has been referred to as "external validity" (e.g., Cook & Campbell, 1979). This second way of generalizing has a parallel in qualitative research.

The parallel occurs on those occasions when a particular part or all of a qualitative research study is the subject of attempted replication. For instance, within a single qualitative research study, a potential occasion for such replication might be the conduct of a multiple-case study, where two or more cases are selected because they are believed to be similar (Yin, 2009). The more similar the findings from the cases, the more a replication might be claimed. However, the opportunity to replicate only may exist when doing a multiple-case study, which is an infrequent design in qualitative research. The more frequent modes of doing qualitative research will not present the same opportunity. For this reason, this second type of generalization is probably a less desirable way of seeking a conclusion from a qualitative study.

RECAP FOR CHAPTER 9: *Terms, phrases, and concepts that you can now define:*

1. Recursive relationships among the various phases of analysis
2. Comprehensive interpretation
3. Description, description plus a call for action, and explanation
4. Thick description
5. Rival explanations
6. Avoiding conclusions that only restate a study's findings
7. Concluding by calling for new research

8. Concluding by challenging conventional generalizations and social stereotypes

9. Concluding with new concepts, theories, or discoveries

10. Concluding by making substantive propositions

11. Concluding by generalizing

EXERCISE FOR CHAPTERS 8 AND 9: DISASSEMBLING, REASSEMBLING, AND INTERPRETING AUTOBIOGRAPHICAL DATA

Portion Related to Chapter 8

Write a short autobiography, organizing it in *chronological* fashion (starting with where and when you were born and bringing it into the present) [do not duplicate the material in the exercise for Chapter 1].

You don't have to try to recall every important experience, but for the experiences you do write down, make sure that you describe the situations so others can feel that they might have been there—for example, covering details such as the geographic location, other people who were involved and your relationship to them, the institutional setting for the experience, and any objects or relevant features of the physical environment. The short autobiography should be about five pages (double-space) in length. Let this version represent the *Compilation* phase, or your compiled database.

After you have finished, return to the entire text and manually code the details. Have at least 8–10 codes, choosing them in either of two ways: (1) Let an item suggest a "higher" conceptual category (*inductive*), or (2) start with concepts you already think might be important and then find items in the text that illustrate these concepts (*deductive*). Write the codes near the relevant text of the autobiography.

Now examine the codes. Decide which ones might be related to each other, totally unrelated, or related in some more complex manner. Add category codes to suit these situations and write them next to the original codes. Let this version represent the *Disassembling* phase of your analysis.

Array the codes and categories in some manner that starts to make sense of your autobiography (e.g., in a hierarchy, matrix, or flow diagram). Let one of the arrays represent the *Reassembling* phase of your analysis.

Portion Related to Chapter 9

Given what you have reassembled, think of broader interpretations about your autobiography and address issues of interest to you (you also can use the following as a suggested set):

1. In 1–2 pages, and citing specific portions of your arrays (from the exercise in Chapter 8), discuss how the experiences you selected share anything in common, or whether they fall under a few major topics (and if so, what are they?). If the experiences do not share anything in common or fall under no major topics, discuss why the experiences tend to be disconnected or unrelated to each other.

2. Continuing your interpretation for another 1–2 pages, cite specific coded materials or arrays to support your claim about what the autobiography might tell a reader about: "The important people in my life" and "Enduring relationships with different kinds of institutions or organizations."

3. In a final page, discuss the extent to which your autobiography is totally unique, compared to one that might provide a basis for generalizing to other people's experiences.

SAMPLE STUDY 1: A STUDY OF UNIVERSITY–SCHOOL PARTNERSHIPS AS AN EXAMPLE FOR CHAPTERS 8 AND 9 (CHAPTER 9 PORTION)

Interpretation in Sample Study 1

Recall that the reassembled data for **Sample Study 1**, described in Chapter 8, highlighted eight types of activities involving faculty–school collaboration. During the interpretation phase, a literature review was introduced as a backdrop for showing that the types of activities that had been found, with one exception, did not differ from those previously reported by other studies.

The literature review also indicated that the various faculty–school collaborations were difficult to sustain over time because the collaborations rarely produced mutual benefits to the partners. In nearly all types of activities, either the faculty or the schools (but not both simultaneously) gained some benefit (e.g., providing inservice training to K–12 teachers benefited the teachers but did not serve the professional advancement of the university faculty). As a result, the prospects for the partnerships being studied, absent continuing external funding, seemed bleak.

In the single exceptional activity, however, both partners appeared to gain some benefit: When inservice training is offered as part of a formal university course (compared to typical inservice training that takes place in ad hoc workshops or summer institutes and are not part of formal university programs), the K–12 teachers still gain the benefit of the training; but now, the university department (and its faculty) may gain the benefit of having an expanded program and increased enrollment in the department. This single activity might therefore be sustained without a continuing infusion of external funds. The interpretation in **Sample Study 1** therefore laid out this whole line of reasoning.

Concluding in Sample Study 1

Based on the identification of one type of activity that appeared to provide mutual benefits to the collaborating partners (inservice training involving formal course offerings by university departments), **Sample Study 1** concluded that future partnerships might be self-sustaining to the extent that they promoted this single activity.

The practical implications of such a conclusion meant that K–12 schools in the future might direct their teachers and their inservice training resources toward university-based coursework rather than to supporting attendance at ad hoc workshops and summer institutes. The schools' teachers could benefit by gaining substantively richer mathematics and science education (because, unlike the curricula for ad hoc workshops and summer institutes, the contents of formal university courses need to be reviewed and approved before being listed by academic departments). The academic departments might benefit, as previously noted, by having broader programs with higher enrollments than existed without their partnerships with the K–12 schools.

PART III

PRESENTING
THE RESULTS FROM
QUALITATIVE RESEARCH

CHAPTER 10

Displaying Qualitative Data

Qualitative studies pose a special challenge in presenting their data because the data usually include narratives from participants. Researchers have a variety of presentation choices, ranging from brief directly or indirectly quoted material to chapter-length life histories. Taking best advantage of these choices assumes that researchers have collected the appropriate data to begin with—such as tape recording interviews if the later desire is to present extensive narrations in a participant's own words. Apart from narrative data, qualitative studies also can benefit from the use of many types of nonverbal presentations, such as the use of graphics, photographs, and reproductions. Some version of any of these types of materials, narrative and non-narrative, also are likely to appear as slides that can augment a researcher's later oral presentations about a study's findings. This chapter discusses how to proceed with all of the preceding situations to create the most accurate but also attractive renditions of a qualitative study's data.

Qualitative data are more alphabetic than numeric. The data are likely to be represented in narratives or in data arrays, such as the word tables, hierarchies, matrices, and other types of diagrams discussed in the preceding two chapters.

At first blush, displaying alphabetic data in these forms would appear not to pose any particular challenge. After all, everyone knows how to put words on a piece of paper or on a slide. However, if you have worked with qualitative data, the exact and best choices are not really easy to know. If you make the wrong choices, your data can appear to be horribly dull, too wordy, or too vague. This chapter tries to help you to avoid such a fate.

Do not overlook the seriousness of the challenge. To begin with, and ignoring the narrative format for a moment, the data arrays used earlier in your analysis may not be the best way of presenting your data for the purpose of communicating effectively with an audience. Although the original arrays should be readily available for inspection, remember that they were intended for your own analysis and for the (likely small) portion of your audience that might want to inspect or check your analytic work. However, the arrays may be too detailed or lengthy to appear within the main body of your final study, much less as part of a slide presentation. They may be better placed in an appendix or as part of other supporting materials.[1]

A safe assumption is that most audiences are interested in learning about your findings and conclusions, as well as a condensed sense of your data, and the original arrays may not readily serve this purpose. How best to present qualitative data to communicate effectively with audiences therefore still remains a challenge.

Turning back to the narrative format, a study's narrative will contain your own words (as discussed fully in Chapter 11)—such as when you interpret your findings. However, narratives also can be the occasion for presenting qualitative data, as is addressed by the present chapter. This use is especially important because the main part of a qualitative study may be based on narrative inquiry, providing the participants with the chance to give detailed accounts of their experiences, including their life stories or life histories (e.g., Labov & Wiletsky, 1997; Murray, 2009).

At a minimum, a common kind of narrative data would take the form of quotations and paraphrased passages, representing your study participants' descriptions of their own lives, actions, and views. In qualitative research, even these briefer descriptions serve as an important form of data. Not surprisingly, the choices about how to present these narrative data are more than a matter of literary style. Methodological issues also are relevant. Yet, this type of narrative—whether brief or lengthy—has not received much attention in existing guides for doing qualitative research.

This chapter therefore focuses on the ways that you might want to display the data in your study. Discussed first in Section A are the narrative forms for presenting the data from participants. Section B then reviews how exhibits or figures—such as tables, graphics, and pictures—might appear in your final study. Finally, Section C gives special attention to the conversion of these materials into slides to accompany an oral presentation that you might make.

---

[1]At least one social science journal is using its electronic archives so readers can access instruments, code books, data arrays, and other documentation to supplement published articles (e.g., see the supplementary materials available in relation to a case study by Randolph & Eronen, 2007). In another field, the distinguished journal *Science*, published by the American Association for the Advancement of Science, follows the same practice (e.g., see the unpublished methods section, tables, and exhibits accompanying a [quantitative] report on student achievement in California by Bryant et al., 2008).

A. NARRATIVE DATA ABOUT THE PARTICIPANTS IN A QUALITATIVE STUDY

PREVIEW—*What you should learn from this section:*

1. The presentation of participants' own words as part of the narrative flow of the entire study.

2. The relationship between the amount of participants' narrative to be included in your presentation and the earlier design of the fieldwork regarding the amount and precision of the data to be collected.

3. The differences between a researcher's narration of a participant's words and the presentation of lengthy and directly transcribed passages representing the participant's own perspectives and meanings.

Nearly all qualitative studies will contain information about the actions and attitudes of individual participants. Whether these people are identified by name or pseudonym, they will be a central part of a qualitative study. Your study may be about a collectivity of people, such as a small group, a culture, or a collective process like a political campaign. In these group settings, an essential ingredient of the study will, at some point, include narrative information about one or more of the individuals who are part of or participate in the small group, culture, or collective process. Thus, every qualitative study is likely to collect data about individual people and to report something about their perceptions, aspirations, beliefs, or behaviors.

In *quantitative* research, a typical strategy would be to collect numeric data and present statistics about individuals' collective features, such as the family composition of people living in a neighborhood being studied; the behaviors among different age groups (e.g., substance abuse rates among teenagers), or the demographic features (e.g., ethnic backgrounds and genders) of the people in an organization. You might have similar statistics as a background feature for your qualitative study, but the essence of your study would be its focus on specific people in their real-world settings, not any statistical profiles. Equally important, you may want to portray the real-world events from the participants' perspectives. Your narrative could then present their voices through the use of extensively quoted material.

Though styles will differ, everyone knows how to write and present such material. Not readily evident is that you have several choices in making these narratives. They can be shorter or longer, and they can contain limited or extensively quoted passages. The choices are not mutually exclusive, so you can use all of them. However, each will require different amounts of data. Each also will require field records with different levels of detail. The choices that follow are organized according to their length and complexity, the shortest and simplest ones coming first.

Interspersing Quoted Passages within Selected Paragraphs

The shortest presentation about individual people usually occurs when the quoted words by one of the participants in a study appear as part of a study's entire narrative flow. Elliot Liebow's (1993) narrative on homeless women provides a good example. The excerpt comes from his broader discussion of homeless women's relationships with their families (p. 114); the participant's words appear in *italics*:

> Conversely, there are certain families that contribute importantly to making women homeless, and having done so, the families then want nothing to do with them precisely because they are homeless. Later, if the women escape from homelessness, they are surprised to find that they are no longer pariahs and at least some family members are prepared to restore relations. Grace was not only surprised at the invitation to rejoin part of her family, she was angry as well. *"I was the same person when I was homeless,"* she said. *"I haven't changed, it's only my situation that's changed. I have my own place and possessions now. That's the only difference."*

The same approach of embedding quoted dialogue within narrative text can be used to capture the interchange between two or more people. By staying overnight in the shelter, which he did many times, Liebow collected such interchanges as the following example in which he writes (p. 132):

> Shirley and the others were preparing for bed. *"Don't forget to wash up,"* said Gretchen [one of the staff persons at the shelter]. Shirley exploded, *"I'm 53 years old!"* she shouted. *"I have children older than you, and I don't need you to tell me to wash up before going to bed."* Having gotten started, Shirley couldn't stop. She denounced Gretchen and the shelter staff for purposely demeaning the women as part of their effort to control them, and continued along these lines until— perhaps to force them to prove her point—she was expelled for the night.

In both of the preceding examples, the quoted passages are short. The combination of the author's own narrative interspersed with the quoted passages produces an easy and attractive presentation style. You can imagine that a prolonged sequence of this kind of writing can induce within the reader the reality of the scene in the homeless shelter and even a sense of being part of that scene.

The brevity of the quoted materials also matches the author's fieldwork methods. On these specific occasions, he did not use a tape recorder. Instead, he took brief handwritten notes. Later, he typed these notes and combined them with his own recollections at his office everyday. Liebow comments (1993, pp. 322–323) on this procedure as follows:

> As best I could, I tried to remember conversations, or part of conversations, verbatim. With practice, one does this pretty well. . . . If I was certain that the reconstruction was so close to the original that the speaker herself would not have known the difference, I retained quotation marks. If I could not achieve this certainty, I used indirect quotation.

On other occasions, Liebow did tape record more extended interviews that led to the development of 20 life histories. They appear in the appendix to his book. (The life histories are mostly narrations by the author, again interspersed by direct quotations from the homeless person in the study.)

Other qualitative scholars respect and practice a similar distinction between quoted and paraphrased dialogues, although they may draw the line between the two situations slightly differently. Some, like Ruth Sidel in her study of single mothers, follow Liebow's practice, feeling confident about using direct quotations because of their note-taking expertise and nightly transcription regimens (Sidel, 2006, p. 15), even when conversations have not been tape recorded. Others, like Mitchell Duneier in his study of the role of street vendors in New York City's sidewalk life, only will use quotations when a conversation has been tape recorded; otherwise, he will use indirect quotes (Duneier, 1999, p. 13).

Using Lengthier Presentations, Covering Multiple Paragraphs

The challenge of presenting information about the individuals in your study—and especially quoting their own words—becomes greater if your study presents more extensive material from the individuals. The need for greater coverage can arise for at least two reasons.

First, a particular person or persons may have an unusual life circumstance that plays an important part in your entire study. Second, a meaningful scene or dialogue may extend over a protracted period of time, unlike the briefer interchanges covered by the examples from Liebow's study. Either of these circumstances would call for material about an individual that might extend over multiple paragraphs, if not a few pages, of your narrative.

If you have not anticipated these needs or opportunities as part of your initial study design, you will have to consider returning to your participants to collect more data from them, whether in verbatim form or not, and then augmenting your database. This revelation is another reason to permit a deliberate overlap between the data collection and data analysis phases of your study.

In other situations, as part of your designed data collection, you might have deliberately decided to limit the greater depth of coverage to a few participants, even though you also had collected smaller amounts of data from all of the participants. For instance, you may have started your study with a two-tiered design— some people being part of your study for longer periods of time and in many different real-world situations, and other people included or interviewed for only shorter periods of time. Such a two-tiered pattern also offers a workable approach (see "Collecting In-Depth Material about a Subgroup of People in a Study," Vignette 10.1).

As another variation, your study might only have focused on a smaller group of people to begin with—as in Valdés's (1996) study of 10 immigrant families (refer also to Vignette 10.3 below). The quoted dialogues reported by Valdés—usually a half-page in length—are especially compelling because they are presented in both

---

VIGNETTE 10.1. COLLECTING IN-DEPTH MATERIAL ABOUT A SUBGROUP OF PEOPLE IN A STUDY

A study by Hochschild (1989) shows how the people in a study were covered at two different levels of intensity.

For a larger group of 50 couples, the author or her assistant conducted interviews of about 2 hours each. For a smaller group of 12 couples, the author herself also made in-depth observations of their household relationships and practices, held more extensive conversations, and collected much more data about the 12 couples.

As a result, the study's findings were based on a modest-sized group (50 couples), but key issues could be covered in greater depth based on the 12 couples studied more intensively. Information about each of the 12 couples covers significant portions of the individual chapters of the book.

This dual pattern, involving two different levels of information about two different-sized groups, can strike the desired balance between the need to cover both the breadth and depth of an issue.

---

the original Spanish language used in the interviews and their English translation. Readers familiar with Spanish then have the choice of deciphering for themselves the original meaning of the dialogues or relying on the English translations.

With any of these variations, your own contact with the participants in your study also likely means that you will have spent a lot of time with them, whether interviewing, participating, or observing. Typically, when in-depth coverage takes place, authors of qualitative studies report spending time in their informants' homes, participating in community and family events together, and being involved in other situations as a participant-observer.

These lengthier presentations still are likely to contain a mixture of a researcher's third-person descriptions interspersed with quoted or paraphrased dialogues. When reporting about a participant-observer experience, the researchers also may have to write about themselves as in an *autoethnography*, and such writing will usually be in the first person. A less frequent style is for researchers to refer to themselves in the third person when reporting such dialogues, as Circe Sturm (2002) does in her study of the racial politics in the Cherokee Nation in northeastern Oklahoma.

Making Chapter-Long Presentations about a Study's Participants

An even greater challenge occurs when the life circumstance of a single participant is so important that an entire chapter is devoted to reporting about that person.

Anderson's (1999) study of the "code of the street," or of life in inner-city neighborhoods, concludes in this manner in its final two chapters. Each chapter is devoted to the main theme of his study, which covers the ways in which young African American males are caught between "the basic tension between the street and the decent, more conventional world of legitimate jobs and stable families" (p. 285). The second-to-last chapter highlights a person who was not able to overcome this tension, whereas the final chapter shows the struggle and adaptiveness by another person who appears to have dealt more successfully with the tension.

In these two chapters, Anderson easily shifts between his third-person descriptions of each participant and extended quotations of their own words. His ability to mix these two modes reflects a mixture of field methods. They included (1) extensive participant-observation (for instance, he serendipitously met one of the persons at a local carryout that he had patronized regularly as part of his daily field routine, and he later tried to find attorneys and jobs for this person over a multi-year period of time), combined with (2) numerous casual conversations as well as extended tape recordings of certain (but not all) of his interactions with the two people (1999, pp. 237–238).

A related example arises when a study not only devotes an entire chapter to a study participant but also dwells on the person's own views and voice rather than any third-person descriptions by the researcher. Such a presentation requires extensive tape recordings of discussions with the participant, followed by thorough reviews of the ensuing transcriptions. To make the material presentable, the researcher may have to edit and reorder the transcribed passages—but this procedure needs to be followed with the utmost care, to avoid reimposing the researcher's perspective on the material that will appear as part of the final study.

Possibly the most well known of this kind of coverage comes from the works of Oscar Lewis. One work, *The Children of Sanchez* (1961), is based entirely on the words of the five members of a Mexican family (see "A Study Based Entirely on the Voices of the People Who Were Studied," Vignette 10.2). Another work, the award-winning *La Vida* (1965), presents a single Puerto Rican family in a book that runs nearly 700 pages.

VIGNETTE 10.2. A STUDY BASED ENTIRELY ON THE VOICES OF THE PEOPLE WHO WERE STUDIED

Except for an introductory chapter, this 500-page study consists entirely of the words of the people who were studied—the members of the Sanchez family (Lewis, 1963). Each chapter covers one of the family's five members, and each member is covered in three separate chapters.

The author, anthropologist Oscar Lewis, suggests that this presentation "tends to reduce the element of investigator bias because the accounts are not put through the sieve of a middle-class North American mind" (1963, p. xi). He further suggests that "The independent versions of the same incidents given by the various family members provide a built-in check upon the reliability and validity of much of the data" (p. xi).

To obtain the needed material, the author made extensive tape recordings of his queries and conversations with the family members over a four-year period. He takes responsibility for arranging and organizing the materials and also omitting his own questions to avoid disrupting the flow of discourse from each family member.

Lewis later expanded this entire approach to family studies in another well-known work, *La Vida: A Puerto Rican Family in the Culture of Poverty—San Juan and New York* (1965).

Presenting Information about Different Participants, but Not Focusing on the Life Story of Any of Them

A more complex and totally different approach arises when the purpose of a qualitative study is to examine cross-cutting issues rather than the life stories of individual people or families. The narrative still includes mixtures of quotations and dialogue with individual participants, but the same individuals are not necessarily tracked from one issue to the next (see "Citing the Experiences and Words of Different People, without Compiling Any Single Life Story," Vignette 10.3).

VIGNETTE 10.3. CITING THE EXPERIENCES AND WORDS OF DIFFERENT PEOPLE, WITHOUT COMPILING ANY SINGLE LIFE STORY

Two studies illustrate this practice.

First, Valdés's (1996) study of 10 newly arrived immigrant families from Mexico makes no attempt to give the life story of any of the families. Thus, the distinctive quality of the study's presentation is that, although it provides extensive information about the 10 families throughout the text, the study is not organized into 10 family histories or cases. Rather, the study sequentially addresses various education and schooling issues, including "raising children" and "interacting with school personnel," citing the particular experiences of one or several of the families within each issue. The result is a "cross-case" presentation (in the absence of presenting any single case) that helps the reader to appreciate the main topic of study—that is, the transitional challenges faced by the families.

Second, Sturm's (2002) study of the Cherokee Nation focuses on a series of cultural patterns related to racial politics. The study has plenty of relevant field scenes describing the actions and perceptions of the people in the study and quoting some of them directly. However, the study again offers no life stories or biographies of any of the people.

See also Vignette 6.9.

An attractive variation is illustrated by Liebow's (1993) study. As his main text moves from topic to topic, the text refers to the experiences of different participants, depending on the relevance and suitability of their experiences to the topic. A reader can then learn more about the fuller background and circumstances of each participant individually by referring to the 20 life histories that appear at the end of the book. As a result of this arrangement, and if wishing to do so, a reader also can go back and forth between the text and the life histories to gain a fuller context for the participants' interactions reported in the text.

When organizing a narrative in a *cross-person* manner, the voices of the participants in a study are not presented in any depth. Although their perceptions and opinions on specific topics still have been preserved, the overall goal is to draw attention to the topics and issues, not to the individual people. This *cross-person* treatment is not to be confused with an entirely different compositional strategy, not desirable from a methodological standpoint, when authors may create a *compos-*

ite but fictitious person comprising the experiences of different real persons. This latter situation, now rarely practiced, presents the composite person as if she or he were a real person.

B. TABULAR, GRAPHIC, AND PICTORIAL PRESENTATIONS

PREVIEW—*What you should learn from this section:*
1. The varieties of ways of presenting data using non-narrative formats.
2. How to create presentable tables and lists—usually different from the data arrays previously used to analyze the same material.
3. The need to exercise extra caution in protecting anonymity (if desired) when individual participants are part of a list, even when pseudonyms are used.
4. Working with graphics, photographs, and reproductions as other formats for presenting a study's data.

Many, if not most, qualitative studies completely limit themselves to narrative presentations covering all of the issues, phenomena, and events that were studied. As just discussed, these presentations also may include individualized descriptions of a study's participants, whether presented in the third person or in varying lengths of first-person voices.

At the same time, some qualitative studies augment their narratives with other modes of presentation that will appear as exhibits or figures, including tables (and lists), graphics, and pictures. Each alternative presents a distinctive opportunity for displaying data, potentially making the data more understandable than when constrained by narrative descriptions alone. The other modes also can create images in a reader's mind to make a study's data more vivid. When presenting the data from your own qualitative study, you therefore may want to consider these other modes in addition to presenting data in a narrative format.

Exhibit 10.1 presents the three modes along with illustrative examples. Each mode is discussed in the ensuing paragraphs.

Tables and Lists

Tables usually represent two dimensions: rows and columns. Multidimensional tables are more complex but also follow similar principles of presentation. The distinguishing feature of tables in qualitative studies is that the tables are likely to consist of words, not numbers (see Chapter 8, Section C). Such tables are commonly regarded as *word tables*.

Also as mentioned at the outset of this chapter, effectively communicating with your audiences may require tables and arrays different from those that you might have amassed to do your analysis. Not readily apparent to many researchers, the desired tables are likely to be shorter and not as detailed as those used in your analysis.

EXHIBIT 10.1. THREE MODES FOR DISPLAYING QUALITATIVE DATA

Type of display	Illustrative example
Word tables and lists	• Summary of findings, placed into a matrix of rows and columns • Chronology • Aggregate characteristics of people studied or interviewed • List of individual people in a study and their *study characteristics* (not necessarily routine demographic characteristics)
Graphics	• Geographic map; census tract map • Spatial layout of a study area • Hierarchical chart (e.g., organization chart) • Flowchart (e.g., sequence of events over a time line) • Family trees and other schemes
Pictures	• Photographs • Reproductions (e.g., of artwork or of others' drawings or pictures)

The desired tables also should have an informative but succinct title (possibly stating the interpretation and not just the subject of the table, in a few choice words) and clear row and column heading structures (including subrows and subcolumns if relevant). Your readers should be able to scan your tables easily, deriving the key relationships between the rows and the columns and quickly interpreting the information in a table's cells (see "Using Word Tables to Summarize an Analytic Finding," Vignette 10.4 and Exhibit 10.2).

VIGNETTE 10.4.   USING WORD TABLES TO SUMMARIZE AN ANALYTIC FINDING

Well-organized word tables can appear to be simple but in fact convey the essence of a study's major findings. For instance, George's (2005) ethnographic study examined the experiences of female nurses who, along with their male spouses, migrated from India to the United States. Among the many complications was the impact on gender roles, as the couples were migrating from a strongly patriarchal society.

A portion of George's interviews focused on how couples divided their household labor, leading to the analytic emergence of four types of households (2005, p. 81). A word table summarizes the key relationships among immigrant patterns, household status, and child-care arrangements (see Exhibit 10.2). A richer and more detailed discussion of the four types then became the subject of an entire chapter in George's book.

See also Vignette 10.5.

A *list* may be considered a one-column version of a table, with any number of rows. Lists also can be helpful in presenting data. For instance, if your study had an important sequence of events over time, you could place the events in chronological order as part of a list. Your readers could scan the entire list. They could possibly

EXHIBIT 10.2. VARIATIONS AMONG HOUSEHOLD TYPES (ACCOMPANIES VIGNETTE 10.4)

Household types	Shaping Factors		
	Immigration pattern	Relationship to labor market	Arrangement for child care
Traditional	• Men are the primary immigrants	• Men have high status • Women have lower or equal status	• Women stay home • Kids are left in Kerala with relatives or at boarding schools
Forced-participation	• Women are the primary immigrants	• Women have high status • Men have lower status relative to their jobs in India and to their wives' jobs in the United States	• Men are forced to participate • Couples work alternate shifts • Some child-care help is available in the United States or Kerala
Partnership	• Women are the primary immigrants	• Women have high status • Men have lower status relative to their jobs in India and to their wives' jobs in the United States	• Men participate • Couples work alternate shifts • There is little outside support
Female-led	• Women are the primary immigrants	• Women have high status • Men are absent, not active, or have low status	• Women are mostly alone • Relatives and the community provide some support

Source: George (2005, p. 81).

follow the chronology more easily than if you had embedded the same sequence as part of your narrative text.

For many qualitative studies, both tables and lists may cover the characteristics of the participants in a study. The characteristics can be reported in aggregate terms—for example, covering the entire group of participants in the study, such as their average age, the percent in each gender, and the distribution of employment specialties. Cable, Shriver, and Mix (2008) used such a table to display these characteristics about the participants they had interviewed as part of their study (p. 387). The table might even compare two different groups of participants—for example, those who had been surveyed and those who had been part of more intensive ethnographic fieldwork (e.g., Moore, 2008, p. 342).

A more delicate situation arises if the list presents the characteristics of individual participants rather than grouping them. For instance, a study of Arab American men and women listed 38 individual participants by pseudonym and also provided detailed demographic data about each person (Read & Oselin, 2008, p. 305). This kind of individualized list can occasionally be found in other studies as well. For instance, such studies include:

- The 54 interviewees in Stone, 2007;

- The 25 focus groups and their composition in Valenzuela, 1999; and

- The tables enumerating the characteristics of the specific parents in Valdés's 10-family study (1996).

Some of these lists, even when using pseudonyms, carry the risk of making the participants identifiable and should be resisted unless the risk of such identification has been agreed upon with the participants.

When the issue of anonymity has been properly addressed, listing the persons who were part of a study is desirable and can enable readers to gain a much stronger sense of a study and its data. For instance, the pertinent characteristics of the persons can reflect directly the topic of study, not just the typical demographic dimensions (see "Listing Information about the People in a Study," Vignette 10.5).

VIGNETTE 10.5. LISTING INFORMATION ABOUT THE PEOPLE IN A STUDY

Two studies provide examples of lists that contain information about the people in each study. In both cases, the lists enumerate characteristics related to the subject of study, not just routine demographic variables.

In the first study, Sheba Mariam George (2005) uses an appendix table to present the individual characteristics of over 50 persons in her study, covering their reasons for immigrating, their occupational status, their year of arrival in the United States, and other features related to her study of gender and class in transnational migration.

In the second study, Deirdre Royster (2007) lists the nearly 40 persons she interviewed, grouped into three categories: low, moderate, and high success. Within each group is listed the name, race, and occupation of each interviewee. The groupings and listed characteristics are directly related to her main topic of study, the exclusion of black men from blue-collar jobs following their completion of high school.
See also Vignette 10.4.

Graphics

Graphics covers any kind of drawing, schema, or crafted work. This kind of presentation offers numerous opportunities to display qualitative data.

Of particular relevance to many qualitative studies is the use of graphics to clarify spatial relationships. A well-chosen *map* or the graphic layout of a study area may orient readers better than any narrative description of the area. Studies therefore often use such maps and layouts to complement narrative descriptions. Such a practice has the greatest relevance when a qualitative study focuses on a geographic area, such as a neighborhood. For instance,

> • Sharman (2006) studied the diverse cultural groups in a single neighbor-hood in New York City. Opposite the title page of his book, he intro-duced his entire text with a schematic map of the blocks and pertinent landmarks in the neighborhood. The map provided readers with a visual image of the spatial relationships within his field setting.

Maps also can be relevant even where the focus of study is not a geographic area. For instance, studies of immigrant groups can depict the immigrants' regions of origin. The maps can be full-fledged or outline maps and are especially helpful when the regions are in less well-known parts of the world. Good examples are:

> • Eastern Spain along the Mediterranean Sea (Narotzky & Smith, 2006, map facing p. 1); or
> • The Southern region of Mexico that falls along the Pacific Coast (Smith, 2006, p. 21).

Maps also can orient readers to complex metropolitan areas, such as the five-county region around Los Angeles (Waldinger & Lichter, 2003, p. 27).

In a similar manner, studies have used census tract maps—and therefore census data—to show the distribution of different population groups relevant to the topic of study (e.g., Edin & Kefalas, 2007, pp. 15, 17–18; Smith, 2006, pp. 31–33). Maps can even be historical, as in one study that showed the geographic relation-ships between two ethnic groups in Eastern Europe in 1910, as a prelude to the more contemporary study of the groups' relationships (Brubaker et al., 2006, p. 31).

Besides maps, census tracts, and historical maps, graphics can cover a broader variety of more abstract topics, such as:

◆ The flow of events across time (e.g., flow diagrams);

◆ Hierarchical relationships (e.g., organization charts);

◆ Family trees; and

◆ Conceptual relationships (e.g., Venn diagrams showing the overlap and nonoverlap of important sets of data).

With sufficient artistic skill, virtually any scheme can be graphically depicted. The main limitation is your own imagination, plus the possible need to find some-one who can render a drawing or even a chart accurately and attractively. Done properly, however, graphics can add life to a qualitative study and its data.

Photographs and Reproductions

These represent a third mode of displaying qualitative data. The photographs may be of the participants or places in a study or of other artifacts and features of the environment relevant to a study. Many of the qualitative studies cited in this textbook make frequent use of such photographs (e.g., Adrian, 2003; Bourgois, 2003; Brubaker et al., 2006; Duneier, 1999; Lee, 2009; Pedraza, 2007; Rabinow, 2007; Sharman, 2006; Smith, 2006).

Given the heavy use of photographs in everyday life, including the fact that anyone with a cell phone can be a photographer, today's audiences have become increasingly perceptive consumers of good photography. Studies that use photographs should therefore set high standards for the quality of the photography—in technical terms (e.g., lighting, focus, and image size) and in artistic composition. Care also should be taken in deciding whether photographs originally appearing as glossy and color photographs will reproduce attractively in the matte and black and white format likely to be required by most academic publications. The photographs, of course, also should be well chosen to reflect a central facet of a study and its context.

Poor photographs can reflect negatively on a study and on the inferred quality of the rest of the study. Good photographs can give meaning to the overused but insightful aphorism of being worth a thousand words (see "Making Good Use of Photographs as Part of Qualitative Studies," Vignette 10.6). Photographs not only appear in books but also can appear in leading contemporary journals. For instance, as a key part of a study of streetcorner interactions, Lee's (2009) article contained 17 photographs organized into five sets of interactions, showing people's gestures and postures.

VIGNETTE 10.6. MAKING GOOD USE OF PHOTOGRAPHS AS PART OF QUALITATIVE STUDIES

Most qualitative studies remain challenged when it comes to presenting photographs as part of the study. Problems run the gamut from the photos being too selective, too glamorous, or glossy (or the reverse—too poorly composed).

Duneier's (1999) study of the sidewalks in New York City overcame all of these problems in a way that other researchers may seek to emulate. His study contains over 50 photos (reducing the selectivity challenge); the photos use a matte and black-and-white presentation that befits the street scenes being studied; and the pictures were candid shots of people on the street. The photos were produced by a photojournalist who had himself been "taking pictures of the inner city for three decades" and who "visited the blocks year-round and came to know the people in the book intimately" (p. 12).

Rabinow (2007) provides a similarly good example. He also relied on an expert collaborator, to whom he gave his deepest thanks on the book's dedication page, for the photographer's "stunning and perceptive pictures, his acute and unique insights, and his friendship."

See also Vignette 7.3.

Reproductions are similar to photographs because they are copies of some existing pictorial work. The reproductions can be copies of artwork, drawings, and old photographs produced by others. They also can represent artifacts, such as pictures of the pages from a person's diary; an old map; a uniform or style of dress; or any number of other items relevant to a qualitative study.

The difference between a reproduction and the photographs just discussed is that you are the creator of a photograph, whereas a reproduction is a copy of someone else's work, including the reproduction of someone else's photographs. Citing the source of the work is therefore an important part of using reproductions properly. As with photographs, any reproductions added to a study's narrative should again be presented in as attractive manner as possible, in terms of both the technical quality of the reproduction and the composition and centrality of the subject matter.

C. CREATING SLIDES TO ACCOMPANY ORAL PRESENTATIONS

PREVIEW—*What you should learn from this section:*
1. Ways of creating attractive slides as part of your oral presentation, to communicate well with viewers.
2. Hints for the best ways of putting words on slides but also for using slides to present matrices or formats other than simple word slides.

In principle, any of the materials discussed in this chapter, including small portions of narrative such as brief quotations, can appear as slides that might accompany an oral presentation of a qualitative study. Available computer software readily enables any of the materials to be converted into a slide format.

But will any set of slides do? Think of the times you have attended presentations at a professional meeting. How often was the information on the slides too small or faint to be easily read or recognized? Did the speaker read what was on the slides to you, using them as a script for her or his presentation? Did the slides impress you in any way—for example, by leaving you with a visual image of the gist of the study's findings?

Good and effective slides are not difficult to design, but presenters may not pay enough attention to their options. The following pages contain some hints that you can consider in designing your slides.

Slide Artwork: Not the Same as the Artwork for Printed Exhibits

The first hint is that, without some reworking, the same item that served well as an exhibit in a printed format is not likely to be reusable as a slide without some formatting changes. Note that readers may scrutinize the exhibits in a written publication for an indefinite period of time. In contrast, an audience only sees a slide for a short period of time (usually minutes), with the speaker's comments also producing a potential distraction.

As a result, you can see why the preferred slides should carry *less* information than their counterpart exhibits. Relative to exhibits, slides need to use larger typeface, be simpler in concept, and be more quickly understandable. For instance, good data exhibits for printed use might have clarifying footnotes, but these will not show well on a slide. Thus, from a practical standpoint, you will need to rework the artwork of exhibits to make them into communicable slides.

A subjective clue is that when you download your slides onto a piece of paper, the preferred slides should appear slightly too large—as if they were a "superstimulus" to your eyes. The slides when printed will appear too "loud." Conversely, the best exhibits will appear too obscure or "faint" when you try to convert them into slides without any reworking.

As a rough guideline, and especially if you are speaking before audiences sitting some distance from your screen, try to use fonts of 18 points or larger in your slides. (Remember that the slides need to be reliably seen by the people sitting or standing at the farthest, not the average, distance from your screen.) Ironically, don't be afraid to create slides with the narrowest possible margins because the unused outer portion of a screen, not covered by a fully projected slide, will add more margin when you show the slides through a projector.

Given the preceding details, you still can get up to 15 easily visible lines of text (including the spaces between the lines) onto a slide. However, only rarely should you use so many lines. Under most circumstances, such a slide will have too much information for your audience to handle.

Text-Only Slides ("Word Slides")

The most basic kind of slide may only contain words on it. For instance, such words may appear on your first slide, displaying a series of numbered items that outline the topics you are going to cover in your presentation. Conversely, such words may appear in a slide at the end of your presentation, capturing your main conclusion(s).

When displaying such texts, many speakers put too many words on a slide. Instead of identifying the key words or phrases to make a point, the slide will contain an entire sentence—or worse yet, an entire (but short) paragraph. The speaker will then proceed to "read" the slide aloud, as if the slide was serving as a script for that portion of the oral presentation.

If you are going to put words on a slide, limit them to the key words, couplets (e.g., adjective–noun or verb–noun couplets), phrases, or sentence fragments that represent the gist of your remarks. Your goal, by designing such slides, is to have audiences remember these key words, couplets, phrases, or sentence fragments as mental cues for recalling your more complete remarks.

Taking Advantage of Slides' Free Form

Putting lines of text onto a slide, regardless of the number that you can fit, would nevertheless not seem to be the most advantageous use of slides to begin with. Better yet would be to fill a slide's blank image with the tables, graphics, and pictorial materials discussed earlier in this chapter. Many of the most attractive oral presentations omit any use of word slides.

For instance, even a two-by-two matrix can be difficult to describe orally. A slide can perform the same function as an exhibit and readily convey this relationship. Exhibit 10.3 comes from a study of school "choice"—an increasingly popular policy whereby students are permitted to select among public schools rather than being assigned to them. The exhibit highlights the different combinations of eligibility produced by a two-by-two matrix. Once the relationship has been established, a speaker can then orally present more details about the contents of the matrix.

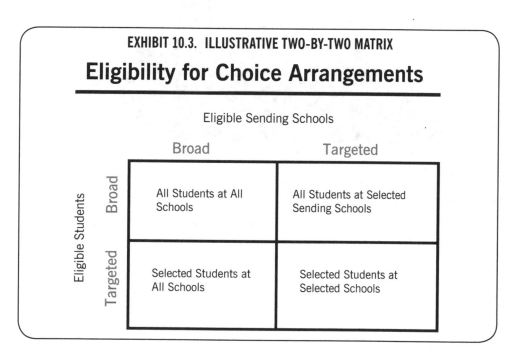

A more creative way of presenting abstract concepts, such as matrices or even lists, involves embedding them within a geometric shape, such as a pyramid. In Exhibit 10.4, even though the main concepts are really just words on a list, audiences may give the slide more attention if such geometric shapes or other objects appear in addition to just plain words. You also can later refer to the shape, such as saying the "pyramid of effectiveness" (which appears as the subtitle of the slide in Exhibit 10.4) as a concrete shorthand that will be easier for audiences to catch aurally than if you refer directly to an abstract concept, such as "evidence-based prevention" (which appears as the title of the slide in Exhibit 10.4).

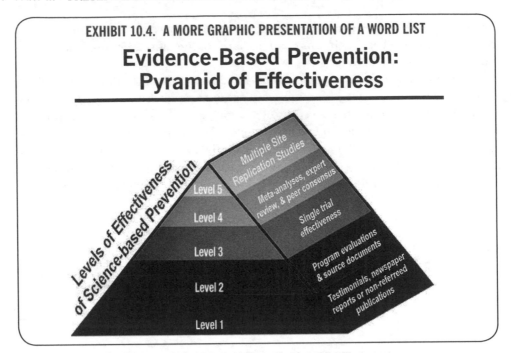

EXHIBIT 10.4. A MORE GRAPHIC PRESENTATION OF A WORD LIST

Evidence-Based Prevention: Pyramid of Effectiveness

Using Icons and Other Symbols

Similarly, icons and other symbols can help to clarify more difficult conceptual relationships. For instance, the study of school "choice" had identified four types of choice arrangements as an important preliminary finding. In addition to listing these arrangements, the slide used "bus" and "school" icons to illuminate the direction of the flow of students from one school to another under each of the four arrangements (see Exhibit 10.5).

In a similar manner, icons and other symbols can add artistic flavor to a slide. An otherwise straightforward set of lines of text can be complemented by a nicely chosen set of icons that illustrate the key concepts, such as the representations of the three other fields—journalism, detective work, and forensics in Exhibit 10.6. Similarly, the collage of reports in Exhibit 10.7 gives an audience concrete images of the reports that were then characterized in the set of bulleted items that follow below the collage.

Choosing Colors and Artistic Style

Software to produce slides has its own default settings so that you can quickly create a slide. The default settings include some modest artwork, including a default color, most commonly some shade of blue.

To give your slides and possibly your entire presentation their own personality, you should try to go beyond the default settings. To begin with, you can discard the default color because attractive slides can be created in black and white. However, if you wish to work with colors, three observations may serve as helpful hints.

EXHIBIT 10.5. USING ICONS TO ILLUSTRATE CONCEPTUAL RELATIONSHIPS

Four Types of Choice Arrangements

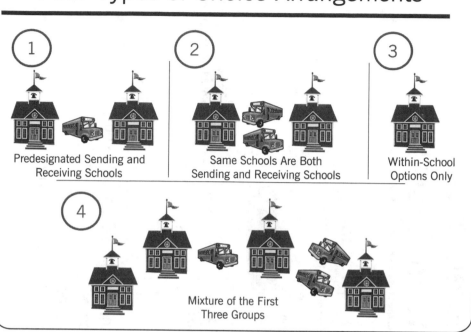

(1) Predesignated Sending and Receiving Schools

(2) Same Schools Are Both Sending and Receiving Schools

(3) Within-School Options Only

(4) Mixture of the First Three Groups

EXHIBIT 10.6. ADDING ICONS TO ILLUSTRATE SPECIFIC TOPICS

Thinking about Rivals

Not much help from existing evaluation or methods textbooks

- How to surface the most compelling and plausible rivals
- How to test rivals

Observed use of rivals in three related (empirical) crafts:

- Journalism

- Detective work

- Forensics

EXHIBIT 10.7. ILLUSTRATING TEXTUAL ITEMS WITH A COLLAGE

Data Collected about State Prevention Systems

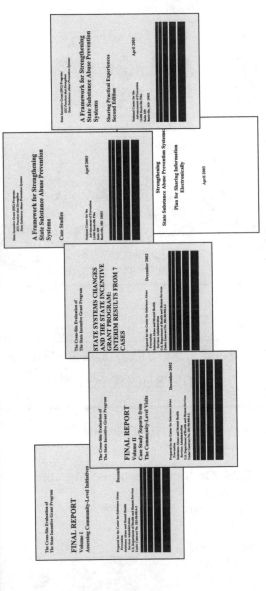

Two reports on subrecipient communities and 10 comparisons

Summary of case materials from 7 cases

Collection of 43 practices from 24 states

In-depth case studies on 8 practices, including replication steps

Over 650 pages of materials

First, colors should not be overused (unless a pictorial image actually contains a lot of color and your slide is a faithful reproduction of that image). A slide's message consists of its substantive content, not its array of colors. Think of colors as accenting your message, not overwhelming it.

Second, some colors are not readily discerned by audiences who sit at the most common distances away from a presenter. The colors on the slide become even more difficult to discern if they are obscured by a background color. For instance, in most cases an audience will have to strain to see the difference between a dark blue and a black line. Similarly, the hues of certain pastel shades may be too close to be distinguished from each other. Background colors that are too strong will aggravate the problem even further, usually making the whole slide too faint and difficult to view or decipher.

You want your audience to attend to the substance of your slides and your presentation, not giving a moment's thought to the coloration of a slide. To strive for such an effect, figure out which groups of colors contrast easily but still remain compatible rather than clashing with each other (e.g., a bright blue, silver, and gold; alternatively, a red, orange, and yellow). Stick to those colors in providing accent to your slides, whose main features can then remain black on white. If you want to reverse the effect of the slides by having white words and figures against a darker or even black background, make sure that the chosen color scheme works easily under this reversed condition.

Third, using the varying shades of the same color (e.g., a dark brown and a light brown) to make substantive distinctions can be a tricky matter. The differences among the shades may be too subtle visually. The problem also exists when you leave your slides in black and white and then use more than two shades of gray. For instance, to represent the different portions of a pie chart, a lighter shade and a darker shade will usually be distinguishable, but going beyond such pairs is risky. For such pie charts and bar charts, consider using different patterns, such as stripes, in place of a third shade.

Slides as an Adjunct to Your Presentation

Even when you have created a set of high-quality slides, remember that they remain a supplementary tool. You and your performance still occupy center stage. Among other controllable strategies, this means: (1) working hard so that you do not simply read your presentation to your audience; (2) being careful not to use too many slides in too short a period of time; and (3) maintaining your audience's focus on the substance of your work.

RECAP FOR CHAPTER 10: *Terms, phrases, and concepts that you can now define:*

1. Narrative data
2. Life histories

3. Direct and indirect quotations of participants' words

4. Two-tiered design for collecting narrative data from participants

5. Presentation of cross-person narratives (cf. a composite of several participants' words blended into the presentation of a fictitious character)

6. Word tables

7. Pseudonyms

8. Photographs and reproductions, including reproductions of photographs

9. Difference between the artwork for slides (to accompany an oral presentation) and the artwork for exhibits (to appear in a printed publication)

10. Icons

EXERCISE FOR CHAPTER 10: MAKING SLIDES

(Be sure to complete this exercise before starting the exercise for Chapter 11.)

Using your fieldwork notes from the exercise in Chapter 5, create two variations of slide presentations, each variation having several (3–5) slides. Both variations should cover the exact same substantive material—either embracing the entire fieldwork experience or summarizing some important portion of it. Both variations also should relate the whole or partial experience from an introductory starting point to a concluding ending point and therefore tell a little "story" to the audience.

The first variation of slides should be limited to verbal material only (i.e., all are to be "word" slides).

The second variation of slides should minimize verbal material and express the relevant ideas through the use of nonverbal materials (e.g., icons, drawings, graphics, or pictures). The second set should have clear verbal titles, however.

Which set was harder to create, and why? Which set will have greater impact on the audience, and why?

CHAPTER 11

Composing Research, to Share It with Others

Whether in a written or an oral form, a final research composition must accurately report a study's findings and conclusions but also in a compelling and attractive manner. The objective is not just to present a study but to communicate it to specific audiences. Qualitative research poses an additional burden by requiring that the composition include narration by a researcher's declarative as well as reflective self. How all of this can come together is the topic of the present chapter.

The chapter starts by describing an "inside out and backwards" strategy for avoiding writer's cramps and then discusses the ways of communicating the declarative and reflective selves. Throughout, the discussion suggests ways of making compositions enticing, while still accurately portraying a study's empirical data. The chapter then ends by describing the reworking process necessary to produce strong compositions, including the ways of responding to various types of reviewers' comments and anticipating the copyediting needs of the final composition.

You are now ready to wrap up your research study. The goal is to render your entire qualitative study, to be communicated with others.

To start, let me tell you a brief story about myself: When I am writing at my computer, people who walk nearby will overhear me speaking sporadically. Some of them think I am saying something to them, and we quickly settle that misunderstanding. Others think that I am muttering to myself.

What I am really doing is reading my own writing aloud. For some reason, I need to hear selected sentences or paragraphs, to decide whether they both contain the substance of what I want to say and also "sound" easy to read. In some way, I keep an imaginary audience in my mind, asking myself whether my former professors, my colleagues and competitors, my friends, and my family will understand the sentence. If a sentence or paragraph passes this (mythical) test, I'm feeling good about it for the time being.

I've had this habit for as long as I can remember. It's so idiosyncratic that I have not compared notes about it with other social scientists. But whether I am peculiar or am one of a large band of people, and whether the habit works well or not, it still provides a helpful clue: You should constantly think of your audiences as you create either your written or oral compositions. Your first impulse needs to resist composing for yourself.

At every turn, think of others when you compose. Think about it this way: Is your message only being sent outwards (*disseminate*), or is it likely to be received and understood the way you want, by those who are important to you (*communicate*)?

Two themes can reflect this orientation toward communication. First, the surface distinctions between writing your findings and presenting them orally may be less important than remembering that both are efforts at communicating with others. You should think of applying most of the ideas about presenting qualitative research to both your writing and your oral presentations. As a result, this chapter uses the terms *composing, presenting*, and *reporting* interchangeably. All are intended to embrace both written and oral modes.

Second, as with all empirical research, your objective must be to share ideas openly and broadly. This second theme is part of a larger one in doing empirical research. The well-known scholar and philosopher Michael Polanyi (1958, 1966) wrote about how scientific progress is dependent on researchers converting their *personal* knowledge into *public* knowledge—to enable others to replicate or challenge their findings. This chapter elaborates on the same theme as it pertains to qualitative research. As shown shortly, you not only need to share your findings, but you also need to provide insights into the *research lens* with which you have conducted your research.

The remainder of this chapter first sets the scene by attending to general matters involved in composing qualitative research. The middle of the chapter emphasizes the fact that your compositions will usually express two selves—a *declarative* self and a *reflective* self. The last portion of the chapter discusses how you might rework your initial drafts, a sometimes extensive process that includes obtaining comments from reviewers as well as revising and editing your work.

As a final prelude, think about acquiring and reading other works on composing, both before and during your compositional efforts. Don't be afraid to look for compositional clues in related fields, such as journalism, history, and nonfiction writing more generally (see "Reading about Composing, in a Variety of Related Fields," Vignette 11.1). The readings can contain sound advice as well as helpful examples. Interspersing your composing with the reading of a chapter or two from these other works every once in a while will not only provide a break but also may stimulate your own writing.

VIGNETTE 11.1. READING ABOUT COMPOSING, IN A VARIETY OF RELATED FIELDS

As with most of the other topics throughout this book, having some reading to do can help to stimulate your thinking. Four favorites on composition should find their way to your bookshelf. They are enjoyable to read, and you should read them before and as you are composing.

 The first is Howard Becker's (1986) book, *Writing for Social Scientists*. It covers many stylistic issues and grapples with the universal challenge of overcoming writer's cramps. The second is Christopher Scanlan's *Reporting and Writing* (2000), aimed at journalists but with plenty of practical suggestions relevant to qualitative research. The third is also from a slightly different field—history—Barzun and Graff's *The Modern Researcher* (1970). Their book covers some nitty-gritty topics such as writing good sentences and paragraphs.

 For a change of pace, also keep on hand Kramer and Call's *Telling True Stories* (2007), a collection of brief contributions by nearly 100 different nonfiction writers from various fields.

A. COMPOSING: GENERAL HINTS

PREVIEW—*What you should learn from this section:*

1. Three types of audiences for a qualitative study and their likely preferences.

2. A specific strategy for getting research compositions started and avoiding writer's cramps.

 Compositions can assume different forms. In social science research, the most prominent form is narrative writing. However, alternative forms may be statistical, visual, oral, or poetic (see "Taking Risks When Using Unconventional Presentations," Vignette 11.2), in any combination. The form it ultimately takes depends on your audience and your sponsors. For qualitative research, the most frequent forms are probably the narrative and visual forms.

Knowing the Audience for Your Qualitative Research

Nearly alone among the social sciences, qualitative research has the ability to reach an extremely diverse array of audiences. Among the potential audiences, those doing research already can be of different types. One type of audience might be other qualitative researchers. They might expect your composition to show innovative and creative techniques and strategies, even if they "push" the boundary between conventional and exotic, conservative and risky.

VIGNETTE 11.2. TAKING RISKS WHEN USING UNCONVENTIONAL PRESENTATIONS

One of my own studies involved a field study of seven urban neighborhoods in the 1970s, when residents suffered severely from poor police, fire, and sanitation services (Yin, 1982, Chap. 10). Toward the end of the study, the fieldworkers (there was one in each neighborhood) had to report their findings, but the form of their presentation was not specified.

   One of the fieldworkers presented his findings as a lengthy, multiversed "street poem." The poem appropriately conveyed both the substance and the "rhythm" of the neighborhood's streets. It carried important implications for urban services and called attention to the often inappropriate (cultural and class) lenses used by service providers.

   The poem appeared in the sponsoring research organization's annual report but drew criticism from board members. They questioned the use of the poem as a meaningful and worthy research product.

   You need to decide how to select the best way of presenting your research, noting that sponsors also have certain expectations for judging whether they have received their money's worth after supporting your work.
   See also Vignette 2.4.

A second type of audience might be other social scientists who, while appreciating qualitative research, also respect alternative and especially nonqualitative research methods. Such an audience might expect your composition to show the pragmatic features befitting what it believes to be "standard" social science methods—or more "realist" tales, in the qualitative jargon (see Van Maanen, 1988, discussed below).

A third type of audience might be more practical minded. It might believe that qualitative research readily leads to usable insights and therefore might seek to find practical lessons from your research.

Effective communication means identifying the audience and selecting the modes that will most likely have meaning to that audience. Because qualitative research can have such a diverse array of audiences, your first goal in reporting your work is to identify and know your audiences and their predispositions.

Be aware of the potentially extreme differences among your audiences and their different preferences. Some will love qualitative research, whereas others will be dubious. What you present at a meeting of anthropologists is not likely to be appreciated by the board members of a private foundation that has sponsored your research. You may need to highlight different aspects of your work with these diverse audiences, including writing different reports and developing different oral presentations.

Having a Way with Words

Nevertheless, for nearly every audience, the communication of qualitative research still has some common features. The first is that qualitative research by definition deals more with words than with numbers and symbols. Whether the words come from your fieldwork, your later field notes, or your data arrays, you need to feel comfortable, if not enthused, by putting words onto paper or into scripting an oral presentation.

If you are to complete your qualitative research successfully, having a way with words—a "flair" for writing—would be a distinct advantage. In fact, many qualitative researchers may have veered toward a pursuit of careers in qualitative research because it gives them an opportunity to write—often to write a lot. Liking to write does not necessarily mean writing finely polished text. You just need to be able to keep a flow of words moving and to be pleased with your choice of words.

To become more comfortable in using words, the most common suggestion offered by others is simply to compose more text, repeatedly and frequently, such as producing term papers or research articles as often as possible. However, even your daily life offers ways of becoming more sensitive to words (see Exhibit 11.1).

EXHIBIT 11.1. SEVEN EXAMPLES OF USING EVERYDAY WORDS

- Keep a diary or journal, making entries daily, if not more frequently.
- Jot down notes when observing something or listening to somebody.
- Work with a keyboard (even your Blackberry) and see how nimbly your fingers can move when writing sentences.
- Send text or instant messages to others frequently.
- Do word puzzles in the daily newspaper.
- When reading, note the writing style, not just the substance, of the text: if the reading is engaging (or not), is it because of a writing style and not just the text's content?
- Watch for word errors in whatever you read.

Having a sufficient way with words still leaves the major challenge of composing your research. Indeed, you already may have experienced problems because you have tried to start at the beginning but didn't know what to say or write. You also may have been advised to start with an outline of your report—at least by defining its likely chapter headings. However, if you are not sure of what to say or write, creating an outline or even a series of chapter headings still may pose difficulties.

Much advice is available for dealing with the problems of not knowing how to start or even how to develop an outline (e.g., Becker, 1986; Wolcott, 2009). Commonly, these are considered ways of overcoming "writers' cramps." If you want to consider yet another alternative that has passed the test of time, my own work has benefited over the years from the option of composing a report "inside out" and "backwards." When I have passed this advice on to others, the option has worked with my colleagues, too. The procedure may therefore represent a reliable way of starting your own writing. Let's see what "inside out" and "backwards" mean.

Composing "Inside Out"

For any given report or oral presentation, the "inside" consists of the specific field experiences or other data arrays and evidence that you intend to present. Such information usually gets presented in the form of:

◆ Quoted dialogues of varying lengths, previously described in Chapter 10 (Section A);

◆ Word tables (tables with words in them);

◆ Vignettes (illustrative case material, such as the vignettes in this book or the presentation of abbreviated life histories;

◆ Graphic displays and other data arrays (e.g., the matrices discussed in Chapter 10, Section B);

◆ Other inserts such as pictures, cartoons, anecdotes, or tales that you would like to see in your presentation; and even

◆ Numeric tables (tables with numbers in them).

The "outside" is the narrative that surrounds these specific field experiences and data, and that contains your entire line of thinking, from introduction to conclusions. The "outside" therefore weaves together all of the ingredients into a full composition.

Starting the compositional process by drafting the inside ingredients first offers two key advantages. One is that you will actually be starting a key portion of your final composition. The second is that the activity forces you to clarify, precisely, the specific field materials, data, or evidence you are going to use. This means reviewing your selected quotations and arrays as described in Chapter 10 and either finalizing the materials in their entirety or selecting the specific portions to be presented in your final composition.

Finalizing these materials will take much careful work, as they need to be edited and refined for their public presentation. However, you can start anywhere with these materials, such as the favorite parts of your analyses. You also can do the easiest parts first. Most importantly, you can proceed with them without worrying about the "outside" of your composition.

Working with the "inside" of your report can continue for some time. You may find that the initially drafted quotations or data arrays do not serve your original objectives, and you may revise them, set them aside, or replace them. In addition, you may find that your original analyses were incomplete. You may then need to revisit your evidence.

Once a minimal set of these "inside" materials has met your satisfaction, you will have a pleasant and surmountable challenge. You can test how you might put these materials into different sequences. The simulated sequence will test which parts of the materials should precede or follow which other parts. For instance, some of your inside materials will describe your time and place of study and the people who are in it; they might normally come early in a sequence. As another example, your data arrays may include a series of brief life stories about the people in your study. You now may play around with these life stories to test the appeal of putting them into different sequences.

By the time you have assembled a tentative rendition of the "inside," including the sequencing of the various parts, you will be surprised to find that you are well on your way to thinking about how to compose the needed "outside." Your sifting through the data and evidence, as well as your testing of alternative sequences, should have automatically stimulated your thinking about the beginning, middle, and end of your entire composition. The process should have led to a mental sketch of the structure of the "outside," if not your ability now to produce a formal outline.

For qualitative research, the inside-out approach has yet more significance. The approach honors the predominantly inductive nature of qualitative research—that many of the initial insights and findings come from concrete and specific events from your empirical work. Although you might have started your entire study with some hypotheses and theoretical issues, a major strength of qualitative research is its attention to what can be learned from field evidence and data. They raise the possibility of discovering or revealing new ideas and explanations not hinted at by the original hypotheses or theoretical issues.

Likewise, the entire inside-out approach is distinctive to empirical research. Composing research differs from composing a novel or other fictional work: You need to build your report around your empirical evidence (and its limitations, for better or worse). Starting with the evidence is not an option available to those writing novels or fiction.

Composing "Backwards"

Whether written or oral, all presentations will have a linear final form. Your final composition even can start with the study's conclusions—which then need to be explained in the remainder of the text. More conventionally, a composition can start with the research questions and literature that initiated the study.

Wherever the composition starts, it will still have a beginning, an end, and a middle. However, although the final composition will be linear, that does not mean you need to produce it in a linear sequence. You can compose the back end before the front end, or the middle before either end.

Most compositions have material at the very back end that falls outside of the main text and its final conclusions or summary. Such materials supplement the main text: end notes, appendices (which can be brief reports of their own), and a list of references. Although the supplemental materials may not be as critical as the main text, they still serve as an integral part of any valued research report.

To work "backwards" is to start by composing as many of these back-end materials as possible, again avoiding the need to attack the body of the presentation. Although you may not be able to compose end notes until the body of the report is started, you can still deal with the appendices and references. Among the appendices, one in particular is essential to qualitative research: some extended statement about the methods used in your study. (More will be said momentarily about the content of this methods section and how it should cover the research lens with which you have done your research.)

You are likely to be ready to draft your methods discussion before dealing with the body of your report. The drafted section may appear at the end of the report in the form of an appendix. The same discussion also may later be brought forward and put into the body of the main text or even appear as an elongated preface. Regardless of where the methods discussion is placed, composing the discussion will give you a big jump in writing your report, even though you might still not be ready to do the main text.

Similarly, you may want to include an illustrative life history, one or more case studies, or a set of supporting tables as additional appendices. Composing these can again help you to complete an actual part of the final report while allowing you to think about how the materials are to be discussed in the main text.

Finally, you can assemble your list of references or other supporting material before attacking other parts of the report. As the earlier phases of your research were taking place, you should have been keeping close track of all your references. You might even have been assembling them in alphabetical order, and adding to the list, throughout your research. When setting them up, be sure to capture the entirety of each reference. Regardless of the format you will later use, certain details (author, title, publisher, place of publication, page numbers for chapters in a book, etc.) will be needed. Nothing is more frustrating than having to attend to these details after everything else has been successfully composed. So, do your best to capture these details when you are first adding a new reference to your list.

B. COMPOSING QUALITATIVE RESEARCH

PREVIEW—*What you should learn from this section:*
1. Using different "voices" in presenting the material.
2. The relevance of creating a sense of "being there" for the reader.
3. Three ways of telling about your learnings from the field.

Beyond general issues of composing, the fact that you will be presenting qualitative research means that you should attend to some features that are distinctive to this kind of research. As one example, an essential quality of qualitative research is that your composition will be putting the reader in touch with the real-world scene or field setting that you have been studying. You have some choices about how to do this.

First, the choices reflect options that are partly methodological (see your "epistemological location" in Chapter 1, Section C) and that also can be associated with the use of different grammatical voices—that is, first, second, and third persons.

John Van Maanen (see "Three Different Ways of Relating Your Fieldwork Findings," Vignette 11.3) defines the several options by describing three ways of telling about your learnings from the field: *realist* tales (told from a third-person, uninvolved perspective), *confessional* tales (told from a first-person style that constantly reminds the reader of your being in the field), and *impressionist* tales (told to make the field vivid, as if the reader was in the field). You may choose any of the three, use them in some combination, or create your own scenarios. However, because each requires slightly different note taking during your data collection, you will want to consider these choices at an early stage of your research, not just when you are ready to compose.

VIGNETTE 11.3. THREE DIFFERENT WAYS OF RELATING YOUR FIELDWORK FINDINGS

John Van Maanen (1988) identifies and contrasts three different "tales of the field" found in qualitative research: realist tales, confessional tales, and impressionist tales. He describes each type in detail, illustratively providing selections of field reports from his own research (e.g., Van Maanen, 1978).

Realist tales are the most commonly found. They present the field "in a dispassionate, third-person voice" (Van Maanen, 1988, p. 45). The author is not part of the tale. Confessional tales "represent the fieldworker's participative presence in the studied scene" (p. 91), explicitly calling attention to the author's role in interpreting the events in the field (e.g., "I saw the police do *X*," rather than "the police do *X*"— pp. 74–75). Authors also may confess how their study might have given them a totally new perspective, compared to what they believed at the outset of their study.

Impressionist tales attempt to "place the audience in the fieldwork situation," to "re-live the tale with the fieldworker, not interpret or analyze it" (Van Maanen, 1988, p. 103). The impressionist tale may be told in dramatic fashion, where "certain unremarkable features of the beginnings . . . become crucial by its end" (p. 104).
See also Vignette 7.1.

Second, the "research" aspect of "qualitative research" means giving careful attention to your empirical evidence. Qualitative research methods do not offer fixed formats for presenting this evidence, as might statistical software that automatically arrays data into contingency tables or into other analytic models. Thus, arraying your qualitative evidence—whether in narrative, graphic, or pictorial form—as part of the display process covered by Chapter 10, but also when now composing, needs to be done with care. Finally, your research-based composition, except where it is properly labeled as being speculative, should not go much beyond the evidence at hand.

Some other valued features of qualitative research are as follows.

Covering the Five Senses

"Being there" means engaging in human interactions in a real-world environment. The more you can convey this experience by depicting what is happening with all five human senses, the more you will be accentuating one of the main strengths of doing qualitative research in the first place.

There is also a "sixth" sense that can be important—intuitions and feelings as experienced either by those in the field or by yourself. Capturing these, again properly labeled, also distinguishes qualitative research from other forms of research.

Representing Multiple Voices and Perspectives, and Also Dealing with Issues of Anonymity

Another virtue of qualitative research is its ability to appreciate differences among human perspectives. Discussed earlier was how to represent the perspectives of the participants in your study in different ways, including the presentation of first-person accounts ranging from brief quoted materials to lengthier, chapter-long life histories (see Chapter 10, Section A).

Whether to identify these participants or to let them remain anonymous is a standard problem that arises when presenting their perspectives (e.g., Guenther, 2009). The issue can be part of a broader question—whether to identify the location where a qualitative study took place. In nearly every study, participant anonymity, together with the use of pseudonyms, is the option of choice. At the same time, most studies still will identify their locations, unless naming them (such as the name of a high school) can readily lead to identifying an otherwise anonymous participant (such as the school's principal). These matters, of course, all should have been considered earlier as part of the process for gaining approval from an institutional review board and protecting human subjects (see Chapter 2, Section E) and as part of your study design (see Chapter 4, Choice 6).

Being Sensitive to the Interpretive Nature of Your Compositions

Qualitative researchers have increasingly understood the interpretive nature of their research reports. Such a situation also derives directly from your role as a research instrument.

The interpretive nature of qualitative research is inescapable and also is an essential strength of doing such research (see "Twitches or Winks?: Interpretive Constructions of Reality," Vignette 11.4). Your constant task is to be aware of and sensitive to the interpretive function, especially when composing. More will be said about how to monitor yourself in this task, under the discussion about your *reflective* self.

Indeed, this reference to the *reflective* self calls attention to the fact that every good qualitative researcher has both a *declarative* and a *reflective* self. Your declarative self wants to tell the world what you know or have learned. Your reflective self needs to admit how you learned what you know, including possible reservations about your methods (of learning and knowing). Good qualitative research expresses both selves. How you might first present your declarative self is described next, followed by Section D on presenting your reflective self.

VIGNETTE 11.4. TWITCHES OR WINKS?:
INTERPRETIVE CONSTRUCTIONS OF REALITY

In a famous and oft-cited essay on qualitative research, Clifford Geertz (1973) cites Gilbert Ryle's work on "thick description." Part of Ryle's message is based on a metaphor—that the muscular contractions associated with a brief closing of an eye (which could be considered a "realist" description) can nevertheless convey two entirely different "meanings," depending on whether the contraction results from a twitch or a wink.

Geertz exploits this metaphor at length, using it to explain a much more difficult concept: that observations of human interactions can involve both an observer and the observed in a complex relationship. The observer may have to interpret the interaction, typically distinguishing between a twitch that has little social meaning from a wink that represents a deliberate social signal. For Geertz, a realist observer may miss the difference between the two. However, interpretive observers also need to be careful because the observed person may deliberately have signaled a fake wink.

C. PRESENTING YOUR *DECLARATIVE* SELF

PREVIEW—*What you should learn from this section:*

1. How to start your composition in an interesting place and keep your readers engaged.
2. Ways of weaving a strong compositional structure together with the needed presentation of a study's empirical data.
3. How to minimize the use of research jargon.
4. Making headings and titles work harder.

You and others may find "storytelling" to be an acceptable metaphor for describing how you will relate your research findings and their implications. However, if you use this metaphor, be extremely careful that it does not convey that your research is unduly based on your imagination only, as in the literal meaning of a true "story." In qualitative research, the "story" needs to be derived from your field experiences and other evidence (with allowances for speculations after they have been preannounced), not a figment of your imagination. Telling your research story is the crux of the declarative self's challenge.

Starting the story at an interesting place, and then keeping the story going in a compelling manner until its conclusion, should be your ultimate goal. However, expect this challenge to be difficult because you are not writing fiction but must build your story around some empirical base. Your data will heavily influence the nature of your story. Sometimes, you will want to tell a stronger story than can be supported by the data. At other times, your data will surprisingly enable you to add a new wrinkle or even a major twist to your story. To avoid becoming prematurely engulfed by these situations, one practical path is to design and complete a modest study first, then to engage in a succession of increasingly larger and more complex and significant enhancements.

As with other forms of composition, no single approach works under all circumstances. In addition, you may already have your own well-developed way of successfully relating your qualitative research to different audiences. However, in case you need more help or are open to additional suggestions in presenting this declarative self, some tips and examples follow. Of course, if you have successfully compiled a set of dialogues, tables, vignettes, and other materials because you have been working "inside out" (see Section A), the broad outlines of your story already should have emerged.

Starting Your Composition at an Interesting Place

The beginning of the story will simultaneously call upon your most creative and analytic thinking. Your goal is to entice the audience into the world of your text, but to use initial paragraphs or pages that are still strongly connected to the main part of your research story and its evidence.

Most typically, you can do this by describing a concrete incident or episode. This strategy again may be considered an inductive one that mimics the strength of qualitative research. However, you also can start by enunciating a broad but provocative generalization. Under many circumstances, such a generalization also can be enticing, even though it represents a deductive start.

As yet another option, consider a readily understood metaphor or a compelling quote from some other work. These devices often present eye-catching words, but you must be sure that they are directly connected to some major part of your study and its themes (see "Three Examples of Attractive Starting Points," Vignette 11.5).

VIGNETTE 11.5. THREE EXAMPLES OF ATTRACTIVE STARTING POINTS

Three studies featured in earlier vignettes offer different examples of ways for you to start your own study. Each start-up is not only concrete but also reflects the main theme of the ensuing study.

Bogle's (2008) study of "hooking up" needs to distinguish between this relationship and that of "dating." She starts her text with *a lengthy quotation* by a popular writer, Tom Wolfe (p. 1). The quote compares the progression in sexual intimacy as if one were running around the bases, noting that whereas "home plate" was once "going all the way," it is now about "learning each other's names." (Third base is "going all the way.")

Anderson's (1999) work is about the "code of the street." He begins his study with *a social tour* down his site's major urban avenue (pp. 15ff). The avenue begins in a well-to-do neighborhood that honors conventional social controls and then ends in areas where urban poverty and joblessness coalesce into an alienating force with a lack of trust in the police and the judicial system—thereby highlighting the code of the street.

Finally, Brubaker et al.'s (2006) study also is about an abstraction—ethnicity and nationhood. Yet, the study begins with *a concrete event*—the removal of a flag from the embassy of the minority group (pp. 1–4)—with the aftermath of the event symbolizing the spirit of the national feelings being studied.

See also Vignettes 2.2, 6.3, 7.1, and 9.3.

Differing "Shapes" of Compositions

At some point after you have set the initial scene and themes, you are then going to have to get the audience involved in additional details about your research.

One conventional compositional structure is the well-known "hourglass" shape (e.g., Scanlan, 2000, p. 168). The composition starts with the broader issues for a section (or chapter) or two, delves into detailed findings and their analyses for several sections, and ends back at a broader level by discussing the general issues and conclusions. These last sections both echo in some way the issues raised by the initial sections and show how the findings and analyses have advanced any lessons and interpretations to a higher plane. The substantive significance of the higher plane then represents your study's contribution to new knowledge.

Most research reports follow this hourglass shape. Following the initial concrete incident or eye-opener, the early chapters then start addressing the broader issues by expanding upon the topic of study and the major substantive concerns that motivated the study. The middle chapters examine the relevant empirical evidence at a highly detailed level. Finally, the latter chapters present the interpretations and conclusions to be drawn from the study, returning to a broader plane by discussing the significance of the research.

Whether you follow an hourglass shape or not, your composition will have long stretches where you need to keep audiences engaged. For instance, the relevant empirical detail cannot be so obscure that the audience loses a sense of its relevance to the broader issues.

A strategy for these long stretches that suits qualitative research well is a strong sense of "being there" that also involves the unfolding of actions (Degregory, 2007). The unfolding action, while gradually shedding the peels of the proverbial onion, should not make the audience feel that it is being dragged into increasingly remote and obscure detail. Rather, you should sequence the sections (or chapters) so that they point increasingly to the essence of your work. The most central portion could then be the highlight of your entire array of evidence, as if finally divulging your study's innermost and precious secrets.

If you accept this general approach to telling your story, you may now have a better appreciation of the benefit of working "inside out." You should be able to see more easily the importance of having arrayed and re-arrayed the inside material without the clumsiness of having to compose and recompose the actual "outer" story. Thus, even before doing much composing, you should have determined the empirical highlight of your study. The highlight could be the presentation of a person whose life history captures the entire scope of your study, the convergence of information about several such persons, or even the occurrence of the key events in the field. As another option, imagine selecting and highlighting the life story of a different person to accompany each of your chapters (see "Using a Different Life Story in Each Chapter to Highlight Its Substantive Message," Vignette 11.6). In addition to the highlight, you also should have begun to know whether your story has an ending, what it might be, and the most venturesome sequence for getting there.

Note that, throughout this process, the uncovering of any gaps in the needed evidence would then permit you to re-inspect remnants of your data that you might

---

VIGNETTE 11.6. USING A DIFFERENT LIFE STORY IN EACH CHAPTER TO HIGHLIGHT ITS SUBSTANTIVE MESSAGE

Edin and Kefalas (2005) collected and tape recorded data from 162 mothers in eight neighborhoods in a major Eastern city, also spending 2 years as participant-observers.

The authors studied how "poor women" might have seen "marriage as a luxury" but judged "having their own children to be a necessity—an absolutely essential part of a young woman's life" (p. 6). The mothers do not see children "as bringing them hardship . . . ; [on the contrary] they believe motherhood has 'saved' them" (2005, p. 11).

The resulting book has six chapters. Each includes an extensive life story of one particular mother. In turn, each life story illustrates the main theme of the chapter. The chapters follow a life-cycle course directly pertinent to the study, with the following titles: "Before we had a baby; When I got pregnant; How does the dream die; What marriage means; Labor of love; and How motherhood changed my life." The life stories help the authors to report their findings with both descriptive and explanatory insight.

---

originally have left unused, to see whether those remnants can now serve a useful purpose in strengthening the flow of your story.

Using Plain Words and Minimizing Research Jargon

Most research fields have their own jargon, shared by the community of scholars of the particular field. Although the community of scholars may feel comfortable with and readily use this jargon, audiences outside of the field—or outside of research more generally—likely will not. They will usually not react well to much jargon, and you should minimize its use in your composition.

The preceding caution pertains to most social science research. However, qualitative research is in a strong position for avoiding the problem. This is because qualitative research and your study are likely to cover human interactions taking place in everyday settings. Take advantage of this facet of qualitative research to use plain words wherever you can. You should continually use:

◆ Concrete, not abstract terms;
◆ Words that your family and personal friends, not just your professional colleagues, are likely to understand; and
◆ Shorter and smaller words rather than longer and bigger ones.

At the same time, if your audience is mainly your own community of scholars, your composition will need to connect carefully with previous research and with important theoretical issues in your field—and hence with selected jargon. In this situation, you may still want to tell the everyday story in plain words but engage in a more jargon-laden discussion in introducing and interpreting the story.

Making Headings (or the Titles of Exhibits) State a Substantive Message

Headings and titles (of exhibits, tables, and slides) can play a special role in attracting your audience's attention. For instance, most people have a certain way of initially examining a social science report. If it is a book or journal article, they will certainly pay attention to the title of the work, and they may read the abstract, if any. Still browsing, they will note the table of contents and then flip or scan through the body of the report to see whether it is worth a more careful reading. Similarly, most people listen at the outset of an oral presentation to know whether they need to continue listening with great care or alternatively can begin to "coast."

Throughout this initial examination (note that the audience's tasks are likely to be qualitative, not quantitative tasks), headings and titles can be critical. If they contain a quick message, they will catch the perusing eye or the half-attending ear. However, some headings, such as the terms *introduction, section 1, method*, or *conclusions*, only convey the superstructure of a composition, not its substance. Worse, some researchers (who tend to write manuscripts as if they were term papers) may not use headings at all.

At the other and more desired extreme, try to make your headings consist of a phrase or even a(n extremely) short sentence that says what you want the reader to know from reading the associated paragraph or section. For instance, the headings to an introductory or concluding section should contain actual content—that is, what the introduction or conclusion is trying to say. Similarly, the title of a table, exhibit, or slide should at least say the topic of the table, exhibit, or slide, if not explicitly stating the finding represented by the data. These practices with headings and titles will not only attract the people browsing your work but also will help serious audiences to gain a better understanding of its content.

D. PRESENTING YOUR *REFLECTIVE* SELF

PREVIEW—*What you should learn from this section:*
1. The main role of the reflective self and need for making your research lens evident, especially in qualitative research.
2. The potential facets of your research lens and how they might have influenced the course of your research.
3. The choices in placing the description of your research lens within your composition.
4. The ways of letting the reflective self get out of control (and how to avoid such ways).

The reflective self expresses *how you know* what your declarative self has presented. You may consider the essence of the task to be one of reporting your research methods or presenting any other important reservations and caveats you have about the information set forth by your declarative self.

The reflective self exists in all scientific inquiry. However, unlike other research fields, qualitative research methods are more complicated in this regard, and the reflective self therefore needs greater exposure. For example, you also may consider the task to include some statement and description of your epistemological position.

Making Your Research Lens as Explicit as Possible

The main complication arises from the fact that you the researcher are likely to be the major research instrument in collecting your data. Unlike other types of research, qualitative research values direct observation and interaction between the researcher and the phenomena being studied, possibly including but certainly going beyond the use of questionnaires and other mechanical instruments for measuring people's behavior and views. And, as pointed out earlier in Chapter 5 (Section D), you as a research instrument bring a particular lens or filter to your data collection process.

No lens is free of bias; every lens has subjective and objective qualities. In presenting your reflective self, the goal is to identify as many of your lens's qualities in as revealing a way as possible. The goal is to provide the audience with sufficient information that it can make its own assessment of the potential (desirable and undesirable) effects of your lens. Thus, you should provide insight into the relationship between what you are reporting (such as information about the participants in your study) and the circumstances of the data collection (e.g., Gubrium & Holstein, 1998). The circumstances could include:

◆ Your cultural orientation and how it might interact with the culture of the people in your study;

◆ The potential relevance of your other physical attributes (gender, age, appearance);

◆ Your motivation, prior interests, and views that might bear in some way on the topic of study; and

◆ How you gained access to the real-world setting and any particular human networks in the real-life setting that you have studied.

In other words, you should try hard to identify the features of your lens that are in any way likely to influence the findings made by your declarative self. Depending on your audience, you can present all of these features in a friendly and insightful manner or as a methodic discussion of strengths, weaknesses, and caveats.

The description of your lens should therefore appear somewhere in your text. The description can appear in any of three places. First, it can be in the preface to your work (see "Using a Preface to Discuss the Fieldworker's 'Lens,'" Vignette 11.7). Such placement is likely to permit the methods to be discussed in a less formal and even friendly rather than stiff manner. Second, the methods can be discussed in the body of the text, as part of a formal section or chapter that also includes other introductory materials (see "Using a Section Titled 'Self-Reflectivity' to Discuss the Fieldworker's 'Lens,'" Vignette 11.8). Finally, the description can be presented in an appendix.

VIGNETTE 11.7. USING A PREFACE TO DISCUSS THE FIELDWORKER'S "LENS"

In his study of homeless women, Elliot Liebow (1993) devotes the entire preface to his methods as a participant-observer. He candidly notes at the outset that "Everything reported about the women in this study has been selected by me and filtered through me, so it is important that I tell you something about myself and my prejudices as well as how this study came about" (p. vii).

The features Liebow then points out about himself include his 3-year affiliation with the emergency homeless shelter where the women stayed (he was a volunteer, staying overnight twice a month); the potential reactions of the women to his age, gender, and appearance; his willingness to help the women by loaning "$2, $5, $10, or even $20 on request to the handful that asked" or by "driving people to social services, a job interview, a clinic or hospital" and other destinations (1993, p. xi); and his belief that participant-observers need to make relationships as symmetric as possible ("the women needed to know as much about me as I knew about them," p. xii).

These self-observations, including ample examples of specific interactions, help to account for the relative closeness with which the women's lives are later described in the book.

See also Vignettes 1.1 and 5.6.

VIGNETTE 11.8. USING A SECTION TITLED "SELF-REFLEXIVITY" TO DISCUSS THE FIELDWORKER'S "LENS"

A section on "self-reflexivity" appears in the methodology portion of Sylvia Pedraza's (2007) study of the Cuban revolution and the ensuing waves of immigration to the United States.

In this section, Pedraza presents many personal details about both sides of her family and their support for or opposition to the events in Cuba. The author also clarifies how these events affected her upbringing and interest in the topic being studied, with specific reference to the fact that she considers herself to be "a child of the American social movements of the '60s" (p. 32).

All these references permit Pedraza to reveal her own lens, which includes her sympathies for "the courageous men and women who struggle at present in the dissident movement in Cuba for universal human rights" (2007, p. 32). At the same time, the study is so carefully executed and replete with archival, survey, and field evidence that the sympathy is not readily seen as unknowingly influencing the main inquiry and its conclusions.

See also Vignettes 4.4 and 7.1.

Describing Your Research Lens as an Important Quality-Control Procedure

From the standpoint of others judging the quality of your research, and especially a qualitative research study, make no mistake that your awareness and sensitivity in presenting the features of your lens assume great importance. Everyone's lens leads to selectivity in the scope of study, the choice of relevant data to be collected in the field, and the interpretation of the findings. Your rendition of the real-world setting and of your entire study are colored by your meanings and interpretations, whether you wish that to be the case or not.

Qualitative research scholars also have pointed increasingly to the lens's role as a filter that may not have been properly divulged in nonqualitative research, where researchers may be sometimes oblivious to their potential biases. For instance, a *postmodernist* critique (Butler, 2002, pp. 37–43) posits that all researchers, including those in nonqualitative fields, reveal their lens by setting study priorities and selecting particular study designs and instruments while ignoring others (see Chapter 12, Section B).

In doing qualitative research, the best studies cannot eliminate these influences but need to recognize them as explicitly as possible. The goal is to provide sufficient information to enable the audience to reinterpret, if needed, your interpretations. That is, a qualitative research composition attains higher quality when the declarative self presents ample evidence and when the reflective self gives sufficient information to know the circumstances whereby the evidence was sought and collected.

Keeping Your Reflective Self Under Control

Revealing your reflective self should not, however, lead to the overuse of either of two textual constructions: narrative footnotes (compared to footnotes only containing a citation) or parenthetical remarks (words in parentheses).

Both forms give you the opportunity to add reflexive detail, either to embellish the text with some additional self-observation or to express a caveat about some point being made in the text. Whichever the function, the tone of these footnotes and parenthetical remarks generally takes that of a theatrical "aside" (also considered a "side comment"). If you were to present such material orally, not just in writing, your tone of voice would probably drop a bit, to indicate to the audience that you were making an aside.

The "aside" is likely to be an expression made by your reflective self. You are commenting about your work, not presenting the actual work covered by the declarative self (otherwise, the material could equally have appeared in the body of the text and not in a footnote or parentheses). (The preceding parenthetical statement, as well as the present one, are examples of the reflective self in this book.)

Nearly all scholars make asides, both in writing and in their oral presentations. However, if you give too much attention to this aspect of the reflective self, you risk confusion: A reader (or listener) must constantly switch attention between the declarative and the reflective selves. As one critic said about narrative foot-notes that were too extensive, "there seem to be two authors, one "above the line" (demarcating the footnote from the text) and the other "below the line." Such a split personality makes for difficult reading or listening. You risk having your audi-ence pay too much attention to the wrong self (the reflective one) and losing track of the main story.

So, limiting your asides and keeping your reflective self under control when writing or making oral presentations will lead to better communication about the main story. An added benefit is that you will have more time to invest in the main story rather than composing and reworking the footnotes and parenthetical remarks.

Making Prefatory Remarks Insightful and Enticing

The reflective self also reveals itself in your prefatory remarks, which may appear in the preface of a book (in addition to any formal methodological statement) or in the introductory remarks of an oral presentation. The substance of most pref-aces, not just in qualitative research, can cover at least two lines of thought. First, the preface may contain a bit of background on how you became interested and engaged in the topic being studied. For qualitative research, you can see how this could readily lead to a more systematic discussion of your research "lens."

Second, a substantive preface also can contextualize the topic being studied. Such prefatory remarks would be different from what otherwise might appear in a study's formal introductory section (or chapter) because the perspective would be more personalized, without the obligation of citing formal references or prior research. The contextual material can be helpful but again should not be over-done, lest the prefatory remarks effectively become your introduction.

For books, the preface is another place for early browsing by potential readers, to help them determine whether the book is worthy of further examination. There-fore, you should compose the preface with some care and present some insight-ful or provocative comments. These comments can then spur potential readers to delve further into your work. Similarly, stating some stimulating prefatory remarks in an oral presentation also will trigger more active listening on the part of your audience.

An unfortunate gap in the literature is the absence of guidance in composing sound but attractive prefaces. Given this lack, you should give careful attention to what appears in your preface. Too personal an approach, which may appear self-centered, risks losing the interest of readers who may want to know whether a work is going to be significant. Too distant an approach risks appearing cold and mechanical, which may be offputting for a work on qualitative research. Reviewing others' prefatory remarks, deciding which ones are appealing and why, and having your colleagues review the drafts of your own can help you to find a comfortable niche.

E. REWORKING YOUR COMPOSITION

PREVIEW—*What you should learn from this section:*
1. The importance of the reworking process in producing research compositions.
2. Two kinds of reviewers who can help in the reworking process.
3. The likely types of reviewers' comments and ways of dealing with them.

After you have created a complete draft of any part of your composition or of the whole composition, you are ready to rework it. A perfect draft, as with Mozart's musical compositions, will require little or no reworking. However, most of us are not able to produce such perfection the first time around, so we have to spend time reworking our drafts.

The time spent on reworking will likely vary with your academic level. For most course assignments, a good guess is that the reworking will only represent 5–10% of the effort you have put into your entire study. However, for theses, dissertations, and more extensive and complex studies, the reworking can require a much greater proportion of the total effort. The reworking also can occur throughout your composing effort, with some portions of the composition having been completed and now being reworked, while other portions are still being completed for the first time.

Helpfulness of Reviews in the Reworking Process

When doing research, your first instinct should be to have your work reviewed by others. Two kinds of "others" matter most: those who were participants in your study and those who are your peers.

Participants

You already should have been verifying your field notes with the participants in your study as part of "checking stuff" throughout your time in the field (see Chapter 7, Section C). However, at this later stage of composing your final draft, you have an opportunity to ask for additional feedback. Ideally, you should be following the procedures that you previously considered during the design of your study (see Chapter 4, Choice 6).

One purpose of such feedback is to confirm the accuracy of the information, and this purpose may be served by showing selected portions of your draft to the participants. Note that the quest for "accuracy" does not imply a singular reality, as in trying to determine the rightfulness of a reported event, but still acknowledges the possibility of multiple perspectives. Thus, checking for accuracy among your participants mainly means confirming that they said what your text says they said.

Another purpose of gaining feedback may be to obtain additional insights and reactions, as the participants can now see what you have pulled together for the first time. In this situation, you might share the entire draft. However, be forewarned that making the entire draft available can produce unanticipated results because participants may find it to be overly academic and in this sense to deviate from their own sense of reality. If you are going to share the entire draft, you probably need to introduce it and discuss its orientation before actually sharing it. You also should anticipate how you might react if participants disagree with important parts of the draft (e.g., Locke & Velamuri, 2009).

Peers

The second type of "others" are your academic peers and colleagues—for example, those who are well informed about the substance or methods in your study (or both) or who, alternatively, just have a keen analytic sense or a critical eye for your work. These peers and colleagues may be similar to those who will be reviewing your work on behalf of journals and other publications and may be considered part of the conventional "peer review" process.

Social science research is not unique in its adherence to peer reviews. Review procedures exist in all other research fields (e.g., the natural sciences and medicine) as well as in such professions as art and architecture. In these practicing professions, the procedures can be quite stringent. The reviews also can be in written or oral form.

Throughout any peer review process, maintain your confidence and be responsive. Having a peer or peer group provide feedback, and then having to revise or rethink your composition as a result of that feedback, will inevitably strengthen the research. Remember that the research will appear under your name, not the names of the peer reviewers. In this sense, you are the beneficiary of others' guidance, and you should be grateful that such guidance is shared freely. I know one senior scholar who made a commitment at the outset of his career that he would always respond to reviewers' comments, regardless of their content. Over the years, this practice has helped the scholar to achieve a 100% acceptance rate for his publications.

Peer reviewers can offer any number of comments. Most journals direct their reviewers toward a positivist orientation—for example, to comment on whether a manuscript's evidence was collected methodically and whether it seems to support the conclusions. Some reviewers may write in a direct manner and openly reveal their greatest trepidations. Other reviewers will write softly but in fact still be raising highly threatening issues. Exhibit 11.2 gives illustrations of reviewers' comments, their deeper threats, and the remedies you might want to entertain in responding to the comments.

As part of the peer review process, journals and others often ask authors to suggest relevant reviewers (if they don't, another common practice is for them to approach individuals whose key works you might have cited in your references). The reviewers will then usually appear anonymously. However, in some situations, such as proposal review committees, or dissertation or thesis review committees, knowledge of the reviewers' identities is readily available. Under these circumstances, you always should try to know something about your reviewers' own research or

EXHIBIT 11.2. RESPONSES TO ILLUSTRATIVE TYPES OF REVIEWERS' COMMENTS

Reviewers' written message	Reviewers' potentially deeper message	Responses/remedies to be considered
1. Conclusions are not supported by the empirical evidence	Study has serious flaws or unimportant conclusions and therefore should not be published	Check whether more evidence is available to be presented, but show how the cited evidence fairly represents all of the collected evidence; rework conclusions to match the cited evidence, making sure that the conclusions have some consequence
2. Findings, interpretations, and conclusions do not logically follow each other	Report is poorly composed, raising possibility that author's research logic is too weak	Reorganize the text, also augmenting, modifying, or deleting substantive arguments; clarify concepts used, in case they may be a source of confusion
3. Fieldwork or other research methods are inadequately described	Choice of methods was poor, for the topic being studied or the study design; or reviewer dislikes the methods	Discuss the choice of method and the options that were considered; augment methodological section(s) with more operational detail, including samples of the protocols that were used, if any; provide more insight into risks from reflexivity
4. Data are not properly treated in analyzing or presenting the data	Report handles data analysis in superficial or sloppy manner	Reconsider analytic techniques, potentially redoing some or all of the analyses
5. Text contains various errors	Inaccuracies reflect poor understanding of literature or sloppy writing	Carefully edit text and tables, also making sure that citations are appropriate and correct

practice. Every reviewer has her or his own implicit view on how research is best done, and these preferences are usually revealed by the reviewer's own work. Thus, one way of learning about reviewers' research or practices is to access and read their own work.

For qualitative research, such preparation is highly recommended. Those who are likely to serve as your reviewers also are likely to have considerably different views toward qualitative research as a whole and also to vary in their preferences for different approaches within qualitative research. You will not have to accept all of a reviewer's comments, but you also don't want to ignore some remarks that you might have misinterpreted because you did not appreciate a reviewer's point of view.

Time and Effort in Reworking

The reworking process may involve several re-drafts of your original composition, with different or the same reviewers providing feedback for each version. Be prepared for the process to be frustrating, but continue to remind yourself that all of the reworking has but one beneficiary: you. The more reworked the composition, the better it is likely to be, and you will be the one who receives the credit for the quality of the work.

Reworking can involve many different facets of your composition. These include:

♦ Correcting technical errors, which may vary from errors in presenting your evidence to errors in citing others' work;

♦ Sharpening your interpretations and the logic connecting your evidence, interpretations, and conclusions;

♦ Reexamining your data in alternative ways, which may still be feasible even though data collection is likely to have been concluded;

♦ Considering alternative interpretations provided by others whose works are called to your attention by reviewers and that you may not have originally cited (or known about); and

♦ Extending (or limiting) your comments about the significance of your work in relation to broader theoretical or practical terms.

Copyediting and Proofreading—and Reviewing Copyeditors' Work

This process also can take place over an extended period of time and over multiple versions of your composition. You should want to know how most of this is done even if others are available to do the copyediting and proofreading on your behalf. You also should want to review what these others might have done to your composition and be sure that you agree with any changes or even may be able to improve upon them. Be leery that in today's publishing world, these external helpers may not be entirely sensitive to the appropriate "lingo" associated either with your substantive topic or with your preferred language. For instance, American English may be different from English spoken in other parts of the world.

In the final analysis, it's your work and your by-line. Your audience will judge you by the quality of the finished product, not knowing or caring whether others might have helped to edit or proofread it. As a result, take pride in your finished work. Sharing ideas and findings in a peer-reviewed public forum is a privilege, not a right. The privilege is extended to only a minority of persons who study or do social science. Be pleased that you are one of them.

RECAP FOR CHAPTER 11: *Terms, phrases, and concepts that you can now define:*

1. Personal compared to public knowledge

2. Inside-out and backwards

3. First, second, and third voices

4. Realist, confessional, and impressionist tales

5. Declarative self and reflective self

6. Hourglass shape

7. Research jargon

8. How you know what you know

9. Research lens

10. Quality control

11. An "aside" or side comment

12. Participants' reviews and peer review

13. Lingo

EXERCISE FOR CHAPTER 11: SUMMARIZING FIELD OBSERVATIONS

Write a summary (three double-spaced pages or longer) of the field observations in the exercise for Chapter 5, based on your field notes. Make sure you develop some conceptual framework so that your summary goes beyond being a simple chronicle or diary of your fieldwork. The summary should therefore arrive at some substantive conclusion.

Write the summary as if it will be submitted for publication to some academic journal. [This assignment can be enhanced, if desired, by selecting a particular journal and making sure that the summary follows the style and substantive themes that are of priority to the journal.]

In doing this exercise, did the sets of slides created under the exercise for Chapter 10 help your thinking in composing the summary, making it easier to do? If so, how? If not, why not?

PART IV

TAKING QUALITATIVE RESEARCH ONE STEP FURTHER

CHAPTER 12

Broadening the Challenge
of Doing Qualitative Research

This chapter places qualitative research within the broader realm of social science research. Covered by the initial portion of the chapter and especially relevant are the similarities and contrasts between qualitative and nonqualitative (or "quantitative") research. The differences also reflect differing worldviews (assumptions about the quality of research and how it is best done), and these differences have been the subject of considerable dialogue and debate. The dialogue includes a postmodernist view that truly objective research, social science or otherwise, may be impossible to achieve under any circumstance.

The chapter reviews the dialogue and indicates how mixed methods research, which combines qualitative and quantitative methods, is one response. The chapter therefore presents an introduction to this type of research, illustrating it in detail with a sample study. Overall, the chapter provides a fuller understanding of the role of qualitative research and concludes by asking readers to think about new ideas for strengthening future qualitative research.

Chapters 1–11 have presented a comprehensive set of ideas and procedures, along with numerous vignettes portraying other scholars' experiences, for doing qualitative research. By absorbing these ideas and understanding the procedures, you already have come a long way in learning about qualitative research. By practicing the procedures, you will have met the main challenge of actually doing qualitative research. Make no mistake: You then will have accomplished a major milestone. You should now be able to draft a completed qualitative study and discuss the pertinent findings and procedures.

At the same time, a greater challenge still lies ahead. You may put it off and confront it later rather than sooner. However, in the long run you probably cannot ignore it entirely, especially if you want to go beyond doing only a single qualitative study and want to pursue or already have been pursuing even a modest career of doing several qualitative studies.

The challenge arises from recognizing that qualitative research does not exist in a vacuum. Rather, qualitative research is part of a broader array of social science methods. Doing qualitative research is only one way of doing social science research. The broader realm includes other, nonqualitative research methods. At some point in your research career you will probably need to demonstrate some knowledge of how qualitative research relates to this broader realm of social science research.

This final chapter helps you to establish some bearings. Throughout the chapter, a major contrast turns out to be between qualitative and nonqualitative research—a cluster of other methods commonly referred to as *quantitative* methods. Until now, this book has only used the quantitative term sparingly, preferring the more global and necessarily vaguer term *nonqualitative methods* because no attempt has been made to define what might be considered as quantitative methods. As a brief preview, such methods might include surveys, experiments, quasi-experiments, or statistical studies of archival data, as might be used in demography, epidemiology, or economics.

Your commitment to learning about the broader realm of social science research deepens as you move through this chapter. Thus, if you are to do a mixed methods research study well, as discussed later in Section C, you will need to know not only how to do qualitative research but also how to use one or more of the quantitative methods. To use these methods properly, you will either have to learn about them yourself or collaborate with someone who does. All this comes on top of your need to have mastered qualitative research. Either alone or with a collaborator, you also will need to know how to mix the qualitative and nonqualitative methods.

By the chapter's end, the deepened perspective should leave you even better equipped to appreciate qualitative research. Thus, as a final consideration, Section D briefly raises the issue of how you might contribute to the continuing development of the qualitative research craft, highlighting three needs that have not yet been satisfied but that might be considered priorities for the future.

A. QUALITATIVE RESEARCH AS PART OF THE BROADER REALM OF SOCIAL SCIENCE RESEARCH

PREVIEW—_What you should learn from this section:_

1. The major similarities and differences between qualitative and other social science research.
2. The assumptions underlying different worldviews in doing social science research.
3. How these assumptions produce additional contrast between qualitative and nonqualitative research.

A good number of qualitative research's procedures mimic more generic procedures that pertain to all of social science research. Other features of qualitative research are more distinctive and contrast with the other ways of doing social science research. You may want to acquaint yourself with these similarities and contrasts.

Examples of Craft Similarities

In several obvious ways, the craft of doing qualitative research does not differ from the craft of doing social science research. Some examples are as follows.

One of the most obvious parallels deals with the procedures for starting a qualitative study (see Chapter 3). The start-up procedures include using prior research, in the form of a study bank, to help suggest new topics for study. This procedure is by no means limited to qualitative research. It also applies to most other social science research. In like manner, parallels exist at the other end of the study cycle. For instance, the suggested ways of reworking a final research composition, discussed in Chapter 11, are relevant to most other social science research, too. All empirical studies can benefit from comments by peer reviewers, regardless of whether a study was based on qualitative or nonqualitative methods.

You may note yet other parallels. For example, among the design features presented in Chapter 4, concerns over *validity*, the use of *triangulation*, and the importance of engaging in *rival thinking*—all to strengthen research findings—are not unique to qualitative research. Similarly, a bona fide quest for *negative instances* as well as the usefulness of *constant comparisons* as analytic benchmarks (see Chapter 8, Section D) represent procedures that move in the same direction as in all other social science research.

With regard to other data analysis procedures, some underlying similarities often have gone unappreciated. For instance, in preparing for analysis, Chapter 8 indicated that a qualitative study could benefit from the creation of a *glossary of terms* special to the study at hand. The role of the glossary has a rough counterpart in analyzing nonqualitative data, because the glossary performs functions similar to the *data dictionaries* used in preparing to analyze nonqualitative data.

Interestingly, even the suggested use of arrays, hierarchies, and matrices in reassembling qualitative data, also as discussed in Chapter 8, may have counterparts in other kinds of social science research. The main caveat still would be that qualitative data largely consist of words and narratives, whereas the data for other methods tend to consist of numbers. In spite of this difference, the use of matrices in qualitative research (as represented by word tables or chronologies) as a preliminary analytic step may not differ functionally from the same preliminary role of conducting *chi-squares* or *correlations* (note that they, too, are matrices) prior to testing more statistical models, in doing nonqualitative research.[1]

---

[1] Two other potential similarities require lengthier probes, beyond the scope of this book. Chapter 1 briefly referred to the first—the possibility that the reflexive role of the researcher in qualitative research resembles the known but underinvestigated "experimenter effect" in experimental research. The second potential similarity also relates to experimental research: the fact that nearly all experiments (whether having positive or negative findings) that are reported in formal publications follow false starts and fine-tuning with earlier variations in the experimental procedures (Streiner & Sidani, 2010). By convention, these earlier variations are not formally reported, but they may be similar to the initial trial-and-error experiences confronted in starting a qualitative study. Vignette 12.2, cited later in this chapter, gives some examples of the earlier variations that are not typically reported in experimental research.

Examples of Contrasting Craft Practices

Qualitative research also has distinctive procedures that differ from those of other social science research. Some examples again follow.

A major difference results from a central feature of qualitative research—the collection of field-based data where you the researcher are the main research instrument. Although you may use a variety of data collection methods, including questionnaires to do structured interviews, your main guide for collecting the qualitative data will be a *research protocol*—whether you formally develop one or not (see Chapter 4, Choice 8).

The protocol specifies the mental framework (or line of inquiry) you will follow as your study progresses. The framework will cover the topics of importance for your qualitative interviews or field observations. The research protocol might then specify the use of other instruments. For instance, these instruments might include a survey questionnaire if your qualitative study is to have structured interviews as part of its data collection. However, the use of a research protocol and the conduct of qualitative or unstructured interviews in the first place (see Chapter 6, Section C) are distinctive to qualitative research, especially in comparison to other social science research methods.

Qualitative research also differs by calling for the collection of narrative data. Your goal is to collect sufficiently rich data so that your study will fully appreciate and better understand the context for the events you are studying. At the same time, as in providing background census data about a neighborhood that might be the setting for your study, numeric data can complement your narrative data. However, the narrative data remain distinctive to qualitative research.

Possibly more difficult to appreciate is another contrast—that between *analytic generalization* and *statistical generalization*. The distinction arises in a qualitative study's design as well as analysis stage (see Chapters 4 and 9). Not all studies, qualitative or nonqualitative, necessarily aim to generalize their findings. However, to the extent that any study concerns itself with generalizing, a succinct summary may be as follows: Qualitative studies tend to generalize to other situations (on the basis of analytic claims) whereas nonqualitative studies tend to generalize to populations (on the basis of statistical claims).

Overall, the preceding and brief summary of similarities and differences should improve your understanding of the place of qualitative research within the fuller realm of social science research. Such an understanding can help you to go beyond doing only a qualitative study. You might consider using both qualitative methods and other methods in the same study, potentially producing more compelling findings. This combined or "mixed" use underlies the interest in *mixed methods research*. Thus, to add to your repertoire for doing qualitative research you may want to consider doing a mixed methods study; Section C of this chapter provides an introduction to this broader challenge.

Differences in Worldviews across Social Science Research

At the same time, the craft contrasts between qualitative research and other forms of social science research also can reflect differences in worldviews.

A worldview consists of a set of beliefs about the acceptable qualities of research and how it should be done. During the recent past, the social science community has not taken the main differences in worldviews lightly. You therefore may want to know a little about the course of events, which are described next.

Chapter 1 presented the multifaceted world within qualitative research. The starting point for the mosaic emerged out of the possibility that the world of human affairs could be interpreted as having not just a single reality but multiple realities (e.g., the *emic* and *etic* views of the same set of events).

The mosaic of qualitative research may in fact mimic much larger differences across social science research more generally. Thus, alternative assumptions about the conduct of social science research (e.g., Hedrick, 1994, pp. 46–49; Reichardt & Rallis, 1994b; Tashakkori & Teddlie, 1998, pp. 6–11) include not only the issue of:

◆ Multiple versus singular realities, but also

◆ Whether research is value-bound or value-free,

◆ Whether research generalizations, when of interest, can be made in a time- and context-free manner (or not), and

◆ Whether causes temporally precede effects, permitting social science methods to strive to identify causal relationships, or whether causes and effects occur virtually simultaneously and may be impossible to distinguish.

To stereotype two different worldviews, people who do qualitative research tend to assume that there are multiple realities that also are value-, time-, and context-bound, and that the complexity of causes and effects makes them virtually impossible to distinguish. People favoring nonqualitative research tend to make the opposite assumptions.

Admitting these differences can lead to the conclusion that qualitative and nonqualitative research are not only different but incompatible. Qualitative researchers can view nonqualitative research, in its quest to use value-free measures that seek to establish cause-and-effect relationships, as being driven to focus on the more trivial, if not irrelevant, aspects of human affairs; nonqualitative researchers can view qualitative research, in its adherence to multiple realities and the complexity of human affairs, as hopelessly entangled in an unending web of preconceived notions and thus untrustworthy research findings (Reichardt & Rallis, 1994b, pp. 7–9). Not suprisingly, the differences have led to sharp and ongoing dialogues.

B. AN ONGOING DIALOGUE

The Positioning of Research

Over the years, the dialogues dealing with these worldviews have produced important understandings about the way that any kind of research is positioned. There is greater sensitivity over such choices as the setting of research priorities and agendas, the selection of research designs and measures to be developed and then used—and therefore the particular reality that then emerges.

Scholars also have vigorously debated the implications of these worldviews, including whether truly "objective" inquiries about human social affairs are possible in the first place (e.g., Eisner & Peshkin, 1990; Guba, 1990; Phillips, 1990a, 1990b; Roman & Apple, 1990). For instance, those inquiries believed to be "objective"—that is, using questionnaires or other instruments external to the researcher—may nonetheless still be influenced (knowingly or unknowingly) by the researcher's definition of the problem to be studied and the questions to be asked.

To illustrate the extremes to which such debates can go, a *postmodernist* view that has drawn increased attention over the past few decades suggests that all human endeavors, from doing abstract painting to conducting scientific research, are implicitly driven by the desire to exercise control over other people (e.g., Butler, 2002, pp. 2–3; Eisenhart, 2006, p. 577).

One postmodernist claim would be that the "objectivity" promoted by natural scientists as required to produce universal truths may in actuality be a way of giving scientists a privileged position over others. Scientists may, for example, use their need to be objective to favor the study of certain topics, people, or specimens, and to ignore other topics because they might not (in the scientists' view) be ready to be studied "objectively." Similarly, the postmodernist critique suggests that qualitative researchers can define the "field [setting]" as a way of propagating the interests of academic disciplines (e.g., anthropology) and an implicit "configuration of western hegemonic power" (Berger, 1993, as quoted by Sluka & Robben, 2007, p. 18).

The postmodernist claim has led not only to strong counterarguments (Butler, 2002, pp. 37–43) but also to the development of conciliatory practices. For instance, to temper the postmodernist critique regarding the exercising of control, qualitative researchers have increased their commitment "to reciprocity—to providing something useful back to research participants for their collaboration—as an ethical requirement of fieldwork" (Sluka & Robben, 2007, p. 21). Moreover, qualitative researchers now acknowledge the possibility of having a variety of relationships between researchers and participants, including relationships that result in the co-production of knowledge rather than following the traditional hierarchical relationship (e.g., Karnieli-Miller, Strier, & Pessach, 2009). In addition, a qualitative study based on *action research* can deliberately define a participatory mode of cooperative inquiry (e.g., Reason & Riley, 2009).

Qualitative versus Quantitative Methods

Across social science research, the ongoing dialogue also has assumed harsher tones, especially in the field of program evaluation in the 1980s and early 1990s. The vying worldviews were split among those who advocated the use of qualitative ("qual") methods and those who advocated the use of quantitative ("quant") methods. The disputes became so severe that they became known as the paradigm wars (e.g., Datta, 1994; Reichardt & Rallis, 1994a). The advocates of the differing worldviews tried to belittle each other, attempting to discredit each other's methods and hence the credibility of their respective research.

The harshness of the debate obscured the fact that contrasting methods had always coexisted in social science, with no method consistently prevailing over any other. Methodological differences had long been recognized and tolerated in such fields as sociology, well predating the disagreements in program evaluation (e.g., Rossi, 1994). Others within program evaluation, including myself, argued the importance of the common ground among all methods—that is, the practices of detailing evidence, thinking about rival explanations, seeking results with significant implications, and demonstrating investigatory expertise in the subject matter (Yin, 1994, p. 82).

Regardless of discipline or field, the traditional and more pressing objective in doing any social science study may consist of the appropriate matching of methods to the research questions being examined, rather than "adhering to some narrow methodological orthodoxy" (Patton, 2002, p. 264). To take but one example (e.g., Shavelson & Townes, 2002, Chap. 5), an evaluation aimed at assessing whether an intervention is effective might call for a quantitative study; however, an evaluation aimed at assessing the nature of the intervention and its implementation might call for a qualitative study. (And evaluations involving both types of questions might call for having both quantitative and qualitative components.)

A Gold Standard?

Although the paradigm wars seemed over and the debate appeared resolved (e.g., Patton, 2002, p. 264)—in part by the reigniting of interest in mixed methods research—not all contentiousness ended. Starting around 2002, supporters of a particular research method, known as *randomized controlled trials*, monopolized major funding sources for education research, also seeking to influence social science research outside of education (Cook & Foray, 2007). The particular method called for individuals or sites to be randomly assigned to experimental conditions— a "treatment" and a "control" condition. The strength of the method had been demonstrated in the conduct of clinical trials in the healthcare field (e.g., Jadad,

2004), and the new advocates believed that advances in education research could result from using such a method.

The advocates referred to the method as the "gold standard," in spite of the paradox that, as a matter of history, the metaphorical reference was to a standard that the United States had long relinquished in 1933, in part to deal with the Great Depression (Patton, 2006). The new funding priority then resonated throughout the federal government, whose central Office of Management and Budget urged all federal agencies—and the research they funded—to use this method (e.g., Caracelli, 2006, p. 85). Failure to do so could result in an agency having its budget cut.

Those who pursued the gold standard accepted other experimental and quasi-experimental methods, but only if proposals first showed why the favored method could not be implemented. However, *non*experimental designs—including most forms of qualitative research—were not welcome, regardless of the research question(s) being addressed. Ironically, surveys, though producing quantitative data, were among the disfavored methods. Proponents of surveys responded by trying to show how surveys could complement the use of the favored experimental method (e.g., Berends & Garet, 2002).

The narrowness of the priority, devoted to a single research method, as well as the forcefulness expressed through the new funding policies, produced renewed clashes that involved dissenting positions taken by major professional associations (e.g., Berliner, 2002).

These clashes have been severe and have produced repercussions throughout much of social science. To this day, you will find reference to the "gold standard" at most professional meetings. Some people still avidly promote the use of randomized controlled trials; others strongly assert the need for studies to select from a portfolio of research methods, depending on the kind of research question(s) being addressed.

Meanwhile, in education, a remarkable encounter focused on the most serious accusation that can occur in the scholarly world—the censoring of research. This accusation, its rebuttal, and its retort are presented in a series of articles (Herman et al., 2006; Schoenfeld, 2006a, 2006b).

The accusation was that a government report of a research project had deliberately omitted research work done on the project, even though the report claimed to present "what the best scientific evidence has to say" (Schoenfeld, 2006a). As an example:

> • A critical problem in assessing an educational curriculum is the nature of the achievement test that is used to test the performance of the students exposed to the curriculum. An artifactual finding may arise if an otherwise worthy curriculum does not fare well because students have been tested with an achievement test whose content does not match the curriculum properly. One remedy is to present a content analysis of the test before making a final interpretation of the students' performance or of the worthiness of a curriculum.

The suppressed research work articulated this need, among other key issues, in highly scholarly terms (Schoenfeld, 2006b, pp. 13–17). The work, pointing to the need to perform a content analysis, originally was to accompany the government report that specified the protocols for evaluating candidate curricula. However, because of the omission, test results were later presented and interpreted without summarizing the content of the achievement tests (Schoenfeld, 2006b, pp. 18–19).

The rebuttal, provided by those leading the government-sponsored project (Herman et al., 2006), was that scholars working on government-sponsored projects always can publish their work independently, but that the official government reports of such projects may omit the same research work, in the interest of streamlining such reports and making them easier for lay audiences to digest. (*N.B.*: You might now be more wary of the nonacademic documents you might download from the Internet as part of your data collection, as discussed in Chapter 6, Section E.)

By entering the policy domain, social science debates can no longer be ended or even aired properly through academic dialogue. The policy arena is a political arena, and any change in the favoring of a particular research method—and more importantly whether any particular research method should ever be the subject of exclusive funding treatment—only can take place as the terms of political offices expire and as new government administrations set their own priorities. The complete story of the role of randomized controlled trials in social science research has therefore yet to unfold.

C. THE PROMISE AND CHALLENGE OF MIXED METHODS RESEARCH

PREVIEW—*What you should learn from this section:*

1. The earlier mixed methods studies that form part of the roots for contemporary mixed methods research.
2. How mixed methods research must occur within the confines of a single study, not multiple studies, and a detailed illustration of such a single study.
3. The challenges and strategies for bringing the needed expertise—covering both a qualitative and a quantitative method—to bear in a mixed methods study.

Mixed methods research offers an option that actually tries to take advantage of the similarities and differences in qualitative and quantitative methods. It represents a pragmatic alternative—showing how research can proceed without resolving the potential conflicts in worldviews. As a result, contemporary supporters of mixed methods research have made an intense effort to define, document, and classify it (e.g., Creswell, 2009; Greene, 2008; Johnson, 2006; Tashakkori & Teddlie, 1998, 2003, 2009).

The Roots of Mixed Methods Research

The supporters have recognized that their efforts represent a renewal of interest (but not any new discovery) because the mixing of qualitative and quantitative methods has had earlier and also deep roots (e.g., Teddlie & Tashakkori, 2009, pp. 8–13, 66).

First, many earlier studies in anthropology and sociology combined some type of fieldwork with the use of quantitative data from surveys or from psychological tests administered to participants (Denscombe, 2008). These earlier studies, previously discussed in Chapter 9, include such classics as Lynd and Lynd's (1929) study of *Middletown*, Warner and Lunt's (1941) six volumes in their series *Yankee City*, and Mead's (1928) study of the *Coming of Age in Samoa*. Similarly, Oscar Lewis, while relying heavily on his own qualitative interviews and fieldwork, also administered a battery of tests to the members of the 100 families in his study—a battery so extensive that it was estimated to require 12 hours per person (Lewis, 1965, pp. xix–xx). More broadly, Samuel Sieber's seminal article (1973) pointed to the benefits but also challenges of mixing field studies and surveys in sociological studies. The combination also had appeared in significant case studies, such as the study of a labor union conducted by an eminent group of scholars in sociology and political science (Lipset, Trow, & Coleman, 1967).

Second, in the evaluation field, mixed methods research has been practiced for a long time and frequently (Greene & Caracelli, 1997). Major evaluations can be traced as far back as the 1960s, supported by the U.S. Office of Economic Opportunity and its antipoverty programs (Datta, 1994) and by the U.S. Department of Housing and Urban Development. The U.S. National Institute of Education supported mixed quantitative–qualitative evaluations in education in the 1970s. Relevant methodological approaches for program evaluations also had been documented early (e.g., Cook & Reichardt, 1979). Finally, a review published in 1989 identified 57 evaluation studies, up to that time, that had used mixed methods (Greene, Caracelli, & Graham, 1989).

Because they cover complex programmatic topics or interventions and often at multiple sites, evaluations tend to need a variety of methods. However, the same kind of broader inquiries also can occur in the absence of formal evaluations. Even the U.S. Census, commonly considered to be the domain of quantitative research, has involved qualitative research for many years (see "Ethnographic Research as a Long-Standing Part of the U.S. Census," Vignette 12.1).

All of these earlier roots have helped to provide a strong foundation for the contemporary revisiting and acceptance of mixed methods research. The later works have assumed the burden of articulating more formally: the research designs for doing mixed methods studies (e.g., Creswell, Shope, Plano Clark, & Greene, 2006; O'Cathain, 2009; Teddlie & Tashakkori, 2006); the procedures for doing mixed methods analyses (e.g., Caracelli & Greene, 1993); and the claims that mixed methods research represents its own research paradigm (e.g., Johnson & Onwuegbuzie, 2004).

VIGNETTE 12.1. ETHNOGRAPHIC RESEARCH AS A LONG-STANDING PART OF THE U.S. CENSUS

Studies and evaluations supported by the U.S. federal government have long included ethnographic research. The research has addressed important policy topics, demonstrating its practical and not just academic value.

Valerie Caracelli (2006, p. 88) points to one of the longest standing efforts— the ethnographies supported by the U.S. Bureau of the Census since the 1960s. A major function of the ethnographic data has been to increase insights into why certain population groups are undercounted. The ethnographies typically involve intensive field-based work. At carefully selected sites, the fieldworkers document the day residence of all persons and also record observations about neighborhood and housing conditions. The results can be compared to the initial, centrally based census count. More importantly, the field data can help to explain any disparities, and this information can be used to improve the accuracy of the census estimation.

A Mixed Methods Study as a Single Study

As an essential feature, a mixed methods study must retain its identity as a single study—addressing a set of research questions that deliberately requires complementary qualitative and quantitative evidence and methods (Yin, 2006). In such situations, the ideal analysis also would reflect an integrated relationship between the qualitative and quantitative components: Both the quantitative and qualitative data would be analyzed and interpreted together, before arriving at a study's main conclusion(s).

In contrast, a mixed methods study is not being done if an initial set of interpretations and conclusions is drawn solely on the basis of either the qualitative or quantitative method alone, apart from another initial set of interpretations and conclusions based solely on the other type of method. Even if the results from both methods are then compared, such separation has effectively split a mixed methods study into two distinct studies. The integration of the two studies would then resemble a research synthesis. Such research syntheses, of course, can be conducted with two or even more studies (e.g., Cooper, 1998). However, the synthesis would not differ from traditional research syntheses and would not meet the definition of a mixed methods study.

When the mixing does occur within a single study, Tashakkori and Teddlie (1998) have provided some straightforward examples of the desired complementary relationships between the quantitative and qualitative components of a mixed methods study (see Exhibit 12.1).

Their examples assume that the qualitative and quantitative inquiries involve individual people as the subject of study. Importantly, both qualitative and quantitative data have been collected from the same individual people. However, many other mixes also can occur, even if organizations or other entities are the subject of study instead of individuals, and even if both quantitative and qualitative data have

EXHIBIT 12.1. THREE GROUPS OF MIXED ANALYTIC METHODS

Combinations for Mixing Quantitative and Qualitative Analyses in a Mixed Methods Study

Parallel mixed analysis
- Interviewing participants (qualitative) at the end of a laboratory experiment (quantitative), to gain insight into the participants' behavior
- Using and analyzing open-ended (qualitative) and closed-ended (quantitative) items as part of the same questionnaire
- Transforming qualitative data into quantitative data through content analysis

Sequential (qualitative first, then quantitative) analysis
- Using qualitative data to define teachers in two groups, based on field observations of their instructional practices (qualitative), and then comparing teachers' responses to a survey (quantitative)

Sequential (quantitative first, then qualitative) analysis
- Using additional qualitative data about individuals who performed extremely well or extremely poorly ("outliers") in a quantitative analysis, to explain their (high or low) quantitative scores

Source: Tashakkori and Teddlie (1998, pp. 128–135).

not been collected from the same sources. As a result, mixed methods research can be based on a wide variety of research designs, and defining and documenting them has been an important task undertaken by contemporary researchers (e.g., Creswell, 2009; Roter & Frankel, 1992; Teddlie & Tashakkori, 2006).

Sample Study 2, found at the end of this chapter, provides an in-depth example of a mixed methods research study. The sample study shows how both qualitative and quantitative methods were mixed to address a research question, with neither alone being sufficient to support a complete study.

> - In Sample Study 2, analyzing the quantitative data (e.g., the correlation) alone would have left a mystery regarding the actual procedures for processing proposals. Conversely, having the qualitative data (e.g., the flow diagrams) alone would not have identified the consequences of each flow, in terms of the number or cost of proposals produced.

The sample study illustrates one type of mixing. Other types are defined in Exhibit 12.1, and to date much of the renewed attention to mixed methods research, as mentioned earlier, has been devoted to classifying the research designs whereby qualitative and quantitative methods can be mixed in a single study.

Expertise Needed for Doing a Mixed Methods Study

At the same time, the texts understate one critical topic: You or others considering mixed methods research need to bring in-depth knowledge about the methods that are being mixed. The most common quantitative methods can include surveys, quasi-experiments, experiments, or even randomized controlled trials.

For instance, research in health services has seen a gradual increase in mixed methods research (e.g., Devers, Sofaer, & Rundall, 1999; Mays & Pope, 1995, 1996; Pope & Mays, 1995; Shortell, 1999). One of the most distinctive contributions claimed for this field has been the mixing of qualitative methods with the use of *randomized controlled trials* (O'Cathain, 2009). By comparison, the mixing in the fields of education and program evaluation has tended to combine qualitative methods with the use of surveys. Beyond these examples, the quantitative methods also may include epidemiology, demography, or economics.

Mixing any of the qualitative and quantitative methods well requires a diverse knowledge base. All methods have their own specialized logic, terminology, procedures, and literature, reflected by separate textbooks and even university courses—and learning about these methods would be hardly a trivial matter. Yet, to ensure the proper mixing of any one of them with qualitative methods, and to avoid embarrassing missteps, require great expertise.

You can bring the needed expertise in two ways. The first is for you to master the complementary quantitative method. However, this can become a demanding task because the quest will come on top of your need to master the qualitative methods. Using quantitative methods also has its own challenges and unanticipated turns, as has been constructively compiled in an edited volume on the research experiences in actual quantitative studies (see "Examples of Pitfalls to Be Overcome in Quantitative Research," Vignette 12.2).

VIGNETTE 12.2. EXAMPLES OF PITFALLS TO BE OVERCOME IN QUANTITATIVE RESEARCH

Not surprisingly, quantitative research has its own pitfalls that need to be overcome if a mixed methods study is to employ both qualitative and quantitative methods. Streiner and Sidani (2010) amassed 42 short articles pointing to such pitfalls and how they were overcome. The pitfalls included:

- The problems of collaborating with therapists, to identify participants for a clinical trial (Joyce, pp. 130–135);
- Working with a tenant organization to gain access for a study of mental health and schooling, only to find the organization requiring attention to its own priority—gaining access to dental services—and extending a 3-year study to one taking over 7 years (Barrette, pp. 119–129);
- Devising the best procedure for reminding participants to complete their diaries for a community health study (Streiner, pp. 223–227), after a postal strike disrupted the planned postcard procedure;
- Substituting a field study for a planned survey of minority businesses, after initial attempts to interview 100 businesses yielded a 3% response rate (Watson, pp. 254–262);
- Finding ways to recruit undergraduates at a small college, compared to the well-established procedures at larger universities, to serve as subjects in psychology experiments (Koch & Tabor, pp. 101–105).

The second way, more commonly found thus far in mixed methods research, is for two or more specialists to collaborate in conducting the same study—each specialist vouching for one of the relevant methods. Now, however, the two specialists need to have a strong collaborative ethic, respecting each other's specialties and then knowing how to mix them. Such collaborations do not necessarily work easily.

If you have been in such situations, you will know that genuine collaboration requires a great degree of patience and empathy for your partner. To start with, you both will have to overcome or ignore any tendency toward reigniting the paradigm wars. Without such a spirit, either the qualitative or quantitative collaborator—and hence method—can overly dominate a study. A typical fear might be the domination of the quantitative over the qualitative (e.g., Creswell, Shope, Plano Clark, & Greene, 2006). A worse possibility is that one of the methods will become distorted. In either situation, the true benefits of mixing the methods will not have been achieved.

Demonstrating the needed patience and empathy, along with the inevitable false starts and trial-and-error learning, automatically consumes another invaluable commodity—time. Thus, by committing to do mixed methods research well, do not be surprised that you may have added immeasurably to the challenge of doing qualitative research alone.

D. MOVING ONWARD

PREVIEW—*What you should learn from this section:*
Ways of thinking about the future of the craft of doing qualitative research.

The preceding jaunt into mixed methods research completes your journey into qualitative research. You should have gained an even fuller understanding of its ins and outs. The rest of this chapter suggests ways in which you might now want to move onward.

Different Motives for Moving Onward

Depending on your situation, you might have different motives for moving onward.

First, you might have read this book because you are doing or thinking about conducting a qualitative study. You wanted to strengthen your approach to such studies or even to strengthen your resolve to start your first qualitative study.

For such readers, the book has presented its ideas in as practical a manner as possible, enabling you to enter the process incrementally. The book does not follow any overarching story line that requires it to be read from cover to cover or in a linear sequence. Therefore, you can continue referring to the chapters in modular fashion as you proceed with your own research, possibly attending more closely to the steps that might be the most challenging to you, such as the ethics of doing qualitative research (Chapter 2), the various ways of recording field data (Chapter 7), or the strategies for interpreting and concluding a qualitative study (Chapter 9).

Second, you might be an instructor teaching a course on qualitative research. Assuming a semester-long course, the book has deliberately been organized into 12 chapters, so that each might be covered during one of the weeks in the semester. The organization of the exercises at the back also matches the chapters, to suggest relevant student work during each week. As an alternative to the weekly exercises, the Appendix presents a semester- or year-long project that can be carried out instead.

To further support coursework, the book's inductive approach means that students can attend to a methodological topic and at the same time be encouraged to examine and work with different qualitative studies as illustrative material. The inductive approach also should be especially helpful because being acquainted with prior studies is one of the best ways of learning to do (any kind of) research. You are now ready to use the book to customize the rest of your syllabus and to start classwork.

Third, you might have scanned through this book because you already know about other social science methods but wanted to learn about (but not necessarily practice) qualitative research. For such readers, the book has tried to make sufficient connections to the other methods, such as the reference to Rosenbaum's observational studies, the contrast between structured and qualitative interviews in Chapter 6, and the discussion of craft similarities and differences in this chapter. You should now be more knowledgeable about the positioning of qualitative research, as well as its foundation and procedures, among the broader array of social science methods.

Fourth, you might be in none of the preceding situations. Possibly, you have used this book to satisfy your curiosity about what your colleagues or friends call "qualitative research," so that you can understand it better. To such readers, Chapter 5's rendition of doing fieldwork might have given you concrete images about the craft as well as the pertinent experiences of notable qualitative researchers, along with references to classic and contemporary works.

Putting Principles, not Just Procedures, into Practice

Independent of your motive for moving onward, and despite the book's practical orientation, the principles of doing qualitative research should draw your longest lasting attention. Doing social science research does not mean searching for and using procedures mechanically, as in following a culinary recipe. Research, whether of the qualitative or nonqualitative variety, calls for many major discretionary choices and judgment calls. Thus, your moving onward should be accompanied by attention to the trustworthiness and credibility of your research, which includes attending to exhaustive searches for evidence and contrary evidence, as well as using research procedures in a transparent way.

By keeping track of the important principles and putting them into practice, you will be honoring all of social science research and not just qualitative research. Your success, as well as the continued success of qualitative research, depends on the conduct of robust and defensible empirical studies.

Making Your Own Contribution to the Craft of Doing Qualitative Research

As a final comment, and reflecting the title of this final chapter, be aware that fresh challenges always will arise. Qualitative research, like all other types of research, has a dynamic quality whereby practices continually evolve. Other than completing your own qualitative research, learning about it, or teaching it, have you thought about how you might contribute to the craft itself?

Three possible needs quickly surface. They deserve your most innovative thoughts. First, and especially compared to developments in using other social science methods, qualitative research remains a rather burdensome craft.[2] Fieldwork can take a long time, increasing the difficulty for scholars, much less students, to do qualitative studies. These days and in contrast, huge quantities of archival data are readily available via websites. The availability can sway researchers from doing a qualitative to doing a quantitative study.

The lengthy time needed to gather qualitative data also can limit its role in addressing pressing issues of public policy, even though such research can be extremely relevant and important to do (e.g., Caracelli, 2006, p. 87). Thus, the first need is to find ways of streamlining the data collection process in qualitative research—but without distorting it in any way. You might agree that this first challenge is not too shabby.

Second, qualitative research also can be cumbersome in its presentation. Typically, the descriptions of a qualitative study and its findings are lengthy. Greater length implies the need for more time and effort to compose the final product. More importantly, greater length also assumes that consumers or readers of qualitative research will be willing to invest more time and effort to learn about any qualitative findings. Thus, the second need is to find ways of reducing this burden—again without distorting the craft in any way. The goal is to make qualitative research more accessible to a wider audience and under a greater variety of conditions.

Third, empirical research derives greater benefits when the lessons from individual studies can be compared and contrasted, producing a cumulative knowledge base. In this manner, the possibility of gaining greater insights based on cumulat-

---

[2]Developments with statistical methods offer an example of methodological progress that can be linked to advances in technology. The example pertains to the now commonplace use of hierarchical linear models as a statistical technique. Although the underlying mathematics for such models had been documented as the "design effect" by the noted social statistician Leslie Kish in his 1965 text, the actual practice of using the models did not start until years later (Bryk & Raudenbusch, 1987). This was because the relevant calculations required a computing power that was not available in Kish's time.

ing knowledge across qualitative studies deserves greater exploration. Despite the surface individuality of most qualitative studies—seemingly precluding such cross-cutting efforts—the growing body of qualitative studies still appears to provide a promising foundation.[3]

In addition to these three needs, you may have your own ideas for improving the craft of qualitative research. Test them. Do some pilot investigations. Share the results with others, in published or unpublished form.

Addressing the preceding or other future needs does not mean that all qualitative research must change in these directions. The depth of inquiry and the insightful narratives that imbue classic qualitative studies still have their place. The main idea is to diversify the craft, while maintaining and raising its standards. In this sense, qualitative research has yet to reach its zenith in becoming a more fulfilling experience for everyone.

RECAP FOR CHAPTER 12: *Terms, phrases, and concepts that you can now define:*

1. Nonqualitative (quantitative) methods
2. Worldviews in social science research
3. Postmodernist claims
4. Paradigm wars
5. Gold standard and randomized controlled trials
6. Mixed methods research
7. A mixed methods study
8. Two strategies for bringing the needed expertise for doing a mixed methods study
9. Needed contributions for improving the craft of qualitative research in the future

---

[3]A cross-cultural database, based on the collection of ethnographic studies and known as the Human Relations Area Files, has existed since 1949 in New Haven, Connecticut. However, the mosaic of qualitative research now goes well beyond ethnographic studies.

**EXERCISE FOR CHAPTER 12: THINKING ABOUT
A MIXED METHODS STUDY**

◆ ◆ ◆

Again use the fieldwork you did for the exercise in Chapter 5 as a starting point. Assuming that the fieldwork led to the collection of qualitative data and that you were able to complete a qualitative study based on the job shadowing (or some alternative choice of field settings), think about how conducting a formal survey of persons, representing others whose jobs you might have shadowed (or other persons related to the alternative choice of field settings) might further strengthen the original study. Respond to the following questions (but you do not need to do any actual data collection):

1. What different research questions can now be addressed by having both types of data rather than having the qualitative data alone?

2. How might (or might not) the survey provide more information about the potential distinctiveness of the job you had shadowed (or the alternative choice of field settings)?

3. What would be one way of conducting an integrated qualitative–quantitative analysis, to avoid creating two separate studies (a qualitative one and a quantitative one)? (*Hint*: Think about how the particular survey questions might directly complement the field queries you had made in your fieldwork.)

4. What part (if any) of the quantitative study could you do alone, and what part (if any) would you need to have done by a more knowledgeable colleague? For instance, comment on whether the survey would be based on e-mail, phone, or face-to-face interviews, and how you would know that the chosen method had met the acceptable standards for using such methods.

SAMPLE STUDY 2: A MIXED METHODS STUDY OF UNIVERSITY PROPOSAL PROCESSING

Introduction to the Sample Study: A study conducted by my own team at COSMOS is presented as **Sample Study 2** and serves as a specific example of a mixed methods study (COSMOS, 1996). The setting for the study is again an educational setting. However, unlike **Sample Study 1** presented earlier in Chapters 8 and 9, the study involves universities alone and not K–12 systems.

Sample Study 2 aimed to assess and explain preexisting university proposal processes, in anticipation of an upcoming conversion to a Web-based (FastLane) submission procedure by a major research-sponsoring federal agency (the National Science Foundation [NSF]). The results were to provide a baseline understanding of the universities' proposal processing experiences.[4] The original plan was then to repeat the study at some later date, to determine the impact, if any, of the new procedure on the universities. (However, the Web-based procedure worked so well that the later study was never conducted.)

The study deliberately engaged 15 universities, chosen to represent differing volumes of proposal submissions. Each also was chosen because a large proportion of its proposals went to NSF or because its records could segregate the NSF proposal experiences from those involving other sponsors. For these reasons, the sample had to be a purposive one.

The fieldwork at each university involved open-ended interviews with a variety of university, school, and department staff and faculty, especially the staff of each university's sponsored research office (SRO). The fieldwork included the collection of extensive archival data, along with reviews of the universities' records and procedures for producing proposals. The data included the length of processing time and the estimated level of administrative staff effort (thus, administrative costs) related to proposal processing. The overall goal was to understand and document the processing at each university.

Among the initial findings, a quantitative analysis found a statistically significant correlation between the universities' costs of submitting proposals and the volume of proposals that had been submitted (see Exhibit 12.2). Each datapoint in the exhibit lies along these two dimensions and represents one of the 15 universities in the study. However, and to everyone's surprise, the direction of the correlation was the exact opposite than one would have expected if using any "economy of scale" logic. According to such logic, services should become cheaper at higher volumes. Instead, *the more proposals that a university submitted, the higher were its costs* per proposal, *measured by the university's administrative expenditures devoted to proposal preparation*.

The next step, following conventional quantitative research procedures, was to test further the strength of the original correlation. For instance, a possible artifact could have been produced by the influence of the two "outliers," or the two datapoints labeled "A" and "B" in Exhibit 12.2. To check this possibility, the correlation was calculated with and without these two datapoints. However, the correlation was still statistically significant, as shown in the box within Exhibit 12.2. Unfortunately, without a much larger sample of universities, other quantitative tests, such as conducting a multivariate analysis, could not be undertaken.

The quantitative analysis also used other routine techniques to search for additional artifacts, including inadequacies in the archival data, but no artifacts could be found. Explaining the counterintuitive direction of the correlation was finally accepted as a genuine and formidable question.

---

[4]The study design deliberately emphasized proposal *processing* rather than proposal *preparation*. A major but unknown part of the preparation process occurs among research investigators before any actual processing starts. Thus, the study design focused on the proposal processes, defined as the steps occurring *after* a principal investigator had formally submitted a proposal to a university, school, or departmental official. Similarly, no attempt was made to assess the extremely difficult aspect of proposal preparation that involves the level of effort and costs of investigators' preparation work. The study design permitted the study to focus on the administrative procedures and costs involved in moving a proposal through the university and on to NSF.

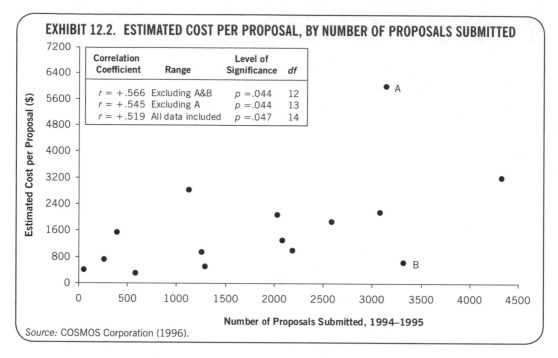

EXHIBIT 12.2. ESTIMATED COST PER PROPOSAL, BY NUMBER OF PROPOSALS SUBMITTED

Correlation Coefficient	Range	Level of Significance	df
$r = +.566$	Excluding A&B	$p = .044$	12
$r = +.545$	Excluding A	$p = .044$	13
$r = +.519$	All data included	$p = .047$	14

Source: COSMOS Corporation (1996).

In the meanwhile, the qualitative data were used to characterize each university's proposal procedures. To make a long story short, the qualitative analysis produced a plausible insight to explain the counterintuitive correlation: To produce a large volume of proposals, universities follow a decentralized process, whereby a university's departments and schools all are involved, compared to a more centralized situation whereby a single sponsored research office (SRO) conducts the entire proposal processing.

With a low volume of proposals, a university relying on a single SRO to do the proposal processing may be efficient. However, at higher proposal volumes, a single SRO becomes a bottleneck and also may not have the specialized expertise to provide substantive oversight. At the same time, the decentralized pattern, while producing more proposals, is more costly because more staff across the entire university—at the department and school levels and in addition to the SRO staff—are collectively involved in the proposal process.

Exhibit 12.3 shows the results of the fieldwork at two contrasting universities, graphically depicting the key processes. The main part of the graphic is a flow diagram, but also important is the time line running along the bottom of each graphic. In the exhibit, the SRO at University "E" becomes involved in the proposal process at an early point and remains centrally involved, and the time to produce the average proposal can take up to 14 weeks. By comparison, University "G" has a more decentralized structure, whereby the departments do most of the early and substantive processing, with the SRO only becoming involved near the end of the process—and the time to produce the average proposal only takes up to 5 weeks. Along with the faster processing time, the decentralized arrangement in University "G" also can produce more proposals because a large number of departments have been involved in processing many different proposals.

These qualitative patterns were then matched against the initial statistical correlation found earlier in Exhibit 12.2. For each of the original datapoints, the university's proposal process was characterized according to varying degrees of centralization or decentralization. The results confirmed that the universities whose datapoints sat at the higher end of the correlation (high volume of proposals but also higher costs per proposal) also had the more decentralized arrangements.

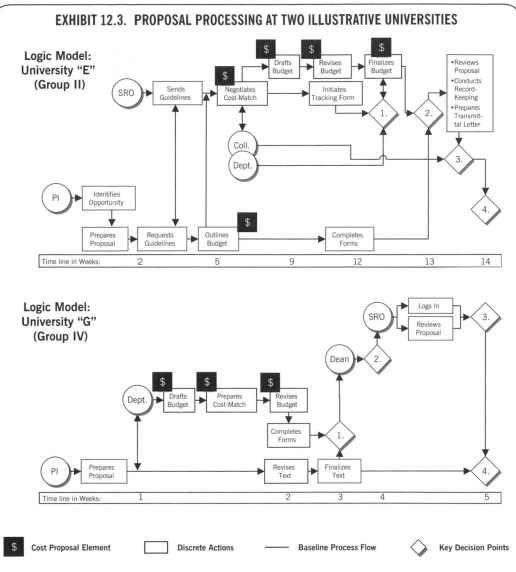

EXHIBIT 12.3. PROPOSAL PROCESSING AT TWO ILLUSTRATIVE UNIVERSITIES

Source: COSMOS Corporation (1996).

APPENDIX

◆ ◆ ◆

A Semester- or Year-Long Project
Career Paths[*]

A. TOPIC OF INQUIRY

Research Question or Curiosity: How do specific events and experiences stimulate or discourage individuals from pursuing particular careers?

Research Relevance: A study of these events and experiences may deepen our understanding of the connections among critical life events in personal histories.

B. START-UP

1. *Defining the Scope of the Study*: Examine your own family, education, and career path to date. State explicitly how far along you are on a career path (e.g., "just thinking about it," "making serious inquiries," "training," "already practicing," etc.). Now identify key events or experiences that influenced or deterred you on this path. Write this as a (not more than) five-page autobiographical statement, with your motivations and feelings, but citing specific events, persons, and experiences from your life history.

2. *Comparative Design*[**]: Select a peer or two (or more, if you like), who are on a *different* path. The peer needs to agree to become a participant in your study, sharing information about her or his own life history, but the peer is not a co-investigator of the study (it's your study).

3. *Literature*: Review one or more key studies of how and why people pursue the specific careers like the ones you and your peer(s) seem to be pursuing. Use the findings of the studies to suggest possible connections and relationships between different kinds of influences and your particular career paths. If the studies' findings do not lend themselves to such relationships, at least use the literature to establish the importance and relevance of your initial research question and its research relevance as stated above. Take notes, with complete citations to the literature you have referenced.

---

[*]For the purposes of the Sample Scenario, a "career" may be a social role (e.g., parent, girl or boy friend, or spouse) and not an occupation. Whatever you choose, substitute it for the word "career" throughout this Sample Scenario.

[**]This part of the Scenario is optional. If you do not exercise the option, ignore the comparative language in the subsequent portions of the Scenario.

C. FIELD PROTOCOL

1. *Protocol Topics/Questions*: Given the main research question (or curiosity) and your insights from the literature review, develop a field protocol to guide your data collection. The protocol should have two parts. Part I should be directed at your career and Part II at your peer's career. The topics/questions in these two parts may overlap but should not be identical, given that the two careers differ.

2. *Identification of Relevant Evidence*: For Part I of the protocol, directed at your career, identify the needed evidence to confirm, separately: (a) how far along you are on your career path, and (b) the events or experiences (from your autobiographical statement) that have influenced you to be on the path. The type of evidence may include interviews, retrieval of personal documents, and even observations of particular field settings, if relevant (see examples in next section). Also, do not hesitate to identify relevant *numeric* data. Critically, if the *absence* of a particular event or experience has been deemed relevant, the protocol needs to identify the evidence that in some way can be used to *confirm the absence*. For Part II of the protocol, be prepared to engage your peer in a lengthy interview, to cover the protocol's topics/questions.

D. DATA COLLECTION

1. *Your Own Career*: Use Part I of the protocol to go beyond your autobiographical statement, by interviewing key other persons or collecting the specific personal documents called for by the protocol. For instance, if a key influence in pursuing your career was early exposure to one or more inspirational role models, try to contact and interview one of them to get their perspective about how they might have influenced you or others as a role model. As another example, if a key influence was your pleasure in completing certain school projects or in obtaining certain grades in your schoolwork on subjects later related to your career choice, retrieve samples of the work or report cards confirming the grades. As an observational example, you might revisit the site of some community service or field internship that might have swayed you toward your career choice.

2. *Your Peer's Career*: For your peer's or other careers, conduct an extensive interview of the peer, covering the topics/questions in Part II of the protocol. Write the results of your interview as a biographical statement about your peer's career (again, not longer than five pages).***

E. SAMPLE ANALYSIS

1. *Description*: Using the field data about your own career, reconstruct your autobiography to produce an *empirically based* account. Think about presenting data by using word tables. For instance, a chronology of the progress along your career path, or a table summarizing key influences with a few sentences about each influence, would be helpful and might make your later analysis more precise.

Make a similar assessment in relation to your peer's career, based on the biographical statement. Think again about using word tables to present data. In this comparative situation, your

---

***For the purpose of this Sample Scenario, you will use your peer's biographical statement as the data for your study and not attempt to corroborate the statement with any other interviews or retrieve any personal documents.

tables might juxtapose information about your career with information about your peer's career. Now summarize how you and your peer(s) are on different career paths and how far you both (all) are along these paths.

2. *Explanation*: Outline and then write what, if any, insights your study has produced. For example, career choices are often thought to be based on "informal" rather than any "formal" or school-based influences. Career choices also may occur as a result of some "critical event," while others occur as a result of a cumulation of separate influences over time. Yet other career choices are thought to derive from culturally based influences rather than any particular events.

With your peer's experiences, compare the differences in the events and experiences influencing the different career paths. Your comparative analysis can cover issues in the preceding paragraph but also should attempt to articulate differences in experience attributable to the differences inherent in the nature of your respective careers.

3. *Conclusion*: State a preliminary conclusion that addresses the original *research question* previously stated above. Separately state and describe how your conclusion bears implications (or not) for the **research relevance** previously stated above.

4. *Significance*: Following the conclusion, return your discussion back to the literature. State whether your findings differ from, corroborate, or help to explain the existing literature in some way, citing and quoting the pertinent parts of the literature.

5. *Caveats and Future Research*: Review and state any methodological reservations or other caveats that might have biased your study and therefore raise doubts about your findings, conclusion, or implications. State how some subsequent study might address and overcome these reservations in the form of suggestions for further research.

A Glossary
of Special Terms Used
in Qualitative Research*

action research: A variant of qualitative research emphasizing researchers' adoption of action roles and active collaboration with participants in support of the topic of study.

analytic generalization: A manner of generalizing the findings of a study to other situations that were not studied, based on logical argument, theory development, or replication (cf. **statistical generalization**). Can be equally applicable to qualitative research (e.g., cross-case generalization) as well as to the findings from any given laboratory experiment (e.g., cross-experiment generalization).

autoethnography: The study of culture that includes the self as an explicit part of the subject of study. By extension, any qualitative study that includes the self in this manner.

CAQDAS: An acronym standing for Computer Assisted Qualitative Data AnalysiS—a generic label for a large variety of commercial and noncommercial software devoted to the analysis of qualitative data.

case study: A study of a particular case or set of cases, describing or explaining the events of the case(s) (cf. **instrumental case study** and **intrinsic case study**). A case study may rely on quantitative or qualitative data (or both) but usually involves some field-based data.

Chicago school: A group of scholars at the University of Chicago, during the early to mid-20th century, who pioneered the development of field-based qualitative inquiry with their highly regarded published studies.

*For larger glossaries that also have fuller explanations, readers should refer to specialized dictionaries that are entirely devoted to such glossaries (e.g., Abercrombie, Hill, & Turner, 2006; Schwandt, 2007).

coding: In qualitative data analysis, the assignment of simple words or short phrases to capture the meaning of a larger portion of (the original) textual or visual data. Whether supported by computer software or not, the analyst must make the coding decisions for every item, including what to code and how (cf. *in vivo* **code**).

confessional tale: The reporting of the findings from a qualitative study, usually engaging a first-person voice, that deliberately includes the researcher's own role and views as one of the persons in the field setting that was studied (cf. **impressionist tale** and **realist tale**).

constructivism: The view that social reality is a joint product, created by the nature of the external conditions but also by the person observing and reporting about these conditions. Following this view, all social reality, because it is constructed in this manner, therefore assumes a relativist rather than absolute nature.

convenience sample: The selection of participants or sources of data to be used in a study, based on their sheer availability or accessibility. Only accepted as a preferred way of doing research under unusual circumstances, such as studying the survivors of a disaster.

conversation analysis: A naturalistic and observational study of the verbal and nonverbal behavior in conversations, including speakers' mannerisms, pauses, intonation, and emphasis. Typically uses audio and video recordings and considers such information as the basic data in a study.

co-production of knowledge: The result when researcher and participant collaborate closely in a research study, compared to the more conventional hierarchical relationship between a researcher and either a survey respondent or a laboratory "subject."

culture: An invisible social structure, embracing groups of people larger than kin groups, who share a common language, religion, or ancestry not always coinciding with political institutions or geographical boundaries. Members of the same culture tend to follow similar everyday practices (or customs), such as cooking, dressing, respecting kin relationships, and celebrating life events such as births, marriages, and deaths.

discourse analysis: An approach to qualitative research that considers language to represent the construction of social reality, especially within the social context of what is said, rather than assuming language only to represent what a person is thinking.

emic: The adoption of an indigenous orientation or perspective, representing those who are part of a study, in contrast to the adoption of an external perspective toward a research topic (cf. **etic**). Originally derived from a loosely analogous distinction between *phonetic* (the external sounds of words) and *phonemic* (the units of words within their internal grammar).

empirical research: Studies based on the collection and presentation of original evidence or data in support of a study's claims. The evidence or data should be amenable to tests of credibility—that is, through the open inspection of the sources and procedures by which the evidence or data were produced (not to be confused with **empiricism**).

empiricism: The philosophical view that all human behavior is learned behavior, with no role for genetic influences. The view relates to qualitative research mainly through its association with **positivism** (not to be confused with **empirical research**).

epistemological location: Characterizing a study's philosophical and methodological underpinnings (e.g., ways of knowing), based in part on its positioning on such dimensions as the relativist–realist or unique–not unique views of real-world events (cf. **epistemological similarity**).

epistemological similarity: Acknowledging that all qualitative studies, regardless of their epistemological location, will be concerned with the common endeavor of establishing their trustworthiness and credibility by being transparent, methodic, and empirically based (cf. **epistemological location**).

epistemology: The philosophical underpinnings of researchers' beliefs regarding the nature of knowledge and how it is derived or created. The particular belief represents a person's *epistemological position*.

ethnography: A field-based study of people in their real-world setting, usually occurring over a sufficiently lengthy period of time to surface people's everyday routines—that is, their norms, rituals, and acceptable social interactions—hence also establishing the distinctiveness of their culture.

ethnomethodology: A variant of qualitative research seeking to understand how people learn and know the social rituals, mannerisms, and symbols taken for granted in everyday life.

etic: The assumption of an external orientation or perspective toward a research topic, in contrast to the indigenous perspective representing those who are part of a study (cf. **emic**). Originally derived from a loosely analogous distinction between *phonetic* (the external sounds of words) and *phonemic* (the units of words within their internal grammar).

feminist perspective: The view that common social as well as methodological relationships (e.g., interviewer and interviewee) embed oft-ignored power relationships that can nevertheless affect the findings of a research study.

fieldwork: Conducting empirical research in real-world settings (the "field"), usually requiring the use of qualitative methods.

focal unit: The unit of study in a qualitative study (e.g., individuals, groups of people, events, or organizations). Defining such units helps to organize the data collection for a study, but not all studies need to have an explicit focal unit.

focus group: A form of data collection whereby the researcher convenes a small group of people having similar attributes, experiences, or "focus" and leads the group in a nondirective manner. The objective is to surface the perspectives of the people in the group with as minimal influence by the researcher as possible.

grand theory: Theoretical constructs attempting to explain large categories of phenomena (e.g., the works of Newton, Einstein, Darwin, Mendel, Freud, Piaget, and Skinner), usually beyond the scope of any single research study.

grounded theory: A variant of qualitative research emphasizing the collection of data about the natural occurrence of social behavior within real-world contexts, unfettered by a researcher's prior categories and preconceptions. Involves the eventual derivation of relevant categories as part of data analysis, but the emergent categories have been derived "from the bottom up" and hence "grounded" in the original reality.

hermeneutics: The aspect of a study that involves interpreting the event(s) being studied to deepen the understanding of the political, historical, sociocultural, and other real-world contexts within which the event(s) occur(s).

impressionist tale: The reporting of the findings from a qualitative study that attempts to place the reader within the real-world setting that was studied and to re-live it (cf. **confessional tale** and **realist tale**).

insider research: Studies conducted by researchers who have privileged connections or real-life roles related to the field settings being studied.

instrumental case study: A case study of a particular situation but, in spite of its uniqueness, being conducted because of its potential applicability to other like-situations (cf. **intrinsic case study**).

intrinsic case study: A case study of a particular situation selected because of its uniqueness and inherent interest, importance, or likely insights, without regard to its applicability to other situations (cf. **instrumental case study**).

***in vivo* code:** A code (assigned in the analysis of qualitative data) represented by a word or phrase that is taken directly from the data being coded (cf. **coding**).

jottings: The initial, sometimes fragmentary set of notes taken while doing fieldwork.

life history: A narrative rendition of a person's life story, attempting to capture the life story and also its turning points and key themes. The life histories of interest come from those persons whose social groups, interactions, or lifestyles have been the main topic of study.

member checks: The procedure whereby a study's findings or draft materials are shared with the study's participants. The "checking" permits the participants to correct or otherwise improve the accuracy of the study, at the same time reinforcing collaborative and ethical relationships.

memos: A set of notes specifically dedicated to a qualitative researcher's ongoing ideas during the coding of qualitative data. The memos help track the coding process and provide reminders about possible refinements as well as tentative thoughts about the relationships among codes and the potential clustering of codes into categories and themes (cf. **personal journal**).

mental framework: The line of inquiry held by a researcher while collecting data, helping to maintain focus on the direction of a study and sensitizing the researcher to the identification of relevant evidence, both supportive and contrary.

mixed methods research: Deliberately designing a study to use quantitative and qualitative methods, both of which are needed to address the research question(s) of interest.

multicultural research: Qualitative research that deliberately highlights participants' perspectives in accurate and valid but also sympathetic ways. Especially pertinent in studies of social groups historically living through the consequences of racism, discrimination, and exclusion from a broader society.

narrative inquiry: Doing a qualitative research study and rendering its findings in a deliberately constructed narrative form. The form accentuates certain features, such as bringing to readers a sense of "being there" that differs from more commonplace narratives.

nonreactive measures: see **unobtrusive (nonreactive) measures**.

ontology: One's philosophical beliefs about what constitutes social reality, and especially whether realities are singular or multiple (see **emic** and **etic**).

participant-observation: A mode of field-based research whereby researchers locate themselves in the real-world field setting being studied, participating and observing in the setting while also collecting data and taking notes about the field setting, its participants, and its events.

participants: The people who are the subjects of a qualitative study (alternatively referred to in the literature as "members").

performance ethnography: A variant of qualitative research focused on analyzing the meaning of drama, art, and other forms of performance in terms of their expression of cultural and related themes.

personal journal: A diary-like record of a researcher's methodological choices, dilemmas, and discretionary judgments used in the course of a research study. Especially includes notes about reflexivity conditions and their likely influence on a study's findings (cf. **memos**).

phenomenology: A variant of qualitative research aiming to study the nature of human events as they are immediately experienced within their real-world context—resisting the prior use of any concepts or categories that might distort the direct experiential basis for understanding the events.

positivism: The view that natural science and hence social science are based on universal truths, with the role of research being to uncover such truths. This view contrasts directly with the view that knowledge and understanding are relativistic, not absolute.

postmodernism: The view that all human endeavors, from doing abstract painting to conducting scientific research, are implicitly driven by the desire to exercise control over other people.

pragmatism: A worldview supporting the selection of appropriate research methods in relation to the research questions being studied. According to this worldview, researchers may choose to use a quantitative method or a qualitative method, or to conduct a mixed methods study using both kinds of methods, all depending on which choice best befits the research questions.

purposive sample: The selection of participants or sources of data to be used in a study, based on their anticipated richness and relevance of information in relation to the study's research questions. Richness and relevance include sources whose data are presumed to challenge and not just support a researcher's thinking about the research questions and therefore should be part of the sample.

qualitative interview: A form of interviewing whereby the researcher's goal is to reveal a participant's meanings and interpretations from the participant's point of view. Such interviewing therefore more likely assumes a conversational rather than a tightly scripted format, in which the researcher must avoid asking "leading" questions.

random sample: The selection of participants or sources of data to be used in a study based on a known statistical relationship between those selected (a sample) and all those who could have been selected (a universe), so that the sample represents a random sample of the universe. At the end of a study, the findings from the sample can then be extrapolated back to the universe.

realist tale: The reporting of the findings from a qualitative study in a dispassionate, third-person voice, with the author not being part of the tale (cf. **confessional tale** and **impressionist tale**).

reflexivity: The dynamic interplay whereby participants (i.e., those being studied) may be influenced by the presence and actions of the researcher, and conversely the influence on the researcher's thinking and observations resulting from the presence and actions of the participants.

research lens: The mental filter present in all qualitative research, affecting researchers' interpretations of the field-based data that will later be reported in a qualitative study.

research protocol: A guide used by a researcher as a mental framework for conducting an inquiry. The guide points to the questions that the researcher is trying to answer and differs from a questionnaire or other research instrument whose questions are posed to a respondent, interviewee, or research subject (cf. **study protocol**).

research questions: The initial questions to be addressed by a research study. The study's findings and conclusions should then provide responses to the questions, including elaborating them.

rival explanations, hypotheses, or thinking: Deliberately engaging in contrary thinking about a study's procedures, data, or findings—to seek procedures, data, or findings that might lead to different results and therefore to reduce biases and to strengthen a study.

self-reflexivity: Researchers' efforts to identify the important reflexive conditions that are present in their study and that might affect the conclusions from the study (see **reflexivity**).

snowball sample: The selection of participants or sources of data to be used in a study, based on referrals from one source to another.

statistical generalization: A manner of generalizing the findings from a study to a larger population that was not studied, based on a known statistical relationship between the study sample and the larger population (cf. **analytic generalization**).

study bank: A collection of references to qualitative studies, amassed to help stimulate thinking about the different topics, methods, and sources of evidence that might be used in a new qualitative study.

study protocol: A plan, usually submitted to an institutional review board (IRB), to gain its approval for conducting a study involving human subjects, such as the participants in a qualitative study. The IRB will usually recommend the structure of the protocol, and its topics may emphasize logistical issues and not cover substantive topics in as great detail as a research protocol (cf. **research protocol**).

symbolic interactionism: A variant of qualitative research emphasizing the importance of people's social interactions and their settings as the basis for deriving the meaning of objects and the social environment. The meanings are usually expressed in language or other symbolic terms.

thick description: The effort to collect data that describe real-world events in great detail. The greater detail not only provides a richer rendition of events but also helps to reduce the researcher's selectivity and reflexive influences in reporting about the event.

triangulation: An analytic technique, used during fieldwork as well as later during formal analysis, to corroborate a finding with evidence from two or more different sources.

unobtrusive (nonreactive) measures: Measures derived from the existing features of a social environment that have resulted from people's natural interactions in the environment—that is, not instigated in any way by a research study or a researcher.

worldview: A broad and deep system of thinking about the methods to be used in social science research, based on having a particular ontological perspective (i.e., how chosen methods do or do not capture real-world realities and whether there is assumed to be a singular reality or multiply constructed realities).

References

QS, qualitative study; CS, case study; IS, interview study (including focus groups); TC, teaching case; MM, mixed methods study

Abercrombie, Nicholas, Hill, Stephen, & Turner, Bryan S. (2006). *The Penguin dictionary of sociology* (5th ed.). London: Penguin.

Addams, Jane, & Messinger, Ruth W. (1919). *Twenty years at Hull-House.* New York: Signet Classic, 1961 (originally published in 1919). (QS)

Addison, Richard B. (1992). Grounded hermeneutic research. In Benjamin F. Crabtree & William L. Miller (Eds.), *Doing qualitative research* (pp. 110–124). Thousand Oaks, CA: Sage. (QS)

Adrian, Bonnie. (2003). *Framing the bride: Globalizing beauty and romance in Taiwan's bridal industry.* Berkeley: University of California Press.

Alexander, Bryant Keith. (2005). Performance ethnography: The reenacting and inciting of culture. In Norman K. Denzin & Yvonna S. Lincoln (Eds.), *The Sage handbook of qualitative research* (3rd ed., pp. 411–441). Thousand Oaks, CA: Sage.

Allison, Graham, & Zelikow, Philip. (1999). *Essence of decision: Explaining the Cuban missile crisis* (2nd ed.). New York: Addison Wesley Longman. (CS)

American Anthropological Association. (1998). *Code of ethics of the American Anthropological Association.* Washington, DC: Author.

American Association of University Professors. (2006). *Research on human subjects: Academic freedom and the institutional review board.* Washington, DC: Author.

American Educational Research Association. (2000). *Ethical Standards of the American Educational Research Association.* Washington, DC: author.

American Evaluation Association. (2004). *Guiding principles for evaluators.* Washington, DC: Author.

American Sociological Association. (1999). *Code of ethics and policies and procedures of the ASA committee on professional ethics.* Washington, DC: Author.

Anderson, Elijah. (1999). *Code of the street: Decency, violence, and the moral life of the inner city.* New York: Norton. (QS)

Anderson-Levitt, Kathryn M. (2006). Ethnography. In J. L. Green, G. Camilli, & P. B. Elmore (Eds.), *Handbook of complementary methods in education research* (3rd ed., pp. 279–295). Washington, DC: American Educational Research Association.

APSA Committee on Professional Ethics, Rights, and Freedom. (2008). *A guide to professional ethics in political science* (2nd ed.). Washington, DC: American Political Science Association.

Auerbach, Carl F., & Silverstein, Louise H. (2003). *Qualitative data: An introduction to coding and analysis.* New York: New York University Press.

Auyero, Javier, & Swistun, Debora. (2008). The social production of toxic uncertainty. *American Sociological Review, 73*, 357–379. (QS)

Bales, Kevin. (2004). *Disposable people: New slavery in the global economy* (rev. ed.). Berkeley: University of California Press. (QS)

Ball, Deborah Loewenberg, Thames, Mark Hoover, & Phelps, Geoffrey. (2008). Content knowledge for teaching: What makes it special? *Journal of Teacher Education, 59*, 389–407. (QS)

Banks, James A. (2006). Researching race, culture, and difference: Epistemological challenges and possibilities. In J. L. Green, G. Camilli, & P. B. Elmore (Eds.), *Handbook of complementary methods in education research* (3rd ed., pp. 773–793). Washington, DC: American Educational Research Association.

Barrette, Philippe. (2010). All aboard!: Using community leaders to keep clinical researchers on track. In David L. Streiner & Souraya Sidani (Eds.), *When research goes off the rails: Why it happens and what you can do about it* (pp. 119–129). New York: Guilford Press.

Barzun, Jacques, & Graff, Henry F. (1977). *The modern researcher* (3rd ed.). New York: Harcourt, Brace, Jovanovich.

Becker, Howard S. (1958). Problems of inference and proof in participant observation. *American Sociological Review, 23*, 652–660.

Becker, Howard S. (1986). *Writing for social scientists: How to start and finish your thesis, book, or article.* Chicago: University of Chicago Press.

Becker, Howard S. (1998). *Tricks of the trade: How to think about your research while you're doing it.* Chicago: University of Chicago Press.

Becker, Howard S., Geer, Blanche, Hughes, Everett C., & Strauss, Anselm L. (1961). *Boys in white: Student culture in medical school.* Chicago: University of Chicago Press.

Berends, Mark, & Garet, Michael S. (2002). In (re)search of evidence-based school practices: Possibilities for integrating nationally representative surveys and randomized field trials to inform educational policy. *Peabody Journal of Education, 77*, 28–58.

Berger, Roger. (1993). From text to (field)work and back again: Theorizing a post(modern) ethnography. *Anthropological Quarterly, 66*, 174–186.

Berliner, David C. (2002). Educational research: The hardest science of all. *Educational Researcher, 31*, 18–20.

Bertaux, D. (Ed.). (1981). *Biography and society: The life history approach in the social sciences.* Thousand Oaks, CA: Sage.

Bloome, David, & Clark, Caroline. (2006). Discourse-in-use. In J. L. Green, G. Camilli, & P. B. Elmore (Eds.), *Handbook of complementary methods in education research* (3rd ed., pp. 227–241). Washington, DC: American Educational Research Association.

Blumer, Herbert. (1969). *Symbolic interactionism.* Englewood Cliffs, NJ: Prentice-Hall.

Bogle, Kathleen A. (2008). *Hooking up: Sex, dating, and relationships on campus.* New York: New York University Press. (QS)

Booth, Wayne C., Colomb, Gregory G., & Williams, Joseph M. (1995). *The craft of research.* Chicago: University of Chicago Press.

Borman, Kathryn M., & Associates. (2005). *Meaningful urban education reform: Confronting the learning crisis in mathematics and science.* Albany: State University of New York Press. (MM)

Borman, Kathryn M., Clarke, Christopher, Cotner, Bridget, & Lee, Reginald. (2006). Cross-case analysis. In J. L. Green, G. Camilli, & P. B. Elmore (Eds.), *Handbook of complementary methods in education research* (3rd ed., pp. 123–139). Washington, DC: American Educational Research Association.

Bourgois, Philippe. (2003). *In search of respect: Selling crack in El Barrio* (2nd ed.). New York: Cambridge University Press. (QS)

Brannick, Teresa, & Coghlan, David. (2007). In defense of being "native": The case for insider academic research. *Organizational Research Methods, 10,* 59–74.

Brenner, Mary E. (2006). Interviewing in educational research. In J. L. Green, G. Camilli, & P. B. Elmore (Eds.), *Handbook of complementary methods in education research* (3rd ed., pp. 357–370). Washington, DC: American Educational Research Association.

Brown, Kathleen M., Anfara, Vincent A., Jr., & Roney, Kathleen. (2004). Student achievement in high performing suburban middle schools and low performing urban schools: Plausible explanations for the differences. *Education and Urban Society, 36,* 428–456. (CS)

Brubaker, Rogers, Feischmidt, Margit, Fox, Jon, & Grancea, Liana. (2006). *Nationalist politics and everyday ethnicity in a Transylvanian town.* Princeton, NJ: Princeton University Press. (QS)

Bruyn, Severyn. (1966). *The human perspective in sociology: The methodology of participant observation.* Englewood Cliffs, NJ: Prentice-Hall.

Bryant, M. J., Hammond, K. A., Bocian, K. M., Rettig, M. F., Miller, C. A., & Cardullo, R. A. (2008). School performance will fail to meet legislated benchmarks. *Science, 321,* 1781–1782.

Bryk, Anthony S., & Raudenbusch, Steven. (1987). Application of hierarchical linear models to assessing change. *Psychological Bulletin, 10,* 147–158.

Bullough, Robert V., Jr. (2001). *Uncertain lives: Children of promise, teachers of hope.* New York: Teachers College Press. (QS)

Burgess, Ernest W., & Bogue, Donald J. (1967). Research in urban society: A long view. In E. W. Burgess & D. J. Bogue (Eds.), *Urban sociology* (pp. 1–14). Chicago: Phoenix Books.

Butler, Christopher. (2002). *Postmodernism: A very short introduction.* Oxford, UK: Oxford University Press.

Cable, Sherry, Shriver, Thomas E., & Mix, Tamara L. (2008). Risk society and contested illness: The case of nuclear weapons workers. *American Sociological Review, 73,* 380–401. (QS)

Campbell, Donald T. (1975). Degrees of freedom and the case study. *Comparative Political Studies, 8,* 178–193.

Campbell, Donald T. (2009). "Foreword," in *Case study design and methods,* by Robert K. Yin (pp. vi–viii). Thousand Oaks, CA: Sage. Originally appeared in the first edition of the book (1984).

Caracelli, Valerie. (2006). Enhancing the policy process through the use of ethnography and other study frameworks: A mixed-method study. *Research in the Schools, 13,* 84–92.

Caracelli, Valerie, & Greene, Jennifer C. (1993). Data analysis strategies for mixed-method evaluation designs. *Educational Evaluation and Policy Analysis, 15,* 195–207.

Carr, Patrick J. (May 2003). The new parochialism: The implications of the Beltway case for arguments concerning informal social control. *American Journal of Sociology, 108,* 1249–1291. (QS)

Charmaz, Kathy. (1999). Stories of suffering: Subjects' stories and research narratives. *Qualitative Health Research, 9,* 362–382.

Charmaz, Kathy. (2002). Stories and silences: Disclosures and self in chronic illness. *Qualitative Inquiry, 8,* 302–328.

Charmaz, Kathy. (2005). Grounded theory in the 21st century. In Norman K. Denzin & Yvonna S. Lincoln (Eds.), *The Sage handbook of qualitative research* (3rd ed., pp. 507–535). Thousand Oaks, CA: Sage.

Chase, Susan E. (2005). Narrative inquiry: Multiple lenses, approaches, voices. In Norman K. Denzin & Yvonna S. Lincoln (Eds.), *The Sage handbook of qualitative research* (3rd ed., pp. 651–679). Thousand Oaks, CA: Sage.

Chaskin, Robert J. (2001). Building community capacity: A definitional framework and case studies from a comprehensive community initiative. *Urban Affairs Review, 36,* 291–323.

Cicourel, Aaron V. (1971). Ethnomethodology and measurement. *Social Forces, 50,* 182–191.

Connelly, F. Michael, & Clandinin, D. Jean. (2006). Narrative inquiry. In J. L. Green, G. Camilli, & P. B. Elmore (Eds.), *Handbook of complementary methods in education research* (3rd ed., pp. 477–487). Washington, DC: American Educational Research Association.

Cook, Thomas D., & Campbell, Donald T. (1979). *Quasi-experimentation: Design and analysis issues for field settings.* Chicago: Rand McNally.

Cook, Thomas D., & Foray, Dominique. (2007). Building the capacity to experiment in schools: A case study of the Institute of Educational Sciences in the U.S. Department of Education. *Economics of Innovation and New Technology, 16,* 385–402.

Cook, Thomas D., & Reichardt, Charles (Eds.). (1979). *Qualitative and quantitative methods in program evaluation.* Thousand Oaks, CA: Sage.

Cooper, Harris M. (1998). *Synthesizing research: A guide for literature synthesis* (3rd ed.). Thousand Oaks, CA: Sage.

Corbin, Juliet, & Strauss, Anselm. (2007). *Basics of qualitative research: Techniques and procedures for developing grounded theory* (3rd ed.). Thousand Oaks, CA: Sage.

COSMOS Corporation. (1996). *The National Science Foundation's FastLane System baseline data collection: Cross-case report.* Bethesda, MD: Author.

Covey, Stephen R. (1989). *The seven habits of highly effective people: Restoring the character ethic.* New York: Simon & Schuster.

Coyle, Adrian. (2007). Discourse analysis. In Evanthia Lyons & Adrian Coyle (Eds.), *Analysing qualitative data in psychology* (pp. 98–116). Thousand Oaks, CA: Sage.

Crabtree, Benjamin F., & Miller, William L. (Eds.). (1999). *Doing qualitative research* (2nd ed.). Thousand Oaks, CA: Sage.

Creswell, John W. (2007). *Qualitative inquiry & research design: Choosing among five approaches* (2nd ed.). Thousand Oaks, CA: Sage.

Creswell, John W. (2009). Mapping the field of mixed methods research. *Journal of Mixed Methods Research, 3,* 95–108.

Creswell, John W., Shope, Ron, Plano Clark, Vicki L., & Greene, Denise. (2006). How interpretive qualitative research extends mixed methods research. *Research in the Schools, 13,* 1–11.

Cronbach, Lee J. (1975). Beyond the two disciplines of scientific psychology. *American Psychologist, 30,* 116–127.

Datta, Lois-ellin. (1994). Paradigm wars: A basis for peaceful coexistence and beyond. *New Directions for Program Evaluation, 61,* 54–70.

Davis, Nancy J., & Robinson, Robert V. (2009). Overcoming movement obstacles by the religious orthodox: The Muslim brotherhood in Egypt, Shas in Israel, Comunione e Liberazione in Italy, and the Salvation Army in the United States. *American Journal of Sociology, 114,* 1302–1349. (QS)

Degregory, Lane. (2007). Finding good topics: A writer's questions. In M. Kramer & W. Call (Eds.), *Telling true stories: A nonfiction writer's guide* (pp. 20–22). London: Plume/Penguin.

Denscombe, Martyn. (2008). Communities of practice: A research paradigm for the mixed methods approach. *Journal of Mixed Methods Research, 2,* 270–283.

Denzin, Norman K. (2003). *Performance ethnography: Critical pedagogy and the politics of culture.* Thousand Oaks, CA: Sage.

Denzin, Norman K., & Lincoln, Yvonna S. (Eds.). (2005). *The Sage handbook of qualitative research* (3rd ed.). Thousand Oaks, CA: Sage.

Devers, Kelly J., Sofaer, Shoshanna, & Rundall, Thomas G. (1999). Qualitative methods in health services research. *Health Services Research, 34*(5), Part II (whole issue).

Drew, Paul. (2009). Conversation analysis. In Jonathan A. Smith (Ed.), *Qualitative psychology: A practical guide to research methods* (pp. 133–159). Los Angeles: Sage.

Duff, Patricia A. (2008). *Case study research in applied linguistics.* New York: Routledge.

Duneier, Mitchell. (1999). *Sidewalk.* New York: Farrar, Straus, & Giroux. (QS)

Dunn, Elizabeth C. (2004). *Privatizing Poland: Baby food, big business and the remaking of labor.* Ithaca, NY: Cornell University Press. (QS)

Edin, Kathryn, & Kefalas, Maria. (2005). *Promises I can keep: Why poor women put motherhood before marriage.* Berkeley: University of California Press. (QS)

Eisenhart, Margaret. (2006). Representing qualitative data. In J. L. Green, G. Camilli, & P. B. Elmore (Eds.), *Handbook of complementary methods in education research* (3rd ed., pp. 567–581). Washington, DC: American Educational Research Association.

Eisner, Elliot W., & Peshkin, A. (1990). Subjectivity and Objectivity. In Elliot W. Eisner & Alan Peshkin (Eds.), *Qualitative inquiry in education: The continuing debate* (pp. 15–17). New York: Teachers College Press.

Emerson, Robert M. (Ed.). (2001). *Contemporary field research: Perspectives and formulations* (2nd ed.). Prospect Heights, IL: Waveland Press.

Emerson, Robert M., Fretz, Rachel I., & Shaw, Linda L. (1995). *Writing ethnographic fieldnotes.* Chicago: University of Chicago Press.

Ericksen, Jeff, & Dyer, Lee. (September 2004). Right from the start: Exploring the effects of early team events on subsequent project team development and performance. *Administrative Science Quarterly, 49,* 438–471.

Erickson, Frederick. (2006). Definition and analysis of data from videotape: Some research procedures and their rationales. In J. L. Green, G. Camilli, & P. B. Elmore (Eds.), *Handbook of complementary methods in education research* (3rd ed., pp. 177–191). Washington, DC: American Educational Research Association.

Fetterman, David M. (2009). Ethnography. In Leonard Bickman & Debra J. Rog (Eds.), *The Sage handbook of applied social research methods* (2nd ed., pp. 543–588). Thousand Oaks, CA: Sage.

Fielding, Nigel G., & Lee, Raymond M. (1998). *Computer analysis and qualitative research.* London: Sage.

Fine, Michelle (Ed.). (1992). *Disruptive voices.* Ann Arbor: University of Michigan Press.

Fontana, Andrea, & Frey, James H. (2005). The interview: From neutral stance to political involvement. In Norman K. Denzin & Yvonna S. Lincoln (Eds.), *The Sage handbook of qualitative research* (3rd ed., pp. 695–727). Thousand Oaks, CA: Sage.

Fowler, Floyd J., Jr., & Cosenza, Carol. (2009). Design and evaluation of survey questions. In Leonard Bickman & Debra J. Rog (Eds.), *The Sage handbook of applied social research methods* (2nd ed., pp. 375–412). Thousand Oaks, CA: Sage.

Gans, Herbert J. (1962). *The urban villagers: Group and class in the life of Italian-Americans.* New York: Free Press. (QS)

Garfinkel, Harold. (1967). *Studies in ethnomethodology.* Englewood Cliffs, NJ: Prentice-Hall.

Geertz, Clifford. (1973). *The interpretation of cultures.* New York: Basic Books.

Geertz, Clifford. (1983). *Local knowledge: Further essays on interpretive anthropology.* New York: Basic Books.

George, Sheba Mariam. (2005). *When women come first: Gender and class in transnational migration.* Berkeley: University of California Press. (QS)

Gilligan, Carol. (1982). *In a different voice: Psychological theory and women's development.* Cambridge, MA: Harvard University Press. (QS)

Giorgi, Amedeo, & Giorgi, Barbro. (2009). Phenomenology. In Jonathan A. Smith (Ed.),

Qualitative psychology: A practical guide to research methods (pp. 26–52). Los Angeles: Sage.

Glaser, Barney G., & Strauss, Anselm L. (1967). *The discovery of grounded theory: Strategies for qualitative research.* New York: Aldine.

Goffman, Erving. (1959). *The presentation of self in everyday life.* Garden City, NY: Anchor.

Goffman, Erving. (1963). *Stigma: Notes on the management of spoiled identity.* Englewood Cliffs, NJ: Prentice-Hall.

Gold, Raymond L. (1958). Roles in sociological field observations. *Social Forces, 36,* 217–223.

Gomm, Roger, Hammersley, Martyn, & Foster, Peter. (2000). Case study and generalization. In Roger Gomm, Martyn Hammersley, & Peter Foster (Eds.), *Case study method: Key issues, key texts* (pp. 98–115). London: Sage.

Grbich, Carol. (2007). *Qualitative data analysis: An introduction.* Thousand Oaks, CA: Sage.

Green, Denise O'neil. (2004). Fighting the battle for racial diversity: A case study of Michigan's institutional responses to Gratz and Grutter. *Educational Policy, 18,* 733–751. (IS)

Greene, Jennifer C. (2008). Is mixed methods social inquiry a distinctive methodology? *Journal of Mixed Methods Research, 2,* 7–22.

Greene, Jennifer C., & Caracelli, Valerie J. (Eds.). (1997). Advances in mixed-method evaluation: The challenges and benefits of integrating diverse paradigms. *New Directions for Evaluation, 74,* whole issue.

Greene, Jennifer, Caracelli, Valerie, & Graham, J. F. (1989). Toward a conceptual framework for mixed-method evaluation designs. *Educational Evaluation and Policy Analysis, 11,* 255–274.

Greenwood, Davydd J., & Levin, Morten. (1998). *Introduction to action research: Social research for social change.* Thousand Oaks, CA: Sage.

Gross, Zehavit. (January 2008). Relocation in rural and urban settings: A case study of uprooted schools from the Gaza Strip. *Education and Urban Society, 40,* 269–285. (CS)

Guba, Egon G. (1990). Subjectivity and objectivity. In Elliot W. Eisner & Alan Peshkin (Eds.), *Qualitative inquiry in education: The continuing debate* (pp. 74–91). New York: Teachers College Press.

Gubrium, Jaber F., & Holstein, James A. (1998). Standing our middle ground. *Journal of Contemporary Ethnography, 27,* 416–421.

Guenther, Katia M. (2009). The politics of names: Rethinking the methodological and ethical significance of naming people, organizations, and places. *Qualitative Research, 9,* 411–421.

Hahn, Christopher. (2008). *Doing qualitative research using your computer: A practical guide.* Thousand Oaks, CA: Sage.

Hall, Rogers. (2000). Videorecording as theory. In Anthony E. Kelly & Richard A. Lesh (Eds.), *Handbook of research design in mathematics and science education* (pp. 647–664). Mahwah, NJ: Lawrence Erlbaum.

Hannerz, Ulf. (1969). *Soulside: Inquiries into ghetto culture and community.* New York: Columbia University Press. (QS)

Hays, Sharon. (2003). *Flat broke with children: Women in the age of welfare reform.* New York: Oxford University Press. (QS)

Hedrick, Terry E. (1994). The quantitative-qualitative debate: Possibilities for integration. *New Directions for Program Evaluation, 61,* 45–52.

Herman, Rebecca, et al. (2006). Overcoming the challenges: A response to Alan H. Schoenfeld's "what doesn't work." *Educational Researcher, 35,* 22–23.

Hesse-Biber, Sharlene Nagy, & Leavy, Patricia Lina. (2007). *Feminist research practice: A primer.* Thousand Oaks, CA: Sage.

Hochschild, Arlie Russell. (1989). *The second shift.* New York: Oxford University Press. (QS)

Holstein, James A., & Gubrium, Jaber F. (2005). Interpretive practice and social action. In N. K. Denzin & Y. S. Lincoln (Eds.), *The Sage handbook of qualitative research* (3rd ed., pp. 483–505). Thousand Oaks, CA: Sage.

Howell, Nancy. (1990). *Surviving fieldwork: A report of the advisory panel on health and safety in fieldwork.* Washington, DC: American Anthropological Association.

Husserl, Edmund. (1970). *The crisis of European sciences and transcendental phenomenology* (trans. by D. Carr). Evanston, IL: Northwestern University Press.

Irvine, Leslie. (2003). The problem of unwanted pets: A case study in how institutions "think" about clients' needs. *Social Problems, 50,* 550–566. (QS)

Jacobs, Glenn (Ed.). (1970). *The participant observer: Encounters with social reality.* New York: George Braziller. (QS)

Jacobs, Rodney N. (1996). Civil society and crisis: Culture, discourse, and the Rodney King beating. *American Journal of Sociology, 101,* 1238–1272. (CS)

Jadad, Alejandro. (2004). *Randomised controlled trials.* London: BMJ Books.

Johnson, R. Burke (Ed.). (2006). New directions in mixed methods research. *Research in the Schools, 13*(whole issue).

Johnson, R. Burke, & Onwuegbuzie, Anthony J. (2004). Mixed methods research: A research paradigm whose time has come. *Educational Researcher, 33,* 14–26.

Jones, Stacey Holman. (2005). Autoethnography: Making the personal political. In Norman K. Denzin & Yvonna S. Lincoln (Eds.), *The Sage handbook of qualitative research* (3rd ed., pp. 763–791). Thousand Oaks, CA: Sage.

Jorgensen, Danny L. (1989). *Participant observation: A methodology for human studies.* Thousand Oaks, CA: Sage.

Joyce, Anthony S. (2010). Changing horses in midstream: Transforming a study to address recruitment problems. In David L. Streiner & Souraya Sidani (Eds.), *When research goes off the rails: Why it happens and what you can do about it* (pp. 130–135). New York: Guilford Press.

Kane, Mary, & Trochim, William. (2007). *Concept mapping for planning and evaluation.* Thousand Oaks, CA: Sage.

Karnieli-Miller, Orit, Strier, Roni, & Pessach, Liat. (2009). Power relations in qualitative research. *Qualitative Health Research, 19,* 279–289.

Karra, Neri, & Phillips, Nelson. (2008). Researching "back home": International management research as autoethnography. *Organizational Research Methods, 11,* 541–561.

Kelly, Anthony E., & Yin, Robert K. (2007). Strengthening structured abstracts for education research: The need for claim-based structured abstracts. *Educational Researcher, 36,* 133–138.

Kidder, Louise H., & Judd, Charles M. (1986). *Research methods in social relations* (5th ed.). New York: Holt, Rinehart & Winston.

Kidder, Tracy. (1990). *Among schoolchildren.* Boston: Houghton Mifflin. (QS)

Kidder, Tracy. (2007). Field notes to full draft. In M. Kramer & W. Call (Eds.), *Telling true stories: A nonfiction writer's guide* (pp. 51–54). London: Plume/Penguin.

Kish, Leslie. (1965). *Statistical design for research.* New York: Wiley.

Kluckhohn, Florence R. (1940). The participant-observer technique in small communities. *American Journal of Sociology, 46,* 331–343.

Koch, Christopher, & Tabor, Anna. (2010). Small colleges and small n's. In David L. Streiner & Souraya Sidani (Eds.), *When research goes off the rails: Why it happens and what you can do about it* (pp. 101–105). New York: Guilford Press.

Kramer, Mark, & Call, Wendy (Eds.). (2007). *Telling true stories: A nonfiction writers' guide from the Nieman Foundation at Harvard University.* New York: Penguin Group.

Kugelmass, Judy W. (2004). *The inclusive school: Sustaining equity and standards.* New York: Teachers College Press. (QS)

Kuzel, Anton. (1992). Sampling in qualitative inquiry. In Benjamin F. Crabtree & William L. Miller (Eds.), *Doing qualitative research* (pp. 31–44). Thousand Oaks, CA: Sage.

Labov, W., & Waletzky, J. (1997). Narrative analysis: Oral versions of personal experience. *Journal of Narrative and Life History, 7,* 3–38. (Original work published in 1967.)

Langness, L. L. (1965). *The life history in anthropological science.* New York: Holt, Rinehart.

Lareau, Annette. (2003). *Unequal childhoods: Class, race, and family life.* Berkeley: University of California Press. (QS)

Lawrence-Lightfoot, Sara. (1983). *The good high school: Portraits of character and culture.* New York: Basic Books. (QS)

Lawrence-Lightfoot, Sara, & Davis, Jessica Hoffman. (1997). *The art and science of portraiture.* San Francisco: Jossey-Bass.

Lee, Jooyoung. (2009). Battlin' on the corner: Techniques for sustaining play. *Social Problems, 56,* 578–598. (QS)

Lee, S. J. (1996). *Unraveling the "model minority" stereotype: Listening to Asian American youth.* New York: Teachers College Press. (QS)

Levitt, Peggy. (2001). *The transnational villagers.* Berkeley: University of California Press. (QS)

Lew, Jamie. (2006). *Asian Americans in class: Charting the achievement gap among Korean American youth.* New York: Teachers College Press. (QS)

Lewin, Kurt. (1946). Action research and minority problems. *Journal of Social Issues, 2,* 34–46.

Lewins, Ann, & Silver, Christina. (2007). *Using software in qualitative research: A step-by-step guide.* London: Sage.

Lewis, Oscar. (1961). *The children of Sanchez: Autobiography of a Mexican family.* New York: Vintage Books. (QS)

Lewis, Oscar. (1965). *La Vida: A Puerto Rican family in the culture of poverty–San Juan and New York.* New York: Vintage Books.

Liebow, Elliot. (1967). *Tally's corner: A study of Negro streetcorner men.* Boston: Little, Brown. (QS)

Liebow, Elliot. (1993). *Tell them who I am: The lives of homeless women.* London: Penguin Books. (QS)

Lincoln, Yvonna S. (2005). Institutional review boards and methodological conservatism. In Norman K. Denzin & Yvonna S. Lincoln (Eds.), *The Sage handbook of qualitative research* (3rd ed., pp. 165–181). Thousand Oaks, CA: Sage.

Lincoln, Yvonna S., & Guba, Egon G. (1985). *Naturalistic inquiry.* Thousand Oaks, CA: Sage.

Lincoln, Yvonna S., & Tierney, W. G. (2004). Qualitative research and institutional review boards. *Qualitative Inquiry, 10,* 219–234.

Lipset, Seymour, Trow, Martin, & Coleman, James S. (1967). *Union democracy: The inside politics of the international typographical union.* New York: Free Press. (CS)

Lipsey, Mark W. (1990). *Design sensitivity: Statistical power for experimental research.* Thousand Oaks, CA: Sage.

Locke, Karen, & Velamuri, S. Ramakrishna. (2009). The design of member review: Showing what to organization members and why. *Organizational Research Methods, 12,* 488–509.

Locke, Mary G., & Guglielmino, Lucy. (2006). The influence of subcultures on planned change in a community college. *Community College Review, 34,* 108–127. (CS)

Lohman, J. D. (1937). Participant-observation in community studies. *American Sociological Review, 6,* 890–897.

Lynd, Robert, & Lynd, Helen. (1929). *Middletown.* New York: Harcourt Brace. (QS)

Lynd, Robert, & Lynd, Helen. (1937). *Middletown in transition.* New York: Harcourt Brace. (QS)

Madsen, Richard. (2009). The archipelago of faith: Religious individualism and faith community in America today. *American Journal of Sociology, 114*, 1263–1301. (QS)

Maginn, Paul J. (2007). Negotiating and securing access: Reflections from a study into urban regeneration and community participation in ethnically diverse neighborhoods in London, England. *Field Methods, 19*, 425–440.

Malinowski, Bronislaw. (1922). *Argonauts of the Western Pacific.* Prospect Heights, IL: Waveland Press. (QS)

Marwell, Nicole P. (2007). *Bargaining for Brooklyn: Community organizations in the entrepreneurial city.* Chicago: University of Chicago Press. (QS)

Maxwell, Joseph A. (1996). *Qualitative research design: An interactive approach.* Thousand Oaks, CA: Sage.

Maxwell, Joseph A. (2009). Designing a qualitative study. In Leonard Bickman & Debra J. Rog (Eds.), *The Sage handbook of applied social research methods* (2nd ed., pp. 214–253). Thousand Oaks, CA: Sage.

May, Reuben, & Buford, A. (2008). *Living through the hoop: High school basketball, race, and the American dream.* New York: New York University Press. (QS)

Mays, N., & Pope, Catherine. (1995). Qualitative research: Observational methods in health care settings. *British Medical Journal, 311*, 182–184.

Mays, N., & Pope, Catherine. (1996). *Qualitative research in health care.* London: BMJ Publishing Group.

McCall, George J., & Simmons, J. L. (Eds.). (1969). *Issues in participant observation.* Reading, MA: Addison-Wesley.

McQueeney, Krista. (2009). We are God's children, y'all: Race, gender, and sexuality in Lesbian and Gay-Affirming Congregations. *Social Problems, 56*, 151–173. (QS)

Mead, George Herbert. (1934). *Mind, self and society.* Chicago: University of Chicago Press.

Mead, Margaret. (1928). *Coming of age in Samoa: A psychological study of primitive youth for Western civilisation.* New York: Perennial Classics Edition published in 2001. (QS)

Menjívar, Cecilia. (2000). *Fragmented ties: Salvadoran immigrant networks in America.* Berkeley: University of California Press. (QS)

Merton, Robert K., Fiske, Marjorie, & Kendall, Patricia L. (1990). *The focused interview: A manual of problems and procedures* (2nd ed.). New York: Free Press.

Miles, Matthew B., & Huberman, A. Michael. (1994). *Qualitative data analysis* (2nd ed.). Thousand Oaks, CA: Sage.

Miller, William L., & Crabtree, Benjamin F. (1992). Primary care research: A multimethod typology and qualitative road map. In Benjamin F. Crabtree & William L. Miller (Eds.), *Doing qualitative research* (pp. 3–28). Thousand Oaks, CA: Sage.

Molotch, Harvey. (1969). Racial integration in a transition community. *American Sociological Review, 34*, 878–893. (QS)

Moore, Mignon R. (2008). Gendered power relations among women: A study of household decision making in Black, Lesbian stepfamilies. *American Sociological Review, 73*, 335–356. (QS)

Morgan, David L. (1992). Doctor-caregiver relationships: An exploration using focus groups. In Benjamin F. Crabtree & William L. Miller (Eds.), *Doing qualitative research* (pp. 205–227). Thousand Oaks, CA: Sage. (QS)

Moustakas, C. (1994). *Phenomenological research methods.* Thousand Oaks, CA: Sage.

Moyer-Packenham, Patricia, et al. (2009). Participation by STEM faculty in math and science partnership activities for teachers. *Journal of STEM Education, 10*, 17–36.

Mulroy, Elizabeth A., & Lauber, Helenann. (2004). A user-friendly approach to program evaluation and effective community interventions for families at risk of homelessness. *Social Work, 49*, 573–586. (QS)

Murphy, Jerome T. (1980). *Getting the facts: A fieldwork guide for evaluators and policy analysts.* Santa Monica, CA: Goodyear.

Murray, Michael. (2009). Narrative psychology. In Jonathan A. Smith (Ed.), *Qualitative psychology: A practical guide to research methods* (pp. 111–132). Los Angeles: Sage.

Napolitano, Valentina. (2002). *Migration, Mujercitas, and medicine men.* Berkeley: University of California Press. (QS)

Narotzky, Susana, & Smith, Gavin. (2006). *Immediate struggles: People, power, and place in rural Spain.* Berkeley: University of California Press. (QS)

National Commission on Neighborhoods. (1979). *People, building neighborhoods.* Washington, DC: U.S. Government Printing Office. (CS)

National Research Council. (2003). *Protecting participants and facilitating social and behavioral sciences research.* Washington, DC: National Academies Press.

Nespor, Jan. (2006). Finding patterns with field notes. In J. L. Green, G. Camilli, & P. B. Elmore (Eds.), *Handbook of complementary methods in education research* (3rd ed., pp. 297–308). Washington, DC: American Educational Research Association.

Neuman, Susan B., & Celano, Dana. (2001). Access to print in low-income and middle-income communities: An ecological study of four neighborhoods. *Reading Research Quarterly, 36,* 8–26.

Neustadt, Richard E., & Fineberg, Harvey. (1983). *The epidemic that never was: Policy-making and the swine flu affair.* New York: Vintage Books. (CS)

Newman, Dianna L., & Brown, Robert D. (1996). *Applied ethics for program evaluation.* Thousand Oaks, CA: Sage.

Newman, Katherine S. (1999). *No shame in my game: The working poor in the inner city.* New York: Russell Sage Foundation. (QS)

O'Cathain, Alicia. (2009). Mixed methods research in the health sciences: A quiet revolution. *Journal of Mixed Methods Research, 3,* 3–6.

Olesen, Virginia. (2005). Early millennial feminist qualitative research. In Norman K. Denzin & Yvonna S. Lincoln (Eds.), *The Sage handbook of qualitative research* (3rd ed., pp. 235–278). Thousand Oaks, CA: Sage.

Palmer, Edward L. (1973). *Formative research in the production of television for children.* Report by Children's Television Workshop, New York (also available through the Educational Resources Information Center, Washington, DC).

Park, Robert E., Burgess, Ernest W., & McKenzie, Roderick D. (Eds.). (1925). *The city.* Chicago: University of Chicago Press.

Patton, Michael Quinn. (2002). Two decades of developments in qualitative inquiry. *Qualitative Social Work, 1,* 261–283.

Patton, Michael Quinn. (2006). Foreword: Trends and issues as context. *Research in the Schools, 13,* i–ii.

Pedraza, Silvia. (2007). *Political disaffection in Cuba's revolution and exodus.* Cambridge, UK: Cambridge University Press. (QS)

Pelto, Pertti J., & Pelto, Gretel H. (1978). *Anthropological research: The structure of inquiry* (2nd ed.). Cambridge, UK: Cambridge University Press.

Pérez, Gina M. (2004). The near northwest side story: Migration, displacement, and Puerto Rican families. Berkeley: University of California Press. (QS)

Phillips, D. C. (1990a). Response to the commentary by Guba. In Elliot W. Eisner & Alan Peshkin (Eds.), *Qualitative inquiry in education: The continuing debate* (pp. 92–95). New York: Teachers College Press.

Phillips, D. C. (1990b). Subjectivity and objectivity: An objective inquiry. In Elliot W. Eisner & Alan Peshkin (Eds.), *Qualitative inquiry in education: The continuing debate* (pp. 19–37). New York: Teachers College Press.

Platt, Jennifer. (1992). "Case study" in American methodological thought. *Current Sociology, 40,* 17–48.

Polanyi, Michael. (1958). *Personal knowledge.* Chicago: University of Chicago Press.

Polanyi, Michael. (1966). *The tacit dimension.* New York: Doubleday.

Pope, Catherine, & Mays, Nicholas. (1995). Reaching the parts other methods cannot reach:

An introduction to qualitative methods in health and health services research. *British Medical Journal, 332*, 413–416.

Powdermaker, Hortense. (1966). *Stranger and friend: The way of an anthropologist.* New York: Norton.

Punch, Maurice. (1989). Researching police deviance: A personal encounter with the limitations and liabilities of field-work. *British Journal of Sociology, 40*, 177–204.

Rabinow, Paul. (1977, 2007). *Reflections on fieldwork in Morocco* (30th anniversary ed.). Berkeley: University of California Press. (QS)

Randolph, Justus J., & Eronen, Pasi J. (2007). Developing the Learner Door: A case study in youth participatory program planning. *Evaluation and Program Planning, 30*, 55–65.

Read, Jen'nan Ghazal, & Oselin, Sharon. (2008). Gender and the education-employment paradox in ethnic and religious contexts: The case of Arab Americans. *American Sociological Review, 73*, 296–313. (QS)

Reason, Peter, & Riley, Sarah. (2009). Co-operative inquiry: An action research practice. In Jonathan A. Smith (Ed.), *Qualitative psychology: A practical guide to research methods* (pp. 207–234). Los Angeles: Sage.

Reichardt, Charles S., & Rallis, Sharon F. (Eds.). (1994a). The qualitative-quantitative debate: New perspectives. *New Directions for Program Evaluation, 61*(whole issue).

Reichardt, Charles S., & Rallis, Sharon F. (1994b). The relationship between the qualitative and quantitative traditions. *New Directions for Program Evaluation, 61*, 5–11.

Reid, M. Jeanne, & Moore, James L., III. (2008). College readiness and academic preparation for postsecondary education: Oral histories of first-generation urban college students. *Urban Education, 43*, 240–261. (IS)

Reiss, Albert. (1971). *The police and the public.* New Haven, CT: Yale University Press.

Rex, Lesley A., Steadman, Sharilyn C., & Graciano, Mary K. (2006). Research the complexity of classroom interaction. In J. L. Green, G. Camilli, & P. B. Elmore (Eds.), *Handbook of complementary methods in education research* (3rd ed., pp. 727–771). Washington, DC: American Educational Research Association.

Riessman, Catherine Kohler. (1993). *Narrative analysis.* Thousand Oaks, CA: Sage.

Riessman, Catherine Kohler. (2008). *Narrative methods for the human sciences.* Thousand Oaks, CA: Sage.

Rivera, Lauren A. (2008). Managing "spoiled" national identity: War, tourism, and memory in Croatia. *American Sociological Review, 73*, 613–634. (CS)

Rolls, Geoff. (2005). *Classic case studies in psychology.* Oxon, UK: Hodder Education.

Roman, Leslie G., & Apple, Michael W. (1990). Is naturalism a move away from positivism? Materialist and feminist approaches to subjectivity in ethnographic research. In Elliot W. Eisner & Alan Peshkin (Eds.), *Qualitative inquiry in education: The continuing debate* (pp. 38–73). New York: Teachers College Press.

Roschelle, Jeremy. (2000). Choosing and using video equipment for data collection. In Anthony E. Kelly & Richard A. Lesh (Eds.), *Handbook of research design in mathematics and science education* (pp. 709–731). Mahwah, NJ: Lawrence Erlbaum.

Rosenbaum, Paul R. (2002). *Observational studies* (2nd ed.). New York: Springer.

Rosenthal, Robert. (1966). *Experimenter effects in behavioral research.* New York: Appleton-Century-Crofts.

Rossi, Peter. (1994). The war between the quals and the quants: Is a lasting peace possible? *New Directions for Program Evaluation, 61*, 23–36.

Roter, D., & Frankel, Richard. (1992). Quantitative and qualitative approaches to the evaluation of the medical dialogue. *Social Science and Medicine, 34*(10), 1097–1103.

Rowe, Michael. (1999). *Crossing the border: Encounters between homeless people and outreach workers.* Berkeley: University of California Press. (QS)

Royster, Deirdre A. (2003). *Race the Invisible Hand: How white networks exclude black men from blue-collar jobs.* Berkeley: University of California Press. (QS)

Rubin, Herbert J., & Rubin, Irene S. (1995). *Qualitative interviewing: The art of hearing data.* Thousand Oaks, CA: Sage.

Ryle, Gilbert. (1949). *The concept of mind.* New York.

Sack, Jacqueline J. (2008). Commonplace intersections within a high school mathematics leadership institute. *Journal of Teacher Education, 59,* 189–199. (QS)

Saldaña, Johnny. (2009). *The coding manual for qualitative researchers.* Thousand Oaks, CA: Sage.

Sarroub, Loukia K. (2005). All American Yemeni girls: Being Muslim in a public school. Philadelphia: University of Pennsylvania Press. (QS)

Sauder, Michael. (2008). Interlopers and field change: The entry of *U.S. News* into the field of legal education. *Administrative Science Quarterly, 53,* 209–234. (IS)

Scanlan, Christopher. (2000). *Reporting and writing: Basics for the 21st century.* New York: Oxford University Press.

Schein, Edgar. (2003). *DEC is dead, long live DEC: Lessons on innovation, technology, and the business gene.* San Francisco: Berrett-Koehler. (CS)

Schoenfeld, Alan H. (2006a). Reply to comments from the What Works Clearinghouse on "what doesn't work." *Educational Researcher, 33,* 23.

Schoenfeld, Alan H. (2006b). What doesn't work: The challenge and failure of the What Works Clearinghouse to conduct meaningful reviews of mathematical curricula. *Educational Researcher, 35,* 13–21.

Schofield, Janet Ward. (1990). Increasing the generalizability of qualitative research. In Elliot W. Eisner & Alan Peshkin (Eds.), *Qualitative inquiry in education: The continuing debate* (pp. 201–232). New York: Teachers College Press.

Schutz, Alfred. (1970). *On phenomenology and social relations.* Chicago: University of Chicago Press.

Schwandt, Thomas A. (2007). *The Sage dictionary of qualitative inquiry* (3rd ed.). Thousand Oaks, CA: Sage.

Schwartz, Morris S., & Schwartz, Charlotte G. (1955). Problems in participant observation. *American Journal of Sociology, 60,* 350–351.

Seidman, Irving. (2006). *Interviewing as qualitative research: A guide for researchers in education and the social sciences* (3rd ed.). New York: Teachers College Press.

Sharman, Russell Leigh. (2006). *The tenants of East Harlem.* Berkeley: University of California Press. (QS)

Shavelson, Richard, & Townes, Lisa. (2002). *Scientific research in education.* Washington, DC: National Academy Press.

Shaw, Clifford R. (1930). *The natural history of a delinquent career.* Chicago: University of Chicago Press. (QS)

Sherman, Jennifer. (2009). Bend to avoid breaking: Job loss, gender norms, and family stability in rural America. *Social Problems, 56,* 599–620. (QS)

Shortell, Stephen M. (1999). The emergence of qualitative methods in health services research. *Health Services Research, 34,* 1083–1090.

Sidel, Ruth. (2006). *Unsung heroines: Single mothers and the American dream.* Berkeley: University of California Press. (QS)

Sieber, Sam D. (1973). The integration of fieldwork and survey methods. *American Journal of Sociology, 78,* 1335–1359.

Sluka, Jeffrey A., & Robben, Antonius C. G. M. (2007). Fieldwork in cultural anthropology: An introduction. In A. C. G. M. Robben & J. A. Sluka (Eds.), *Ethnographic fieldwork: An anthropological reader* (pp. 1–28). Malden, MA: Blackwell.

Small, Mario Luis. (2004). *Villa Victoria: The transformation of social capital in a Boston Barrio.* Chicago: University of Chicago Press. (QS)

Small, S. (1995). Action-oriented research: Models and methods. *Journal of Marriage and the Family, 57,* 941–955.

Smith, Robert Courtney. (2006). *Mexican New York: Transnational lives of new immigrants.* Berkeley: University of California Press. (QS)

Spradley, James P. (1979). *The ethnographic interview.* New York: Holt, Rinehart & Winston.

Spradley, James P. (1980). *Participant observation.* New York: Holt, Rinehart & Winston.

Stack, Carol. (1974). *All our kin.* New York: Basic Books. (QS)

Stake, Robert E. (1995). *The art of case study research.* Thousand Oaks, CA: Sage.

Stake, Robert E. (2005). Qualitative case studies. In Norman K. Denzin & Yvonna S. Lincoln (Eds.), *The Sage handbook of qualitative research* (3rd ed., pp. 443–466). Thousand Oaks, CA: Sage.

Stewart, David W., Shamdasani, Prem N., & Rook, Dennis W. (2009). Group depth interviews: Focus group research. In Leonard Bickman & Debra J. Rog (Eds.), *The Sage handbook of applied social research methods* (2nd ed., pp. 589–616). Thousand Oaks, CA: Sage.

Stewart, Moira. (1992). Approaches to audiotape and videotape analysis: Interpreting the interactions between patients and physicians. In Benjamin F. Crabtree & William L. Miller (Eds.), *Doing qualitative research* (pp. 149–162). Thousand Oaks, CA: Sage. (QS)

Stewart, Thomas, Wolf, Patrick J., Cornman, Stephen Q., & McKenzie-Thompson, Kenann. (2007). *Satisfied, optimistic, yet concerned: Parent voices in the third year of the DC Opportunity Scholarship program.* Washington, DC: Georgetown University Public Policy Institute. (QS)

Stone, Pamela. (2007). *Opting out?: Why women really quit careers and head home.* Berkeley: University of California Press. (QS)

Strauss, Anselm, & Corbin, Juliet. (1998). *Basics of qualitative research: Techniques and procedures for developing grounded theory* (2nd ed.). Thousand Oaks, CA: Sage.

Streiner, David L. (2010). Hoist on our own postcard. In David L. Streiner & Souraya Sidani (Eds.), *When research goes off the rails: Why it happens and what you can do about it* (pp. 223–227). New York: Guilford Press.

Streiner, David L., & Sidani, Souraya (Eds.). (2010). *When research goes off the rails: Why it happens and what you can do about it.* New York: Guilford Press.

Stritikus, Tom, & Nguyen, Diem. (2007). Strategic transformation: Cultural and gender identity negotiation in first-generation Vietnamese youth. *American Educational Research Journal, 44,* 853–895. (QS)

Sturm, Circe. (2002). *Blood politics: Race, culture, and identity in the Cherokee Nation of Oklahoma.* Berkeley: University of California Press. (QS)

Sudman, Seymour, & Bradburn, Norman M. (1982). *Asking questions: A practical guide to questionnaire design.* San Francisco: Jossey-Bass.

Suttles, Gerald D. (1968). *The social order of the slum: Ethnicity and territory in the inner city.* Chicago: University of Chicago Press. (QS)

Tashakkori, Abbas, & Teddlie, Charles. (1998). *Mixed methodology: Combining Qualitative and Quantitative Approaches.* Thousand Oaks, CA: Sage.

Tashakkori, Abbas, & Teddlie, Charles (Eds.). (2003). *Handbook of mixed methods in social and behavioral research.* Thousand Oaks, CA: Sage.

Tashakkori, Abbas, & Teddlie, Charles. (2009). Integrating qualitative and quantitative approaches to research. In Leonard Bickman & Debra J. Rog (Eds.), *The Sage handbook of applied social research methods* (2nd ed., pp. 283–317). Thousand Oaks, CA: Sage.

Teddlie, Charles, & Tashakkori, Abbas. (2006). A general typology of research designs featuring mixed methods. *Research in the Schools, 13,* 12–28.

Teddlie, Charles, & Tashakkori, Abbas. (2009). *Foundations of mixed methods research.* Thousand Oaks, CA: Sage.

Tedlock, Barbara. (1991). From participant observation to the observation of participation: The emergence of narrative ethnography. *Journal of Anthropological Research, 47,* 69–94.

Tetley, Josephine, Grant, Gordon, & Davies, Susan. (2009). Using narratives to understand older people's decision-making processes. *Qualitative Health Research, 19,* 1273–1283. (QS)

Thomas, William I., & Znaniecki, Florian. (1927). *The Polish peasant in Europe and America.* Chicago: University of Chicago Press. (QS)

Thrasher, Frederic M. (1927). *The gang: A study of 1,313 gangs in Chicago.* Chicago: University of Chicago Press. (QS)

Valdés, Guadalupe. (1996). *Con respeto: Bridging the distances between culturally diverse families and schools.* New York: Teachers College Press. (QS)

Valenzuela, Angela. (1999). *Subtractive schooling: U.S.–Mexican youth and the politics of caring.* Albany: State University of New York Press. (QS)

Van Maanen, John. (1978). On watching the watchers. In Peter K. Manning & John Van Maanen (Eds.), *Policing: A view from the street* (pp. 309–349). Santa Monica, CA: Goodyear.

Van Maanen, John. (1988). *Tales of the field: On writing ethnography.* Chicago: University of Chicago Press.

Van Manen, Max. (1990). *Researching lived experience: Human science for an action sensitive pedagogy.* Albany: State University of New York Press.

Vidich, Arthur J., Bensman, Joseph, & Stein, Maurice R. (Eds.). (1964). *Reflections on community studies.* New York: Wiley. (QS)

Waldinger, Roger, & Lichter, Michael I. (2003). *How the other half works: Immigration and the social organization of labor.* Berkeley: University of California Press.

Warner, W. Lloyd, & Lunt, Paul S. (1941). *The social life of a modern community.* New Haven, CT: Yale University Press (in six volumes).

Wasonga, Teresa, & Christman, Dana E. (2003). Perceptions and construction of meaning of urban high school experiences among African American university students: A focus group approach. *Education and Urban Society, 35,* 181–201. (IS)

Watson, Dennis. (2010). Community-based participatory research: A lesson in humility. In David L. Streiner & Souraya Sidani (Eds.), *When research goes off the rails: Why it happens and what you can do about it* (pp. 254–262). New York: Guilford Press.

Webb, Eugene T., Campbell, Donald T., Schwartz, Richard D., & Sechrest, Lee. (1966). *Unobtrusive measures: Nonreactive research in the social sciences.* Chicago: Rand McNally.

Webb, Eugene T., Campbell, Donald T., Schwartz, Richard D., Sechrest, Lee, & Grove, Janet Belew. (1981). *Nonreactive measures in the social sciences* (2nd ed.). Boston: Houghton Mifflin. Previously published as *Unobtrusive measures: Nonreactive research in the social sciences* (1966).

Weick, Karl E. (1968). Systematic observational methods. In Gardner Lindzey & Elliot Aronson (Eds.), *The handbook of social psychology,* Vol. 2 (2nd ed., pp. 357–451). Reading, MA: Addison-Wesley.

Weiss, Robert S. (1994). *Learning from strangers: The art and method of qualitative interview studies.* New York: Free Press.

Weitzman, Eben A. (1999). Analyzing qualitative data with computer software. *Health Services Research, 34,* 1241–1263.

Whyte, William Foote. (1955). *Street corner society: The social structure of an Italian slum* (3rd ed.). Chicago: University of Chicago Press. (Original work published in 1943) (QS)

Whyte, William Foote. (1984). *Learning from the field: A guide from experience.* Thousand Oaks, CA: Sage.

Whyte, William Foote. (1989). Introduction to action research for the twenty-first century: Participation, reflection, and practice. *American Behavioral Scientist, 32,* 502–512.

Whyte, William Foote. (1992). In defense of Street Corner Society. *Journal of Contemporary Ethnography, 21,* 52–68.

Wilkerson, Isabel. (2007). Interviewing: Accelerated intimacy. In M. Kramer & W. Call (Eds.), *Telling true stories: A nonfiction writer's guide* (pp. 30–33). London: Plume/Penguin.

Williams, Christine L. (2006). *Inside toyland: Working, shopping, and social inequality.* Berkeley: University of California Press. (QS)

Willig, Carla. (2009). Discourse analysis. In Jonathan A. Smith (Ed.), *Qualitative psychology: A practical guide to research methods* (pp. 160–185). Los Angeles: Sage.

Wilson, William Julius, & Taub, Richard P. (2006). *There goes the neighborhood: Racial, ethnic, and class tensions in four Chicago neighborhoods and their meaning for America.* New York: Vintage Books. (QS)

Wolcott, Harry F. (1999). *Ethnography: A way of seeing.* Walnut Creek, CA: AltaMira.

Wolcott, Harry F. (2009). *Writing up qualitative research* (3rd ed.). Thousand Oaks, CA: Sage.

Wolfinger, Nicholas H. (2002). On writing field notes: Collection strategies and background expectancies. *Qualitative Research, 2,* 85–95.

Wong, Kenneth K., Yin, Robert K., Moyer-Packenham, Patricia S., & Scherer, Jennifer (Eds.). (2008). Special issue on the Math and Science Partnership program. *Peabody Journal of Education, 83*(4).

Yardley, Lucy. (2009). Demonstrating validity in qualitative psychology. In Jonathan A. Smith (Ed.), *Qualitative psychology: A practical guide to research methods* (pp. 235–251). Los Angeles: Sage.

Yin, Robert K. (1982a). Patrolling the neighborhood beat. In R.K. Yin (Ed.), *Conserving America's neighborhoods* (Chapter 3, pp. 26–50). New York: Plenum Press. (MM)

Yin, Robert K. (1982b). Using participant-observation to study urban neighborhoods. Chapter 10 in *Conserving America's neighborhoods* (pp. 132–157). New York: Plenum Press. (QS)

Yin, Robert K. (1994). Evaluation: A singular craft. *New Directions for Program Evaluation, 61,* 71–84.

Yin, Robert K. (2000). Rival explanations as an alternative to "reforms as experiments." In Leonard Bickman (Ed.), *Validity & social experimentation: Donald Campbell's legacy* (pp. 239–266). Thousand Oaks, CA: Sage.

Yin, Robert K. (2003). A case study of a neighborhood organization. *Applications of case study research* (2nd ed., pp. 31–52). Thousand Oaks, CA: Sage. (CS)

Yin, Robert K. (2006). Mixed methods research: Are the methods genuinely integrated or merely parallel? *Research in the Schools, 13,* 41–47.

Yin, Robert K. (2009). *Case study research: Design and methods* (4th ed.). Thousand Oaks, CA: Sage. (First published in 1984)

Yin, Robert K. (in press). Case study methods. In Harris Cooper et al. (Eds.), *The handbook of research methods in psychology.* Washington, DC: American Psychological Association.

Yow, V. R. (1994). *Recording oral history: A practical guide for social scientists.* Thousand Oaks, CA: Sage.

Zorbaugh, Harvey Warren. (1929). *The Gold Coast and the slum.* Chicago: University of Chicago Press. (QS)

Author Index

Subject Index

Page numbers in italic indicate figures and tables; page numbers followed by *n* indicate note.

About the Author

Robert K. Yin, PhD, has directly overseen, led, or participated in nearly 200 studies, most using qualitative methods. He serves as the president of COSMOS Corporation, a firm devoted to social science research. Most recently, he has had an extensive assignment with the United Nations Development Programme, helping its staff to strengthen the use of qualitative research in its evaluations. Dr. Yin has taught methods courses in the Department of Urban Studies and Planning at the Massachusetts Institute of Technology, and he advises doctoral students in preparing the prospectuses for their dissertations, most recently at the University of Copenhagen. Currently, he holds the position of distinguished scholar-in-residence in the School of International Service at American University.

In all, Dr. Yin has authored six books, edited four others, and published nearly 100 journal articles. His research has covered a wide array of fields, such as primary, secondary, and postsecondary education; health promotion, HIV/AIDS prevention, and substance abuse prevention; organizational development and program evaluation; neighborhood, community, and urban development; and technological innovation and communications.